Deborah and Her Sisters

JEWISH CULTURE AND CONTEXTS

Published in association with the Herbert D. Katz Center for
Advanced Judaic Studies of the University of Pennsylvania

Steven Weitzman, Series Editor

A complete list of books in the series is available from the publisher.

DEBORAH AND HER SISTERS

How One Nineteenth-Century Melodrama
and a Host of Celebrated Actresses Put Judaism
on the World Stage

Jonathan M. Hess

UNIVERSITY OF PENNSYLVANIA PRESS

PHILADELPHIA

Copyright © 2018 University of Pennsylvania Press

All rights reserved. Except for brief quotations used for purposes of review or scholarly citation, none of this book may be reproduced in any form by any means without written permission from the publisher.

Published by
University of Pennsylvania Press
Philadelphia, Pennsylvania 19104-4112
www.upenn.edu/pennpress

Printed in the United States of America on acid-free paper
10 9 8 7 6 5 4 3 2 1

Library of Congress Cataloging-in-Publication Data
ISBN 978-0-8122-4958-3

In loving memory of my mother,
Frances Aaron Hess (1933–2015)

Contents

Introduction. Shylock's Daughters: Philosemitism,
Theater, and Popular Culture in the Nineteenth Century   1

Chapter 1. Anatomy of a Tearjerker: The Melodrama
of the Forsaken Jewess   26

Chapter 2. Sensationalism, Sympathy, and Laughter:
Deborah and Her Sisters   65

Chapter 3. Playing Jewish from Rachel to the Divine Sarah:
Natural Acting and the Wonders of Impersonation   110

Chapter 4. Shylock and the Jewish Schiller: Jews, Non-Jews,
and the Making of Philosemitism   164

Concluding Remarks. Jewishness, Theatricality,
and the Legacy of *Deborah*   196

Notes   209

Index   249

Acknowledgments   259

Introduction

Shylock's Daughters: Philosemitism, Theater, and Popular Culture in the Nineteenth Century

Playing Jewish

In June 1866, Annie Lewis, a prostitute in Memphis, Tennessee, was arrested for being drunk and disorderly. As the Memphis *Public Ledger* reported, when Lewis was carted off to the police station, she caused "much merriment" by performing scenes from Shakespeare.[1] When the aspiring actress's friends refused to pay her fine the following morning, however, Lewis quickly took on another role. She cursed the police by spontaneously giving her rendition of the Jewish maiden in *Leah, the Forsaken*, the American adaption of Salomon Hermann Mosenthal's *Deborah* that had recently catapulted Kate Bateman to star status on both sides of the Atlantic. Performing a scene that would come to earn a secure place in late nineteenth- and early twentieth-century acting manuals, Lewis drew her power from the language of Old Testament vengeance that Leah used to rebuke the Christian lover who had abandoned her: "Curse, thrice cursed may you be for evermore, and as my people on Mount Ebal spoke, so I speak thrice, Amen! Amen! Amen!"[2] Apparently "outcursing Leah in the vehemence with which she upbraided the police," Lewis delivered an extravagant performance that marked both the beginning and the end of her career as an actress. "What a pity!" the *Public Ledger* explained to its readers: "So young, so beautiful, and yet so fallen."[3]

Over the course of the nineteenth century, the theater gained an unprecedented level of respectability in Europe and North America. Yet deep-rooted cultural suspicions about working women putting themselves and their bodies on display persisted, fueling the long-standing popular associations between actresses and prostitutes that helped make this news item from Memphis of interest.[4] But wherein lay the special appeal of taking on a Jewish role, whether

Figure 1. F. W. Lawson's sketch of Kate Bateman in the role of Leah appeared in the November 1863 issue of *London Society* a month after Bateman opened in *Leah* at the Royal Adelphi Theatre in London. Francis Wilfred Lawson (1842–1935) / Museum of the City of New York, 40.160.329.

Figure 2. Kate Bateman as Leah, carte-de-visite photograph. Hess private collection.

for Lewis, her impromptu audience at the police station, or the readers of the evening newspaper? In an era where Jews were rapidly integrating into non-Jewish society, speaking new languages and adopting new modes of behavior, Jews often stood out for their adaptability. In this context, some contemporaries characterized Jews as inveterate masters of the art of dissimulation. "What good actor today is *not*—a Jew?" the German philosopher Friedrich Nietzsche asked in 1882, posing a question that drew on a long tradition of regarding the Jews' integration into the modern world as a phenomenon akin to acting (or aping)—a form of pretense to be approached with the same level of suspicion traditionally reserved for the theater.[5] The involvement of Jews with the theater in the nineteenth century never approached the level of Jewish engagement in the music business or the film industry in the twentieth century. The visible roles that Jews often played in theater, however, reinforced these associations between Jews and actors, and between Jewish women and actresses in particular. To cite one telling example, the most famous European actress of the mid-nineteenth century, the international celebrity Elisabeth-Rachel Félix (1821–1858), often known simply as "Rachel," was not just herself Jewish; her Jewishness was very much in the public eye for much of her illustrious career in France and on her many tours abroad.[6]

By taking on a Jewish role that allowed her to indulge in the excesses of Old Testament vengeance, Lewis thus gave a performance that reveled in its own theatricality at the same time as it disclosed a certain ambivalence about Jews. But there is more at stake in the Memphis news story than deep-seated reservations about actresses, Jews, and other women of ill repute bubbling to the surface. Let us consider another amateur reenactment of *Leah*, this one in a far more upscale social milieu. Several years earlier, Lady Clementina Hawarden, an eminent British portrait photographer, created a study of her two favorite subjects—her adolescent daughters—at her home in London (Figure 3).[7] Using the first floor of her South Kensington residence as her studio, Hawarden dressed up Clementina and Isabella Grace in slightly different costumes, imitating Bateman in the same role that Lewis used as a script for her confrontation with the police. Hawarden's daughters lack the distinctly Orientalist turban that Bateman famously wore in the role, an accessory that nineteenth-century theatergoers would have associated with the "Eastern dress" of the beautiful Jewess Rebecca of York in Sir Walter Scott's best-selling historical novel *Ivanhoe* (1820).[8] But they each wear versions of the blouse, dress, necklace, and sash that were the hallmarks of Bateman's exotic Leah costume. The peaceful, restful poses in Hawarden's costume tableau do not foreground the grandiose performance of the curse scene that served as Lewis's inspiration in Memphis. Hawarden placed her duplicate Leahs in close proximity to each other, each of them

Figure 3. Lady Clementina Hawarden, *Photographic Study*, 1863–1864. © Victoria and Albert Museum, London.

looking away from the natural light coming in from the window and off to the side. Indeed, they both avoid eye contact with the spectator in a more decisive manner than Bateman did in the widely disseminated carte-de-visite photographs that helped inaugurate her new celebrity status. As a result, Hawarden's teenage models appear oblivious to the maternal camera staging and capturing this intimate, reflective moment, giving viewers the voyeuristic pleasure of being able to gaze not at one but at two Leahs at once.

Neither Bateman, nor Hawarden, nor Lewis was Jewish. Whatever ambivalence they may have harbored about Jews, all these women obviously found the role of Mosenthal's exotic Jewish maiden attractive. But why did these non-Jews find taking on the role of Leah so alluring? Just as importantly, why did our nineteenth-century forebears take such an interest in the spectacle of young women putting themselves on display as Jews? What was the draw for viewers of Hawarden's photographs, readers of the Memphis *Public Ledger*, and theatergoers more generally of experiencing the high drama of Jewish women cursing or being able to focus their gaze on exotic Jewesses in a state of repose? A final

Figure 4. Kate Bateman as Leah, carte-de-visite photograph. Hess private collection.

example illuminates a further dimension of the allure of Mosenthal's material. When twenty-year-old Kathi Frank made her debut playing Deborah in Mosenthal's adoptive city of Vienna in 1867, Memphis streetwalkers and Victorian art photographs of adolescent girls were likely far from her mind. But this Jewish actress no doubt recalled her first appearance in this drama at age seven while visiting her grandmother in a small town in Hungary. Thirteen years earlier, when she heard that a traveling theater troupe was in need of a child actress for the "famous Jewish play *Deborah*," the seven-year-old future star presented herself to the director, explaining how eager she was to play the daughter of the Christian man "who likes the Jews so much." Frank must have made a convincing case. She got the role of the young Christian child Deborah, whom Deborah's former lover and his new wife name after the forsaken Jewess and who enjoys a heart-wrenching embrace with the Jewish Deborah in the play's final scenes. But there was a hitch. Frank had to promise the director to bring along a Jewish prayer shawl from her grandmother's home so that the actress playing the adult Deborah might have an authentic costume to enhance her performance. Frank gladly acquiesced, and so began her career on the boards.[9]

The Jewess Whose Woes Made a Million Weep

Before *Fiddler on the Roof*, before *The Jazz Singer*, there was *Deborah*. *Deborah and Her Sisters* offers a cultural history of one of the great blockbusters of the nineteenth-century stage, exploring the popularity that Mosenthal's *Deborah* and its exotic vision of Jewishness came to enjoy among Jews and non-Jews alike. Initially, the German Jewish elite complained that Mosenthal—himself a Jew—had written a drama that bore little authentic Jewish content and did even less to foster Jewish solidarity.[10] Coming from a different angle, mainstream Central European literati typically protested that the play was overly sensational and lacked formal coherence as a tragedy.[11] Much to the dismay of many of its critics, nevertheless, Mosenthal's melodrama about a Jewish maiden forsaken by her non-Jewish lover quickly became one of the most commercially successful German plays of the era. Hailed by friends as the most popular German play of the century and acknowledged by foes as the only German drama of its generation that achieved genuine success abroad, *Deborah* became a veritable international sensation.[12]

Following its 1849 premiere in Hamburg, *Deborah* took German and Austrian stages by storm and came to be widely performed throughout Europe, the British Empire, and North America. Over the course of the nineteenth century, *Deborah* was translated not just into English but into fourteen other languages: from French, Italian, and Spanish to Hebrew and Yiddish, and from Dutch, Danish, and Norwegian to Czech, Hungarian, Polish, Russian, Serbian, and Slovenian. The product of an era that had yet to institute the protections of international copyright, *Deborah* proved as malleable as it was mobile, circulating in more than fifty different print and manuscript versions, most of which never came to Mosenthal's attention in Vienna. *Deborah* gave rise to a particularly rich tradition of adaptations and spin-offs in Great Britain and North America, where theater was more brazenly market-driven than in continental Europe, where court theaters still maintained cultural hegemony. In the English-speaking world, the interest in Mosenthal's material yielded versions of the play that were far less bound to the original script and often far more creative in their reworking of it than standard European translations of the play.

Whether they saw the play as *Deborah*, *D'vorah*, *Débora*, *Leah*, *Miriam*, *Naomi*, *Rebecca*, *Ruth*, *Lysiah*, *Clysbia*, or simply *The Jewess*, Mosenthal's drama gave millions of nineteenth-century theatergoers the pleasures and thrills of compassion with female Jewish suffering. A favorite star vehicle for international celebrities from Adelaide Ristori and Fanny Janauschek to Kate Bateman and Sarah Bernhardt, *Deborah* spawned operas in Italian and Czech, burlesques, poems, musical selections for voice and piano, a British novel fraudulently marketed in the United States as the original basis for the play, and three American silent films—not to mention thousands of souvenir photographs of actresses in character as Mosenthal's forsaken Jewess. The vast majority of those who saw the drama and relished in its spin-off merchandising were non-Jews. Yet *Deborah* also came to enjoy particular popularity among Jewish audiences as well, whether performed in Hebrew in Istanbul, in German in Vienna or Cincinnati, in Yiddish in Warsaw, London, and New York, or in English across North America.[13]

For generations of theatergoers, Mosenthal's drama of the forsaken Jewess who vows vengeance but eventually comes to reconcile with the Christians who wronged her was the ultimate tearjerker. Yet *Deborah* did not just give audiences a good cry by enabling them to identify with an exotic and alluring Jewish woman. It was a theatrical spectacle that gave spectators the sense that their tears shed in identification with female Jewish suffering meant something. In an era that witnessed the rise of new forms of political and racial antisemitism, theatergoers often celebrated the pleasure taken in feeling the pain of the suffering Jewish woman as the ultimate litmus test for liberal feeling. "If there was a dry eye in the house last night," a Chicago reviewer noted in 1875, "it must have belonged to some being not connected with our common humanity."[14] Or as a comic sketch in the *New York Clipper* noted in 1869, using the mock German American English known as Dutch dialect: "Und if I see a gal vot don'd gry [cry] in dot piece, I voodn't marry dot gal efen if her fader owned a pig prewery [big brewery]. Und if I see a feller vot don'd gry, I voodn'd dook a drink mit him."[15] As a physical manifestation of compassion with Jewish suffering, weeping over Deborah's or Leah's woes gave theater audiences a pleasurable way of experiencing and celebrating their own liberal-mindedness.

As a vehicle for unleashing liberal feelings of compassion, *Deborah* offered a foil to Shakespeare's *The Merchant of Venice*, a drama that experienced unprecedented popularity on the nineteenth-century stage. In the second decade of the nineteenth century, distinguished actors such as Ludwig Devrient in Germany and Edmund Kean in England began to reinterpret Shakespeare's Jewish villain Shylock as a sympathetic and tragic figure. In the latter half of the nineteenth century, this tradition of the noble Shylock held great appeal for prominent Jewish actors, whether Bogumil Dawison, a Polish Jewish star actor who performed in German, or Daniel E. Bandmann, a German Jew who began his career on the German-language stage in New York but soon switched over to English and became an internationally known Shakespearean actor.[16] Bandmann, in fact, made his English-language debut playing Shylock at Niblo's Garden in New York immediately before Bateman opened in *Leah, the Forsaken* at the same theater just three days later. Starting with Jacob Adler's *Shylock* in 1901, *The Merchant of Venice* subsequently earned a secure place in the repertoire of the American Yiddish stage.[17] Yet however sympathetic Shylock may have occasionally managed to appear on the nineteenth-century stage, performances of Mosenthal's material fueled a broad-based cultural fascination with a Jewish woman who was far more appealing—and decidedly more alluring—than Shakespeare's vengeful middle-aged Venetian moneylender. Devrient's, Kean's, Dawison's, and Bandmann's renditions of Shylock often managed to surprise spectators with a glimpse into Shylock's humanity. Performances of *Deborah*, however, routinely transformed their audiences into a "chorus of tears" that "took hold of man and woman alike."[18]

Figure 5. German Jewish actor Daniel E. Bandmann as Shylock in *The Merchant of Venice*. Harvard Theatre Collection, TCS 44, Houghton Library, Harvard University.

Deborah and its various incarnations left behind a vast paper trail in both theater archives and the press in Europe, North America, and the British Empire. In recent years, much of this material has become accessible digitally in ways earlier generations of theater historians could not have fathomed.[19] *Deborah and Her Sisters* mines these physical and digital archives to offer a new vision of the productive role that theatrical performances of Jewishness played in nineteenth-century popular culture. This book focuses on both the remarkable ability of a drama to adapt itself to a dizzying number of different contexts and the diverse cast of characters—actresses, writers, adapters, advertisers, theater managers, and fans—key to its commercial success. For decades, *Deborah* could be relied on to pack the house, whether performed in New York, London, or Barcelona, by itinerant theater troupes in small towns in Eastern Europe, or in theaters in newly established mining communities in Australia and the American West. Paying careful attention to local performances as well as the dynamics of transnational exchange, *Deborah and Her Sisters* offers a history of the most popular Jewish drama of the era that probes the legacy of nineteenth-century liberal culture and its universalist aspirations.

In his controversial best-seller *Hitler's Willing Executioners*, Daniel Goldhagen famously characterized philosemites—non-Jews who express positive attitudes toward Jews and Judaism—as "antisemites in sheep's clothing."[20] Indeed, Jews and scholars of Jewish history alike have often approached the phenomenon of philosemitism with suspicion, either regarding expressions of philosemitism as a mask for anti-Jewish sentiments or stressing the problematic disjunction between philosemitic idealizations of Jews and Judaism and the way Jews generally perceive of themselves. In its origins in late nineteenth-century Germany, philosemitism was hardly a neutral term. Following on the heels of that other late nineteenth-century neologism, antisemitism, it was first used not by those who felt solidarity with or respect for Jews but by card-carrying antisemites seeking to denigrate and denounce their opponents.[21] Particularly in the aftermath of the Holocaust, understandably, scholarship in Jewish history has often taken the study of antisemitism to be a more urgent task than analyzing the positive roles that idealizations of Jews among non-Jews may have played in relations between Jews and non-Jews and the ways Jews understand themselves. To some extent, philosemitism has continued to be a contested term today. In recent years, nevertheless, scholars have argued that philosemitism needs and deserves to be studied on its own terms rather than simply mined for its ambivalence or antagonism toward Jews and Judaism.[22] As Jonathan Karp and Adam Sutcliffe write in a recent anthology of essays on philosemitism, "the vast human cost of antisemitism, and of the Nazi genocide in particular, does not warrant the simple conflation of these idealizations into their negative shadow. . . . If we are to understand the meanings and associations with which Jews have long been freighted in Western culture, we must recognize their complexity and approach them from all angles, without a predetermined assessment of their underlying essence as monolithically negative."[23]

Studying the rich and long performance history of *Deborah* is valuable here for two reasons. First, it opens a window onto one of the most widely circulated romanticized visions of Jewishness in the nineteenth-century world, one whose appeal cut across linguistic and national boundaries as well as those of class, gender, and religion. Second, and just as importantly, it forces us to confront moments when Jews and non-Jews worked together—as actors, translators, writers, composers, orchestra conductors, musicians, set painters, theater managers, and, not least of all, audience members—to produce and experience these idealized conceptions of Jews. As the example of young Kathi Frank borrowing a male Jewish prayer shawl from her grandmother's home for the actress playing Deborah sets into particularly sharp relief, the Jewishness that performances of *Deborah* and *Leah* brought onto the stage differed considerably from the modes of Jewishness experienced in other settings, whether the synagogue, the Jewish home, institutions of Jewish learning, or the pages of the numerous Jewish newspapers that emerged during this period. Rather than indicting Mosenthal's melodrama for its lack of authentic Jewish content, *Deborah and Her Sisters* underscores the value of studying these theatrical performances of Jewishness as a discrete phenomenon unto itself, one distinct from—and yet, at times, also related to—the experiences of those who identify as Jews. Rather than measuring performances of *Deborah* and *Leah* against a fixed standard of what constitutes genuine Jewish experience, this study acknowledges the relative autonomy of such theatrical experiences of Jewishness while also exploring their relationships to the empirical Jews and non-Jews for whom they served as a source of pleasurable entertainment.

As one might expect for an era that witnessed an explosive growth in commercial theater, the beginnings of modern celebrity culture, and the heyday of stage melodrama, the performances of Jewishness that *Deborah* promoted trafficked in stereotypes—of passionate and beautiful Jewish women, of vengeful Jewish men, of Jewish suffering as the ideal theatrical spectacle, and of Judaism as a disruptive force. As we shall see when considering scripts for *Deborah*, *Leah*, and their offshoots, ambivalence about Jews was no stranger to the *Deborah* phenomenon. Indeed, the thrilling invocation of Old Testament vengeance in the play's renowned curse scene was key to its commercial success and central to the way it ultimately sought to cultivate its audience's sympathies for its suffering heroine. Not surprisingly, there have been no sustained revivals of *Deborah* or *Leah* since the Holocaust. Yet focusing on the mere presence of stereotypes or their patent lack of realism runs the risk of blinding us to their function. Dismissing the Jewishness of the *Deborah* craze as stereotypical, melodramatic, or inauthentic diverts our gaze from the productive role that this theatrical phenomenon played in nineteenth-century culture. For a sixty-year period, Mosenthal's drama provided its audiences with the ultimate feel-good experience of tearful sympathy and liberal universalism, and it often did so for Jews and non-Jews alike. *Deborah* may not offer a vision of Jewishness that strikes us today as unequivocally positive. But the ambivalence of this drama's vision of Jewishness cannot be grasped without a fuller sense of its tremendous allure and appeal. We need to take seriously the tears that the drama provoked as it sought to provide Jews and non-Jews alike the pleasures of compassion with Jewish suffering.

The *Deborah* phenomenon stood at the center of a liberal culture of taking pleasure in feeling the pains of Jewish suffering. But how can we gain a historical understanding of the significance or the function of the tears that Mosenthal's material elicited? Studying spectator response in the past always poses methodological challenges, even when we have access to a large and diverse set of contemporary sources, as is the case here. Contemporaries noted occasionally that the pleasurable experience of a shared humanity that performances of *Deborah* and *Leah* unleashed could easily promote smugness and complacency rather than generate real desire for social or political change. As an American Jewish newspaper noted as the nineteenth century was drawing to a close, Mosenthal's heroine was arguably a "Jewess whose woes have made a million weep without effecting any special reduction in the amount of prejudice vented against the race in actuality."[24] Tears shed by Jews and non-Jews in identification with Deborah or Leah may not have directly undercut the rise of political antisemitism, prevented pogroms, or forestalled incidents of anti-Jewish violence. For the most part, indeed, *Deborah* and *Leah* were not performed as a conscious mode of resistance to antisemitism. There is certainly no evidence to suggest that Annie Lewis in Memphis, Clementina Hawarden in London, or Kathi Frank in Hungary found the drama and its title figure attractive specifically for this reason.

As we shall see repeatedly throughout this book, nevertheless, the philosemitic feelings that *Deborah* fostered were not bereft of all efficacy. For the millions of spectators who flocked to see the many different versions of Mosenthal's drama that played such a prominent role in the nineteenth-century theater world, identification with Jewish suffering proved to be deeply alluring, offering an experience of Jewish exoticism that afforded them the pleasure of feeling their own liberal sense of humanity. Nineteenth-century antisemites who disliked the play for ideological reasons were keenly aware of the play's power to promote liberal modes of feeling, vilifying *Deborah* for its "bold expression of

Semitism," its "glorification of Judaism," and its dramatic "representation of the sufferings of the Jewish people."[25] In his seminal antisemitic tract of 1879, *Der Sieg des Judenthums über das Germanenthum* (The Victory of Judaism over Germandom), Wilhelm Marr cited the popularity of *Deborah* as irrefutable proof that the theater had become a place where Jews yielded tremendous power, the "forum" of the Jews.[26] In an explicitly antisemitic literary history published two decades later, the prominent German literary historian Adolf Bartels singled out *Deborah* for manipulating "harmless German minds" with a "Jewish-pathetic" form of sentimentality.[27]

Of course, Marr and Bartels hardly represent credible authorities, much less mainstream voices. Far more individuals in the nineteenth century bought tickets to see Mosenthal's play than heeded Marr's and Bartels's advice to steer clear of this sentimental spectacle of Jewish suffering. The hysteria over the emotional power of Mosenthal's play that these antisemitic writers give voice to, however, underscores how important it is to take the philosemitism of the *Deborah* craze seriously. By doing so, we shall not only gain insights into the greatest Jewish blockbuster of the nineteenth century; we shall put ourselves in a position to understand the affective world of the nineteenth century. At stake here will not just be a better appreciation of how our Jewish and non-Jewish forebears thought and felt about Jewish difference. We shall come to grasp the key role that theatrical performances of Jewishness played in giving rise to modes of liberal feeling.

Shylock's Daughters: Jews and Jewesses in Nineteenth-Century Culture

Not all or even most nineteenth-century interpretations of Shylock tended to be sympathetic. Moreover, from Fagin in Charles Dickens's *Oliver Twist* (1837) to Veitel Itzig in Gustav Freytag's *Soll und Haben* (Debit and Credit, 1855), the best-selling German novel of the period, nineteenth-century literature developed a rich repertoire of stereotypes of Jewish villains. *Oliver Twist* appeared in the first of many stage adaptations already in 1838, when Dickens's novel was still in the process of being serialized, and the popular role of the criminal Fagin was one of numerous Jewish villain types on the English-speaking stage. For much of the nineteenth century, indeed, the stock image of the stage Jew was overwhelmingly negative, one enhanced at times by the artificially large noses that actors playing Jews tended to wear.[28]

To be sure, there were prominent exceptions. In the German-speaking world, Gotthold Ephraim Lessing's classic drama *Nathan der Weise* (Nathan the Wise, 1779) inverted *The Merchant of Venice* to present a prototype of the "noble Jew," a wealthy Jewish merchant who preaches religious tolerance and earns the friendship and respect of non-Jews through his wisdom, generosity, and benevolence.[29] In England, Richard Cumberland's comedy *The Jew* (1794) similarly created in its hero, Sheva, an image of a kindly Jewish moneylender, a figure calculated to elicit sympathy rather than fear or laughter. Lessing's and Cumberland's philosemitic dramas, moreover, were both translated into numerous languages, including Hebrew and Yiddish, and *The Jew* was widely performed on both sides of the Atlantic during the nineteenth century. The dominant image of the Jew on the European and American stage nevertheless remained a deeply negative one, whether a sinister, evil figure or a less menacing comic type. During this period, Lessing's once-controversial *Nathan der Weise* became required reading in schools and a staple of theater repertoires in the German-speaking world, and the newly minted canonical status of Lessing's drama is significant. Yet it needs to be seen against the backdrop of the rich tradition of anti-Jewish farces that developed during the early nineteenth century as well. These plays did not just give older anti-Jewish stereotypes a new lease on life. They often explicitly singled out Lessing's *Nathan* for parody, rendering Lessing's idealized figure of the noble Jew a source of laughter.[30]

Whether an idealized (or travestied) Nathan, a tragic Shylock, a benevolent Sheva, a nefarious Fagin, or a pushy, comic Jew selling secondhand clothes and speaking in Yiddish-inflected tones, these figures have one obvious trait in common. They are all men, and often middle-aged or elderly men. Jewish women have tended to play a fundamentally different role in the Western cultural imagination from their male counterparts. In literature and on the stage, Jewish women have generally appeared far more erotically charged, much more ambivalent, and also considerably younger than the typically black-and-white extremes of Shylock the evil moneylender and Nathan the wise and benevolent. In *The Merchant of Venice*, for instance, Shylock's late wife, Leah, never makes an appearance, but his beautiful daughter Jessica plays a crucial role in the plot, stealing her mother's turquoise ring and other treasures from her father, whom she abandons in order to elope with Lorenzo and convert to Christianity. Like Shylock, Nathan is a widower, one whose wife and seven sons were murdered by Christian crusaders long before the drama begins. One of the ways in which Lessing inverts Shakespeare is by having Nathan's beautiful adoptive daughter Recha pledge love and loyalty to her Jewish father even after it is revealed that she is not, in fact, a Jewess but a Christian, the product of a union between a Christian woman and a Muslim man.

Since at least the early modern period, European literature has often denigrated male Jews while idealizing the Jewish woman as an alluring and exotic object of desire. The literary type of the *belle juive*, or beautiful Jewess, that arose

Figure 6. This oft-reproduced engraving of W. Drummond's sketch of the "beautiful Jewess" Rebecca in Walter Scott's *Ivanhoe* features the turban characteristic of her "Eastern dress" that served as a model for Bateman's Leah costume. Charles Heath, *The Waverley Gallery of the Principal Female Characters in Sir Walter Scott's Romances and Poems* (London: Tilt and Bogue, 1840). Hess private collection.

in this context was not just erotically charged and typically more virtuous (and more appealing to non-Jews) than her often less-than-righteous father. As the object of Christian desire, the beautiful Jewess was often highly ambivalent, able to mediate between Judaism and Christianity in ways rarely open to the male Jews of the literary imagination.[31] In the aftermath of the popularity that Walter Scott's best-selling historical novel *Ivanhoe* (1820) achieved across Europe, the beautiful Jewess became an established trope in European literature as never before. Whether following Scott's Rebecca of York and forsaking a Christian lover to remain true to the faith of her fathers or finding love and redemption in the arms of a Christian suitor, the beautiful Jewess was ubiquitous in nineteenth-century literature. Part of the unique power of this figure, as Nadia Valman has demonstrated, lay in its ability to represent tensions between ideals of inclusion and mechanisms of exclusion central to the liberal models of secular nationhood that became prominent during this era. As a figure that could represent both the "ideal object of liberal tolerance" and "its demonized Other," the ambivalent figure of the Jewess often figured at the center of narratives concerned with demarcating the shape of modern liberal models of nationhood.[32]

Figure 7. Salomon Hermann Mosenthal, autographed carte-de-visite photograph. Hess private collection.

In writing a drama about a young and beautiful Jewess caught up in a love affair with a young Christian man, Mosenthal was thus hardly breaking new ground. He was relying on a tested formula for success. In the decade and a half before Mosenthal wrote *Deborah*, moreover, the sensation that Fromental Halévy's grand opera *La Juive* (The Jewess, 1835) had made in Paris and outside France thrust the figure of the beautiful Jewess even further into the public eye. Eugène Scribe's libretto for *La Juive* drew liberally on both *The Merchant of Venice* and Lessing's *Nathan*, culminating in the spectacle of its heroine Rachel's dramatic choice to die as a Jewish martyr in a cauldron of boiling water even as it is revealed that she is not, in fact, a Jewess but the daughter of her Shylock-like father's adversary, the Cardinal.[33] Performed in Vienna already in 1836 under the title *Die Jüdin*, Halévy's opera was a fixture in the Viennese opera repertoire during the early 1840s, when Mosenthal first moved to Vienna. During this period, this international blockbuster was performed widely throughout the German-speaking world.[34] When *Deborah* had its world premiere in Hamburg, in January 1849, the Hamburg Stadttheater advertised Mosenthal's play with the title *Deborah, die Jüdin* (Deborah, the Jewess), hoping to draw in fans of Halévy's grand opera to see the new drama by a still-unknown German Jewish playwright.[35]

Some Jewish writers in the nineteenth century recognized the beautiful Jewess as a problematic figure. Rahel Meyer, in the German-speaking world, for instance, wrote novel after novel where she created an alternative type of Jewish woman, often explicitly challenging the figure of the beautiful Jewess. In the late 1850s, Meyer even wrote an idiosyncratic biographical novella about the actress Rachel Félix that refused to eroticize the international star known for her many love affairs with high-profile non-Jewish men.[36] Even when writing primarily for Jewish audiences, many Jewish writers wholeheartedly embraced the trope of the beautiful Jewess, simply retooling it for Jewish purposes.[37] In Ludwig Philippson's historical novel *Jakob Tirado* (1867), for instance, a beautiful crypto-Jewish woman escapes from Portugal to Elizabethan England, only to find herself disgusted by a performance of *The Merchant of Venice* at the Globe Theatre. In an episode invented for the novel, Philippson has Queen Elizabeth take his female protagonist Marie Nunes to the Globe, where she is appalled by the figure of Shylock and outraged by the apostasy of his daughter. Rejecting Queen Elizabeth's overtures of friendship (and her conversionary zeal), Marie refuses to follow in Jessica's footsteps. Instead, she marries the novel's male protagonist, Jakob Tirado, a man whom her pious mother regards as an ideal replacement for Marie's late father. Rather than stealing her father's money and betraying her paternal legacy, Marie joins forces with Tirado to create a flourishing Jewish community of former conversos in Amsterdam.[38]

Focusing on how Jewish writers strategically sought to reformulate dominant modes of representing Jews and Judaism casts light on an important dimension of modern Jewish culture. Juxtaposing dominant tropes and figures to their subversion or appropriation by Jewish writers, however, can run the risk of blinding us to the extent to which figures like the beautiful Jewess were often part of a shared culture of representing and experiencing Jewishness among Jews and non-Jews. In focusing on the transnational performance history of Mosenthal's drama, *Deborah and Her Sisters* offers a dynamic snapshot of how this shared culture was constructed and sustained in a variety of different contexts, from Vienna and San Francisco to small towns in Ukraine and the Idaho Territory. As we shall see in Chapter 1, when we examine the original script for *Deborah*, there is little that was subversive in Mosenthal's use of the figure of the beautiful Jewess. What Mosenthal did do was to mine this figure as never before to create a powerful melodrama, one uniquely suited to pull at its spectators' heartstrings, bring them to tears, and give them the sense that tears shed in identification with Jewish suffering had moral value.

The *Deborah* craze, importantly, was hardly the only example of Jews and non-Jews coming together to enjoy the sentimental pleasures of identifying with Jews. The most prominent genre of nineteenth-century Jewish fiction on the continent was ghetto literature, a tradition of tales about the recent Jewish past launched in the 1840s by writers such as Alexandre Weill in France and Leopold Kompert in Austria.[39] Often focusing on the trials and tribulations of ordinary Jews caught up in conflicts between traditional Jewish life and the lures of the modern world, ghetto literature generally promoted nostalgia for a tradition-bound Jewish world that was quickly disappearing while also exploring the promise of life beyond the ghetto. The distinctive mode of sentimental nostalgia for Jewish tradition that characterizes this French- and German-language ghetto fiction was one of nineteenth-century Jewish literature's most vital legacies, familiar to us today through the 1964 Broadway musical *Fiddler on the Roof* and its 1971 film adaptation. Like the musical by Jerry Bock, Sheldon Harnick, and Joseph Stein, moreover, Weill's and Kompert's sentimental tales of traditional Jewish communities caught up in the transition to modernity did not just happen to appeal to non-Jews. Ghetto tales were explicitly designed to represent traditional Jewish life in a way that would make sense to a non-Jewish audience. Jews also were not the only Europeans to produce these nostalgic tales about the Jewish past in the nineteenth century. One of Kompert's and Weill's most prominent successors in the field of ghetto literature was the prominent Austrian writer Leopold Sacher-Masoch, a non-Jew.

Over the course of his career, Mosenthal wrote more than twenty libretti for opera, from Otto Nicolai's *Die lustigen Weiber von Windsor* (The Merry Wives of Windsor, 1849) to Karl Goldmark's *Die Königin von Saba* (The Queen of Sheba, 1875). As a playwright, he tried repeatedly, largely in vain, to recapture the phenomenal success he achieved with *Deborah*. In his final years, Mosenthal himself turned to the genre of ghetto literature, publishing tales of Jewish life in his native central German city of Kassel in illustrated magazines with mass circulation such as *Die Gartenlaube* and *Über Land und Meer*. After Mosenthal died suddenly, following a heart attack at age fifty-six, in 1877, his *Erzählungen aus dem jüdischen Familienleben* (Tales of Jewish Family Life) appeared posthumously as a set and were frequently republished and translated into other languages.[40] When he published his ghetto tales in the final two years of his life, he accompanied them with illustrations by the celebrated Jewish painter Moritz Daniel Oppenheim, an artist second to none when it came to creating shared spaces of experiencing Jewishness in nineteenth-century Europe.

Oppenheim's *Bilder aus dem altjüdischen Familienleben* (Scenes of Traditional Jewish Family Life), a nostalgic cycle of paintings glorifying traditional Jewish folkways was, as Ismar Schorsch has pointed out, among the most widely circulated Jewish books ever published in Germany.[41] Oppenheim's images appeared in book form four times between 1866 and 1913; they were published in numerous portfolio editions; and they were frequently sold as postcards,

Figure 8. Moritz Daniel Oppenheim's popular 1867 painting of a Passover seder, *Der Oster-Abend*, was frequently reproduced, appearing in 1867 in the mass-market family journal *Die Gartenlaube*, on postcards, and elsewhere. The Jewish Museum, New York / Art Resource, NY.

reproduced on kosher margarine containers, and featured on pewter and porcelain plates used for Passover and the Sabbath. Oppenheim is routinely heralded as the first modern Jewish painter. As Andreas Gotzmann has pointed out, we nevertheless misunderstand the original context and function of his images of traditional Jewish life if we position them in an entirely Jewish milieu. Like *Deborah* and Mosenthal's Jewish tales, Oppenheim's prints were produced for and marketed primarily toward a non-Jewish audience in the nineteenth century.[42] Indeed, when Oppenheim first prepared grisaille versions of his paintings to facilitate the transition to mass reproduction in the 1860s, his images often appeared in mainstream illustrated weeklies such as *Die Gartenlaube* and *Über Land und Meer*; only a small fraction of the hundreds of thousands who read these popular family journals were Jews. In the realm of mass-produced nostalgic images of Jews, moreover, Sacher-Masoch has a clear equivalent. Hermann Junker, a Christian artist from Frankfurt, was inspired by Oppenheim to create his own set of scenes of traditional Jewish family life, and his prints also circulated in postcard form.[43]

The nostalgia for traditional Jewish folkways in nineteenth-century culture was largely a print phenomenon, without a clear equivalent on the stage. As popular as ghetto tales and Oppenheim's prints may have been, and as important as they are as cultural-historical phenomena, they pale in comparison to this "Jewish play" or "Hebrew drama" that millions of theatergoers came together to see performed for decades, in fifteen languages, across Europe, North America, and the British Empire.[44] In its various versions, Mosenthal's play did not just reach more people over a longer period of time than ghetto fiction or reproductions of Oppenheim's paintings. As a mode of live performance featuring a lead actress playing a Jewess cursing and then reconciling with the Christian world, *Deborah* also functioned differently from sentimental fiction enjoyed privately in the domestic sphere of the home or mass-produced images that might end up on the coffee table or one's walls at home. In the affective experience it offered, Mosenthal's melodrama was a far cry from the quiet reverence for the dignity of traditional Jewish family life fostered by ghetto tales and Oppenheim's images. The pleasures that *Deborah* afforded Jews and non-Jews alike, moreover, were public pleasures, pleasures enjoyed in social spaces where Jews encountered Jewishness produced on stage for a live audience that was almost always mixed.

When Sarah Bernhardt was performing her new version of *Leah* on her 1892 American tour, Boston theater critic Charles Wingate noted that Mosenthal's play was "the only play with a Jewish woman as the heroine which has survived to the present day."[45] Indeed, at mid-century, *Deborah* was not an isolated phenomenon but one of several new Jewish dramas that appealed to Jews and non-Jews alike in this way. Victor Séjour's *La Tireuse de cartes* (The Fortune-Teller, 1859) was widely performed in France, Italy, and the German-speaking world well into the late 1860s. In England and the United States, it circulated in at least four different versions: as *The Fortune-Teller; or, the Abduction of the Jew's Daughter*; as *The Woman in Red*; as *Gamea, or the Jewish Mother*; and as *The Sorceress*.[46] In North America, actresses such as Avonia Jones, Matilda Heron, and Felicia Vestvali included both *Leah* and *Gamea* in their touring repertoires, and the London publisher Ward and Lock advertised its novel version of *The Woman in Red* alongside the unauthorized novel *Leah, the Jewish Maiden*.[47] Séjour, a non-Jew, was a native of New Orleans with a Creole background who lived in France, and his play focused on a mother, Géméa, whose infant, Noémi, was forcefully removed from her after being baptized by a nurse. Particularly in Europe, theatergoers were aware that *La Tireuse de cartes* was a response to the ongoing high-profile case of Edgardo Mortara, an Italian Jewish boy removed from his home by papal authorities in 1858 after it became known that his nurse had baptized him.

The nineteenth-century stage saw the performances of other new Jewish-themed and biblical plays as well. Karl Gutzkow's *Uriel Acosta* (1846) used the situation of Jews in seventeenth-century Amsterdam as a backdrop to argue against religious fanaticism and celebrate freedom of thought and liberty of conscience. A staple of the German theater repertoire, *Uriel Acosta* also enjoyed a long afterlife on the Yiddish stage, circulating in four different versions.[48] After his success creating *Leah* for Kate Bateman, Augustin Daly, the American drama critic who would later emerge as one of the leading impresarios of the American theater, tried his hand at another Jewish drama. Daly adapted Friedrich Hebbel's tragedy *Judith* (1840), a classic of the nineteenth-century German stage, for Avonia Jones, a prominent American actress whose performances of *Gamea* and *Leah* Abraham and Mary Todd Lincoln enjoyed in the months before President Lincoln was assassinated.[49]

Neither *Uriel Acosta* nor *Judith* ever became an international sensation on the level of *Deborah*. The success that *La Tireuse de cartes* enjoyed was short-lived, no doubt because of its topical nature and its unusual concern with the fate of a Jewish mother rather than the more typical beautiful Jewess. When it came to live performances of Jewishness that appealed to Jews and non-Jews alike over a series of decades, *Deborah* had no real peer in the nineteenth century. For precisely this reason, a transnational performance history of this highly mutable drama offers a powerful perspective on the dynamic encounters between Jews and non-Jews that helped frame the experience of Jewishness in the latter half of the nineteenth century.

In focusing on the role of interactions between Jews and non-Jews in producing Jewishness in this way, *Deborah and Her Sisters* joins the works of a growing group of scholars who have sought to conceptualize the relationship between Jewish and general history in more dynamic ways than concepts such as assimilation and integration, minority and majority, typically allow. In his work on the role of Jews in German culture between the world wars, Steven Aschheim introduced the notion of "co-constitutionality" to underscore the extent to which Weimar culture was not "Jewish" but rather "jointly constructed by both Jewish and non-Jewish intellectuals who were not acting in their 'Jewish' or 'non-Jewish' capacities."[50] Arguing along similar lines, Jeanette R. Malkin and Freddie Rokem's recent volume of essays, *Jews and the Making of Modern German Theatre*, similarly stresses the ways in which German theater in the decades before the Nazi seizure of power was a "co-creation" of Jewish and non-Jewish Germans working together.[51] Scholars working on popular culture in the late nineteenth and early twentieth centuries, such as Marline Otte and Klaus Hödl, have made similar arguments in recent years, exploring the way popular entertainment often "blurred and redrew the boundaries between insiders and outsiders" to create spaces where Jews and non-Jews came together.[52]

However blurred boundaries between Jews and non-Jews may have been in creating and sustaining the commercial success of the *Deborah* craze, the product was an experience of Jewishness that was anything but fuzzy. In this sense, what we shall encounter studying the nineteenth century differs considerably from the way Jewish ethnicity has figured into popular forms of entertainment in more recent years. Andrea Most's *Theatrical Liberalism: Jews and Popular Entertainment in America*, for instance, offers a fascinating exploration of the extent to which Jews used the theater and other media in twentieth-century America to create a distinctly Jewish model of secular liberal culture, one whose Jewish origins were often obscured from the millions of Americans who enjoyed musicals like *Pal Joey, Oklahoma!, My Fair Lady*, or *Hair*.[53] Focusing on the postwar period, Henry Bial's *Acting Jewish: Negotiating Ethnicity on the American Stage and Screen* provides a probing investigation of the ways in which American popular culture engages in an elaborate strategy of double-coding, subtly providing Jewish American audiences with behavioral models that non-Jewish spectators typically did not pick up on.[54] One of the distinctive traits of the *Deborah* craze is that Jewishness here was not obscure but firmly and explicitly on the surface, equally legible to Jews and non-Jews alike. As a melodrama, we shall see, *Deborah* offers little in the way of behavioral models or authentic Jewish content. Studying the transnational performance history of Mosenthal's drama, however, affords us a window on a vibrant culture where Jewish difference was not hidden but celebrated, a culture where Jews and non-Jews joined together to indulge in the pleasures of identifying with Jewish suffering as the ultimate experience of a feel-good universalism.

Writing Transnational Theater History

When Mosenthal died in 1877, the Viennese writer Karl von Thaler joked in an obituary in *Die Gartenlaube* that the epigraph for his tombstone should read: "Here rests a poet from the attacks of his critics."[55] Mosenthal received numerous awards, honors, and medals during his lifetime, starting with the breast pin that the Austrian emperor Franz Joseph I conferred on him after seeing an early performance of *Deborah* in 1849.[56] In his final years, Mosenthal was famous for being photographed wearing his many decorations.[57] Rarely, though, did he ever receive the approval of the cultural elite. To be sure, the drama to which he owed his fame and fortune was often performed at prestigious venues such as Booth's Theatre in New York, Her Majesty's Theatre in London, and the Burgtheater in Vienna. And there were members of the elite such as Theodor Fontane, Germany's foremost novelist in the late nineteenth century, who harbored a soft spot for *Deborah*.[58] In the eyes of many critics, however, particularly in the German-speaking world, Mosenthal's sensational melodrama was anything but a masterpiece of the nineteenth-century stage. Nineteenth-century literary histories typically mention *Deborah* only to deride it for its commercial success. Not surprisingly, *Deborah* has met the same fate as much literature and culture that was popular in the dual sense of achieving success at the box office while failing to earn the cultural elite's stamp of approval. Few scholars of German literature and culture today are even aware of Mosenthal's play. Of those who are, even fewer regard *Deborah* as a drama that merits rigorous study.[59] Daly's *Leah, the Forsaken* has garnered somewhat more attention from scholars of both British literature and American theater, particularly among those interested in Anglo Jewish and American Jewish studies.[60] A comprehensive investigation into the transnational sensation of the *Deborah* craze, however, has never been attempted.

In Chapter 1, we shall turn our attention to Mosenthal's original script, exploring the formal complexity of the play and the highly sophisticated manner in which it went about the task of eliciting the sympathy—and the tears—of its audience. In this context, we shall come to recognize *Deborah* as a masterfully constructed melodrama, one whose success at the box office was neither an accident nor a generic symptom of the commodification of affect in nineteenth-century culture. As crucial as Mosenthal's text was, *Deborah and Her Sisters* is ultimately less interested in the script itself than in the adaptation, circulation, and performance of Mosenthal's material.[61] To this end, the remaining three chapters of the book direct their energies less at Mosenthal and his text than at the cultural mobility and adaptability of his material. I focus here less on texts than on performances, on the theatrical events and the theatrical public spheres they participated in and help constitute, whether in continental Europe, the British Empire, North America, or elsewhere. In terms of method, *Deborah and Her Sisters* thus owes far more to recent developments in theater and performance studies than to literary studies.[62]

Chapter 2 concerns itself specifically with the dynamics of adaptation and cultural mobility, exploring the creative (and sometimes not so creative) ways in which *Deborah* was adapted, rewritten, and retooled throughout the nineteenth century. In this context, I discuss not just published scripts for *Deborah* and *Leah* but versions of the play that circulated in manuscript and performances that can be reconstructed only from secondhand reports. I position the multiple versions of the play alongside their offshoots, whether poetry, sheet music, or opera; the British novel *Leah, the Jewish Maiden* and its pirated American version; the proliferation of carte-de-visite photographs of actresses posing as Deborah

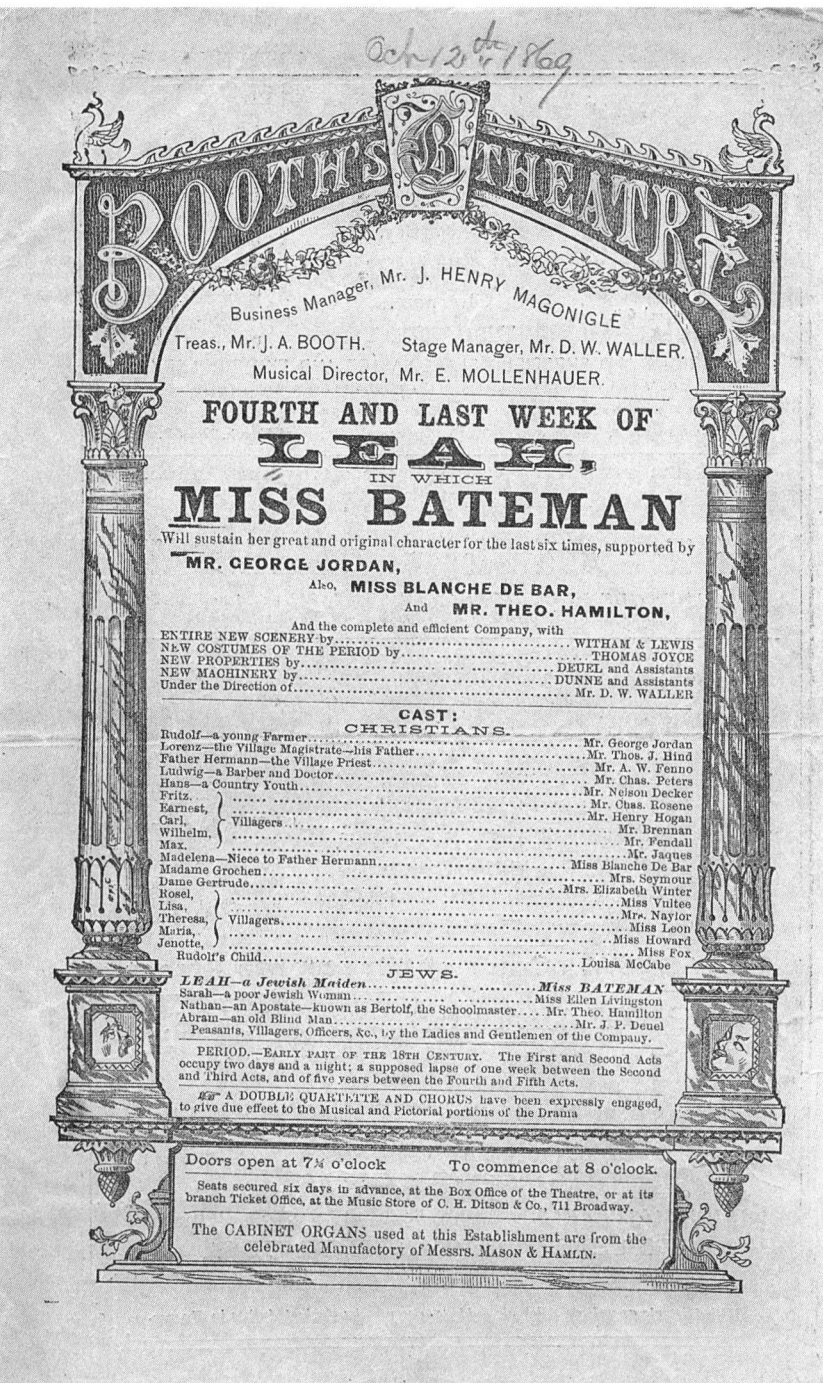

Figure 9. Program for 1869 performance of Bateman's revival of *Leah* at Booth's Theatre, New York. Billy Rose Theatre Division, New York Public Library for the Performing Arts, Astor, Lenox and Tilden Foundations.

and Leah; and the rich tradition of burlesques and parodies of this material that developed in the United States and the United Kingdom.

Continuing this deliberate move outward from the original text, Chapter 3 concerns itself with the individuals who were generally perceived to be at the center of the *Deborah* craze on both sides of the Atlantic. I focus here on the actresses as well as the mode of acting characteristic of performances of *Deborah* and *Leah* from the 1849 premiere in Hamburg through the American silent films produced in the second decade of the twentieth century. Highlighting the complexity of nineteenth-century emotional acting styles—a phenomenon often obscured by modernist polemics against actors' and audience's identification with roles—I consider here the interaction between actresses and their audiences in performances of the play and the role of the play in nineteenth-century star culture. Actresses performing *Deborah* and *Leah* invited identification at the same time as they encouraged audiences to develop a keen sense of the theatricality of their performances. Against the backdrop of an analysis of the elective affinity between the figure of the actress and the figure of the Jewess in nineteenth-century culture, Chapter 3 explores how Jewish and non-Jewish audiences experienced the Jewishness performed on stage—paradoxically—as theatrical and authentic at the same time.

Approaching the *Deborah* craze from the perspective of social history, Chapter 4 explores how performances of *Deborah* and *Leah* created spaces where Jews and non-Jews came together to produce and experience these highly theatrical modes of Jewishness. In both Europe and North America, the sentimental vision of Jewishness central to the history of *Deborah* was hardly peripheral to Jewish life. Rather, this was a phenomenon that Jews helped mold, working together with non-Jews in a variety of settings to create images of Jewishness for Jews and non-Jews alike that shaped the relations between them. Offering case studies of this phenomenon in diverse locales from San Francisco and Idaho City to small towns in Moravia and Ukraine, Chapter 4 explores the roles that Jews played—whether as actors, advertisers, audience members, translators, musicians, or theater owners—in launching, sustaining, and promoting widespread interest in *Deborah*. The tradition of philosemitic liberalism produced in this manner often did not earn the stamp of rabbinic authority or the approval of Jewish community leaders, particularly in Central Europe. As Chapter 4 makes clear, however, Mosenthal's drama did not only enjoy a robust following among Jews; whether performed at fund-raising benefits or at gatherings in Jewish community settings, it came to play an important role in Jewish institutional life as well.

The juxtaposition of Annie Lewis in Memphis, the Hawarden girls in London, and Kathi Frank in Hungary that I used to open this introduction may seem jarring to us today. Indeed, on one level, these instances of non-Jews pretending to be Jews almost seem designed to make those who identify as Jews uncomfortable. We shall see repeatedly throughout this study, indeed, that there were individual Jews in the nineteenth century who took offense at *Deborah*. There was also a long tradition of anti-theatricality among religious Jews as well as leaders of the Haskalah—the Jewish Enlightenment—that made some Jews predisposed to approach all theatrical performances with suspicion, whether or not Jews were being represented on stage.[63] It is certainly possible today to approach the *Deborah* craze with a fundamental skepticism, questioning the authenticity of these nineteenth-century spectacles of Jewishness performed largely by non-Jews for a largely non-Jewish audience.[64] In forcing this sort of suspicion on the broad-based fascination with Mosenthal's drama of the suffering exotic Jewess in its many iterations, we lose sight of the ways in which nineteenth-century audiences experienced the grandiose theatricality of *Deborah* itself as a heightened form of authenticity. To be sure, this cultural phenomenon belonging to the heyday of stage melodrama did not survive the first two decades of the twentieth century, much less the Holocaust. In the second decade of the twenty-first century, it is difficult to imagine bringing a revival of *Deborah* to the Burgtheater or Broadway. For so many Jews and non-Jews in the nineteenth century, nevertheless, the highly theatrical performances of Mosenthal's play offered an experience of Jewishness that boasted its own form of authenticity—one that Jews helped decisively to shape, and one that held particular urgency for Jews precisely because of its broad appeal to non-Jews all over the world. It is this experience that this book seeks to reconstruct and give its due.

Chapter 1

Anatomy of a Tearjerker: The Melodrama of the Forsaken Jewess

Uncle Schneider and the Theater of Compassion

In December 1869, "Uncle Schneider," a fictional German American columnist in the *New York Clipper*, shared his excitement over having the opportunity to see *Leah*, the adaptation of Mosenthal's *Deborah* that had taken American and British stages by storm following its New York premiere in January 1863. Writing in the mock German American English known as Dutch dialect, Uncle Schneider imparted his impressions of this "putty nice play" and produced a comic sketch that was widely performed and reprinted well into the twentieth century.[1] "Schneider Sees Leah" consisted largely of a charmingly naive scene-by-scene synopsis. Schneider told the story of the persecuted Jewess Leah, abandoned by the Christian Rudolf—"dot[']s her feller"—after his "fader" and the village schoolmaster—"dot's de Villen"—conspire and misrepresent to Rudolf that Leah accepted their bribe "and "dook some money to go vay." The appeal of this and other Uncle Schneider sketches derived, to some extent, from their unrelenting mockery of immigrant speech. Yet in taking an American reworking of a German play as its subject matter, "Schneider Sees Leah" also offered a commentary on the newfound prestige of German drama on the New York stage that Augustin Daly's *Leah, the Forsaken* and J. Guido Methua's 1863 adaptation of Albert Emil Brachvogel's *Narziß* (Narcisse) had helped establish. American advertisements routinely marketed *Leah* as a masterpiece of the contemporary German stage and a "great emotional play."[2] Uncle Schneider concluded his synopsis, accordingly, with a description of *Leah*'s famous ability to bring audiences to tears.

According to legends that Mosenthal helped perpetuate, Jakob Lutzberger, the stage director of the Theater an der Wien, Vienna's largest commercial theater in the 1840s, decided to put on *Deborah* after reading through the script caused him to break out in tears.[3] Tears, indeed, were inextricable from *Deborah* from the beginning of its long career on stage. The earliest advertisements for *Leah* in the United States promised theatergoers an experience of "tearful sympathy,"[4] and initial reviews stressed how the play's concluding scenes, in particular, brought "tears to the eyes of the most phlegmatic individual in the house."[5] In the action-packed final sequence that takes place five years after Rudolf abandons Leah and marries his village sweetheart, Leah returns to see whether the curse that she pronounced on Rudolf and his family has borne fruit. Much to her surprise, she finds a thriving young family ridden by guilt over the way she was treated years before, and she learns that Rudolf has had an audience with the emperor to plead for equal rights for the Jews. After she meets Rudolf's daughter and discovers that she was named Leah, after her, her heart melts. She subsequently recants her curse, blesses Rudolf's family, and forgives the Christian world that has wronged her. Sensing that she is about to die, Leah sinks into Rudolf's arms and is taken for dead. Immediately thereafter, the schoolmaster, the play's scheming villain, shows up with a mob of villagers to enforce the soon-to-be-antiquated laws banning Jews from the village. When Leah shocks the villagers by rousing herself and denouncing the schoolmaster

Figure 10. *Closing Scene in "Leah the Forsaken," Frank Leslie's Illustrated Newspaper*, October 9, 1869. Hess private collection.

as a Jewish apostate, the schoolmaster lunges at her, inadvertently revealing himself as the murderer of the last person who discovered his identity, the blind Jewish patriarch Abraham. As the authorities take the schoolmaster into custody, Leah renounces vengeance once and for all and dies peacefully, a symbol of reconciliation between Jews and Christians.[6]

Uncle Schneider spends more time describing this sensational final sequence than any other part of *Leah*, offering a detailed account of the response that it provoked among theatergoers. Once Leah meets the "leedle child" Leah and discovers her name, both she and the audience are overwhelmed:

> Oh! my goodnessness, don'd Leah gry orful ven she hear dot. I dold you vat it is, dot's a shplaindid ding. Und quick comes dem tears in your eyes, und you look up ad de vall, so dot nobody can'd see dot, und you make out you don'd care aboud it. But your eyes gits fulled up so quick dot you couldn'd keep dem in, und de tears comes down of your face like a shnow-storm, und den you don'd care a tarn if efery body sees dot. Und Leah kisses her and gries like dot her heart's broke, und she doks off dot gurse from Rudolf und goes away. De child den dell her fader und muder about dot, und dey pring her back. Den dot mop comes back und vill kill her again, but she exposes dot skoolmaster, dot villain, und dot fixes him. Den she falls down in Rudolf's arms, und your eyes gits fulled up again, und you can'd see someding more. I'd like to haf as many glasses of beer as dere is grying chust now. You couldn'd help dot any vay.

Amid clichés of German men whose sole frame of reference is a glass of beer, Uncle Schneider's sketch offers a compact analysis of *Leah*'s workings as a tearjerker. Confronted by the spectacle of Leah crying in her encounter with her namesake, spectators find themselves overwhelmed by tears, embarrassed by a seemingly involuntary welling up. They try at first to look away to avoid being seen by others. Yet recognizing that the tears cannot be stopped, they give in, initially indifferent to others present in the theater. Once Leah recants her curse, exposes the schoolmaster, and begins to die, however, members of the audience self-consciously embrace crying as a collective experience. No longer able to see the stage because of the volume of tears streaming down his face, Schneider turns his attention to his fellow playgoers, all of whom are weeping, and he celebrates this intense feeling of human solidarity. Focusing on those around him in the theater, he pronounces men and women who are not in tears as somehow beyond the pale of humanity. Naturally, he expresses these sentiments with reference to beer: "Und if I see a gal vot don'd gry in dot piece, I voodn't marry dot gal efen if her fader owned a pig prewery. Und if I see a feller vot don'd gry, I voodn'd dook a drink mit him."

Leah's power, for Schneider, lies in its ability to create affective bonds between members of the audience, in the ways it uses the pleasures of crying to remind theatergoers of their common humanity. In this sense, "Schneider Sees Leah" links the popular American adaptation of Mosenthal's *Deborah* to the theory of sentimental drama put forth by Gotthold Ephraim Lessing in the eighteenth century.[7] To be sure, Schneider does not make this connection explicit. Lessing's grand vision of the theater as a site where human beings learn the civic virtue of compassion was likely far from the mind of Charles M. Connolly, the Irish American journalist and composer who created the Uncle Schneider sketches, not to mention the many people who heard this sketch performed in subsequent decades. Yet Schneider's reflections on the nature of collective, involuntary weeping offer an intriguing extension of Lessing's vision of the impact of tragic drama. Schneider focuses less on an ideal spectator in his or her relation to what is presented on stage than on the interactions among theatergoers, on the way bonds of sympathy are forged among those attending a particular performance. Departing from Lessing's idealism, he also implicitly questions the influence of the sympathy practiced in the theater, underscoring the difficulty of moving from the communal pleasure of crying over the play to the exigencies of the world outside. Whatever civic virtue one learns by experiencing compassion with Leah's woes, Schneider suggests that theatergoers take action to prepare themselves to get on with their lives: "Vell, afder de piece is oud, you feel so bad, und so goot, dot you must ead a few pieces of hot stuff do drife avay der plues." Like the process of telling the story of seeing *Leah*, spicy food provides the beer-drinker the cathartic agent needed to purge the complex emotions aroused by Mosenthal's play.

Much of the humor of the Uncle Schneider sketch derives from its combination of sophistication and naïveté, and, for our purposes, "Schneider's Sees Leah" is as important for what it obscures as for what it illuminates. In identifying great theater with tearjerkers, our immigrant beer-drinker reveals himself at odds with contemporary German visions of high culture, whether those in the New York German-language theater scene or those back in the old country.[8] By the time of *Deborah*'s German premiere in 1849, the cultural cachet that Lessing's poetics of compassion had enjoyed eighty years earlier had long since become a thing of the past, eclipsed by Goethe's and Schiller's establishment of the classical drama as the new gold standard for serious drama. In his widely disseminated theoretical writings, Schiller, in fact, defined the ethical grandeur of tragedy in opposition to contemporary forms of consumer culture whose chief effects were a "mere emptying out of the tear sacs" and finding "sensual

Figure 11. Kate Bateman as Leah, carte-de-visite photograph. Hess private collection.

Figure 12. Kate Bateman as Leah, carte-de-visite photograph. Hess private collection.

release for the vessels."[9] Lessing may have aspired to a world in which heartfelt tears of compassion would come to replace applause in the theater.[10] For all his insights into the audience's response to the involuntary crying provoked by *Leah*, Schneider's vision of weeping as a barometer of aesthetic value betrays a charming ignorance of the ways in which critics and literary elites saw a good cry in the theater not as the lofty goal of dramatic art but as a deplorable sign of the commercialization of culture.

In the Anglo American context, *Leah*'s success at the box office had set this nexus between weeping and show business very much in the public eye. Kate Bateman, the American actress who created the role of Leah in New York in 1863 in Daly's adaptation, wrote Daly after the play's London premiere in October 1863 that from her vantage point at the center of the action on stage, she experienced the final scenes with delight as a constant alternation between an audience in tears and roaring applause.[11] In this self-consciousness about working over her public, Bateman hardly exemplifies Lessing's fantasy of tears of compassion coming to replace clapping in the theater. With an initial run of 210 performances at the Royal Adelphi Theatre, Bateman's *Leah* was among the greatest commercial successes of the London stage in the 1860s. When the play closed in June 1864, an English weekly commented that theatergoers had wept a veritable "ocean of tears" over the sorrows of Bateman's "fair Hebrew,"[12] and both the British and the American press reported on the enormous profits that the newly established star reaped as she went on tour playing *Leah* in English provincial theaters.[13] "Schneider Sees Leah," moreover, appeared in 1869 on the heels of widely circulated reports that the "water-power" generated by audiences "weeping over Leah's woes" had helped set up a very wealthy Bateman as part owner of a profitable silk mill in Paterson, New Jersey.[14] The commerce in tears that *Leah* made possible was not limited to the 1860s or to Bateman. Forty years later, the great emotional American actress Nance O'Neil was famous for provoking the same alternation between weeping and applause in her audiences as Bateman while performing *The Jewess*, a version of *Deborah* that she included in her touring repertoire well into the second decade of the twentieth century.[15]

In his unapologetic enjoyment of crying in the theater, Schneider is oblivious to this theatrical dimension of weeping; he comments neither on the ways the particular performance of *Leah* he saw brought its audience to tears nor on the broader institutional context in which tearjerkers became such popular and profitable entertainment. Readers of the *New York Clipper* might have assumed that Schneider was referring to Bateman's highly publicized revival of *Leah* at Booth's Theatre in September and October 1869.[16] Connolly, however, has Schneider mention neither the actress who played Leah, nor the name of the theater, nor any other details that might indicate that Schneider had spent time thinking about how *Leah* functioned as a performance. By 1869, international celebrities such as Adelaide Ristori and Fanny Janauschek had performed *Deborah* (in Italian and German, respectively) on their American tours; countless American actresses had adopted versions of *Deborah* or *Leah* as star vehicles; and the play had been performed in New York alone at fourteen theaters, from the upscale Booth's Theatre on 23rd Street to venues downtown on the Bowery. In his charming naïveté, Schneider is as unaware of the broader theater scene as he is blind to the way virtuoso actresses were interacting with their audiences to afford them the pleasures of crying.

In studying how *Deborah* functioned as a tearjerker, this chapter foregrounds what Schneider fails to see—namely, the ways in which performances of the drama brought audiences to tears not despite their theatricality but because of it. In this sense, a nineteenth-century melodrama like *Deborah* that was used as a star vehicle differs considerably from eighteenth-century dramas geared at cultivating compassion. Lessing's domestic dramas were typically predicated on an aesthetic of the viewer's complete absorption in the happenings on stage, with the spectator suspending disbelief to accept the illusion of the theater. In Lessing's inaugural domestic tragedy *Miss Sara Sampson* (1755), theatricality itself is famously vilified on stage, with the villain Marwood's dissimulation, deception, and duplicitousness set in stark contrast to the heartfelt tears and transparent emotions of Sara Sampson and her virtuous father, Sir William. Mosenthal produced over the course of his career more than twenty libretti for operas, from Otto Nicolai's *Die lustigen Weiber von Windsor* (The Merry Wives of Windsor, 1849) to Karl Goldmark's *Die Königin von Saba* (The Queen of Sheba, 1875). Critics sometimes complained that his dramas were too "operatic," drawing their energy from grandiose performances, elaborate stage effects, and melodramatic excess.[17] The fictional Uncle Schneider may not be able to pierce the illusion of theatrical representation. Most theatergoers who purchased tickets to attend *Deborah* or *Leah* tended to be more sophisticated, cognizant that they were walking into a theatrical event whose focal point was the extravagant performance of a lead actress.

German newspapers frequently noted that playing Mosenthal's Jewess required actresses to display the "entire range of affects" as few other roles did.[18] Charles Lamb Kenney, the drama critic for the London *Times* who prepared the English libretto for Ristori's Italian performance of *Deborah* at Her Majesty's Theatre in July 1863, made similar comments in the promotional pamphlet he wrote for Bateman later that year. To perform Deborah or Leah, he explained, an actress has to express "almost every grade and shade of serious emotion" and show her "command . . . over every chord of human passion."[19] Reviewers on both sides of the Atlantic routinely noted that the play was organized around two grand scenes for actresses to display their virtuosity. Following on the heels of the tender romantic scenes with Rudolf (or Joseph, as he was called in the German original), actresses in the title role had to perform, first, the elaborate curse scene at the end of the third act of *Deborah* (Act IV in Daly's *Leah*), which required a tremendous modulation of the voice and the performance of fury, wrath, and a demand for Old Testament vengeance that audiences often experienced as "blood-curdling" or "electric."[20] Moving into the play's final act, actresses faced the challenge of making a convincing transition to display tenderness, forgiveness, and overflowing compassion as the protagonist either died on stage (as was the case in Bateman's version of *Leah*) or set off with her people, in the oft-cited words of Mosenthal's original, "a symbol of the tribe that has renounced its hatred now we know that you can love us."[21]

Whether in the newly created Idaho Territory or the southern Moravian town of Znaim (Znojmo), audiences were anything but lost in the illusion of the reality of events depicted on stage. Inevitably, they took performances of *Deborah* or *Leah* as an opportunity to express admiration and adulation for the actresses able to master this demanding role, frequently interrupting performances with boisterous applause and repeated demands for curtain calls.[22] Audiences delighted in extravagant performances where leading actresses managed to bring Deborah or Leah to life, converting the theater into a seemingly magical arena that transcended its own materiality. The tears that these performances provoked, however, were not tears that supplanted applause but tears that were accompanied by the audience's keen sense of the theatricality of the spectacle they were witnessing, tears that audiences experienced as heartfelt as the same time—paradoxically—as they revered the virtuoso actresses whose performances made such weeping possible.

In future chapters, we will study the transnational circulation of Mosenthal's material (Chapter 2) and explore the interplay of authenticity and theatricality in actual performances of *Deborah* and *Leah* (Chapter 3). Before doing so, we need to understand how and why Mosenthal's drama was able to provoke "oceans of tears" to begin with. In the heyday of sentimental literary culture in the eighteenth century, public crying was often celebrated as a sign of a healthy masculinity. By the mid-nineteenth century, however, intellectual elites had cordoned off the private realm as the appropriate sphere for crying, typically deriding weeping as feminine.[23] As Franco Moretti pointed out decades ago, since the mid-nineteenth century, tears and weeping have typically provoked shame rather than serious interest in intellectual circles; only recently has there developed a small body of scholarship in literary and film studies that takes the phenomenon of spectator crying seriously.[24] Not surprisingly, the reception history of *Deborah* is peppered by a tendency to dismiss the tears that the play produced as unworthy of serious critical attention. One critic, referring to the 1890s, has noted that *Leah* was "one of those perennially popular 'four-hanky' melodramas" that did little more than allow "the affluent ladies of New York to have a good cry without ever exposing them to the misery of real life."[25] Critics in the German-speaking world complained that in "arousing compassion ad nauseam," Mosenthal's deeply manipulative drama helped set the tone for the ascendancy of cheap melodrama on the German stage.[26] To be sure, by the latter half of the nineteenth century, crying in the theater was a highly commodified affair, and Schneider himself alerts us to the disjunction between weeping in the theater and the challenges of the world outside. The problem here is not just that polemical statements of this nature are typically armed with a paucity of historical evidence, a pejorative use of the term "melodrama" that derives from its nineteenth-century detractors, and deeply rooted cultural suspicions about crying. They divert our attention from the complex ways in which Mosenthal's drama elicited the sympathy of its audiences.

Despite occasional matinées that catered to women, Mosenthal's drama hardly deserves to be caricatured as a cultural form whose main task was to enable "affluent ladies" to deflect their attention from real-world suffering. Bateman, at the Royal Theatre in Glasgow, once brought a crowded house of sailors from the Channel Fleet to tears and held them spellbound.[27] Whether she was performing *Deborah* in German or English, Fanny Janauschek was famous for transforming her audiences into a "chorus of tears" that "took hold of man and woman alike."[28] In his autobiography, British journalist George Augustus Sala recalled the male bonding that *Leah* could engender. During Bateman's initial run of *Leah* in 1863–1864, Sala and fellow journalist friends Horace and Augustus Mayhew and Charles Kenney used to go to the Adelphi together "at least three times a week . . . for the express purpose of weeping bitterly over the woes of the persecuted Hebrew maiden, and of being thrilled by the terrific curse which she uttered."[29] The forms of sympathy that Mosenthal's drama produced were also not narrowly circumscribed by class. American advertisements for *Leah* often stressed the drama's appeal to "fashionable" audiences,[30] and eventually, after its success in New York and London, *Deborah* did make it to the Burgtheater in Vienna, the revered bastion of German high culture, where it was regularly performed for nearly four decades. But versions of the play also proved successful at venues catering to less elite patrons, whether working-class theaters in London's East End, makeshift theaters in mining towns in Australia and the American West, or wandering theater troupes in the German-speaking world.

Rather than speculating about theatergoers unself-consciously partaking in an escapist, commercial culture of sentimentality or vilifying *Deborah* for its popularity or its appeal to women, this chapter turns its attention to Mosenthal's original script, bringing to light the complex poetics of compassion that was written into the play from the beginning. Rehabilitating Mosenthal from the charges of cheap sentimentalism and crude, effect-driven melodrama that some of his nineteenth-century critics leveled at him, my discussion of the text will take seriously the affective power that Mosenthal's drama exerted over its audiences, exposing the formal complexity of the play and the highly sophisticated manner in which it went about the task of transforming its spectators into a "chorus of tears." More than a generic symptom of the commercialization of affect, *Deborah* needs to be recognized as a masterfully constructed melodrama.

In the wake of Peter Brooks's *The Melodramatic Imagination* (1976), literary critics and film scholars have come to take melodrama seriously as an object of study, salvaging melodrama from both nineteenth-century polemics denigrating it as bad tragedy and twentieth-century diatribes against its alleged deviations from cinematic realism. In this context, melodrama has often come to be understood less as a discrete genre unto itself than as a mode, and one that lies at the core of more canonical cultural formations, whether the fiction of Honoré de Balzac or Henry James or realist cinema itself. In his seminal work from the 1970s, Brooks defined melodrama as a secular form that had the function of rendering legible "the conflict of good and evil played out under the surface of things"; for Brooks, the evil villains and suffering heroes and heroines whom we identify with melodrama work together with its polarized words and grand gestures "to locate and to articulate the moral occult."[31] More recent work has tended to focus less on melodrama's function of imagining a clear-cut ethical universe than on the affective work it performs. Steve Neale, in a key essay from the 1980s, stressed the unique combination of powerlessness and fantasy that melodrama unleashes in its spectators through the tears it provokes.[32] Building on Neale's analysis and on Christine Gledhill's work on melodrama and the woman's film, film critic Linda Williams has also defined melodrama in terms of the bodily fluids—the tears—it produces in its spectators. Zoning in on the unique power that lies in the way melodrama encourages identification with suffering victims, Williams has sought to rehabilitate the way melodrama helps "negotiate moral feeling" and produces feelings of righteousness that deserve to be taken seriously.[33]

Focusing on the original text of *Deborah*, this chapter explores why Mosenthal's tearjerker was able to command such success at the box office in the latter half of the nineteenth century. What was there about this play about a suffering, forsaken Jewess that enabled it to become one of most popular German dramas of its generation and the only German drama that became a true international sensation during this era?[34] As the esteemed literary historian Julian

Schmidt protested in an early critique of *Deborah* published in the prominent cultural review *Die Grenzboten*, Mosenthal was clearly counting on a familiar exotic figure to play well with the theatergoing public.[35] Indeed, as we noted in the Introduction, Mosenthal was working solidly within the tradition of the figure of the "beautiful Jewess" that had become an established fixture of European culture in the wake of Walter Scott's best-selling historical novel *Ivanhoe* (1820) and Fromental Halévy's enormously successful grand opera *La Juive* (1835). We shall discover in this chapter, however, that there was more at stake here than a cynical use of an exotic type to which the discussions over Jewish emancipation during the 1848 revolution had lent new relevance. Mosenthal used the figure of the suffering beautiful Jewess in innovative and creative ways, offering a powerful rewriting of both Lessing's famous idealization of Jewish figures on stage and the vision of compassion central to Lessing's dramaturgy. *Deborah* was artfully designed not just to tug at its spectators' heartstrings and bring them to tears. Through an elaborate alternation between provoking feelings of powerlessness and promoting spectators' utopian desires for a political order where Jews and Christians might live side by side, Mosenthal's drama actively promoted liberal modes of feeling, giving theatergoers the sense that their tears shed in identification with Jewish suffering meant something. The political significance we should attribute to these pleasurable experiences of sentimental liberalism is the issue we shall address in this chapter's conclusion.

Recasting Lessing's Legacy: *Deborah* and the Poetics of Compassion

Rejecting the grand public figures who were the traditional heroes of classical drama, Lessing put forth a vision of tragedy that rests on what Paul Fleming has aptly termed "the posited similarity—and thus exchangeability—between average hero and average audience."[36] "The names of princes and heroes can give a play pomp and majesty," Lessing explains in an oft-quoted passage from his *Hamburgische Dramaturgie* (Hamburg Dramaturgy, 1767), "but they contribute nothing to its emotional impact.... If we feel compassion with kings, we feel it for them as human beings, and not as kings."[37] Lessing calls for a complete identification with the suffering hero or heroine that precludes any hierarchical relationship. It is for this reason that he was so eager to dismantle the aesthetic category of "admiration" central to his friend Moses Mendelssohn's vision of tragedy. Lessing's famous reinterpretation of the fear that Aristotle associates with the response to tragedy as "compassion applied to ourselves" reinforces this ideal of a fundamental lack of distance between theatergoers and the figure on stage whom they claim as one of their own.

Just decades later, Lessing's successors came to regard this type of identification less as an aesthetic ideal than as a social problem and, at times, as a public health hazard as well. Already in the 1770s and 1780s, literary elites complained about the "reading fever" fueled by the sentimental novel and its invitation to identify with its protagonists and consume literature excessively, reading one novel after the next.[38] As Goethe and Schiller enshrined the classical drama as a new ideal for the German stage, theater critics engaged in analogous diatribes against the huge volume of sentimental plays by August von Kotzebue, August Wilhelm Iffland, and Charlotte Birch-Pfeiffer that seemed to transform Lessing's dramaturgy of compassion into a commercially successful mode of theater catering to the lowest common denominator of public taste.[39]

Faced with *Deborah* taking German stages by storm, Mosenthal's detractors often subsumed this play that allegedly "aroused compassion ad nauseam" into this tradition of denigrating popular culture. Schmidt complained in his article in *Die Grenzboten* that *Deborah* blended a "banal pathos" reminiscent of Schiller's imitators with a heavy dose of exoticism and melodrama.[40] Elite commentators like Schmidt and the drama critic Heinrich Theodor Rötscher argued that Mosenthal fundamentally lacked "a receptivity for tragic problems" and was "incapable of comprehending the laws of poetic composition."[41] The problem here was not just that *Deborah* ended on a relatively upbeat note, with Deborah reconciling with her former lover before setting off with her people. "Chance," rather than "necessity," drove the plot; in the pivotal scene in Act II, the schoolmaster, entrusted with the task of offering Deborah money in exchange for her promise to abandon Joseph and leave town, actually gives the bribe to a different Jewish woman, sending word back to the village that Deborah accepted the money.[42] As Rötscher pointed out, misunderstandings and miscommunications of this nature transpire in real life but have no place on the tragic stage. Deborah's rapid transition from the Old Testament vengeance of the curse scene to the reconciliatory tone of the final act appeared similarly lacking in motivation. According to one critic, the sole purpose of this feel-good denouement was to set Deborah up to pronounce the famous "slogan" about "the tribe that has renounced its hatred now we know that you can love us."[43]

When we consider how *Deborah* reworks Lessing's poetics of compassion, the internal logic of the play will come more clearly into focus, and *Deborah* will emerge less as a failed tragedy than as a play that sought to elicit the sympathy of its audience in a highly complex manner. For Lessing, compassion is not an emotion to be awakened merely at the end of a drama. Tears are to be provoked, rather, throughout the play, facilitated by a central figure with whom spectators readily identify from the beginning.[44] From the opening scene of Mosenthal's drama, however, Deborah appears as a challenging object of sympathy for both the audience and the villagers on stage. As the play continues, the plot hinges increasingly on the difficulty of developing and practicing compassion with this Jewess from Hungary, with her oft-noted strange clothing, her "bushy black eyebrows," and her "long dark hair hanging down on her naked brown shoulders" (I.ii). One critic noted that Deborah was a figure "calculated rather to repel than to attract sympathy—a woman of fierce passions, and rendered almost demoniac by the circumstances in which she is placed."[45] The fact that Deborah speaks almost exclusively in blank verse, in elevated and, at times, biblical language, whereas scenes between the Catholic villagers are mostly in prose, underscores further what Lessing sought to preclude: the distance between heroine and audience.

Mosenthal does more than build on the long tradition of the figure of the beautiful Jewess and traffic in a mode of exoticism that happens to disrupt the workings of sympathy. *Deborah*'s power as a tearjerker, we shall see, derives from the tensions it introduces into Lessing's identificatory model of compassion, from the way it probes the limits of the implicitly Christian models of sympathy that shaped eighteenth-century ideals of compassion. In this sense, *Deborah* is not just the *Tendenzstück* or topical drama about Jewish emancipation that its peers took it to be. It is a drama that reflects on the parochial nature of Christian sympathy and seeks to develop, on the formal level, a new, secular ethos of liberal compassion able to acknowledge and accommodate Jewish difference.

A consideration of the genesis of Mosenthal's *Deborah* project helps illuminate the motivations behind this revision of Lessing's model of tragedy and Mosenthal's interest in writing a Jewish-themed drama along these lines. In the early 1870s, after Jews had earned complete civil rights in the Austro-Hungarian Empire, Mosenthal celebrated *Deborah* as a direct product of the revolutionary fervor of 1848. He himself briefly served in the civilian militia in spring 1848 in his adopted city of Vienna, and he claimed to have composed the play while hearing cannons firing on the imperial arsenal.[46] Yet despite its commitment to principles of Jewish emancipation that were part of the agenda of the failed revolutions of 1848, *Deborah* was neither the work of a radical liberal nor the product of a sustained interest in politics. Nor was the drama considered politically controversial when it was first performed. Indeed, its Viennese premiere in March 1849 was used as a special event to celebrate the new constitution that Emperor Franz Joseph had just enacted into law—without any involvement of parliament.[47] Later that summer, when Franz Joseph decorated the author of *Deborah* with a brilliant breast pin, no one registered surprise. In 1851, once Mosenthal was established as a successful playwright, he had no qualms about allowing himself to be appointed to a titled position in the Ministry for Education that enabled the empire to flaunt its goodwill toward Jews in the absence of extending Jews complete civil and political rights.[48]

In contrast to the "Young German" writers of the previous decade, Mosenthal never regarded himself as politically engaged.[49] As the Viennese *Neue Freie Presse* noted in its obituary when Mosenthal died in 1877, Mosenthal was known as apolitical in his private life as well as in his writings.[50] In the following section, we will explore how *Deborah* draws its energy from tensions between Christian modes of compassion and the quest for a more secular ethos of liberal sympathy able to accommodate Jewish difference in new ways. But secular sympathy was of interest to Mosenthal primarily as a dramaturgical project. The reasons that Mosenthal gravitated toward Jewish subject matter and the figure of the beautiful Jewess in the late 1840s have far less to do with liberal politics than with his ongoing quest to write a powerful drama that would establish him as a significant playwright in the Viennese theater world.

As a dramatist, Mosenthal faced the perennial challenge of coming up with original material.[51] Indeed, in the opera libretti that he produced, from *Die lustigen Weiber von Windsor* (1849) until his death in 1877, he honed skills recycling and retooling texts written by others that had shaped his career as a playwright from the beginning. Mosenthal's first play, *Der Holländer Michel* (Michel, the Dutchman, 1845), was an adaptation of Wilhelm Hauff's popular tale "Das kalte Herz" (The Stone Heart). While theater programs advertised Mosenthal's second work for the stage, *Die Sklavin* (The Slave Girl, 1847), as an "original drama," Viennese newspapers noted that this sensationalist play set in South Africa was more than a tad reminiscent of *Toni*, an 1812 play by the Schiller-imitator Theodor Körner.[52] On the surface, the drama that catapulted Mosenthal to international fame was no less derivative. Mosenthal borrowed both the concept for *Deborah* and the skeleton of its plot from his friend Otto Prechtler, who had been planning to make a drama out of the libretto he had written for *Mara*, a romantic opera about a gypsy woman forsaken by her non-gypsy lover that had played to mixed reviews since its 1842 premiere.[53]

It was with Prechtler's blessing that Mosenthal transformed Mara, the daughter of a deceased gypsy chieftain, into Deborah, the daughter of a deceased rabbi, and the similarities between Mosenthal's drama and Prechtler's libretto are striking. In *Mara*, as in *Deborah*, the villagers conspire to offer the title figure a bribe to abandon her Christian lover; both women deliver elaborate curses when their lovers get married; and both women eventually forgive those who wronged them. The popularity of Prosper Mérimée's *Carmen* (1845)—a novella translated into German in 1846 and set, like *Mara*, in Spain—no doubt reinforced Mosenthal's sense that a drama about an exotic and transgressive heroine might become his key to success at the box office.[54] His reworking of

Prechtler's libretto, moreover, was facilitated by a long tradition that rendered the beautiful Jewess and the beautiful gypsy parallel objects of exotic and erotic fascination.[55] Even though the genealogy of *Deborah* seems to have been unknown in the English-speaking world, some of Bateman's most widely reproduced poses as Leah picked up on this elective affinity between the Jewess and the gypsy (Figure 13).

In adapting Prechtler's material, Mosenthal did not mechanically substitute one exotic heroine for another. He fundamentally and creatively reworked the

Figure 13. *Miss Bateman as Leah, at the Adelphi Theatre, Illustrated London News*, April 9, 1864. Hess private collection.

concept of Prechtler's libretto, inserting his heroine into a drama that revolved from the beginning around the question of compassion with the exotic outsider and that drew its energy from the tensions between this figure and her surroundings. *Mara* opened with a series of choruses and arias that characterized gypsies as wild children of nature without a homeland, who harbor an irrational hatred and distrust of those outside their tribe. As we shall see shortly, the opening sequence that Mosenthal devises for *Deborah* focuses not directly on Jews but on Christian attitudes and behavior toward Jews. *Deborah* begins by exposing the limitations of Christian modes of sympathy, introducing a problem that structures the entire drama and finds resolution only in its final scenes.

In this context, it makes sense that Mosenthal found the verdict on the drama pronounced by his idol Franz Grillparzer, the towering figure of nineteenth-century Austrian theater, so devastating. "Grillparzer found nothing to criticize in my drama—except for its main point," Mosenthal wrote in an essay in the popular illustrated weekly *Über Land und Meer*. Unaware of his borrowings from Prechtler, Grillparzer complained to the up-and-coming playwright that he had made a fatal mistake in making a Jewess his protagonist; Mosenthal would have done well, Grillparzer commented, to make Deborah a "gypsy" or some other "vagabond girl," as this would have lent his play a more timeless quality, allowing the "purely human" dimension of the conflict to take center stage.[56] For Mosenthal, the Jewishness of his heroine was essential to the way his drama constructed the "purely human," central to the way his drama functioned as a tearjerker and revisited the implicitly Christian models of compassion undergirding Lessing's poetics of sympathy.

In making a passionate, emotional Jewish woman the central figure of *Deborah*, Mosenthal was not just after timeliness. By transforming Prechtler's gypsy heroine into a beautiful Jewess, he created a drama that gave his largely non-Jewish audiences the thrill of experiencing a new way of identifying with Jewish suffering. In this sense, his revision of Lessing's dramaturgy goes hand in hand with a revision of the function that Jewish figures played in Lessing's dramas. Critics well disposed toward *Deborah* inevitably compared Mosenthal's play with Lessing's celebrated *Nathan der Weise* (Nathan the Wise, 1779), noting that *Deborah* was far more moving and much more gripping than Lessing's philosophical parable about religious tolerance.[57] Gustav Heckenast, Mosenthal's publisher, marketed the print edition of *Deborah* with a quotation from a review of the play in Frankfurt am Main that related it to *Nathan* along these lines.[58] Lessing is famous in the annals of German theater history for breaking with the legacy of Shakespeare and Marlowe to create the prototype of the figure of the "noble Jew," first in his early play *Die Juden* (The Jews, 1749) and later in much more elaborate form in *Nathan*.[59] Nowhere in Lessing, however, do Jewish figures appear in tragedies or other plays where they might invite compassion, and nowhere in Lessing do we ever see Jewish women. Both *Nathan*, a "philosophical poem" that had its origins in a theological dispute, and *Die Juden*, a comedy, feature noble Jewish men who invite admiration rather than sympathy. In keeping with Lessing's Enlightenment vision of universalism, moreover, characters on stage in both dramas overcome prejudice to learn to venerate these idealized Jewish men as human beings, not specifically as Jews. While these dramas clearly call for respect for religious differences under the banner of a universal humanity, they encourage little interest in their main characters' Judaism.[60] In keeping with this level of abstraction, Lessing's idealized Jewish figures are not just men; they are largely sterile figures, male Jews who find emotional fulfillment through male-male friendship (or adoptive fatherhood, in the case of *Nathan*), not through erotic relationships with Jews or non-Jews.

In both her eroticism and her exoticism, Mosenthal's Deborah is anything but an abstract embodiment of a universal human rationality that transcends religious differences and commands respect and admiration. Indeed, as a character, she—like so many other nineteenth-century literary Jewesses—is far more complex and far more ambivalent than Lessing's Nathan, Shakespeare's Shylock, Richard Cumberland's Sheva, Charles Dickens's Fagin, or the scores of other male Jewish villains (and the occasional hero) who populate the pages of nineteenth-century fiction and drama.[61] Deborah both invites and repels sympathy, marking compassion with Jews the desideratum that the play struggles with in a sustained and systematic manner from its very first scene to its concluding sequence. In this way, Mosenthal revisits Lessing's dramaturgy of compassion to create a tearjerker that renders an exotic Jewish woman the focal point of an affective poetics that makes Jewish difference the object of a new, distinctly secular, form of compassion. How all this makes for such a good cry is the question we shall explore in what follows, as we focus on how tensions over the issue of sympathy structure the drama, its plot, and the way it engages its spectators.

The Elusiveness of Compassion

In one respect, my discussion of the text of *Deborah* will support the nineteenth-century critics who charged Mosenthal with being concerned more with dramatic effect than with the theater's potential to stage fundamental ethical conflicts. From its first scene until its last, indeed, *Deborah* was a drama written with its audience in mind, systematically built around its goal of using the stage to create a spectator-position from which a distinctly secular mode of sympathy becomes possible and enables tears to flow. Before Deborah even appears on stage, several scenes into Act I, her future rival—Hanna, who eventually marries Deborah's love interest, Joseph—describes her in terms that stress the exoticism of her outward appearance and invite compassion with her and her fellow Jews who have escaped an episode of anti-Jewish violence in Hungary and are seeking "shelter among the animals of the forest" (I.ii). The type of sympathy that Hanna has in mind, however, is a distinctly Christian one and quickly reveals itself as problematic, setting the tone for the remainder of the drama's quest to develop a mode of compassion that enables spectators to connect with Deborah's suffering.

The play opens on Good Friday, as Hanna walks out of the village church with her uncle the priest, telling him that his sermon has inspired her to follow the example of Christ and suffer for humanity. When the priest tells his niece that she should emulate Jesus not with grandiose deeds but through love and good works, Hanna immediately suggests reaching out to the suffering Jews in the forest, perhaps even going so far as to help Deborah's companion, a poor Jewish woman with a newborn, by taking in her child and raising it as her own. Hanna's overzealous fantasy of benevolence toward Jews in the name of Christ quickly exposes itself as a dead end. As the schoolmaster is quick to point out, the laws do not allow Jews to stay overnight in the Austrian province of Styria, and in the world that Mosenthal initially creates on stage, these legal restrictions are buttressed by popular anti-Jewish sentiment. Immediately before Deborah arrives on stage, hauled in by the mob that wants to stone her and drag her into the river, the villagers rehearse a litany of complaints about Jewish penchants for usury, well-poisoning, witchcraft, and kidnapping of Christian children.

In the fast-paced opening act of *Deborah*, anti-Jewish sentiments quickly yield to anti-Jewish violence, creating a spectacular entrance for Deborah that some Jews found disturbing for its graphic portrayal of anti-Jewish persecution.[62] Deborah emerges here dragged in by *"the peasants, from whom she wrests herself away, and steps boldly to the front of the stage"* (I.iv). Deborah's grand entrance and the scene that follows include a minimal number of spoken lines, providing actresses a tremendous opportunity to demonstrate their talents for nonverbal acting. An actress who worked with Kate Bateman reported that Bateman "practiced the one single feature of rushing on the stage pursued by the town rabble, during two long hours every day regularly for a week, before she trusted herself to do it before the public on the first night. The consequence was that the effect was magnificent—the persecuted and lovely Jewess flying with swift feet before the vile rabble of a bigoted German town, hooting at her, stoning her—she as a climax turning and defying them—that one effect was enough to carry the weight of the entire play and make it a success."[63] The spectacle of the beautiful Jewess resisting mob violence obviously encourages spectators to follow Hanna and regard Deborah as an object of compassion. But even as the audience is encouraged to identify with the persecuted Jewess, Deborah is hardly willing to be a passive object of Christian sympathy. This scene that begins with Deborah's bold steps to the front of the stage culminates in an extravagant rejection of any vision of Jews as the object of Christian benevolence.

When Deborah appears on stage, Hanna initially seeks to rush to her assistance but proves powerless to create a buffer against the mob. After Hanna's vain attempt to stop the violence, it is her uncle the enlightened priest who tries to help Deborah. He offers her a mode of protection that she explicitly refuses—without uttering a single word:

> PRIEST. Step back, you blinded people! I shall lay my priestly hand upon her. Daughter of Judah! Do not tremble. The priest of Christ lays his holy hand on your head. Come to me. (*He tries to place his hand on her head. Deborah lets out a dull cry and escapes to the other side of the stage.*)
> CROWD (*chasing her*). Look at her! She's shaking!
> OLD LISE. She can't bear his touch! Stone the godless woman!
> PRIEST. And if she's godless, come now! Let he who is without sin among you cast the first stone at her. (*They all grow quiet, and the crowd disperses. The priest gestures at Deborah.*) Go forth in peace! (*Deborah slowly turns to go. The crowd grumbles.*) (I.iv)

As a Jewess and an innocent victim of Christian persecution, Deborah rejects Christian benevolence, showing the villagers that the touch of the enlightened priest is unbearable to her. Daly cleverly ups the ante on this scene, having *Leah, the Forsaken*'s Father Herman raise a cross as the crowd bows in submission and Leah cowers beneath him in a tableau vivant that he uses to conclude Act I (Figure 14). In both Mosenthal's *Deborah* and Daly's *Leah*, the heroine does more than express discomfort with traditional symbols of Christianity; she explicitly refuses the model of Christian compassion introduced in the play's opening scene. Well-meaning characters like Hanna and the priest want to extend sympathy to Jews and act on what Hanna identifies as basic principles of "humanity" and "justice" (I.ii). At this point in the play, however, compassion in the name of Christ, no matter how heartfelt, is revealed as problematic.

The first four scenes of *Deborah* thus institute a disjunction between the initial compassion with Deborah that the audience is encouraged to feel and the Christian framework that well-intentioned characters in the play use to identify with Deborah's suffering. Mosenthal establishes this discrepancy between the perspective of the spectators and the limited viewpoint of figures on stage, moreover, not primarily through dialogue but—as one might expect for a play

Figure 14. This sketch of the tableau vivant that concludes Act I of Daly's *Leah, the Forsaken* originally appeared in the *New York Clipper*. Promptbook for unidentified production of *Leah, the Forsaken*, Harvard Theatre Collection, THE TS 2378, Houghton Library, Harvard University.

often branded with the moniker "melodrama"—through nonverbal acting and carefully managed stage effects. The scenes that follow build on this tension between the affective response of the spectators and the limitations of what is possible within the confines of the world depicted on stage, using a jarring juxtaposition of Christian symbols and Jewish symbolic language to develop a model of secular compassion for the spectators.

In the eighth scene of Act I, Mosenthal shifts from one Christian milieu to another, moving from the square outside the village church to the cross in the woods where Deborah and Joseph have agreed to meet. The audience encounters Deborah waiting in the moonlight, one of those special effects for which Mosenthal was famous. The scene begins in moonlight but with no moon visible. At a dramatic point in Deborah's opening monologue, the moon rises, and with some Hebrew tossed in for exotic flavor, Deborah greets "Levana" and then recites, in German, the prayer sanctifying the moon and yearning for the restoration of Israel that she recalls from her rabbi father. Waiting alone in the woods, Deborah expresses discomfort over the presence of the cross and the figure of Christ beside it: "Uncanny image! Why do I shudder so when I see you? Why do your pale features provoke such ghastly horror in me?" (I.viii). Deborah's prayer for the restoration of Israel and her horror in the presence of Christian symbols not only situate her decidedly outside the reach of Christian compassion; they set her up to gesture at a world that transcends religious differences. Indeed, at this point in the drama, we learn that Deborah has clearly moved beyond her father's Jewish piety. As she waits for Joseph next to the cross, Deborah speaks of Joseph as her "messiah," and she prays to the moon not for the "sunken city of Zion" or for the restoration of Israel but "only for him, whom my soul loves" (I.viii).

In this setting, oversaturated with Christian symbols and Jewish symbolic language, Deborah and Joseph imagine a decidedly secular future for themselves, setting up the spectators to root for a grand dream of a union that will negate the religious differences between them. Neither Deborah nor Joseph raises the specter of conversion, which would have been the only way for a Jewish woman to marry a Christian man when the play was set in 1780 as well as when it premiered in 1849. Rather, Deborah, still speaking in a Jewish register, describes this Jewish-Christian union as an "exodus" from *Mitzrayim* (Egypt) through the "desert" into the "Promised Land" of a love in which God resides as in the "burning bush." Joseph, too, envisions their love as the fulfillment and negation of traditional Jewish dreams of exile and redemption. Calling himself a "priest of human rights," he promises Deborah salvation in America, where they can escape "Egyptian darkness" and build an "altar to the new religion, human love," in a country where religious differences apparently do not matter (I.ix).[64] The star-crossed lovers' dialogue in this scene raises the hopes for a secular happily-ever-after in America; at the same time, it presages the tragic outcome that theatergoers familiar with the conventions of serious drama would expect. Deborah, in particular, worries ominously that their love will not survive, and even as they promise to meet at the hundred-year-old linden tree to set off for foreign shores, Deborah and Joseph each struggle with the emotional ties binding them to their communities of origin. Daly here, characteristically, adds dramatic excess to this scene. He places the evil schoolmaster in the bushes to eavesdrop and adds a lengthy dialogue where Leah makes Rudolf promise not to "forsake" her while insisting desperately that she "*will not* be betrayed" (Figure 15).[65]

As Act I concludes, *Deborah* thus already places theatergoers in the position of wishing for the impossible happy end, creating what Steve Neale, in the seminal essay "Melodrama and Tears," defined as the classic spectator-position for melodrama, with its characteristic mix of powerlessness and fantasy.[66] The play here encourages spectators to develop sympathy for Deborah and Joseph in

Figure 15. Dress rehearsal of *Leah, the Forsaken*, April 1896, Opera House, Wheeling, West Virginia. In this production of *Leah*, we see the schoolmaster as well as another character eavesdropping on Leah and Rudolf. Linna Hennig Sherman Collection. Courtesy of the Local History Collection of the Ohio County Public Library Archives, Wheeling.

their vision of a Jewish-Christian union, nurturing hopes that they fully expect to be dashed; the fact that *Leah, the Forsaken* identifies the schoolmaster as an additional threat that the lovers themselves do not perceive—and as a spectator-position to be rejected by the audience—only further intensifies the audience's double sense of helplessness and hope here.

Within the context of the drama as a whole, the secular mode of compassion that emerges at the end of Act I figures not as a lasting phenomenon but as an ephemeral beginning. Indeed, even as the play encourages spectators to develop sympathy for Deborah and Joseph in their utopian love, it also stresses the dark side of compassion, the fundamental dangers to the self that can ensue from developing sympathy with an exotic Jewess. In recounting to Deborah how he developed feelings for her, Joseph recalls the night when he first met her in the forest and was "touched" by her "pain." Feeling Deborah's suffering led immediately to an instinctive act of benevolence, as Joseph offered Deborah his hand and helped her find the hut in the forest where she and her fellow Jews are now camping out. Soon thereafter, however, compassion and benevolence yielded to other feelings:

> JOSEPH. Since that night an uncanny bond draws me to you, you poor, beautiful woman, and leaves me no peace and quiet. When I try to sleep, I see your image, with your moist, black eyes staring at me. Your long, dark hair envelops my hand and draws me to your breast. When the dignified priest looks me up and down, when my father and my dear friend [Hanna] knock at my heart and ask where the old love is, it is you whom I see. Your mouth, your kiss seals the secret on my lips. For this I am angry at you. You have taken from me everything that I have held dear since my youth. Yet I feel that you have given me more. Thus I'm angry, I fear you, and I lament you. Anger, fear, and pain are my love. (I.ix)

There is more at stake here than compassion morphing into a romantic interest in a dark and beautiful stranger. As sympathy with Deborah's sufferings yields to passion, Joseph loses all control, ceding his autonomy to the uncanny force of the dark-haired, dark-eyed woman who engages in exotic rituals with the moon. At the same time as the play invites spectators to identify with Deborah and Joseph's dream of a secular world in which Christians and Jews might be able to live together in harmony, it also casts Deborah, here again, as an unruly object of compassion, underscoring how easily the hierarchical act of condescending to perform an act of benevolence can result in a loss of all agency. Stephen Watt, in a recent discussion of Daly's *Leah*, picks up on this dynamic to foreground the metaphoric connection between Jewishness and vampirism in the play.[67]

When Joseph describes his love for Deborah in Act II, in conversation with his childhood friend Hanna the next day, he again stresses the uncanny powers of the Jewish seductress. Recalling the "sufferings of her people," he tells Hanna of his initial compassion and his subsequent oath to become Deborah's "rescuing angel," plans that were thwarted when "passion took hold of me so painfully, so wildly, as if she were controlling me with a prayer, with magic signs" (II.vi). By this point in the drama, Joseph's feelings of powerlessness vis-à-vis Deborah are compounded by intense feelings of guilt toward his father, Lorenz. When, the night before, Joseph confessed to his father his love for Deborah and plans to elope, Lorenz suffered a stroke just as he was about to curse his son. Hanna's solution to Joseph's conflict between romantic love for the exotic Jewess and guilt over betraying his father is that Joseph simply redirect his passion, channeling it back into the type of sympathy that motivated her Christian feelings of benevolence in the play's opening scene: "You should love her, but love in her the humanity that suffers innocently" (II.vi). Joseph, however, lacks all power to control his feelings concerning Deborah. In conversation with his father and the priest in the next scene, he is not merely indecisive; he cedes all power whatsoever, presenting himself as a passive object of pity: "If you could gaze into my heart, priest, you would have compassion with me. I am so attached to you yet also so firmly attached to her. My heart is about to break into pieces. Demand no decision from me; I do not want to bother you anymore. Tell me what I should do, and I will do my best to do it. God will have mercy upon me" (II.vii).

It is in this context that Joseph agrees to go along with his father and the priest's scheme to test Deborah's love by offering her money to leave town. After all, as Joseph's otherwise fairly liberal father points out, opening the door to anti-Jewish sentiments, "these people do anything for money" (II.vii). As Act II progresses, the powerlessness of the audience is compounded as spectators witness the schoolmaster's machinations and the series of fateful misunderstandings that follow. We first see Deborah readying herself for a rendezvous with Joseph that the audience knows will never happen. Once Joseph fails to show up at the linden tree at the appointed time, a frantic Deborah appears at the gate of Lorenz's home, where Lorenz, Hanna, and Joseph, all believing that she has accepted the bribe, accuse her of bewitching Joseph with her charms (Figure 16). Joseph, still fearful of her power over him, nominally forgives Deborah for making him so miserable while accusing her of "trading for her people" and taking his love "to market like a commodity," indifferent to the pain and suffering she was causing a "Christian heart" (II.xix). And immediately after the misinformed Joseph presents himself as an object of pity victimized by a conniving Jewess, Joseph ascends to a clear position of power over Deborah. Before going inside, he hurls an additional bag of money at her feet, leaving a desperate Deborah behind, calling out his name. In Daly's version, Leah runs after Rudolf, shrieking, "You will not, shall not leave me!" prompting Rudolf to slam the door in her face.[68]

If Act I closes by placing theatergoers in the position of still wishing for the impossible happy end, Act II creates a situation where all hopes are dashed and where the audience shares Deborah's sense of powerlessness as Joseph and the other liberal-minded villagers turn on her and adopt the antisemitic mind-set of the mob that pursued her so graphically in Act I. At this point in the drama, Deborah is not an unruly object of compassion but the perfect object of sympathy and identification for the audience. From the perspective of a dominant theory that celebrated tragedy's potential to rise above the arbitrary nature of everyday life to stage grand moral conflicts between free and self-conscious individuals, the series of misunderstandings that undoes Deborah and Joseph's relationship was undoubtedly a flaw in the play. The literary historian Hermann

Figure 16. This illustration of the concluding scene of Act III of Bateman's London production of *Leah* (Act II in *Deborah*) appeared in the October 17, 1863, edition of the London *Illustrated Times*, mislabeled as the curse scene. *Scene from the Drama of "Leah," at the New Adelphi Theatre.* © National Portrait Gallery, London.

Hettner made this point in an influential 1852 book on modern drama, noting with irony that if only a member of the audience were to get up onto the stage and explain this "disastrous error" to Deborah and Joseph, all their problems would be averted.[69] Nineteenth-century melodrama, however, inevitably placed its characters in situations beyond their control, routinely giving spectators privileged knowledge that its characters lacked. In this context, it was not just a sense of decorum that prevented theatergoers from interrupting performances to let Deborah and Joseph know about the machinations of the schoolmaster. Spectators would have been robbing themselves of the pleasure that came from experiencing their own sense of powerlessness in the theater, the pleasure that came from feeling the pain of Mosenthal's Jewish protagonist.

The Thrills of Old Testament Vengeance: Sympathy Gone Awry

Focusing on how Deborah emerges as an object of compassion over the course of the first two acts of the play thus sheds light on a level of formal complexity in *Deborah* that was lost on nineteenth-century critics eager to delineate the play's failures to conform to their model of tragedy. The sympathy with Deborah that emerges at the end of Act II ultimately proves a fleeting phenomenon, and the challenges leading up to it reemerge in an amplified fashion in Acts III and IV, ultimately finding resolution—and finally achieving a less ephemeral mode of compassion—only in the play's concluding scenes. Act III, in fact, performs a complete reversal of the dynamic established at the end of Act II. Deborah's uncanny power reasserts itself here to become a source of terror, creating a situation where it is not Deborah but Joseph who emerges as the object of sympathy. At first, as the villagers happily prepare for Joseph and Hanna's wedding just eight days later, Deborah's pain and Joseph's betrayal obviously lurk in the background. When Deborah appears in the cemetery at the back of the church, pale, disheveled, and forlorn, she enters into a long monologue reflecting on the suffering inflicted on her by Joseph. In this scene, she again speaks in an explicitly Jewish register, explaining that she has spent the last seven days mourning her love as one sits shivah. After she peeks into the church window and discovers that she is witnessing Joseph's nuptials, however, her ire is provoked. In the famous curse scene that follows, she ends up placing the audience in the same position as Joseph found himself in Act II. No longer the object of sympathy or identification, she becomes here a source of fear.

Over the course of the curse scene, feelings of sympathy quickly yield to terror. At the beginning of her confrontation with Joseph, Deborah continues to function as an object of compassion, crying out to Joseph: "You believed I took it [the money]? Miserable Christian! You went along and gave me up. The Jewess was not worth even a question?" (III.xi). But soon she begins mocking Joseph's Christian God of love, pledging her allegiance to the Lord of Israel, whom she characterizes here as the God of vengeance. Unwilling to accept Joseph's pleas for mercy and forgiveness, she rekindles her relationship with "her old riches," "the excess of hatred," pronouncing that the Lord her God demands an "eye for an eye, a tooth for a tooth, and a heart for a heart." Speaking not just with melodramatic excess but *"with prophetic ecstasy"* called for in Mosenthal's stage directions, she uses fiery biblical language to list Joseph's transgressions: "'Thou shalt not bear false witness,' and you perjured yourself; / 'Thou shalt not be unfaithful,' and you broke faith; / 'Thou shalt not steal,' and you stole my heart; / 'Thou shalt not kill,' and you killed my heart." Disregarding Joseph's pleas for her to stop as well as his desperate apologies, Deborah proceeds in similarly extravagant language to curse Joseph, his future progeny, and his father as well: "Curse! Three curses! And just as my people said on Mount Ebal, I say three times: Amen, Amen, Amen!" (III.xi). After announcing that she will return in the future to witness the effects of her curse, Deborah steals Joseph's rosary and departs. Joseph, overwhelmed by her fury, loses consciousness and falls to the ground.

Figure 17. *Scene from the Drama of "Leah" at the Adelphi Theatre—the Curse*, originally published in the *Illustrated London News*. Billy Rose Theatre Division, New York Public Library for the Performing Arts, Astor, Lenox and Tilden Foundations.

No longer an object of compassion, Deborah here offers a spectacular display of Old Testament wrath that terrorizes a repentant Joseph and causes him to faint. Audiences generally experienced this scene as the most thrilling moment in the play. Playing Deborah in Prague in the summer of 1850, local celebrity Marie Frey caused several women in the audience to faint.[70] Bateman, performing Leah in Manchester in November 1867, similarly caused a woman to pass out in the theater "from excess of feeling."[71] In at least one case in 1864, experiencing the power of Bateman's performance of Leah in London reportedly proved fatal.[72] Regardless of whether theatergoers actually lost consciousness—most, of course, did not—the curse scene gave audiences a fundamentally different experience from the concluding sequence of the previous act. If the final scene of Act II invited spectators to identify with Deborah's powerlessness and suffering at the hands of Christians, Act III concludes by displaying Deborah's terrifying dominion over the man who wronged her, presenting her as a woman who uses her connection to Jewish tradition to threaten to annihilate the domestic tranquillity of the Christian world. More than a seductive stranger who robs Joseph of his autonomy through her "wild" love, Deborah presents herself as an uncanny force of Old Testament fury whose wrath is pleasurable because of its terror. The Jewish woman whose powerlessness invited compassion and identification at the end of Act II becomes in Act III a force threatening to wreak havoc on the Christian world.

A critic at *Deborah*'s Viennese premiere in 1849 complained that the drama placed its audience in emotional overdrive, simply giving rise to too many different feelings.[73] Indeed, Mosenthal's play invites its audience to identify with Deborah's powerlessness as a victim of Christian persecution and feel her pain, only soon thereafter causing theatergoers to fear Deborah's power and identify with her potential victims. Nothing could be further, it seems, from Lessing's ideal of a central figure drawing a steady stream of tears of sympathy from his or her audience. In this sense, *Deborah* supports Linda Williams's insistence that melodramatic pathos is never "merely a matter of losing oneself in overidentification"; rather, Williams notes, melodrama hinges on suspenseful action and on forcing its spectators constantly to "negotiate between emotions and between emotions and thought."[74] Over the course of its first three acts, *Deborah* presents its protagonist both as an ideal object of a new form of secular compassion and a source of terror threatening to destroy the Christian world. From the perspective of its content, the curse scene could prove troubling, particularly to Jewish critics who found the extravagant performance of Old Testament vengeance either embarrassing or out of place in a drama ostensibly committed to the idea of integrating Jews into the modern world.[75] How Jews reacted to the play and what they did with it is a topic we shall return to in Chapter 4. For now, it suffices to point out that within the formal structure of a drama that reworked Lessing to use the theater to develop a new, secular mode of sympathy focused on Jewish suffering, the curse scene served a clear purpose, setting the stage for the fourth and final act's resolution to the challenge of the drama as a whole.

Spectatorship, Sympathy, and the Promise of Secular Redemption

The first three acts of *Deborah* take place in largely Christian locales—in front of the village church, at the cross in the woods, in the cemetery behind the church—and against the backdrop of religious celebrations, whether Good Friday and the anticipation of Easter or Joseph and Hanna's wedding. Mosenthal creates a (counterfactual) world where Good Friday in 1780 coincides with the first night of Passover, and this enables Deborah's traveling companion, the blind Jewish patriarch Abraham, to voice specifically Jewish hopes for messianic redemption that run parallel to Christian visions of rebirth (II.ix). In great contrast, the final act, Act IV, which takes place five years later, in 1785, stages its reconciliation of Christians and Jews in decidedly nonreligious spaces: first, among ruins outside town, where a group of Jews are camping out en route to America; and then, in front of Lorenz and Joseph's farmhouse. In terms of time, the world that Mosenthal's characters inhabit in Act IV is similarly structured not by a cycle of religious celebrations anticipating redemption but by the promise of secular modernization, by a change in political tides ushered in by the Habsburg emperor whose name coincides—not so subtly—with the name of Deborah's love interest. Mosenthal offers here an idealized vision of Joseph II and his famous Edict of Tolerance, an act of modest reform that abolished some medieval restrictions and extended Jews rights somewhat. It is under the banner of this new era of Joseph II that Jews and Christians find their way to mutual understanding and that the play creates a stable spectator-position that enables the audience to feel a lasting mode of secular compassion with Jewish suffering.

Act IV begins elaborating this vision of secular redemption not with reference to Joseph II but in an entirely Jewish milieu, focusing on Deborah's relationship to a group of Jews camping out in the ruins of a castle preparing to immigrate to America. Seeing itinerant Jews in ruins likely reminded some contemporary audiences of Adalbert Stifter's widely discussed 1842 novella *Abdias*, with its opening scene of dirty, degenerate Jews residing in the ruins of a Roman fort in North Africa.[76] Yet Mosenthal's Ruben, the idealistic Jewish leader who sings the praises of America as a land where "Christians and Jews" are treated as "human beings" and joined in "brotherly love" (IV.i), could not be more different from Stifter's ambivalent Jewish protagonist. Ruben's vision that Jews denied equal rights in their beloved homeland should emancipate themselves by heading off to America was a blatant anachronism, an echo of Austrian debates in the aftermath of the failed 1848 revolution rather than anything related to the play's historical setting in the 1780s.[77] Within the structure of the play itself, nevertheless, Ruben's mythic vision of America as a secular political paradise continues the unfinished business of Joseph and Deborah's romantic scene in Act I. It marks Ruben as Joseph's successor as an America-bound "priest of human rights" while also reestablishing Jews—in the aftermath of the excesses of Deborah's curse scene—as proper objects of compassion for the audience.

As Ruben calls on his fellow Jews to ready themselves to make the journey to the seashore, Deborah remains obsessed with revenge. Deborah, who celebrated Joseph as her messiah in Act I, is unable even to comprehend Ruben's hopes for the New World and his despair over having to leave his Austrian homeland. Indeed, she calls Ruben a "sinner" for forsaking the traditional dream of a messiah who will lead Jews back to the Holy Land, prompting Ruben to proclaim that the "old city of Zion is dead and will never be resurrected" (IV.i)—a position that she herself had accepted five years earlier as she prayed to the moon to find salvation with Joseph. For Ruben, the prospect of Christians and Jews living together in peace and harmony serves as evidence that "the hour of the messiah" is near and that the New Jerusalem of brotherly love has displaced the "beautiful fairy tale" of the Promised Land to become the proper object of messianic longing. America is important here not just as the destination that Ruben has chosen but as a shorthand for a secularized Jewish messianism on the brink of being realized across the world. In this context, it is crucial that the idealistic Ruben finds turning his back on his "dear homeland" painful: "Beloved land that has cast us out, look, your children are moving away in tears, for their love, mother, remains with you!" (IV.i). Deborah's cynical retort that the emigrant Jews will not be missed and that "no tear will be shed for them" (IV.i) only further encourages spectators to embrace Jews as objects of compassion, as fellow human beings and potential fellow citizens whom they and their countrymen have forced to seek a homeland elsewhere.

Following on the heels of the curse scene, the opening of Act IV establishes a difference between Deborah and other Jews, rendering Jews as a collective the object of sympathy while marking Deborah once again as a challenging object of compassion. Deborah, indeed, explicitly scorns Ruben's ideal of brotherly love and his modern interpretation of Judaism and its mission. Obsessed with revenge, she insists on stealing back to the village to witness the "rich harvest of her hatred." When Ruben advises her to "think of God and forget revenge," she pledges her undying allegiance to her vision of a vengeful God who visits the sins of the fathers on children and children's children. Ruben points out that it is the nature of the divine to love and forgive, stressing that the notion of a God of hatred is the product of centuries of exile and persecution and not an essential feature of Judaism. Impatient with Ruben's attempts to rob her of her personal God of vengeance, Deborah tells Ruben to let her be; she will meet him at the coast after she has taken care of her business in the village.

The opening of Act IV, then, invites sympathy with Jewish potential fellow citizens while making clear that the excesses of the curse scene are not to be equated with Judaism itself. It also stresses the need for Deborah to be reeducated so that she, too, might find a place within Ruben's grand vision of a liberal community where Christians and Jews are joined in brotherly love. In this context, the change in political tides brought about by the reign of Joseph II prove monumental. The scenes among the villagers that take place before Deborah arrives at Joseph's farmhouse show a collective eager to develop more liberal attitudes toward Jews. As Lorenz explains with enthusiasm, the new emperor treats Jews and Christians as equals, provided they are good citizens, and he has already created a situation where "even the peasant learns to think quite differently" and "overcome the cursed prejudice imbibed along with his mother's milk" (IV.iii). The village priest has begun to devote sermons to the importance of extending neighborly love toward Jews, encouraging the villagers to reflect on how they had treated Deborah five years earlier. Lorenz suffers from particularly strong guilt over his role in arranging that Deborah be removed from the picture, and we learn that Joseph, who fell severely ill the night of his wedding, lives his life in the shadow of remorse over his betrayal and mistreatment of Deborah. Once his secret identity was revealed, the schoolmaster has become for the villagers the very model of a "Jew with a heart" and a beneficiary of the villagers' newfound goodwill toward Jews. Nine days earlier, we learn, Joseph set off to meet with the authorities to ask that the schoolmaster be given back his job and that his brother and his family from Hungary be allowed to settle in the village. (As we shall see in Chapter 2, Daly and others put the figure of the schoolmaster to different uses in their adaptations of Mosenthal's material.)

In this context, when Hanna discovers that a group of poor Jewish refugees headed for America is camping out in the castle ruins, "fearful of the dwellings of the human beings in this land that still exiles them so cruelly" (IV.iv), she welcomes this information as a godsend, an opportunity for the villagers to make amends for their maltreatment of Deborah five years earlier. Hanna and Lorenz make immediate plans to send food and wine to Ruben and his followers. They aid Jews here, moreover, not in the name of Christ, as was the case in Act I, but under the banner of the new, secular vision of tolerance and brotherly love instituted by Joseph II—an ideal of coexistence first elaborated for the spectators by Ruben. As Deborah makes her way toward the village to witness the effects of her curse, the play's goal of developing a secular mode of sympathy with Jewish suffering has largely been achieved, and Jews and Christians alike have embraced a liberal vision of tolerance and mutual respect. Much like in Act II, where the audience witnessed Deborah preparing herself for a rendezvous with Joseph that was never going to happen, here, as Deborah heads off to witness the effects of her curse, the plot hinges on a disparity between Deborah's knowledge and that of the spectators. The difference here is that this time around, Deborah hardly figures as an object of identification whose victimhood provokes compassion. Rather, it is Deborah who needs to be taught sympathy here, and this happens in a highly theatrical scene where she herself comes to occupy the position of spectator.

Initially, Deborah shows up at Hanna's doorstep and, without being recognized, she enters into dialogue with her former rival, hoping to ascertain the effects of her curse. Despite Hanna's goodwill, her offers of food, water, and shelter, and her clear explanations that Joseph has set off "to demand justice for a man who had to suffer because he is a Jew" (IV.vi), Deborah is unable to perceive the obvious change in attitudes in the village. Understandably, her questions—whether Joseph has abandoned his wife, whether she thinks he might perish in an accident during his absence, and so on—make Hanna uncomfortable. When Hanna asks her to leave, Deborah is overjoyed that "the old power is awakening" in her (IV.vi). Soon thereafter, Hanna changes her mind. She insists that Deborah stay the night and then recites the Lord's Prayer. Unable to respond to Hanna or process any of the information presented to her in this conversation, Deborah winces and hides in the bushes.

In the subsequent scene, Deborah eavesdrops on Hanna's reunion with Joseph. Her position as spectator here provokes the change of heart that face-to-face dialogue with Ruben and Hanna did not. She first witnesses heartfelt embraces between Joseph, Hanna, and their child and then hears Joseph tell Hanna of his meeting with Joseph II. As Joseph reports on the emperor's grand vision of a "new era" where Jews will be valued as citizens, he expresses joy but also confesses to Hanna that he is still plagued by memories of Deborah: "It is no longer her curse that I fear—her hatred was but the touchstone of her love—but her pale, mild face, which visits me in my dreams and says in a pained voice, 'I have forgiven you!' Oh, Hanna, if I could see her just once and confess how severely I feel I wronged her. If I could bathe her hand with my tears, then I would be able to make amends for the curse. Then I would finally find peace again" (IV.vii). Hearing this, Hanna tells Joseph of the Jews headed toward America, wondering whether the beggar woman to whom she just offered shelter might know them and be able to help find Deborah so that Joseph might make amends. Just as zealous in her benevolence as she was in Act I, Hanna suggests inviting Deborah to share "the blessing of our home" and become "a dear sister to me."

Mosenthal's text contains no stage directions for Deborah during her eavesdropping, but her position as a spectator to Joseph's fantasies of forgiveness provided actresses ample opportunity to display their skills working with gestures, body language, and facial expressions. In the following scene, after Joseph and Hanna head inside to look for her, Deborah emerges from her hiding place and expresses in a monologue how the scene she has just witnessed is moving her:

> DEBORAH (*stepping out from the bushes*). What was that? Eternal One, did I hear properly? The sheets of ice covering my heart are melting, I feel my old sense of life returning. Joseph! (*Melting into tears*)

> O God, what are you doing with me! No, no, I no longer love the way I once did. The altar flame [of love] has taken its offering, and now only the eternal flame of human kindness [*Menschenliebe*] burns once again in the cemetery of my breast. No, Hanna, I shall not remain here with you; I do not wish to be a silent reproach and disturb the beautiful peace of your souls. I shall set off with my people, a symbol of the tribe that has renounced its hatred now we know that you can love us. (*Sneaking off*) I must be quiet so that no one sees me, the gate is open. (IV.viii)

Moved by the spectacle that she has just witnessed, Deborah melts into tears, her humanity rekindled as she feels compassion for Hanna and Joseph. Recognizing that God has restored her love of humanity through this scene, Deborah renounces her quest for vengeance. Following Ruben's pronouncements at the beginning of the act, she concedes that hatred is not an essential aspect of Judaism but a product of centuries of Christian persecution. Taught by her tears that her love for Joseph is gone, she embraces in its place not a quest for revenge but a compassionate love of all humanity, a position she claims here as part of her Jewish legacy.

Melting into tears in this way in a monologue, the character who threatened to wreak havoc on the Christian world at the end of Act III becomes the ideal object of sympathy, one who develops compassion for those who wronged her at the same time as she invites the sympathy of the audience. Yet these are not the last tears shed on stage. The love of humanity that Deborah embraces in her de-eroticized state does not just give voice to a renunciation of vengeance and an abstract expression of goodwill. Once she recognizes that the "altar flame" of romantic love has died out, Deborah is given the opportunity both to witness and experience the joys of motherhood. Immediately after her monologue, Joseph and Hanna's daughter comes outside, and she responds to Deborah's question as to her name by telling her that she is named Deborah, after "the other Deborah. Father and Mother speak of her often, and I pray for her every night" (IV.viii). Hearing that Joseph and Hanna have chosen to atone for the way they treated her by naming their child Deborah, Deborah cries again, and as the stage directions indicate, "*she covers the child with kisses, with extreme emotion.*" Handing young Deborah the rosary she took from Joseph after cursing him in Act III, Deborah hugs the child again before pronouncing her blessings on the child, her home, and the entire village. Reconciled in this way, Deborah sets off to meet Ruben and the other Jews at the coast, leaving Joseph and Hanna to discover, through the rosary, that Deborah has come and forgiven them. In

Figure 18. Kate Bateman as Leah with young Leah. Carte-de-visite photograph of Kate Bateman as Leah at the Adelphi Theatre. London, 1863. © Victoria and Albert Museum, London.

the final scene, Deborah appears on the hill above the house, visible to the audience but not to Joseph and Hanna, as Joseph exclaims, "Yes, it was she! We are reconciled!" and Deborah disappears behind the hill (IV.ix).

In this final scene, Deborah becomes far more than an object of compassion. For the theatergoers, who are the only ones to see both her and Joseph's family at the same time, she becomes the symbol of a new liberal political order, a model of Jews and Christians living together in fraternal love cemented by tears of sympathy. The fact that she and her fellow Jews are headed off for America at precisely the moment when the Christian villagers are ready to accept them further underscores the utopian nature of this project, placing the audience, once again, into the familiar tearjerking position of wishing for the elusive happy end. Unlike in Act I, however, the audience here wishes not for two lovers from different worlds to be united against all odds but for the realization of a political order grounded in the secular model of compassion that allows the Jews and Christians in the drama to reconcile. In this scene, it is fitting that Deborah and Joseph never reconcile face-to-face; the reconciliation that takes place here is mediated entirely by the spectators, whose tears express both their own powerlessness and the fantasy that tears shed in the theater might somehow herald the beginning of a new political order in which Jews and Christians might live together as equals. *Deborah* does not just give audiences the pleasures of a good cry. It is designed to give spectators the sense that their tears of compassion mean something, the sense that their collective crying in the theater anticipates the liberal community that the play invokes as the curtain falls.

As it culminates in this final tearjerking sequence, *Deborah* affords its spectators the pleasures of feeling their powerlessness at the same time as it underscores the power of tears to express a utopian desire for liberal community. Crying here functions neither simply as self-soothing behavior nor as an infantile reaction to distress. As Mosenthal's drama sets it up, rather, crying has value: it has the power of producing liberal feeling, of enabling spectators to identify with Deborah and to recognize the symbolic significance of their identification with this figure who presents herself as "a symbol of the tribe that has renounced its hatred now we know that you can love us." Of course, the feel-good universalism that the play promotes in its final scenes as it encourages non-Jews to feel the pain of Jewish suffering and congratulate themselves on their liberal sentiments hardly marked a radical politics. For all its power to promote a utopian desire for a liberal political order, the feelings of compassion produced in the theater could easily become pleasurable ends in themselves and, as such, a substitute for political change. In this regard, the liberal fantasies that the play promotes in its final moments were both political and nonpolitical at once. *Deborah* encouraged spectators to embrace a utopian political vision while also enabling them to feel good about how bad they felt about Jewish suffering.

Tears shed in identification with Jewish suffering were thus double-edged, fostering the desire for a liberal political future while also promoting complacency in the present. In this context, the fact that Mosenthal's drama conflated the unrealized goals of the 1848 revolution with Joseph II's Edict of Tolerance—implying that the sense of shared humanity it wanted to promote had a juridical foundation in the Austrian Empire under Joseph II—only supported the way it could nurture liberal political fantasies and promote smugness at one and the same time. Exactly how this all played out politically is the issue we shall explore in the next and final section of this chapter. In coming to terms with the affective power that *Deborah* wielded over its audiences, however, it may make sense not to approach the mode of liberal feeling that Mosenthal's play engendered with too much suspicion: the unique way *Deborah* combined utopian politics with complacency was no doubt key to the tremendous success it enjoyed among theatergoers.

Deborah's success at the box office was thus hardly an accident or a generic symptom of a more general commodification of affect in nineteenth-century popular culture. Mosenthal's play was elaborately constructed around the goal of making sympathy with Jewish suffering into the ultimate theatrical pleasure, one that allowed spectators to revel in their own liberal sentiments. As a playwright, Mosenthal hardly points the way toward Ibsen, Strindberg, Brecht, or any of the giants of theatrical modernism. Mosenthal's achievements with *Deborah* were of a different magnitude. *Deborah* went about its task of bringing its spectators to tears with a level of formal complexity and sophistication that was lost on nineteenth-century critics who complained that Mosenthal lacked a sense for the grandeur of tragedy and failed to create a drama depicting free and self-conscious individuals caught up in fundamental moral conflicts. For its nineteenth-century naysayers, *Deborah* may have indeed epitomized the four-hanky melodrama. *Deborah* did so, however, because it was a masterfully constructed tearjerker.

Liberal Feeling and the Politics of Sympathy

Mosenthal's critics, as we noted earlier, routinely took issue with the way *Deborah* functioned as a drama. They objected to its special effects, they censured its emotional pyrotechnics, and they complained about the role that chance and misunderstanding played in a plot whose central conflict allegedly lacked sufficient motivation. Yet criticism of the way Mosenthal's tearjerker "aroused compassion ad nauseam" occasionally drew ammunition from another source—from Richard Wagner's "Das Judenthum in der Musik" (Judaism in Music), the antisemitic rant that the composer published anonymously in 1850 and rereleased under his own name in 1869. In "Das Judenthum in der Musik," Wagner complained that those who argued for Jewish emancipation were typically driven by abstract liberal principles rather than by any "real sympathy" with Jews. Challenging the notion that Jews should be granted equal rights, Wagner sought to vindicate the "instinctive dislike" and the "involuntary repellence" that Jews incited in non-Jews. He attempted in this way to put an end to German liberals' misplaced political sympathies and to alert his contemporaries to the ways in which Jews were defiling the art world and transforming the sacrosanct realm of culture into a commodity.[78]

Published one year after the premiere of *Deborah*, "Das Judenthum in der Musik" targeted Wagner's rivals—the Jewish composer Giacomo Meyerbeer and Felix Mendelssohn-Bartholdy, a Protestant convert from Judaism—rather than Mosenthal, whom Wagner never deigned to mention in any of his writings.[79] In the wake of Wagner's essay, nevertheless, some critics came to denounce the commercial success that Mosenthal enjoyed with *Deborah* in Wagner's terms as a distinctly Jewish encroachment into the hallowed halls of German high culture. The celebrated Swiss writer Gottfried Keller, for instance, noted in an

1855 essay that Mosenthal's talents lay in creating the type of "melodramatic hodgepodge of effects" only to be found in "the stuff of the most profit-hungry and most impish haggling Jew."[80] As Keller explained privately in a letter to Hermann Hettner, Mosenthal engaged in grand financial "speculation" in the theater, taking advantage of "the weaknesses of the public" to present his audiences with "a collection of tiny little effects stubbled together with a truly Jewish baseness and impertinence."[81] The prominent Viennese writer and critic Ferdinand Kürnberger argued in similar terms, complaining that Mosenthal and other Jews helped ruin the Austrian stage by selling out tragedy to cheap, sensationalist consumer culture.[82]

Franz Dingelstedt, director of the Burgtheater in Vienna in the 1870s, published an essay on the occasion of Mosenthal's death that deserves to be mentioned here. Dingelstedt, a friend and former teacher of Mosenthal, integrated into his obituary a two-page digression, "The Jew on the Stage," that blamed *Deborah* for being the "progenitor of the popular Jewish plays." Dingelstedt's tribute to his former pupil repeatedly echoed the anti-Jewish hysteria of Wagner's essay when discussing Mosenthal's prominence and relative lack of artistic talent.[83] Given how the terms of Wagner's antisemitic diatribe crept into complaints about Mosenthal's success at the box office, it may not be surprising that Wilhelm Marr's seminal antisemitic tract of 1879, *Der Sieg des Judenthums über das Germanenthum* (The Victory of Judaism over Germandom), cited the popularity of Mosenthal's *Deborah* as irrefutable proof that the theater had become a place where Jews yielded tremendous power, the "forum" of the Jews.[84] In a distinctly antisemitic literary history published two decades later, the prominent literary historian Adolf Bartels singled out Mosenthal's *Deborah* for manipulating "harmless German minds" with a "Jewish-pathetic" form of sentimentality.[85]

Critics with antisemitic tendencies clearly found in Wagner's essay a convenient vocabulary with which to dismiss *Deborah*'s commercial success. But Marr's and Bartels's concerns about the power that this sentimental play wielded over "harmless German minds" also underscores the flip side of this phenomenon, namely, the way Mosenthal's commercially successful drama offered a powerful challenge to the logic at the core of Wagner's attack on both the liberal principles of the 1848 revolution and the alleged Jewish influence on German culture. Whether or not this was its goal, *Deborah* used the theater to generate goodwill for Jews, and it did so through a theatrical mode of sympathy that performed particularly well at the box office. Mosenthal's play drew its energy, indeed, from the way it afforded audiences the thrill of identifying with Jews, reveling in precisely the mode of liberal sympathy that Wagner sought to discredit. Unlike Gustav Freytag's best-selling novel *Soll und Haben* (Debit and

Credit, 1855), Mosenthal's blockbuster drama did not cast Jewish otherness as the symbolic foil for the creation of a liberal national community that had no real place for Jews as Jews. *Deborah* placed Jews and compassion with Jews, rather, at the center of both its ruminations on the nature of a liberal polity and its workings as a theatrical spectacle, making sympathy with Jewish suffering the litmus test of liberal feeling.

Mosenthal, of course, did not write *Deborah* in the late 1840s in order to issue a conscious challenge to nascent antisemitism or the fateful treatise that Wagner would publish one year after *Deborah* premiered in Hamburg, Vienna, Berlin, Prague, Frankfurt, Munich, and elsewhere in the German-speaking world. Mosenthal's goals and motivation had far more to do with experimenting with the affective power of the stage than with engaging with contemporary politics. But whatever his original intentions may have been, the culture of compassion with Jewish suffering that *Deborah* promoted in the aftermath of the 1848 revolution was not without broader political significance. *Deborah* helped foster the liberal sympathy that Wagner's antisemitism sought to challenge, giving theatergoers precisely that pleasure of compassion with Jewish suffering that "Das Judenthum in der Musik" wanted to obliterate. As we shall see in Chapter 3, there were moments when critics heralded the virtues of Mosenthal's play as a challenge to rising antisemitism. For the most part, however, there is little evidence that the huge volume of theatergoers who flocked to see the play typically conceived of their enjoyment of it in explicitly political terms; audiences crying at performances of *Deborah* were hardly performing a self-conscious challenge to rising antisemitism. Jews and Jewish suffering provided such riveting material for a melodramatic tearjerker less because of the drama's political intent than because Mosenthal's play skillfully used them to provoke a powerful and pleasurable mode of compassion among his spectators. Through promoting sympathy with Jewish suffering, *Deborah* clearly challenged the rising tide of antisemitic sentiment. This phenomenon emerged as a by-product of the play, however. It was hardly its primary function or goal.

As we commented in the previous section, the tears that *Deborah* provoked were both political and nonpolitical at once. *Deborah* engendered desires for a liberal political order at the same time as it enabled spectators to feel that tears shed in identification with Jewish suffering could be sufficient in themselves. Yet rather than exposing this tension as a flaw—as a sign of the play not being political enough—it may make more sense to recognize its productive function. *Deborah* may have indeed promoted smugness and complacency. Against the backdrop of Wagner's antisemitism, however, it also helped convert the theater into a place where non-Jews came together to enjoy feeling compassion with Jewish suffering. The fact that it accomplished this task in a nonthreatening way, while fostering smugness and complacency, was crucial to the cultural work that it performed. As a melodrama, *Deborah* did not just produce tears; it produced moral feeling, encouraging spectators to take pleasure in their ability to rise above the anti-Jewish prejudices over which the play sought to triumph. How the particular mode of liberal feeling that *Deborah* unleashed related to actual Jews both inside and outside the theater is an issue we shall address in Chapter 4. Before we can tackle this issue, however, we need to leave the German-speaking world behind and explore yet another dimension of *Deborah*'s tremendous success: the spectacular way in which Mosenthal's melodrama of the forsaken Jewish woman became an international sensation.

Chapter 2

Sensationalism, Sympathy, and Laughter: *Deborah* and Her Sisters

In March 1863, *Harper's Weekly*, the most widely read American periodical of the Civil War period, published a tirade against the ways in which "hatred of race" and the "desperate pandering to the meanest and most inhuman prejudice" were threatening to "abase, divide, and destroy" the American nation: "The staple of all the speeches against the Government, and in favor of the rebellion and anarchy is . . . an appeal to the popular prejudice against an outcast race. The argument is simply—'Is a negro equal to a white man? Will you fight for the negro? Do you want your daughter to marry a black man? Do you want the bread taken from your mouths and the work from your hands by negroes? Will you have black Senators and a negro President?'"[1] The genius of the Confederacy, we read, is that its leaders know how to mobilize racism politically, ensuring that fears over the abolition of slavery morph into anxieties over miscegenation and hysteria over the specter of black power. Thankfully, *Harper's* offers an antidote to the rhetorical excess of politically manipulated popular prejudice. Readers are enjoined to go to the theater, to see Kate Bateman star in the smash hit of the 1863 New York theater season and a play that has apparently never been more "timely": "[W]henever and wherever you can, go and see Leah, and have the lesson burned in upon your mind, which may help to save the national life and honor."

Despite the grand expectations that *Harper's Weekly* broadcast to its more than 200,000 readers, there seems to be little evidence that American performances of *Leah, the Forsaken* contributed directly to "saving the national life and honor" or bringing about an end to the war between the states. Both President Lincoln and General Grant did see the play, and Tony Kushner even smuggled a reference to it into the opening scenes of his screenplay for *Lincoln* (2012).[2] Yet the argument in *Harper's* that *Leah*'s graphic depiction of the "loathing . . . felt in Christian Europe for the Jews" would be a wake-up call to the "condition of our public affairs" was not widely echoed in the American press. Even in the wake of the *Harper's* exhortations, few critics and spectators made connections between the way *Leah* elicited compassion for Jews and the sort of sentimental abolitionism promulgated at the time by Harriet Beecher Stowe's *Uncle Tom's Cabin* and its many popular stage adaptations.[3] During the Civil War, tellingly, *Leah* was enjoyed in the South as well as in the North—apparently without generating anti-Confederacy sentiments.[4]

The discussion in *Harper's* is significant less as a window into the play's actual impact than because it illuminates how easily the fundamental aesthetic of Mosenthal's tearjerker maintained itself as the play crossed national boundaries and was adapted for new audiences. In Chapter 1, we explored how *Deborah* gave its spectators the sense that their tears of compassion meant something, the feeling that the sympathy with Jewish suffering they experienced in the theater was helping to anticipate the liberal community that the play invoked as the curtain fell. Augustin Daly's *Leah*, we shall see, differs considerably from Mosenthal's original in the way it functioned as a tearjerker. According to *Harper's*, however, *Leah* produced a feel-good universalism in the United States that was analogous to the effects of Central European performances of Mosenthal's play. Like *Deborah*, *Leah* was a drama that could be relied on to produce and reinforce liberal modes of feeling, enabling spectators to feel themselves rise above prejudice as they enjoyed the thrills of identifying with "outcasts."

As the Austrian writer Leopold Sacher-Masoch noted with pride in 1878, defending a recently deceased Mosenthal from the attacks of his critics, Mosenthal deserved credit for being the only German dramatist of his era who wrote a play that became a true international sensation.[5] Indeed, even Mosenthal's harshest opponents conceded that *Deborah* achieved a level of international success that surpassed that of any other German play.[6] German and Austrian commentators, however, were occasionally puzzled that a play as topical as *Deborah* was able to find such success abroad, among theatergoers unfamiliar with Joseph II's Edict of Tolerance or the European debates over Jewish emancipation.[7] Seeking to explain a phenomenon that baffled many of Mosenthal's German and Austrian critics, this chapter explores how *Deborah* became one of the German-speaking world's most prominent cultural exports in the latter half of the nineteenth century. Whether it was regarded as the "powerful sermon" that *Harper's* celebrated or experienced simply as a riveting night at the theater, the play's tearful mode of liberal universalism allowed itself to be adapted and retooled for a staggering number of different audiences and contexts.

Before we can trace how Mosenthal's sentimental liberalism crossed linguistic, national, and cultural boundaries with such ease, an overview of the basic dynamics of the play's circulation is in order. By the end of the nineteenth century, Mosenthal's play had been translated into Czech, Danish, Dutch, English, French, Hebrew, Hungarian, Italian, Norwegian, Polish, Russian, Serbian, Slovenian, Spanish, and Yiddish.[8] *Deborah* was performed not only across Europe and throughout North America, Australia, and New Zealand, but in places as diverse as Calcutta, Honolulu, Istanbul, and Kingston, Jamaica.[9] Given how "operatic" some critics felt Mosenthal's drama was, it should not come as a surprise that *Deborah* was not just performed as a spoken drama. Soon after the London premiere of *Leah*, the Italian composer Francesco Schira, an orchestral conductor in London, began working on the opera *Lia*, which was based on Bateman's version of *Leah* and premiered in Venice in 1876.[10] Schira's opera never approached the success of the play it was modeled on. Josef Bohuslav Foerster's Czech folk opera *Debora,* which was based loosely on Jiří Kolár's 1852 Czech translation of *Deborah*, achieved somewhat greater longevity. *Debora* premiered in Prague in 1893 and continued to be performed in interwar Czechoslovakia until the late 1920s, with a revival in 1949 and a radio recording ten years later.[11] As one might expect for a Czech opera written during an era of rising nationalism, *Debora* situates the action of Mosenthal's play in an entirely Czech rural milieu seemingly outside of history, deleting any and all references to Austria, Austrian imperial politics, and even Jewish emancipation. Foerster's opera transforms Mosenthal's topical drama into a distinctly Christian story of reconciliation and redemption, often drowning out Debora's cries of vengeance with both organ music and choruses about the redemptive power of Christ's love.

As we shall see in Chapter 3, the success of Mosenthal's *Deborah* was inextricable from its power as a dramatic star vehicle. Whatever attention the operas garnered pales in comparison to the sensations that actresses produced playing the role. Enabled by new technologies of photography and printing, carte-de-visite photographs became a cottage industry starting in the 1860s, and during this period, images of Bateman and other actresses in costume as Deborah or Leah quickly flooded the market.[12] As such collectibles proliferated, the *Deborah* cult gave rise to a significant volume of both authorized and unauthorized spin-off merchandising, particularly in the English-speaking world. In the United States in 1863, piano selections for the incidental music that Robert Stoepel composed for the New York production of *Leah* were published with a large autographed lithograph of Bateman as Leah on the cover that made Stoepel's *Reminiscences of Leah* an attractive piece of theater memorabilia.[13] Stoepel's music was used at the Adelphi Theatre in London but never sold as a collectible item in Great Britain. Local composers Brinley Richards and Augustus Greville took this as an opening to compose their own music inspired by the play. While Bateman was appearing in *Leah*, Richards and

Figure 19. Kate Bateman as Leah, carte-de-visite photograph. Hess private collection.

Figure 20. Lucille Western as Leah, carte-de-visite photograph. Western's costume updated Bateman's Orientalist turban, replacing it with something resembling an Arab headscarf. Western was the first American actress after Kate Bateman to adopt *Leah, the Forsaken* into her repertoire and played the role throughout the country until her death, in 1877. Harvard Theatre Collection, THE GEN TCS 19, theatrical cartes-de-visite photographs of women, ca. 1854–1879, Lucille Western folder, Houghton Library, Harvard University.

Greville each published competing pieces for voice and piano called "Leah's Song," with different portraits of Bateman in Leah costume on the cover.[14]

In June 1864, Edward W. Price, a teenager from Highgate, then a village outside London, was so inspired by Bateman's performance and the hype it was generating that he sought to re-create *Leah* in a 150-page epic poem in heroic couplets. That Price did so in the absence of a published script is impressive. He must have seen the play numerous times and owned several carte-de-visite photographs of Bateman; some sections of the poem read like descriptions of Bateman's poses as Leah, and, as reviewers noted, its teenage author seems to have been taken by the erotic power of Bateman's exotic Jewess. Ultimately, however, Price's *Leah: A Poem in Six Cantos* was little more than a painful-to-read work of fan fiction. It received attention due to its subject matter but was lambasted by critics for its mediocrity. It never saw a second printing.[15]

After the mass-produced photographs of actresses as Deborah or Leah, hundreds of which have survived in theater archives (and some of which pop up occasionally on eBay), the most enduring piece of memorabilia related to the *Deborah* craze proved to be the anonymously published novel *Leah, the Jewish Maiden*. Released initially in April 1864 with a cover image reminiscent of one of Bateman's poses during the curse scene (Figure 24), this novel grafted a long, action-packed backstory onto the plot of *Leah*, giving Bateman's version of the play a cumbersome, almost incoherent, prequel of more than 240 pages. A critic writing for a prominent American magazine described *Leah, the Jewish Maiden* as a "sensation novel of the lowest school, which all intelligent readers, were it not for the interest which it borrows from the drama . . . would lay aside in disgust before half a dozen leaves were cut."[16] Still, the novel often received favorable notices in the press and went through numerous editions in England, the United States, and Australia, no doubt appealing largely, if not exclusively, to fans of the play.[17] When the prominent Philadelphia publisher T. B. Peterson & Brothers released the American edition of the novel in 1868, it not only gave *Leah* a new subtitle, calling it *Leah; or, the Forsaken*; it fraudulently marketed the novel as a German American "scholarly" translation of the original novel by Dr. Mosenthal that was the basis for the play.[18] The American edition of the *Leah* novel was reprinted in 1877 and again in 1892, when Sarah Bernhardt performed her new version of *Leah* on her American tour. At no point does anyone seem to have questioned Peterson & Brothers' claims to be publishing an authoritative translation of an original novel by Mosenthal.

As the example of the *Leah* novel makes clear, much of the piggybacking on the *Deborah* and *Leah* craze was commercially motivated and facilitated by a lack of international copyright. In North America and the British Empire, publishing and theater were much more brazenly market-driven than in a continental

Figure 21. Cover image of Robert Stoepel's piano selections, *Reminiscences of Leah*, with lithograph of Kate Bateman as Leah. Hess private collection.

Figure 22. Cover page of Brinley Richards's *Leah's Song*. Harvard Theatre Collection, THE b TCS 79, sheet music about personalities, women, ca. 1800–2000, Folder: Music Women Bat-Bayes, Houghton Library, Harvard University.

Figure 23. Cover page of A. Greville's "It Is the Hour: Leah's Song." Harvard Theatre Collection, THE b TCS 79, sheet music about personalities, women, ca. 1800–2000, Folder: Music Women Bat-Bayes, Houghton Library, Harvard University.

Figure 24. The cover design of the anonymously published British novel *Leah, the Jewish Maiden* imitates Bateman's performance in the curse scene. (OC) 250 r. 10, front cover, Bodleian Libraries, University of Oxford.

Europe, where court theaters still maintained cultural hegemony. Not surprisingly, a richer tradition of adaptation and spin-offs developed in the English-speaking world than anywhere else on the globe, yielding versions of the play that were far less bound to Mosenthal's original and often far more creative in their reworking of it than standard European translations of the play. Indeed, the *Deborah* craze gained a momentum in the Anglo American world that has no equivalent elsewhere. The primary focus of this chapter, accordingly, will be the innovative—and, frankly, sometimes not so innovative—ways in which *Deborah* was adapted and rewritten in North America and the British Empire.[19]

Mosenthal was famous in the German-speaking world for the pride he took in *Deborah*'s international stature, collecting theater programs of performances of *Deborah* and *Leah* from places as far away as New York, California, and the gold mines of Australia.[20] Yet he was also consumed at times by his inability to reap profits from foreign productions of the play. For Mosenthal, the success of his play in the Anglo American orbit proved to be a double-edged sword. German performances of *Deborah* were required by law to pay royalties through Mosenthal's agent Hermann Michaelson, and, in many cases, Mosenthal was able to enter into agreements with foreign translators to ensure that their versions of the play yielded revenue. Both Léon Halévy's original French translation of *Deborah* and the Italian translation prepared by Gaetano Cerri, which Adelaide Ristori performed from Barcelona to Moscow, for instance, were authorized versions of the play that produced profits for Mosenthal.[21] As Mosenthal noted in a desperate letter to Augustin Daly after he learned of *Leah*'s initial success on the New York and London stages, there were no copyright agreements with England or the United States that obligated translators or adaptors of German plays to pay royalties.[22] When it served their needs, playbills and advertisements indicated that *Leah* was the celebrated play by "Dr. Mosenthal" (or, as he was sometimes referred to in the English-speaking world, "Dr. Mozenthal"). Daly's adaptation, nevertheless, was not an authorized version of *Deborah* but a play that took on a life of its own in North America and the British Empire.

After Bateman learned that Mosenthal was, in fact, not dead, as she had originally thought, she gave him great pleasure by sending him half of her earnings from the hundredth performance in London and inviting him to come see the play.[23] Nevertheless, the play that made Bateman an international star in the English-speaking world was quite literally her property, with a copyright securely registered in her name.[24] In 1865, Mosenthal traveled to London to enjoy a performance of *Leah* and enjoyed the standing ovation he received at the Adelphi Theatre.[25] The phenomenon he experienced there, however, had in many ways little to do with him. Despite the pleasure that Mosenthal took in the play's international success, he never seems to have been aware of many of the offshoots of the *Deborah* craze—the novel, the Italian opera, the sheet music, and Price's epic poem, not to mention the numerous competing English-language versions of the play we shall be discussing.[26]

German performances of *Deborah* were by no means uniform in the way they rendered the play's key scenes. Within the German-speaking world, nevertheless, most productions of *Deborah* tended to follow Mosenthal's script, with occasional lines cut here and there. The Italian translation that Ristori used and the version of the drama performed in Spain remained close to the original text as well.[27] Many other translations of *Deborah* into languages other than English also tended not to deviate in significant ways from the German text. The Slovenian translation that was published in 1883 in Ljubljana—then part of the Austro-Hungarian Empire—stayed extremely close to Mosenthal's original German script.[28] David Radner's Hebrew translation, first published in Vilna in 1880, rendered the entire drama into prose, translated Mosenthal's German freely at times, and included far more Hebrew liturgical language than was in Mosenthal's original. Radner, nevertheless, did not change the act or scene structure or the constellation of characters, nor did he alter the plot or the key scenes we discussed in Chapter 1 in any significant way.[29] The Polish translation published by Jozef Unger in 1858 also followed Mosenthal closely, with the main exception being that it used the character names that Ristori used in her oft-performed Italian version of the play—Lorenzo rather than Lorenz, Albert rather than Joseph, and Anna rather than Hanna.[30]

Ristori typically insisted in her promotional materials that she was presenting the play "as originally written by Dr. Mosenthal."[31] In her hands, nevertheless, *Deborah* often took on a life of its own. Theatergoers at Ristori's high-profile Italian performances across Europe had access to bilingual libretti that enabled them to follow along in their native languages. In the aftermath of her tours, these bilingual editions provided future adapters a convenient substitute for the difficulties of working through Mosenthal's German original. The 1858 Polish translation that appeared in Warsaw two years after Ristori visited that city did not just borrow the character names from Ristori. It also used the unique alternate ending that Ristori used in her performances of *Deborah*. At the end of the play, the Polish Deborah does not silently disappear behind the hill and leave her former lover to proclaim, "Yes, it was she! We are reconciled!" Rather, she follows her Italian precursor to climb to the summit of the hill and have the last word in the play, making a final dramatic speech: "Yes, Deborah, disarmed by love, leaves you and departs into exile, Deborah, the true image of her unfortunate race, has forgotten her hatred and, persuaded by your love, she pardons you. May the one God who is the God of all bless you all; farewell forever!"[32]

Three months before Bateman opened in *Leah*, Ristori performed *Deborah* in London, with an English-language libretto prepared by Charles Lamb Kenney (and with Bateman and her father sitting in the audience).[33] In the wake of Bateman's success with *Leah* in London, Kenney's translation of Ristori's *Deborah* gave rise to three different versions of the Mosenthal material, each of which ended the play just as the touring Italian star had: George August Conquest's *Deborah; or, the Jewish Outcast* (1864); *Rebecca, the Jewish Wanderer* (1864); and *Ruth, the Jewess* (1868).[34]

It was not just Conquest's *Deborah*, *Rebecca*, and *Ruth* that were several degrees removed from Mosenthal's original. Daly, who knew no German, created *Leah* specifically for Bateman, based on a rough translation of *Deborah* that his friend Emile Beneville prepared for him.[35] Transforming Mosenthal's four-act drama into a standard five-act play, Daly rendered the entire drama in prose, pruned numerous minor scenes, deleted some of the biblical language, and, most importantly, changed the ending. But Daly's script never commanded the authority in the English-speaking world that Mosenthal's original had in Europe. In the closing scenes of the version of *Leah* that Daly had printed privately in 1863 and that appeared in *French's Standard Drama* series starting in 1874 and *Lacy's Acting Editions* soon thereafter, an ailing Leah reconciles with Rudolf (Joseph) and Madalena (Hanna) against the backdrop of a reprise of the mob violence in Act I and Leah's outing of the schoolmaster as a Jewish apostate. Yet even during *Leah*'s initial two-week run in Boston in December 1862 and in the weeks following its premiere at Niblo's Garden in New York the following January, the Bateman production made continual alternations to Daly's script, particularly when it came to the ending. In Boston, the play ended with Leah accepting the asylum of the church.[36] By the end of the second week of the New York production, Leah was dying on stage rather than following Daly's stage directions and "*slowly and feebly*" exiting as she pronounced that she would now go "away with my people."[37] (Tellingly, Stoepel's *Reminiscences of Leah*, published later that spring, included a piece of incidental music titled "Leah's Death.")

Before the play opened in London in October 1863, Bateman's illustrious manager-father arranged for John Oxenford of the London *Times* to rework Daly's script even further. As we shall see later in this chapter, both the official manuscript copy of *Leah* submitted for licensing to the Lord Chamberlain's Office in London and Bateman's personal manuscript copy of the script used in subsequent years indicate numerous departures from Daly.[38] Many productions of *Leah* in the nineteenth century followed Daly's script. In Bateman's version, however, Leah always died. The same was the case for adaptations inspired by Bateman's performance of *Leah* at the Adelphi Theatre: Price's epic poem *Leah*; the novel *Leah, the Jewish Maiden*; and the Italian opera *Lia*.

The discrepancies in the performance of Daly's script pale in comparison to the proliferations of competing versions of *Leah* and *Deborah* that followed Bateman's success. Just days after Bateman closed her production of *Leah* in New York and set off for a European vacation, Isaac C. Pray prepared an original translation of *Deborah* for Catherine Selden that was performed at New York's Winter Garden Theatre under the title *Deborah of Steinmark; or, Curse and Blessing*.[39] Pray's translation was praised, but Selden, who had chosen *Deborah* for her debut, earned devastating reviews.[40] In October 1863, just two weeks after Bateman opened in *Leah* in London, the British actress Mary Gladstane created the role of Miriam in a Baltimore production of *Miriam, the Deserted*, a play that similarly alleged to be a fresh translation from the German original.[41] In Boston that December, Charlotte Thompson premiered in yet another version of the Deborah material, *Clysbia, the Deserted*, and played the role in Washington, DC, Chicago, and elsewhere.[42] While Bateman was performing in England from 1863 to 1866, Daly held the American rights to the play. During this period, he and his brother Joseph spent an inordinate amount of time scanning newspapers from around the country to track down performances and collect fees, publishing notices in the *New York Herald* warning that those performing *Deborah of Steinmark*; *Naomi, the Deserted*; *Clysbia, the Persecuted*; *Esther, the Jewish Maiden*; and *Miriam, the Deserted* would be "prosecuted to the utmost extent of the law."[43]

The rapid proliferation of competing versions of *Leah* and *Deborah* characterized the early career of Mosenthal's play throughout the English-speaking world. While Bateman was engaged in her initial run of *Leah* in London, Conquest's *Deborah*, based on the Ristori version, opened at the Grecian Theatre in East London, starring Edith Heraud. Soon after *Leah* closed in April 1864, the Royal Victoria Theatre, also in the East End, presented Charles Smith Cheltnam's three-act drama, *Deborah; or, the Jewish Maiden's Wrong!*[44] The following years witnessed a seemingly endless parade of different versions: a play called *Leah, the Forsaken* that a San Francisco German-born rabbi presented as his original translation from the German (1864);[45] *Naomi, the Jewish Maiden* (Baltimore, 1864);[46] *Deborah, the Jewess* (Manchester, 1864);[47] *Rebecca, the Jewish Wanderer* (London, 1864); *The Jewish Wanderer* (Manchester, 1864);[48] *Lysiah, the Abandoned* (New York, 1864);[49] *The Maiden's Curse* (Boston, 1865);[50] *Deborah, the Deserted Jewess* (New York, 1866, based on Pray's *Deborah of Steinmark*);[51] *The New Leah* (Brooklyn, 1867);[52] *Leah, the Outcast* (Boston, 1867);[53] *Ruth, the Jewess* (London, 1868); *Hagar, the Outcast Jewess* (London, 1869);[54] a second *New Leah* (New York, 1875)[55]—and many, many more.

Like Daly's *Leah*, Cheltnam's *Deborah; or, the Jewish Maiden's Wrong!* appeared in paperback in a prominent series of acting editions of popular plays.[56]

By the late 1870s, Daly's *Leah* and Cheltnam's *Deborah*, the only English-language versions of *Deborah* to circulate in print, naturally came to dominate. Still, new adaptations of the Mosenthal material continued to be created well into the twentieth century. Sarah Bernhardt, whom we will discuss in detail in Chapter 3, arranged for her own edition of the play to perform, in French, on her 1892 American tour. In 1898, in New York City, Reverend Oliver J. Booth, a minister with a checkered past who enjoyed writing for the stage, created a version of *Leah* with a happy ending. In Booth's recasting of the material, Leah was not forsaken but lived happily ever after with Rudolf.[57] The American stage and early film actress Nance O'Neil had her own adaptation of *Deborah*, called *The Jewess*, which McKee Rankin created for her based on a version of *Leah* prepared by Louis Ludovici; O'Neil used *The Jewess* for her British debut in 1899 and continued to perform it well into the second decade of the twentieth century.[58] The first two decades of the twentieth century yielded three different silent film treatments of the material as well: *Leah, the Forsaken* (1908); a second *Leah, the Forsaken* (1912); and *Deborah, the Jewish Maiden* (1914), sometimes marketed as *The Jewish Maiden's Wrong*.[59]

Subjecting scripts of *Leah* or *Deborah* to close textual study is difficult not simply because many circulated in manuscript form and no longer exist. Scripts and promptbooks that have survived indicate that some productions cobbled pieces of Daly's *Leah* together with sections from Cheltnam's *Deborah*, while sometimes also going back to Mosenthal's original or translations of it.[60] The Australian actress Ada Lawrence, for instance, used a version of the play that followed Daly's adaptation, except for a few key scenes borrowed from Cheltnam's *Deborah*; the language used throughout, however, was neither Daly's nor Cheltnam's but often a translation of relevant scenes in Mosenthal.[61] Other versions cut liberally and inserted new scenes into the play. Many productions that advertised themselves as *Leah* were, in fact, versions of Cheltnam's *Deborah*—and vice versa.[62] Sometimes actresses changed the name of their play when on tour, performing *Naomi* in one city and *Leah* in the next.[63] In October 1867, while the touring Austrian actress Fanny Janauschek was performing *Deborah*, in German, at the Academy of Music in New York, Julia Dean was appearing as Leah at one New York theater and Fanny B. Price was performing *Naomi* at another, prompting one critic to poke fun at the "various aliases of Leah, Naomi, Rebecca, Judith and all the Hebrew female names in the catalogue" used for new and not-so-new versions of Mosenthal's play.[64] In some instances, the creation of new adaptations of the Deborah material may have been dictated by an honest quest for innovation. Particularly in the first decades of its popularity, new adaptations of Mosenthal's drama were at times not novel at all but simply an advertising scheme or an attempt to escape paying royalties.

In coming to terms with the ways Mosenthal's play was reworked for English-speaking audiences, it will prove fruitful to focus our energies on the Daly and Cheltnam adaptations that remained the basis for so many nineteenth-century productions of *Deborah* and *Leah*, examining the surviving manuscript versions of Bateman's version of *Leah* as well. For even as they moved away from the original, these versions of the play are remarkable for the way they zoned in on how Mosenthal's *Deborah* elicited the sympathy of its audience and drew its energy from its attempts to create a spectator-position for compassion with Jewish suffering. German critics never tired of complaining about the sensationalism of the American and British theater,[65] and indeed, both Daly and Cheltnam wrote plays that were far more melodramatic than Mosenthal's *Deborah*, much richer in spectacle and the performance of emotional excess. Yet sensationalism never served as an end in itself for either Daly or Cheltnam. Their reworkings of the Mosenthal material certainly sought to give American and British audiences the type of thrill and excitement they came to expect from popular entertainment.[66] They did so, however, as part of an effort to create even more powerful tearjerkers than Mosenthal's *Deborah*, dramas that would promote modes of liberal feeling requiring minimal familiarity with the play's and the material's German and Austrian context. One of the unique features of the *Deborah* craze in the English-speaking world, finally, was that the sentimental liberalism so crucial to the play's appeal did not always take itself seriously. *Deborah* and *Leah* provoked tearful sympathy, indeed, at the same time as Mosenthal's material could become the source of laughter. We will conclude this chapter by examining the rich tradition of parodies and burlesques that *Deborah* gave rise to, exploring how comic inversions of Mosenthal's philosemitism commented on the power and the significance of the modes of liberal feeling that the play was able to give rise to, at such far remove from its place of origin.

The Americanization of *Deborah*

German critics frequently registered that the character of Ruben—the idealistic leader of the Jewish refugees who appears at the beginning of the final act, invoking a modern interpretation of Judaism and celebrating America as a land where "Christians and Jews" are treated as "human beings" and joined in "brotherly love"—was key to the drama's topical relevance in the aftermath of the failed revolutions of 1848.[67] When Daly set to work adapting *Deborah* for an American audience in the summer of 1862, a year into the Civil War, Jewish emancipation was hardly a burning political issue in the United States. Daly, accordingly, deleted the figure of Ruben and excised the lengthy scene in which he appeared from his version of the play, opening his final act with a "Reaper's Chorus" that introduced the material that Mosenthal used in the second scene of Act IV of *Deborah*. To be sure, Daly retained references later in the act to the group of Jewish emigrants "cruelly driven" out from their homes and headed for America, and his Madalena is as eager to help these unfortunates as was Mosenthal's Hanna.[68] Ruben's secular messianism and the elaborate construction of Jews as a collective object of sympathy that open the final act of *Deborah* and that we discussed in Chapter 1, however, are both notably absent from Daly's *Leah*.

In this way, Daly altered the framework in which tears for Jewish suffering were shed. He retained the scene where Joseph tells his wife about his meeting with the emperor and the sense of a grand new day where Jews and Christians are equal before the law; like *Deborah*, moreover, *Leah* moves from religious celebrations and anticipations of religious redemption in Act I to more secular visions of redemption in the play's final act. Daly systematically purged the play, however, of specific references to Joseph II and the Edict of Tolerance. Indeed, there is no one named Joseph in Daly's *Leah*. The emperor is never referred to by name, and Daly gave Deborah's love interest the more Germanic-sounding name Rudolf, just as he changed Hanna to Madalena and Deborah to Leah, likely to avoid biblical names commonly used in nineteenth-century America.[69] Despite Rudolf's meeting with the emperor and the imperial letter he carries back to the village spelling out new laws regarding Jews, moreover, the final act of Daly's *Leah* hardly presents a world where the liberal sentiments of reform have already trickled down to the peasantry. Egged on by an unrepentant schoolmaster, the villagers seek to stone and drown Leah at the beginning of Act V, just as they did in Act I, and the mob returns in the play's final scene with the intention of having the officers of justice arrest Leah. Daly followed Mosenthal closely in the key scenes where Leah eavesdrops on Rudolf and Madalena and then encounters their child Leah. But he set this reconciliation against the backdrop of a mob that continues to nurture anti-Jewish sentiments.

Leah figures as an object of sympathy at the end of Daly's play thus without the trappings in Mosenthal's *Deborah* that cultivated a distinctly secular form of compassion with Jewish suffering and invested it with broader historical and political significance in the aftermath of the failed revolutions of 1848. Daly did not just turn Joseph II into a generic emperor. In a move that would have baffled German audiences, he also moved the action of the play from the 1780s to the "early part of the eighteenth century."[70] Both the initial production of the play in Boston in 1862 and much of the publicity material that Daly helped prepare for performances in New York and Philadelphia in 1863 situated the action even further in the past, having *Leah* take place in the mid- or early seventeenth century, sometimes explicitly in Austria, sometimes vaguely in "Germany," a term that was often used broadly in the period before the creation of a German nation-state in 1871.[71] The rare critic aware of the play's European context noted the play's call for Jewish emancipation and its challenge to the political status quo.[72] For the most part, American reviewers stressed the "medieval" nature of the anti-Jewish prejudices evident in Daly's depiction of village life without any sense that this remote world bore any direct relationship to the European (or American) present. Even a review in the New York *Jewish Messenger* praised this drama about "German manners and village life" for capturing the "terrible influence of the bigoted and crushing superstitions" of the "fanatic age" of the "Seventeenth century."[73] Advertisements made clear that the management at Niblo's Garden had spared no expense in scenery and costumes to capture the "historical period of the story."[74] But this remote, "medieval" historical period did not speak directly to the American present. Even amid the controversy set off by General Grant's infamous General Order No. 11, banning Jews from his military district in late 1862 and early 1863, no commentators drew direct parallels between *Leah* and current events affecting Jews in the United States.[75]

The "memoir" that Daly wrote for Kate Bateman, which was sold in theater lobbies in early 1863 and quoted in early promotional material for the play, explains the logic undergirding this shift to a more remote historical past: "As a voice from the past, this beautiful drama brings to us of the present day a complete picture of German village life, as it existed two centuries ago. The bigotry and crushing superstition of that age are painted in the same life like colors that glow upon the pages of Hawthorne, or give a somber grandeur to the early chronicles of New England History."[76] *Leah* appears here in good company, as a companion to *The Scarlet Letter* (1850), a portrayal of bigotry, superstition, and intolerance reminiscent of Hawthorne's re-creation of Puritan Salem in the 1640s. In this way, Daly's *Leah* domesticates Mosenthal's *Deborah*, making it a drama that teaches American Christians to confront the brutality of their own past with its Puritan-like fanaticism and intolerance. Unmoored from its Austrian context, *Leah* helps American theatergoers appreciate anti-Jewish animus as a phenomenon out of sync with what Daly terms here "true Christian love and forbearance," invoking a phrase used on the earliest playbills as well.[77] In the absence of Ruben's secularized Jewish messianism and the distinctly secular mode of sympathy with Jews that it made possible, Daly's play channeled the energies of the Jewish-Christian love affair into a celebration of Christian compassion, giving its audiences a decidedly nonthreatening and seemingly noncontroversial feel-good mode of liberal universalism. In this way, Daly's *Leah* promoted an even greater level of smugness and complacency than Mosenthal's *Deborah*.

In turning Beneville's rough translation of Mosenthal into an effective star vehicle for Bateman, Daly rendered it in a familiar idiom, giving the secular mode of compassion in *Deborah* a Christian inflection. The brave new world envisioned at the end of *Leah* derives its inspiration as much from the secular spirit of imperial reform as from the renewal of Christian sympathy. Nowhere was this shift of emphasis clearer than in the final scenes of the play. After Daly's heroine experiences the power of compassion by eavesdropping on Rudolf and Madalena and relinquishing her quest for vengeance, she, too, has a heart-wrenching encounter with her namesake and then plans to set off with her people. Leah's ailing health, however, causes her to collapse, and she never makes it up the hill that Deborah ascends at the end of Mosenthal's play as Joseph exclaims that they are reconciled. Reconciliation in *Leah* takes place face-to-face, rather. Leah, near death, gives Rudolf and Madalena her blessing, takes Rudolf's hand, and places it in Madalena's as she sinks into their arms, passes out, and is assumed to be dead. In Daly's play, however, there is unfinished business that needs to be wrapped up before a final reconciliation between Jews and Christians can ensue. Adapting *Deborah* for the American stage meant creating a melodramatic villain who needed to be disposed of in the final scene. Daly accomplished this task by reworking the figure of the schoolmaster. He not only placed Bateman's sympathetic Leah alongside a duplicitous Jewish apostate who sets the workings of compassion in relief; he structured the entire final act of *Leah* around the conflict between the Jewish apostate's paranoid persecution of Jews and the (Christian) spirit of reconciliation.

Before we can discuss what this means, it will prove useful to discuss Daly's innovations in some detail. In Act II of *Deborah*, Abraham, the blind Jewish patriarch traveling with Deborah, recognizes the scheming schoolmaster by his voice as a Jewish apostate from Pressburg (modern-day Bratislava), the son of his old friend Nathan. After the schoolmaster's identity is revealed in this scene, he never again appears on stage. Subsequent conversations among the villagers reveal that after he no longer felt compelled to keep his Jewish origins a secret, the schoolmaster became a model member of the community, and this transformation helps set the stage for the reconciliation in the play's final act. Reflecting on the anti-Jewish prejudice that used to be common in the village, Lorenz, Joseph's father, recognizes that "it was actually our fault that the schoolmaster was against his people." Lorenz takes pride in the fact that the schoolmaster has now reconnected with his Jewish family and wants them to settle in the village (IV.iii). It is on behalf of the schoolmaster and his family that Joseph turns to the imperial authorities to make a plea for more liberal laws concerning Jews.

Daly had as much use for a scoundrel who never resurfaces on stage after the first half of the play as he did for the lackluster tale of repentance and transformation that the villagers recount about the schoolmaster. In *Leah*, accordingly, the schoolmaster becomes a far more paranoid and menacing figure than in Mosenthal's play. In Daly's play, it is the schoolmaster's idea—not Lorenz's—to bribe Leah to leave town. He spies and eavesdrops on others; he makes frequent asides to the audience, revealing his fear of being discovered; and he lives in constant anxiety that other Jews will step forward and reveal the secret that he is not really "Master Carl"—or "Bertolf," as he came to be known when Oxenford rewrote Daly's script—but rather "Nathan of Presburg [sic]." In Daly's *Leah*, the schoolmaster strangles Abraham as soon as Abraham recognizes him, and his fear of Jews revealing the secret of his past leads him to pursue Leah in Act V, riling up the mob to stone her and drag her into the river, just as the villagers attempted to do in Act I. After Madalena thwarts Nathan's scheme to drown Leah and offers her temporary refuge in her home, Nathan vows to return with the police, whom he will count on to enforce the laws banning Jews from the village. Immediately after Leah is taken for dead, Nathan shows up with a warrant for her arrest, accompanied by the officers of justice, a notary, and the villagers, all of whom are unaware of the new laws outlined in the imperial letter that Rudolf has brought back from Vienna.

At the conclusion of *Deborah*, Joseph, Hanna, and their child stand alone at the center of the stage as Joseph proclaims that they are reconciled, while Deborah slinks away behind the hill, unseen by them but visible to the audience. In this way, Mosenthal quietly stages the reconciliation between Deborah and the Christian world through the spectators and the compassion they feel. The final scene of *Leah* involves its audience in a fundamentally different way, enacting a grand spectacle that gives the audience the chance to witness a confrontation between Nathan and Leah and enjoy the thrill of one final performance of Jewish vengeance. No one in this particular scene talks about legal reform or waxes on about a New Jerusalem where Jews and Christians can live together in peace and harmony. This conclusion of *Leah* draws its energies instead from a series of shocks experienced by the villagers and the audience alike.

First, when Nathan rushes onto the scene armed with officers of justice to take Leah into custody, he is surprised to hear from Rudolf that Leah is already dead. Nathan's presence shocks Leah, however, and she rouses herself, much to the astonishment of the villagers present (and the members of the audience seeing the play for the first time as well). Yet the villagers' wonder at Leah's apparent return from the dead is nothing compared with their reaction when Leah, referring to herself as the "daughter of Rabbi David," addresses the schoolmaster familiarly, as Nathan. In unison, the villagers cry out their confusion and horror that Nathan is a "Jewish name!" When the schoolmaster calls Leah a liar, Leah denounces him as "Nathan of Presburg, who left his old father to die in poverty, and became a Christian!" As soon as his identity is revealed, Nathan panics and lunges at Leah, disclosing a much greater secret as he warns her—in front of the entire village—that she will meet the same "fate" as "the driveling Jew [i.e., Abraham] who, like you, dared to tell my secrets to the world."[78]

All of this—Leah's apparent return from the dead, her revelation of Nathan's secret identity, Nathan's inadvertent confession of murder, and his attempt to kill Leah—is packed into just twenty lines of script. This series of shocks that the villagers on stage experience could not be more different from the quiet, comforting compassion that spectators feel at the conclusion of Mosenthal's play. Yet all this is nothing compared with the sensational sequence that follows. When Rudolf signals to the officers to take Nathan into custody, Leah responds in a manner that indicates that her newfound feelings of compassion and solidarity with humanity have not entirely displaced the wrath and anger that surfaced in the curse scene:

> LEAH. You hear him?—he confesses! You, then, killed the poor old man who tottered blindly on the borders of the grave. As Judith to Holofernes, so I to you. (*goes toward him, and draws a knife from her girdle*) I tell thee, apostate—(*overcome by sudden faintness, she staggers, drops her dagger, and is falling as* MADALENA *catches her; she leans on* MADALENA'S *shoulders—after a pause, and faintly*)[.] Thine, thine is the vengeance, vengeance, madness and folly. To him above, and not to me, even as he said it. Alas, alas! (*suddenly starting*) Who embraces me? Who dares (*softly*) Rudolf, you—But I must not remain. I must now [go] away with my people, for this night I shall wander into the far-off—the promised land! (LEAH *separates from them, and is going off slowly and feebly, while* RUDOLF, MADALENA, *and* CHILD *kneel*; NATHAN, *bound, cowers in on side*; VILLAGERS *group.—Music, as curtain falls, demi-slow*)[79]

Leah's first response to Nathan's confession and his arrest is not to take comfort that the secular authorities seem to have everything under control. Daly's Leah hardly models the sense of relief that spectators of Mosenthal's *Deborah* have as they look forward to a bright future at the end of the play. Instead, she grabs her knife and tries to behead Nathan, reminding the audience of the Old Testament wrath of the curse scene as she cites Judith as her precursor. In her frailty, however, Leah quickly comes around and renounces the role of the vengeful Jewess. She forsakes revenge once and for all, reiterating the faith in the loving God that she had affirmed just minutes before, as she witnessed Rudolf and Madalena's reunion and hugged the young Leah.

At the end of *Deborah*, Mosenthal's protagonist sets off with her people, a vital "symbol of the tribe that has renounced its hatred now we know that you can love us." Daly's Leah, however, ends the play defeated once she performs the public service of helping to unmask the schoolmaster. As she sets off slowly and feebly, entertaining fantastic visions of joining her people and entering the "promised land," Leah is not part of the new world that the play envisions. As good triumphs over evil—the wicked Jewish apostate is taken into custody, and Leah reconciles with Rudolf and his family—the play clearly invokes a future world where Jews and Christians might come to live together in harmony. (Given the spectacular exposé and removal of the rabble-rousing schoolmaster and the new laws concerning Jews on the horizon, it certainly stands to reason that these villagers will not so easily be riled up to chase, stone, and try to drown the next Jewess who wanders into their town.) Yet unlike in Mosenthal, in Daly's play this sense of harmony is predicated on the removal of both an unrepentant Jewish apostate-villain and the Jewish woman whose wild and unruly passion created such havoc in the first place.

The tears that Daly's *Leah* sought to produce were thus not quite the same tears of compassion through which Mosenthal's spectators expressed their utopian desire for Ruben's vision of a liberal political order in which Jews and Christians could live together as citizens. The final scene of *Leah* hopes for a secular world where Jews and Christians might live together in peace and harmony at the same time as it gives theatergoers the pleasures of Christian compassion with a Jewish woman who, despite her heart-wrenching reconciliation with the Christian world, is apparently still prone to Jewish outbursts of violence and vengeance. The thrill of witnessing a final flare-up of Jewish wrath before vengeance is superseded by love and death is inextricable here from the spectatorial pleasures of witnessing the duel between Leah and Nathan as secrets are unveiled, the villain is removed, and the harmony of village life restored. The pleasure of the final scene is, to some extent, contingent on the relief that comes from knowing that Leah's sufferings will end as she goes off feebly to a likely demise amid fantasies of joining her people in the Promised Land. As Leah heads off and Nathan is taken into custody, the conclusion of the play celebrates tolerance at the same time as it removes the two characters who have posed a threat to public order. "Christian love and forbearance" work best, it seems, when Jews are taken out of the picture.

Ambivalence about Jews was no stranger to European and North American liberalism in the nineteenth century.[80] Indeed, as we noted in Chapter 1, such ambivalence was already present in Mosenthal's original script, both in the curse scene's extravagant performance of Old Testament vengeance and in the frequent references to the uncanny power that Deborah yielded over Joseph. In reworking Mosenthal, however, Daly amplified this ambivalence considerably. There is no evidence to suggest that Daly had any sustained interest in the question of Jewish emancipation or that his revisions to Mosenthal were motivated by ideological concerns or any ideas that he may have held about Jews. The ambivalence about Jews that he reinserts into the drama's concluding sequence is important less because of its politics than because of its dramaturgical function, because it enables him to give *Leah* a conclusion that was more complex and more sensational than anything in Mosenthal. *Deborah* was a drama written with its audience in mind, built systematically around its goal of bringing the audience to tears. Daly used Mosenthal's material, accordingly, to create an even more dramatic tearjerker, bringing nearly the entire cast on stage to create a far more gripping and far more spectacular finale than the rare American theatergoers familiar with Mosenthal's original play would have expected.

Of course, compared with other commercially successful plays of the 1860s in London and New York, the conclusion of *Leah* was measured and tame, perhaps even dignified. The actor-playwright-manager Dion Boucicault helped launch the genre of the "sensation drama" in 1860 with *The Colleen Bawn*, a play that hinged on a spectacular scene involving a shooting and a stunning rescue from drowning, all presented with dramatic stage effects.[81] Daly's highly successful melodrama *Under the Gaslight* (1867) ended on an even more extravagant note, taking advantage of new technologies to stage the rescue of a one-armed man tied to the railway tracks just in the nick of time before a train rolled onto stage. The concluding scene of *Under the Gaslight* experienced a long afterlife on the stage and the screen, not least of all in Boucicault's *After Dark* (1868), which landed Boucicault in legal trouble for plagiarizing the concluding scene of *Under the Gaslight* and staging a dramatic rescue from an oncoming train. In the case of Daly's *Leah*, the sensation scene took place without special effects, using classic melodrama rather than dramatic illusions produced by newfangled technology to thrill, surprise, and entertain its audience as it gave them a comforting sense of compassion with Leah's sufferings.

Giving Mosenthal's drama a more riveting ending in this way clearly generated a mode of compassion with Jewish suffering that served to bolster rather than challenge Christian modes of compassion. In this sense, *Leah* departs significantly from Mosenthal. But we need not regard the Christian underpinnings of the feel-good universalism that Daly reinserts into the drama as overly exclusive or as antagonistic toward Jewish difference. As much as Daly's Christian-inflected liberalism shies away from Mosenthal's celebration of a more thoroughly secular mode of compassion with Jews, the sentiments of "Christian love and forbearance" that *Leah* cultivated seem not to have been a phenomenon that nineteenth-century American Jews regarded with suspicion. Commentators routinely noted that Jews were overrepresented in audiences attending *Deborah* and *Leah*—and not just in New York, Philadelphia, and Cincinnati, but in Memphis and Shreveport, Louisiana, as well.[82] Jews in the United States expressed no less enthusiasm for Daly's *Leah* than for Mosenthal's *Deborah*.[83] Rather than criticizing the liberal Christian framework into which Daly set Mosenthal's material, the American Jewish press celebrated the play's powerful arguments against prejudice and praised Bateman's performance of a Jewish woman wronged who finds comfort in returning to her "imperishable religion" to "feel those pure emotions of Divine love" and extend forgiveness.[84] Just as importantly, Jewish newspapers welcomed the schoolmaster as a figure demonstrating the "great punishment which surely follows apostasy."[85] Daly's adaptation of the play clearly reinserted a nominally Christian form of love into Mosenthal's topical play about Jewish emancipation and amplified the ambivalence about Jews already present in the drama. It did so, however, without getting in the way of Jews and non-Jews coming together in the theater to partake of the same pleasure of feeling the Jewess's pain as their European counterparts.

In understanding the impact of the play, the ambivalence central to the conclusion of Daly's *Leah* is important less because of its content than because of its form, because it enabled Daly to craft a powerful ending for the play that introduced a level of depth and complexity absent from Mosenthal's original. Leah is unable to make as easy a transition as Deborah from hatred and vengeance to love, compassion, and human kindness, and she becomes the perfect object of compassion only in a demise set against the backdrop of the dramatic undoing of the schoolmaster and the shock of the villagers. The occasional German critic pronounced the conclusion of *Leah* an improvement over Mosenthal's original.[86] Others, however, regarded it as typical for the sensationalism of the English and American stage.[87] Wherever one came down on this issue, it was indisputable that the innovations that Daly introduced lent Mosenthal's material a much more interesting and far more exciting conclusion than *Deborah* had in its original form. In the German-speaking world, Mosenthal himself was frequently charged with playing to the audience and caring more about sensational effect than dramatic form. In this sense, Daly was simply surpassing Mosenthal at his own game.

Death and Redemption in London

At the time he was hired to adapt *Deborah* for Bateman, Daly was a drama critic for several New York papers who had yet to make it as a playwright. Fearing the jealousy and potential ill will of his fellow journalists, he was particularly anxious that the "paternity of Leah" be kept secret.[88] Early performances of *Leah* in Boston and New York, accordingly, attributed the adaptation of Mosenthal not to Daly but to an anonymous "gentleman of distinguished literary ability," a term that provoked occasional ridicule in the press.[89] Daly's fears proved not to be unfounded. As rumors of his authorship of the popular play surfaced, devastating reviews by his peers singled out his script for special attack.[90] New York drama critics described his adaptation of Mosenthal as "dramatic hash" written in "poverty-stricken" language, and they complained about the "weak and commonplace prose" and the "redundant, tame, unsuitable, and often incorrect language" of the "illiterate and unskillful dramatist" who produced this poor translation of Mosenthal.[91] To be sure, most reviews were not this negative. By May 1863, Daly's authorship of the successful play was public knowledge. Bateman dedicated her final New York performance of *Leah*, on May 23, to a benefit in his honor.[92] By the end of the 1860s, after he had opened his own theater on Fifth Avenue, Daly had little difficulty casting himself as the playwright and theater impresario whose illustrious career had begun with his adaptation of *Leah*.[93]

Given the fresh memory of the bad press that Daly's language earned in New York, Bateman and her manager father proceeded with caution when preparing for the play's London premiere in fall 1863. Before opening night, H. L. Bateman arranged for John Oxenford—the drama critic of the London *Times*, a prolific playwright, and a noted translator from German—to rework Daly's entire script. And Oxenford was not the only contact at the *Times* whom Kate's father cultivated. Rather than using Daly's memoir in London, he commissioned Charles Lamb Kenney—another drama critic at the *Times*, who had produced the English libretto for Ristori's Italian performance of *Deborah* that the Batemans attended in July—to write a new promotional pamphlet for his daughter and her new play.[94] Not surprisingly, following opening night on October 1, 1863, the *Times* gave both Bateman and *Leah* a brilliant review, helping to set the stage for the play's spectacular initial run of 210 performances.[95]

Oxenford's version of *Leah* incorporated the changes introduced early in the play's New York run, having Leah die on stage rather than head off feebly to join her people. With some minor alterations and changes, it was this unpublished version of the play that Bateman performed for twenty-six years. During Bateman's 1866 revival of *Leah* in New York, some critics in Daly's camp made polemical assertions that Oxenford's revisions to his script were insignificant.[96] The surviving two manuscript copies of Bateman's script, however, indicate that Oxenford's changes were anything but superficial.[97] Oxenford, indeed, gave Daly's language a complete stylistic makeover, creating a drama that reads much better and more smoothly than Daly's text, which still retains at points the marks of an adaptation that began with a crude, literal translation from the

German. Oxenford was known for his translations of Goethe and Heinrich von Kleist, and he was familiar with Mosenthal's work. Soon after reworking *Leah* for Bateman, he began preparing, with Mosenthal's blessing, an English version of Mosenthal's *Pietra* for Bateman that she eventually performed, briefly, in 1868; he also wrote the libretto for George Alexander Macfarren's 1864 opera *Helvellyn*, which was based on Mosenthal's other internationally successful drama, *Der Sonnwendhof* (Sunny Vale Farm, 1854).[98] Interestingly, despite his German skills, Oxenford did not go back to the text of *Deborah* in reworking Daly's *Leah*. In cleaning up Daly's prose for Bateman, Oxenford seems to have worked solely with Daly's script. In many cases, his thorough revision of Daly's language produced a text even further from the original than Daly's *Leah*.

In terms of content, many of Oxenford's changes were minor. In a likely effort to avoid conflict with Haymarket Theatre manager John Baldwin Buckstone, whose melodrama *Henriette, the Forsaken* launched its career at the Adelphi in 1832–1833, Oxenford and the Batemans called the revised version of the play simply *Leah* rather than *Leah, the Forsaken*; this became the title that Bateman used for the next twenty-six years. Retooling the play for a British audience, Oxenford deleted the concrete references to America and the land across the sea from Rudolf and Leah's romantic scene in Act II, having his star-crossed lovers hope to elope simply to a "western land of promise, where none may suffer for their creed";[99] in Act V, however, he maintained Madalena's reference to a "tribe of emigrant Jews, going to America" camping out in the castle where they "seem to be terribly afraid of our villagers."[100] At some points in the drama, Oxenford further toned down biblical language and deleted Hebrew terms such as *Mitzrayim* (Egypt), and he also trimmed back some of the scenes where villagers engage in gossip. Apart from detailed instructions about sound effects, props, and the music used to accompany the most dramatic scenes in the play, the most characteristic feature of Oxenford's version was the way the final scene was staged.

Oxenford retained nearly all the dialogue from Daly's concluding sequence, including Leah's reference to herself as Judith during her last flare-up of Old Testament vengeance. The main differences lay in the stage directions. Leah here does not draw a knife from her own girdle, as she did in Daly. Arriving on the scene unarmed, rather, she "*snatches [the] knife from Rudolf*" instead, making her appear a bit more impulsive. As she totters here, most importantly, it is not Madalena who catches her but Rudolf, and it is in his arms that she finds peace in death: "LEAH. Rudolf! *Staggers towards him, he catches her.* I must not remain . . . *sinks, as he kneels.* I will wander on with my people to the far-off, the Promised Land! MUSIC. *She turns her face towards Rudolf, and dies in his arms. When Leah's right arm falls, Lorrenz* [sic] *raises his hat. All the male villagers raise their hats. Madalena+child too.*"[101] As in Daly's *Leah*, here we see the victory of Christian compassion over the lingering threat of Jewish vengeance. This version of the drama, however, provides far more closure than was the case in Daly. Leah here does not go off to an uncertain demise. As she proclaims her hope to find messianic redemption with her own people, she dies on stage, in Rudolf's arms, and in such a way as to command the respect of all the villagers, including those who had joined the schoolmaster in seeking to stone and drown her minutes before. Leah remains the focal point of the concluding scene in a far more powerful manner than was the case in the conclusion of Daly's script. In this recasting of Daly's finale, Leah dies a redemptive death that gives her suffering meaning. Leah's melodramatic death on stage enables the villagers to feel good about how bad they feel about the fate she has met. She becomes, in death, a symbol of reconciliation between Jews and Christians, dying a Jewish death designed to provoke the compassion of the Christian world.

Having Leah die in this way altered both Daly's and Mosenthal's play significantly. But this innovation that Bateman introduced in New York and that Oxenford formalized in his revisions to the play hardly came out of nowhere. Leah's redemptive death marked an ingenious innovation, a concluding sequence that harkened back to the beginning of the drama, to the celebration of Good Friday and anticipation of Easter in the opening scene. In Daly and Oxenford, as well as in Mosenthal, Madalena leaves the church on Good Friday, inspired by her uncle's sermon, hoping to follow Jesus' example and make sacrifices for humanity by helping Jews. Building on Mosenthal, Daly had already made this invocation of Jesus more pointed, opening his version of the drama with a hymn that the villagers sing as they walk out of church on Good Friday afternoon. The hymn, retained in its entirety in Oxenford's *Leah* and sung to Stoepel's music, invokes Jesus to stress the value of seeking to "imitate His works / and walk His holy ways."[102] In Oxenford, tellingly, Madalena makes an explicit link between her desires to practice the virtues of Christian compassion and the all-embracing mode of liberal universalism invoked in the play's final scene: "For all of us ... all the children of Adam ... are all brethren, are we not?[103] Like Mosenthal's *Deborah*, *Leah* migrates from anticipations of religious redemption in Act I to the more secular models of redemption that emerge at the end of the play under the banner of imperial reform and the spirit of Jewish-Christian coexistence. But by staging Leah's death, the finale of Bateman's version of the play situates secular redemption in much closer proximity to its Christian precursors than was the case in either Mosenthal or Daly. In the final scene, Leah's Jewish suffering provokes a community-building exercise for those on and off stage who are encouraged to cultivate compassion for her and create a world in which Jews and Christians might live together in peace and harmony. The play that begins with the anticipation of an Easter celebration concludes here not with Jesus' death and resurrection but with Leah's suffering and redemptive death, rendering the Jewess's dead body the focal point of a scene that gives audience members the clear sense that tears shed over Leah's sufferings mean something.

As an article in the *Musical World*, a London journal, stated emphatically in 1864, the goal of Bateman's *Leah* was not to perform the "victory of Christ over Jehovah."[104] As Kenney commented in the promotional pamphlet that appeared soon after *Leah* opened in London, Bateman's play certainly portrayed the "eventual triumph" of the "Christian principles of love, forgiveness, and toleration," giving expression to a "feeling that has been long growing in the hearts of Jew and Christian throughout Europe."[105] Dramaturgically speaking, however, the great advantage of the liberal principles of tolerance and goodwill that *Leah* coded as both Christian and universal was that they allowed the Jewess Leah, for a moment, to take the place of Jesus, giving audiences the pleasure of experiencing her suffering and death. The play that begins in church with a ceremony anticipating Christian redemption concludes outside Rudolf's farmhouse with Christian onlookers learning how to feel compassion with Jewish suffering: Leah's spectacular death encourages the villagers and the spectators to practice the Christian virtues of tolerance and goodwill that Madalena defended in the first scene of the drama.

Tellingly, much of the fan fiction and spin-off merchandising that Bateman's *Leah* generated in England focused on the slippery way Leah's redemptive death in Rudolf's arms mediated between Judaism and Christianity. Of the two British pieces of music inspired by Bateman's *Leah*, Brinley Richards's "Leah's Song" was the more popular. Indeed, apart from the extravagant color image of Bateman sitting in front of the cross on its cover, Augustus Greville's "It Is the Hour: Leah's Song" actually had little to do with the play whose success it was seeking to take advantage of.[106] Richards's "Leah's Song" was routinely advertised as the "most popular song of the day" and was republished several times, including in a version for solo piano.[107] Marketed as a "Beautiful Drawing-Room Song" with a one-octave range "adapting itself to any voice,"[108] Richards's song focuses on a moment in Leah's development never actually presented on stage. "Leah's Song" gives singers and their audiences in Victorian living rooms the unique sense of experiencing both Leah's despair over being forsaken and her enduring hope that she will eventually come to find peace in death in Rudolf's arms:

Deceiv'd, and broken hearted,
Ah! who shall be my stay!
JUDAEA veils her face,
The GENTILE turns away.

> Yet when pale death shall come,
> To give the wand'rer rest,
> Oh! may my latest sigh,
> Be drawn upon his breast.[109]

Paired with a cover image of an exotic Bateman as Leah being pursued by the mob, this song crystallizes around the anticipation of Leah's redemptive death. Leah here does not just style herself as the object of Christian compassion, longing for consolation in death upon the breast of the Gentile lover for whom she regrets she "gave up all! / My People, yea, my God."[110] Indeed, in terms of its musical form, Richards's "Leah's Song" resembles a typical Victorian hymn. Richards, that is, uses an explicitly Christian register to sing the tale of Leah's Jewish woes. In this sense, "Leah's Song" offers the perfect antipode to the hymn with which the drama opens, creating a musical number that does for Leah what the opening hymn did for Jesus.

Price's epic poem *Leah* similarly promotes a distinctly Christian mode of compassionate liberalism, one that Price sets into relief by emphasizing that the Jews' ancient crime of killing Jesus should now, finally, be consigned to the past: "Surely their race's stain / Has faded now, for centuries have rolled, / Long cycles passed, since that dark crime of old / Proved their great downfall, and their country's bane." Here, too, Leah dies a redemptive death, with "more than earthly beauty," crowned with a "heavenly halo" as she staggers and dies in Rudolf's arms.[111] The novel *Leah, the Jewish Maiden* was in the unique position to narrate Leah's ascent to heaven. At the conclusion of the novel, Leah gasps, "ADIEU, RUDOLPH," as she dies in her former lover's arms: "*His* name was the last word her lips uttered; and then departed to her God—the soul of LEAH, THE JEWISH MAIDEN."[112] As an opera, Schira's *Lia* picked up where the novel left off and managed to stage Lia's Jewish death and her ascension to heaven in an even more spectacular manner. As Schira's Lia dies on stage, the chorus proclaims that the gates of paradise are opening to welcome her as a saint and a martyr. Here, as well, however, Lia dies an explicitly Jewish death. Indeed, as Maddalena sings that the children of Israel ascend to the same heaven as Christians do, Lia dies, departing from the earth singing that she is going off to the "Promised Land" with her people. As Rudolfo leans over Lia's corpse in tears and Maddalena throws herself into the arms of her father-in-law, Lorenzo, the priest extends his hands to bless Lia from heaven, performing the reconciliation between Jews and Christians in an unequivocally Christian register.[113]

Of course, none of these adaptations of Bateman's material marked a radical innovation. They all built off the ambivalence about Jews that Daly highlighted in rewriting Mosenthal's concluding sequence and that Bateman's version mined even further for its melodramatic potential. By creating a drama that concluded with Leah's death and her transformation into a symbol for the cause of reconciliation and peaceful coexistence between Jews and Christians, Bateman's *Leah* enacted a grand spectacle of Jewish martyrdom geared at generating Christian compassion. In Mosenthal, Deborah heads off, reconciled and in good health, to join her people and set off for America, part of a robust Jewish collective that appeared on stage at the beginning of the play's final act; in keeping with the clear trajectory of the play's conclusion, one Austrian production even gave the play the title *Deborah, oder: die Auswanderung der Juden* (Deborah, or: the Emigration of the Jews).[114] By the time the play made it to London, it had proved effective to dispense with the collective of wandering Jews and kill off Leah on stage. Rather than focusing the energies of the spectators on Jewish emigration, it proved expeditious to present a sensational scene of Jewish suffering and death that gave spectators a thrill and a clear sense, once again, that their crying in the theater served a higher purpose.[115]

Cheltnam's *Deborah* and the Wonders of Spectatorship

Daly's two major innovations—the transformation of the schoolmaster into a villain to be unmasked in the final scene of the play and Leah's illness and brush with death in the closing scene—became defining features of the long career of Mosenthal's *Deborah* on the English-language stage, particularly after his *Leah* appeared in *French's Standard Drama* series as Augustin Daly's *Leah, the Forsaken* in the 1870s. To be sure, there were occasional English-language versions that remained close to the original and avoided these changes. Conquest's *Deborah; or, the Jewish Outcast*, for instance, opened at the Grecian Theatre in London while Bateman was still performing *Leah* at the Adelphi and advertised itself as a faithful translation of the version of *Deborah* that Ristori had performed in London, in Italian, at Her Majesty's Theatre, in July 1863.[116] As mentioned above, Conquest most likely created his play working off Kenney's libretto for Ristori's performance rather than going back to Mosenthal's script. Following the Ristori version, Conquest retained both Mosenthal's four-act structure and his use of blank verse. His *Deborah* steered clear of the melodramatic excesses that Daly introduced in relation to the schoolmaster and the final scene, concluding instead, following Ristori, with Deborah's statement of forgiveness and reconciliation to Joseph, Hanna, and young Deborah.[117] None of this went unnoticed in the press. Conquest's *Deborah* was often praised for its "elevated" style and its "moral" message, and critics at numerous performances in the 1860s noted that the audience burst into loud applause whenever sentiments in favor of religious toleration were voiced.[118]

The Ristori libretto also gave rise to other London versions that failed to earn this level of approval. After *Rebecca, the Jewish Wanderer* opened at the Marylebone Theatre in August 1864, it was rejected out of hand as yet another unoriginal *Leah* knockoff; apparently, the play's grand innovation of introducing a sensation scene where Rebecca saves young Rebecca from an avalanche before delivering her final speech on stage did not impress the critics.[119] In 1868, a new adaptation of *Deborah* at the Princess Theatre called *Ruth* was written off as an unintentional travesty of *Deborah* and repeatedly singled out for parody in the British, German, and Austrian press.[120] Whatever the differences were between Conquest's *Deborah*, *Rebecca*, and *Ruth*, none of these plays achieved any lasting success.

Of all the English-language versions of Mosenthal's material, it was Charles Smith Cheltnam's *Deborah; or, the Jewish Maiden's Wrong!* that came to compete the most with Daly's *Leah*. Like the authors of *Deborah; or, the Jewish Outcast*, *Rebecca*, and *Ruth*, Cheltnam, a prolific playwright, likely created his script using the English translation of Ristori's Italian version that was distributed to theatergoers at her performance the previous summer. Indeed, he restored the main characters their original German names, with the telling exception of Hanna; following Ristori's script, he called Joseph's wife Anna (a more appropriate change for a Romance language that does not aspirate its *h*'s than for English). He also went along with Ristori's *Deborah* in rendering the name of one of Mosenthal's villagers, Old Lise, as Martha, and in spelling Ruben's name Reuben. Whatever his sources were, Cheltnam departed significantly from other adaptations of Ristori's *Deborah*. He transformed Mosenthal's four-act play into a three-act prose drama, the conventional genre for popular theater. While he retained the lengthy scene with Reuben that Daly cut, he lent the encounter between Reuben and Deborah a melodramatic twist that it lacked in both the original and Ristori's version. At the end of this scene, Deborah does not promise to meet Reuben at the coast to sail off to America. When Reuben asks, "On the sea-shore you will join us?" Cheltnam's Deborah responds, "If I live. Farewell!" The stage directions indicate that Deborah "*waves him off, and totters slowly out*" as Reuben "*watches her sadly*" before exiting along with the other Jewish emigrants.[121] Cheltnam retains the sense in Mosenthal's original of Jews on a mission to find a secular Promised Land in America as they separate themselves painfully from a beloved fatherland. But he amplifies the rift between Deborah and her fellow Jews, making Deborah's death a melodramatic inevitability.

The logic behind Cheltnam's adaptation becomes clear when we examine both its explicit borrowings from *Leah* and its efforts to create a drama that would be even more sensational than Bateman's successful play in the West

End. Following *Leah*, Cheltnam's *Deborah* is set not in the 1780s but also in the "early part of the last century," and the description of the "white bodice, brown skirt, turban, and scarf for waist" required for Deborah's costume clearly indicates that the mass-produced photographs of Bateman as Leah that were sold by the thousands in London shops framed Cheltnam's vision of how his heroine should dress.[122] As was the case in Mosenthal, Cheltnam's schoolmaster does not kill Abraham after the recognition scene. But his schoolmaster becomes a far more devious villain than Daly's apostate, one who gets more stage time than his counterpart in *Leah*. After his encounter with Abraham, Cheltnam's schoolmaster goes mad with paranoia, hears voices, and accuses his friends of being spies, all of which he expresses in a series of elaborate monologues and dialogues with his neighbor Martha, whom Cheltnam's dramatis personae describes as a "Fanatic Old Woman."[123] All this paranoia takes its toll. At the beginning of the third and final act, the stage directions indicate that the schoolmaster "*appears haggard, and ten or twelve years older than in the preceding Act*" even though just five years pass between Act II and Act III.[124]

Here, as in Daly, whatever visions of liberal reform the emperor and Joseph and Anna have embraced are not yet shared by the peasantry. In the final act of Cheltnam's play, the schoolmaster plays an even greater role riling up the mob than in Daly. When the schoolmaster and Martha hear of the presence of Jews in the next valley, they are outraged. Complaining that the priest and the magistrate are "wanting in sense of Christian duty," they feel compelled to take the law into their own hands and "drive out" these "pestiferous Jews" from "our district, even with fire and sword."[125] By beginning the final act with this dialogue set in the schoolmaster's house—the scene between Deborah and Reuben follows[126]—Cheltnam thus structures his play even more explicitly than Daly's around a conflict between the paranoia and violence of the apostate's anti-Jewish mindset and the drive toward reconciliation between Deborah and the Christian world.

Cheltnam's final scene similarly builds on *Leah* to create something even more sensational than the conclusion that Bateman had been performing in London. Even though Cheltnam's Deborah is not ill, reconciliation here takes place face-to-face instead of being quietly mediated through the spectators. In Cheltnam, as in Bateman's *Leah*, the schoolmaster storms onto stage followed by a crowd of villagers to interrupt Deborah's final reunion with Joseph and Anna. Cheltnam's fast-paced conclusion, however, makes *Leah*'s sensation scene look tame. Cheltnam integrates a murder and a dramatic suicide into a sequence that for Bateman included only an arrest by the police and Leah's quiet demise after one last flare-up of Jewish vengeance:

MARTHA. *(L.)* See, neighbours! see! I told you we should find here one of the abominable tribe! *(murmurs)* Seize her, Schoolmaster.
DEBOR. Touch me not—apostate!
S. MASTER. *(shrieking)* She lies! she lies! do not listen to her lying tongue!
DEBOR. I speak the truth—Nathan, son of Nathan, the Jew of Presburg!
S. MASTER. *(wildly)* Silence! *(plunging his hand into his breast)* She's mad! Neighbours, heed not her words!—she's mad! *(movement of amazement in the crowd)*
DEBOR. Hypocrite! Deserter of his aged father! Disgrace of Israel!
S. MASTER. *(frantically)* I am lost! Woman!—die! *(he suddenly, scarcely seeming to know what he is doing, plunges a knife into her bosom, then, after looking wildly around for a moment rushes up the hill-path, reaching the top at the moment LORENZ and two PEASANTS appear at the brow of the hill)*
JOSEPH. *(who has rushed forward and caught DEBORAH in his arms)* Seize him! Seize the murderer! *(general movement)*
S. MASTER. *(seeing no way of escape)* Lost! Lost! *(he springs from the rocky edge of the path into the stream—a cry of horror from all—the PASTOR enters hurriedly and crosses to JOSEPH, who is supporting DEBORAH—DEBORAH takes ANNA's hand and places it, with JOSEPH's, upon her heart, then raises her other hand towards heaven and dies—ANNA sinks upon her knees, the child kneeling by her side—the PASTOR reverently takes off his hat, and the CROWD do the same—OLD MARTHA sinks upon her knees, and buries her face in her hands—LORENZ remains upon the hillside, hat in hand, a wondering spectator—the curtain descends slowly)*[127]

Deborah dies here without the relapse into Jewish vengeance that she demonstrated at the conclusion of *Leah*. The spectacle of Cheltnam's final scene hinges, instead, on the expressions of Jewish pride that are Deborah's last words as she publicly brands the schoolmaster a hypocrite, the betrayer of his father, and the disgrace of Israel. Here, too, Deborah helps restore public order by unraveling the schoolmaster, who murders her, barely aware of what he is doing, and then dies a dramatic death as he jumps off a cliff into the river.

In reworking the final scene of Bateman's *Leah*, Cheltnam retains the ambivalence that Daly introduced and makes the restoration of public order go hand in hand with the removal of Jewish figures. Indeed, at the conclusion of his *Deborah*, the Jews on stage kill themselves off, the innocence of the once-vengeful Jewess restored as she becomes the victim of male Jewish vengeance. In her victimhood, however, Cheltnam's Deborah takes on far greater power in the dramatic duel between her and the schoolmaster than she had at the end of Bateman's *Leah* or Mosenthal's *Deborah*. Deborah not only gets to pronounce her Jewish pride. As soon as the schoolmaster commits suicide, she stages her own final moments, orchestrating a scene of reconciliation and redemption where she joins Joseph and Anna together and places their hands on her heart as she gestures melodramatically toward heaven and takes her last breath. In Cheltnam's *Deborah*, the final scene is a spectacle of Deborah's own making that sets the villagers in a state of shock. Following the example of Anna and young Deborah, who kneel, and the pastor, who takes off his hat in reverence, the entire cast is rendered speechless as they take off their hats and stand in wonder, watching the scene that has just transpired. In this way, Deborah creates a spectacle for the villagers—and, by extension, the audience—that lends a clear meaning to her murder at the hands of the schoolmaster. Styling herself as a martyr for the cause of Jews and Christians living together in harmony, she takes her last breath, confident that she commands the sympathies of the entire crowd of villagers assembled on stage, with the fanatical Martha the exception that proves the rule.

Cheltnam thus amplifies the sensationalism that characterizes the final scene of Bateman's *Leah*, transforming the reconciliation that is mediated by the spectators' tears of compassion in Mosenthal's play into a breathtaking spectacle performed before both the villagers and the audience. In this sense, the final scene repeats the thrills of the curse scene at the end of Act II, replacing fear of Deborah's Old Testament wrath with a sense of awe and admiration over Deborah's ability to dedicate her own death to the project of reconciliation. In its staging, in fact, the final scene of Cheltnam's *Deborah* carefully reiterates key innovations that he introduced into the curse scene. At the end of the curse scene in Act II, Cheltnam did not merely have Deborah snatch Joseph's rosary as she exits. Immediately after Cheltnam's Joseph faints, Anna, Lorenz, the pastor, and the villagers all rush out from the church where Joseph and Anna have just gotten married. As the scene comes to an end, Anna screams and rushes to Joseph. She kneels down beside him and raises his head, in front of all the villagers, creating a tableau with which Cheltnam concludes the act. Act III concludes, subsequently, by bringing nearly the entire cast on stage again for an even more grandiose crowd scene where, amid murder, death, suicide, kneeling, and screaming, Deborah styles herself as the ideal object of compassion and assigns a clear symbolic significance to the sympathy that she counts on from the villagers and the audience. Like Mosenthal's Deborah and Bateman's Leah, Cheltnam's heroine also learns the power of compassion as a spectator witnessing Joseph and Anna's reunion before she has her heart-wrenching encounter with the young Deborah on stage. But she hardly goes off with her people, "a symbol of the tribe that has renounced its hatred now we know that you can love us." Rather, she stays behind, dying melodramatically on stage so that her well-staged death might enable the audience to feel a lasting mode of compassion with her suffering.

Building on Bateman's *Leah*, Cheltnam concludes his drama in such a way that Deborah also finds deliverance in death. Here, too, the play that begins with the anticipation of an Easter celebration concludes not with Jesus but with Deborah's suffering and redemptive death. In this sense, the feel-good conclusion of Cheltnam's *Deborah* further changes the direction of Mosenthal's play, with its clear celebration of Reuben's secularized Jewish messianism in the final act. With her death pronounced as an inevitability in her conversation with Reuben, Deborah steals Reuben's thunder, becoming a figure whose martyrdom for the cause of tolerance and religious harmony gives Anna and the other villagers an experience of awe, reverence, wonder, and inspiration in the play's final scene that is far more spectacular and likely far more moving than anything they would have seen in church in the scene before the drama opened. Fashioning Deborah as a proud Jewish martyr whose death invokes Christian models of redemption may appear problematic to us today. But from the perspective of a play that sought to transform Mosenthal's *Deborah* into an even more powerful and even more sensational tearjerker than both the version that Ristori had performed in London the summer before and the version that Bateman had had such success with at the Adelphi Theatre, these innovations made perfect sense. Like Daly, Cheltnam was simply surpassing Mosenthal at his own game, mining Mosenthal's Jewish material for its potential to give the audiences the pleasure—and the thrills—of a good cry.

Forsaken or Forsook? Tears, Laughter, and the *Deborah* Craze

Moving from the analysis of texts to the discussion of actual performances, the following chapter will explore how *Deborah* and *Leah* hinged on a unique mode of interaction between actresses and their audiences. Before investigating the types of acting and the forms of theatricality that sustained the *Deborah* craze, it will prove illuminating to expand our discussion of how the most common scripts for *Deborah* and *Leah* sought to elicit emotional responses with a consideration of a set of nineteenth-century adaptations that poked fun at both the tears that the drama produced and the idealized visions of Jewish martyrdom characteristic of Anglo American versions of Mosenthal. The English-speaking world produced, alongside the huge number of different versions of the play, a rich tradition of parodies. The much more sensational brand of sympathy with Jewish suffering that Mosenthal's material promoted in the Anglo American world was not just marked by the heightened theatricality that we saw in our analysis of Daly's, Bateman's, and Cheltnam's scripts. It also lent itself to and embraced a level of irony about both the play and the tearful compassion it provoked that is worth exploring for the self-conscious way it comments on the sentimental universalism propelling the *Deborah* craze.

The Viennese press occasionally singled out Mosenthal's *Deborah* for parody, but often in a malicious way. The tradition of satire that we will be exploring here had no real equivalent in the German-speaking world. As one example among many, let us consider the cartoon "Mutter Deborah" (Mother Deborah, Figure 25) that ran in the Viennese satirical weekly *Figaro* in 1858, just after Ristori performed her Italian version of *Deborah* in Vienna.[128] In this image, a Deborah bearing a faint resemblance to Ristori boasts exaggerated Jewish features, sporting bushy eyebrows, long, jet-black hair, and an oversize nose, the darkness of her features accentuated by crosshatching. Surrounded by wreaths, Ristori/Deborah holds in her arms a baby Mosenthal, who proudly waves a letter of recommendation in the air. The writing on Mosenthal's clothing—

Figure 25. "Mutter Deborah," *Figaro*, March 7, 1858. Austrian National Library.

Deboraleben, Dichterleben—pokes fun at both his 1850 drama *Ein deutsches Dichterleben* (A German Poet's Life) and the fact that his only claim to fame as a poet (*Dichter*) is the play that enables Ristori and other stars to shine. While Ristori holds Mosenthal in her arms, paying far less attention to the playwright than to the audience tossing wreaths at her, another man-baby, Cajetan or Gaetano Cerri, Ristori's Italian translator and the editor of the Austrian women's magazine *Iris*, tries to crawl up her skirts to get a piece of the action. "We want a wreath too, Mama!" reads the German caption, mocking dramatist and translator alike in their vain quest for recognition—and their relative insignificance in the star performance that their labors made possible.[129]

It is illuminating to compare "Mutter Deborah" to the widely circulated image of Bateman that the American political cartoonist Thomas Nast featured in the series of eighteen caricatures he sketched for a high-profile masquerade ball at the New York Academy of Music in April 1866, just after Bateman's first American revival of *Leah*. Subsequently reproduced in *Harper's Weekly*, this image mocks one of the most widely disseminated cartes-de-visite of Bateman as Leah.[130] Nast transforms Bateman's fearful countenance in the photograph into a pose that looks grumpy (and dumpy), with exaggerated black eyebrows, beady eyes, and an oversize nose that emphasize the foreignness of Bateman's Jewess at the expense of the figure's eroticism. With its massive head, this caricature of Bateman "leans from the frame in a most unnatural way," as the *New York Times* commented.[131] Nast's Leah repels rather than attracts viewers. Neither the object of compassion nor a character who provokes fear, Bateman's Leah here is rendered an unpleasant figure: not a *belle juive* but an ugly Jewess, and one who appears uniquely ill equipped to give spectators the thrill of a good cry.

While both "Mutter Deborah" and the Bateman cartoon indulge in Jewish stereotyping and poke fun at the popularity of the figure of Mosenthal's Jewess, they do so to different ends. Put on display and published alongside caricatures of political and cultural luminaries of the day, including Andrew Johnson, Ulysses Grant, P. T. Barnum, Edwin Booth, Henry Ward Beecher, the director of the Academy of Music Max Maretzek, and Nast himself, Nast's image offered up a mockery of Bateman's *Leah* that contributed to her celebrity rather than the unrelenting ridicule of Mosenthal in the *Figaro* cartoon. Like the German American sketch "Schneider Sees Leah," which we explored in Chapter 1, this image displayed at the opera ball under the title "The Forsook—Miss Bateman" hardly sought to undermine Bateman or the fame she gained playing the Jewish maiden.[132] Indeed, by rendering Miss Bateman a figure incapable of eliciting compassion, one who lacks the erotic appeal of Bateman's Jewish maiden and who is "forsook" rather than "forsaken," Nash's cartoon offers an illuminating (and humorous) commentary on both Bateman's success playing the role and the

Figure 26. Thomas Nast, *The Forsook—Miss Bateman*, *Harper's Weekly*, April 14, 1866. Hess private collection.

Figure 27. Kate Bateman as Leah, carte-de-visite photograph. Hess private collection.

Figure 28. E. Dexter, engraving of Dan Setchell. Billy Rose Theatre Division, New York Public Library for the Performing Arts, Astor, Lenox and Tilden Foundations.

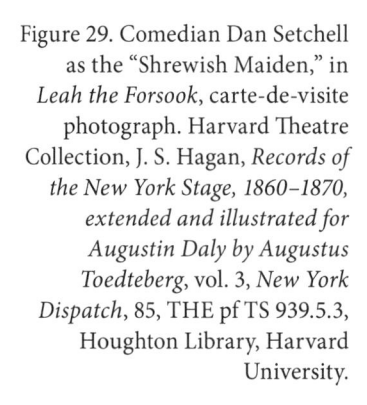

Figure 29. Comedian Dan Setchell as the "Shrewish Maiden," in *Leah the Forsook*, carte-de-visite photograph. Harvard Theatre Collection, J. S. Hagan, *Records of the New York Stage, 1860–1870, extended and illustrated for Augustin Daly by Augustus Toedteberg*, vol. 3, *New York Dispatch*, 85, THE pf TS 939.5.3, Houghton Library, Harvard University.

drama itself. Setting Bateman's Leah alongside the president of the United States, General Grant, and others, this celebrity roast clearly contributed to the *Deborah* craze rather than ridiculed those profiting from it. By labeling his caricature "The Forsook—Miss Bateman," moreover, Nast lent it an impressive pedigree. The grammatical infelicity in its title invoked the popular burlesque *Leah the Forsook* that opened in New York in July 1863 and that the renowned comedian Dan Setchell had performed to great acclaim across the country until he died, in early 1866, in a shipwreck while bound for New Zealand.[133]

Leah the Forsook was but the most famous of a series of good-natured satires and parodies that Mosenthal's play provoked in the English-speaking world. It was so well known, in fact, that other comic skits followed Nast in borrowing its title. Alfred Post Burbank, the noted elocutionist who first performed "Schneider Sees Leah" starting in the mid-1870s, often listed this sketch in his recital programs as "Leah the Forsook."[134] During the same period, Rollin Howard, the well-known American minstrel performer often credited with the authorship of the song "Shoo Fly, Don't Bother Me," introduced a new burlesque, "Leah the Shook, or Was She Forsook," blacking up and cross-dressing to play Leah. By the time Howard published a (now lost) print version of this burlesque in 1881, he, too, was marketing this skit as *Leah the Forsook*.[135] William Routledge's burlesque, *Leah, a Hearty Joke in a Cab Age*, performed in London in January 1869 and put on the boards in New York two years later under the title *Leah—a Curse-Sorry Burlesque*, never made claims to the title of Setchell's routine. In terms of content, as we shall see, it owed much to the way *Leah the Forsook* poked fun at the way *Deborah* and *Leah* functioned as tearjerkers.[136]

In the 1860s, there were harsh critics of *Leah* who claimed that a burlesque was not necessary since the play was already a parody of itself, and there were others who felt that *Leah the Forsook* was so funny that it ruined the original, making spectators unable to shed tears watching *Leah*.[137] For the most part, however, *Leah the Forsook*'s parody was part and parcel of the *Leah* craze rather than an effort to subvert it. Frank Wood, the author of *Leah the Forsook*, first developed an interest in *Leah* in his capacity as the drama critic for *Wilkes' Spirit of the Times*, an elite New York weekly that had published more glowing reviews and notices of Daly's play than any other paper.[138] Soon after the initial success of *Leah the Forsook* in July 1863, Wood became friends with Daly and began collaborating with him, working together to transform Emile Beneville's crude translation of Victorien Sardou's comedy *La Papillonne*—Beneville had translated *Deborah* for Daly the year before—into a viable play for the New York stage.[139] The advertising for *Taming a Butterfly* the following February underscored the reciprocal relationship between Daly's adaptation of Mosenthal and Wood's burlesque. Daly and Wood marketed *Taming a Butterfly* in good humor as the combined effort of "Augustin Daly, author of Leah, the Forsaken, and Frank Wood, author of Leah, the Forsook."[140] Wood died of consumption in 1864, but Setchell continued to perform *Leah the Forsook* until he died. He typically did so, not surprisingly, in cities where *Leah* had enjoyed success—first in New York, then in Boston (at the Howard Athenaeum, where Bateman first performed *Leah*), and subsequently in New Orleans, Buffalo, Washington, DC, Cincinnati, and San Francisco.

Like the *Leah* music and the *Leah* novel, *Leah the Forsook* appealed primarily to fans of the play, functioning less as a critique of *Leah* than as an index of its popularity and as a commentary on the culture of sentimental compassion with Jewish suffering that it engendered. To a certain extent, the appeal of *Leah the Forsook* was inseparable from Setchell, whose comic acting Mark Twain once praised with his characteristic wit: "I have experienced more real pleasure, and more physical benefit, from laughing naturally and unconfinedly at his funny personations and extempore speeches than I have from all the operas and tragedies I have endured, and all the blue mass pills I have swallowed in six months."[141] Playing the "Shrewish Maiden" in *Leah the Forsook*, the "very large" Setchell earned uniformly rave reviews for his "make up" and his hilarious and "grotesque" parody of Bateman's Leah and her various poses and "attitudes" in the role.[142] In San Francisco, Setchell had no difficulty adjusting his performance to caricature Matilda Heron, who played Leah at the San Francisco opera house, earning enthusiastic reviews for his impersonation of her as well.[143]

As brilliant as Setchell may have been, the success of *Leah the Forsook* was also a function of the ingenious way in which Wood rewrote Daly's play, and this is what requires our attention. To some extent, Wood's burlesque was a standard piece of work, composed in mock heroic verse, with cross-dressing for all its main roles and original lyrics written to popular songs such as "When the Cruel War Is Over" and "Sally Come Up."[144] But part of the reason that the *New York Herald* celebrated *Leah the Forsook* as the best burlesque in years was no doubt Wood's subtle ability to zone in on how the original *Leah* functioned as a drama.[145] Parodying the well-known reference to five years elapsing between Leah's curse scene and the reconciliation of the final act, the playbill for *Leah the Forsook* indicated that a "period of five minutes is supposed to elapse between the first and second acts." Before the final scene, subsequently, a "period is supposed to elapse. Due notice will be given of the elapsing of the COLON and SEMI-COLON." Wood cleverly set the action of *Leah the Forsook* not in "ancient Steiermark" but more locally, on New York's Lower East Side, that is, in "that region flowery, / Where Chatham Street is joined unto the Bowery."[146] By having the action of *Leah the Forsook* take place in *Kleindeutschland* (Little Germany), an immigrant neighborhood where "Jews and Teutons" lived side by side, Wood found ample opportunity to poke fun at both Germans and Jews. He inserted seemingly constant references to beer and pretzels for the Germans and ham and pork for the Jews. In *Leah the Forsook*, the blind Jewish patriarch Abraham becomes a Jewish old-clothes dealer, and in keeping with the level of deference one might expect for a burlesque, Wood dispenses with any attempt to portray Judaism or Jewish rituals authentically or romantically. At a key point in the first half of the drama, we find ourselves outside "Leah's ancestral home," where she lives with "Old Abe and his Cabinet of Curiosities." Wood has Leah and Abraham here perform a "pork offering": "Ham! Headcheese!!! Horror!!!" This scene is followed, accordingly, by the "Jew d'shus indignation of Leah."[147]

But *Leah the Forsook* does not just make fun of Jews. It systematically robs *Leah* of its sentimentality at the same time as it subverts the romantic idealization of Jewish suffering central to the play's success. In rewriting *Leah*, Wood zoned in on each of the scenes that were crucial for the way the play functioned as a tearjerker, divesting each of its ability to elicit compassion for Jewish suffering. In Daly's and Bateman's *Leah,* Act I concluded with a tableau where Leah, pursued by the mob, cowers beneath the village priest and the cross he raises above her. Wood's Leah, when chased by the mob, does not became transfigured into an image of Jewish suffering calling out for sympathy. Instead, she "takes refuge in a pair of Boxing Gloves," which she dons repeatedly over the course of the play.[148] In *Leah the Forsook*, Leah's grand curse scene hardly electrifies the audience and creates an atmosphere where one might hear a pin drop. In Wood's scene called "THE CUSS," Leah does not just curse Rudolph; she threatens him with a lawsuit for breach of promise. Wood retains Leah's heartfelt encounter with young Leah, played in New York by the twenty-seven-year-old character actor Charles T. Parsloe, Jr., who would later become famous for his creation of the "Chinese coolie" type on the American stage.[149] No one seems to have wept as these two grown men hugged in the "heart rending interview with infant child" that the press celebrated as "excessively comic and effective."[150] Rather than provoking tears, accordingly, *Leah the Forsook* ends on an upbeat note, with a reference to precisely the sort of prejudices about Jews and money that Rudolf and his family learn to renounce by the end of the original play. In *Leah the Forsook*, Leah neither wanders off with her people nor dies on stage. Instead, she accepts an offer of free rent and decides to stay on and live happily ever after with Rudolf and Madalena.

After its New York premiere, one critic wondered about Wood's use of Jewish stereotypes, doubting "if the degradation of an unfortunate people be a fit theme for satirical illustration." Was it really appropriate to substitute the themes of "love, apostasy, and gold" in *Leah, the Forsaken* for "[l]ove, theft, and pork" in *Leah the Forsook*, this critic asked, fully aware that his concerns would likely fall on deaf ears.[151] Interestingly, these sorts of anxieties about the political correctness of Wood's burlesque rarely reared their head at the time, even among Jews. When Setchell visited Cincinnati in February 1865, for instance, Pike's Opera House took out special advertisements in the prominent Jewish newspaper the *Israelite*, where notices for the "first appearance of the inimitable comedian, Dan Setchell" in *Leah the Forsook* appeared alongside advertisements for Jewish businesses, Jewish marriage announcements, and Jewish death notices.[152] As readers of the *Israelite* no doubt were aware, Samuel Naphtali Pike, the successful whiskey dealer and entrepreneur who built Pike's Opera House, was himself Jewish.[153] By 1865, several different versions of *Deborah* and *Leah* had been performed in Cincinnati, and it stood to reason that Jews—like other fans of the play—would be in a unique position to enjoy *Leah the Forsook* as well, attending a performance in a grand venue built and owned by one of their own. A decade later, the New York *Jewish Messenger* recalled "poor Dan Setchell's burlesque" of Bateman's *Leah* not as offensive but as "shockingly funny" and "ridiculous," clearly assuming a Jewish readership familiar with the burlesque and well disposed toward it.[154]

What, then, was at stake in *Leah the Forsook*'s flagrant use of seemingly anti-Jewish stereotypes? Whatever their original intentions, they may have served as a diversionary tactic in the earliest performances. *Leah the Forsook* opened at the Winter Garden Theatre on Monday, July 13, just as the New York City draft riots were beginning. The "good-hearted mischief" of *Leah the Forsook* was welcomed in the press as a "refreshing" antidote to the drama playing out on the streets as working-class white men (mostly Irish immigrants) directed their anger and violence at African American residents of New York.[155] At one performance in late July, Setchell made this connection explicit, bringing down the house when he appeared on stage as Leah, chased by the mob, and before using his boxing gloves, turned to his persecutors and exclaimed, "I do not see a riotous face among you."[156] Contrary to what *Harper's Weekly* would have expected back in March, few critics seem to have made connections between *Leah*'s obvious attempt to overturn anti-Jewish sentiment and the persistence of antiblack racism. Indeed, for a moment in July 1863, laughing about Jews and German immigrants in the theater may have functioned as an escape valve, a way not to think about ethnic tensions outside the theater doors.

After mid-July, however, and certainly in performances outside New York City, it is hard to imagine that audiences felt that enjoying jokes about Jews had anything to do with street wars between Irish immigrants and African American New Yorkers. *Leah the Forsook* appealed to fans of *Leah*, to those who took pleasure in identifying with Leah's Jewish suffering. If Wood's burlesque enabled them to laugh about Jews, it did so in an effort to travesty the sentimental identification with Jewish suffering central to the power of Mosenthal's play. In this context, laughing at Jews and rejoicing in Leah's ability to live happily ever after, rent-free, with Rudolf and his family had less to do with antisemitism than with the powerful mode of compassion with Jews that was key to the draw of *Leah* in the first place. In this sense, it makes sense that *Leah the Forsook* could prove popular among Jews as well. Audiences laughing at Setchell's performance of the "Shrewish Maiden" and his impersonation of Bateman (or Heron) were hardly subverting the pleasures that they took in feeling Leah's woes. Rather, in an elaborate game of inversion, they were augmenting them, just as Nast's caricature of Bateman as Leah at the opera ball enabled viewers to recall the tears shed through compassion with Leah's suffering by confronting them with an image of Leah that made precisely such compassion seem ridiculous. As a burlesque, *Leah the Forsook* clearly played with anti-Jewish stereotypes but did so in a subversive manner, rendering these stereotypes the stuff of burlesque.

In this context, a few words about the other significant *Leah* burlesque are in order. Routledge's *Leah, a Hearty Joke in a Cab Age* (1869) was not performed nearly as often as *Leah the Forsook*, though Routledge did play the part of Leah on both sides of the Atlantic, apparently producing "roars of laughter."[157] Written, like *Leah the Forsook*, in mock heroic verse, Routledge's *Leah* also features cross-dressing and musical numbers, many of which border on the nonsensical (and some of which are seemingly never-ending). At its best, it appears as a takeoff on Wood's burlesque. Like Wood, Routledge pokes fun at the time that elapses before the final act of Leah, with a minor twist, noting that an "interval of six years" is to be imagined between his final two scenes: "The author regrets he cannot satisfy the realistic tendencies of the present day on this point, as the performance might be too long to please all."[158] When the mob pursues Leah at the beginning of the play, she takes refuge not in boxing gloves but in an umbrella.[159] Like Wood, most importantly, Routledge relishes in an excess of seemingly anti-Jewish stereotypes. Abraham here is a "general and unfair dealer, merchant in anything that pays" and an "advocate of the early worn-out clothing movement,"[160] and both Abraham and Leah are constantly seeking to peddle their wares and make good deals. Abraham, in particular, speaks a Germanic or Yiddishized English, and he eventually comes to recognize Nathan the Schoolmaster as Ike Moses, a Jew who owes him money and who converted to Christianity to escape paying debts. Nathan's surname links him to E. Moses & Sons, the prominent London manufacturer of inexpensive ready-made clothes whose merchandise was often advertised alongside notices for performances of *Leah*.[161] Here, too, all ends happily in the final scene. Abraham and Ike Moses agree to go into business together, and Leah quickly forgives Rudolph, pleased that he has hung up a sign saying, "All Jews to be received kindly."[162] In an absurd coda that comes out of nowhere, "Father Bede," the village priest, decides to marry Leah: "O, my heart! / This Jewish beauty's caused it quite to start; / I vowed I'd not re-marry, but then she / Has made me hate what's called celibacee."[163]

As a cultural phenomenon, Routledge's *Leah* never achieved the visibility of Wood's burlesque. But the flagrant trafficking in anti-Jewish stereotypes that it shares with Wood's *Leah the Forsook* underscores the particular way in which burlesques of *Leah* zoned in on the way the drama elicited the emotions of its audience. By playing with anti-Jewish stereotypes on stage, Routledge's *Leah* and *Leah the Forsook* hardly sought to encourage audiences to embrace these prejudices and adopt, say, the initial mind-set of the villagers who seek to stone and drown Leah as she enters the stage. Indeed, both burlesques dispense with any notion of Leah as a melodramatic victim. Whether she uses boxing gloves or an umbrella, Leah in both plays yields power; rather than suffering or dying a redemptive death, she manages to live happily ever after in a world where the anti-Jewish prejudices depicted on stage no longer matter. By giving Leah's tragedy such ridiculous endings, these burlesques did not just forestall the weeping that the play was famous for producing and poke fun at the romantic idealization of Jewish suffering that was crucial to all versions of Mosenthal's *Deborah*. By interrupting the pleasures of identification with the sufferings of Mosenthal's Jewish heroine, these burlesques shed light on the fundamental aesthetic experience of *Deborah* and *Leah*, enabling fans of the plays being travestied to be self-conscious about their joys of feeling the Jewess's pain. Playing with the anti-Jewish prejudices that *Deborah* and *Leah* sought to dismantle was, of course, potentially a double-edged sword, as the comments of the reviewer quoted above make clear. Yet this ambivalence was precisely what made these burlesques funny. In an indirect way, laughing at Germans and Jews on stage fueled the sentimental identification with Jewish suffering.

* * *

As a mode of caricature that revels in its own excess, burlesque celebrates its own theatricality and typically engages with its audience in a far more self-conscious manner than the often very serious dramas that it puts under its microscope. In the fairly innocuous British burlesque *Debo-Leah* performed at the Britannia Theatre in London in 1864, for instance, "Debo-Leah" (known also as "Debby") gives a speech à la Ristori in which she reconciles with Hannah and "Joe" (sometimes referred to as "Joey"): "I forgive all and recalls what I called you to your face / cause in the long run you've shown Pity to my Race." In a ridiculous coda that follows, Debo-Leah agrees to marry her nemesis Nathan the schoolmaster—a man not "much bigger than an umbrella"—but only after addressing the audience directly: "If this wasn't a Burlesque, I couldn't think of doing it / but as it is, there's another way of doing it / and when it's known my affections you've managed to inveigle / won't it astonish [']em at the Adelphi and the Eagle."[164]

Certainly, one would be hard-pressed to find a serious performance of *Deborah* or *Leah* where the lead actress disrupted theatrical illusion so deliberately. As we shall see in the following chapter, nevertheless, we make a fateful error if we assume that nineteenth-century audiences seeing *Deborah* or *Leah* were somehow passive as they allowed performances of Mosenthal's play to bring them to tears. Indeed, contrary to modernist clichés about nineteenth-century spectators' penchant for losing themselves in dramatic illusion, we shall find that audiences attending performances of *Deborah* and *Leah* on both sides of the Atlantic were keenly self-conscious about theatrical spectacle. Turning our gaze from texts to performances, it is time to consider the role that actresses played in interacting with their audiences to bring Mosenthal's Jewess to life. Self-consciousness about the way *Deborah* and *Leah* used romantic idealizations of Jewish suffering to bring audiences to tears was not the exclusive property of burlesques, parodies, and cartoons engaging in good-hearted mockery of the play. It was, as we shall see, a constitutive element of performances of Mosenthal's *Deborah* from the very beginning, and on both sides of the Atlantic.

Chapter 3

Playing Jewish from Rachel to the Divine Sarah: Natural Acting and the Wonders of Impersonation

> Daughters I care little about especially if it means love for father; I have never felt it, and cannot act it.... As you have not seen me act, I must tell you that my style is passionate. When I love, it must be madly, not the tender, gentle love that shrinks from observation, but love that would sweep away, all before it, and if thwarted, would end in despair, madness, and death. In fact in acting I am more fond of being bad than good. Hate, revenge, despair, sarcasm, and resistless love I glory in; charity, gentleness, and the meeker virtues I do not care for. I should like to play "Leah," I think in Louisville, and if we see fit in Philadelphia.
> —Avonia Jones, January 11, 1863, letter to Augustin Daly

> In moving situations ... if real tears do not come to my eyes I do not truly feel what I am acting, nor can I impress my audience to the same extent when I feign emotion as when I really feel it. I have acted the part of Leah for twenty-four years, and the tears always come to my eyes when the little child says "My name is Leah."
> —Kate Bateman, from an 1887 interview

As a prelude to considering the theatrical pleasures that actresses afforded their audiences through their performances of Deborah and Leah, let us consider one of the most prominent models of modernist theater that sought to consign nineteenth-century tearjerkers to the past. In his vision of epic theater, Bertolt Brecht famously underscored the pitfalls of actors—like Bateman and Jones—who sought to move audiences through their thorough identification with their roles:

> [T]he actor has to discard whatever means he has learnt of getting the audience to identify with the characters which he plays. Aiming not to put his audience into a trance, he must not go into a trance himself. . . . At no moment must he go so far as to be wholly transformed into the character played. The verdict: "he didn't act Lear, he was Lear" would be an annihilating blow to him. He has just to show the character. . . . [H]is feelings must not at bottom be those of the character, so that the audience's may not at bottom be those of the character either. . . . This principle—that the actor appears on the stage in a double role, as [Charles] Laughton and as Galileo [in Brecht's *Life of Galileo*]; that the showman Laughton does not disappear in the Galileo whom he is showing; from which this way of acting gets its name of "epic"—comes to mean simply that the tangible, matter-of-fact process is no longer hidden behind a veil; that Laughton is actually there, standing on the stage and showing us what he imagines Galileo to have been.[1]

Epic theater continually disrupts theatrical illusion to foreground its own process of representation. Rather than appearing to become the characters they represent, actors render their acting transparent as they *show* audiences their characters, appearing on stage in double roles as both themselves and the figures they represent. For the spectator, the perception of the difference between actor and character creates a situation where identification becomes impossible. Spectators here are not moved to cry tears of compassion; instead, they are empowered with critical distance from the events depicted on stage.

Theater historians routinely note that the denigration of feeling and empathy was central to the radical break that Brecht sought to perform with the Aristotelian tradition, with its typical emphasis on theater's immediate appeal to the emotions. What requires our attention is the polemical language that Brecht uses as he calls on actors to lay bare processes of representation that their precursors were allegedly all too eager to endow with an aura of mystery. In prescribing detachment and distance, Brecht reduces both the identification of actors with roles and the empathy that spectators feel with characters on stage to aesthetic phenomena of a lower order than epic theater. Rather than stressing the complex physical and imaginative labor that actors require to identify with their roles or the cognitive work that spectators engage in as they watch a staged performance, Brecht insists that theater predicated on identification places both actors and spectators in a "trance," a mental state that represents the antithesis of the enlightened, rational stance that he wants audiences of epic theater to embrace. Epic theater thus does not merely promote the self-consciousness of spectators in the theater. It does so by putting forth a caricature of earlier modes of acting as fostering a mind-numbing escapism that renders spectators blind to both the workings of theatrical representation and the realities of the world outside the theater.

The immediate target of Brecht's polemics against theatrical illusion and the identification that it fosters were the naturalistic acting techniques promoted by the Russian theater director Constantin Stanislavski. But the method that Stanislavski began to develop in the early decades of the twentieth century grew out of the serious attention that an earlier generation of critics had given to the "emotionalist" school of acting that gained such a foothold on the nineteenth-century stage. In his influential 1888 book *Masks or Faces? A Study in the Psychology of Acting*, the British drama critic William Archer offered a spirited defense of actors' imitation of the emotions of the characters they play, stressing the importance of actors' thorough identification with their roles. Writing at a time when Denis Diderot's *Paradoxe sur le comédien*, posthumously published in 1830, had just appeared in English translation under the title *The Paradox of Acting*, Archer challenged Diderot's vision of actors being unmoved by the emotions they represent. Archer argued that the essence of acting lay instead in "mimetic emotion"; in this context, he stressed actors' ability to "play from the heart" rather than "from the head alone." Archer claimed that to be effective, actors must do exactly what Brecht forbids (and what Bateman and Jones revel in): actually feel the emotions that they bring to life on stage.[2] Archer based his challenge to Diderot on a series of extensive interviews with working actors, including Bateman; her comments about *Leah* above appeared in his chapter exploring the role that imagination and identification play in actors' abilities to produce credible tears on stage.

By characterizing actors who become one with their roles and the spectators who enjoy such performances as caught up in a mind-numbing trance, Brecht obscures both the novelty and the complexity of the emotional acting that proved crucial to the success of Mosenthal's *Deborah* and its various incarnations. Nineteenth-century audiences often found performances of emotional acting thrilling because they marked a dramatic departure from earlier, more rhetorical, acting styles with actors making well-defined "points" and then stopping to enjoy applause. Nineteenth-century audiences were riveted, indeed, by actors who seemed able to tap into spontaneous feeling while bringing roles to life on stage.[3] So much of the allure of international celebrities such as Edmund Kean, Fanny Janauschek, Henry Irving, Sarah Bernhardt, and others lay in these artists' ability to portray intense emotions and changing emotional states so powerfully. In the case of performances where leading actresses appeared to become Deborah or Leah on stage, spectators were hardly blind to the work of acting in the theater. Consider, for instance, how Grover's Theatre in Washington, DC, advertised an upcoming performance of *Leah, the Forsaken* in January 1865. An initial ad in the *Evening Star* noted that the "Renowned Tragedienne MISS AVONIA JONES" would be appearing in her "CELEBRATED TRAGIC IMPERSONATIONS," debuting on Monday, January 2, in "her magnificent impersonation of LEAH."[4] After puff pieces in the *Evening Star* hailed the "complete and genuine triumph" of this "high priestess of tragedy" in her "famous impersonation of Leah,"[5] Jones performed the play again on Tuesday. Tuesday's performance apparently generated enough interest to encourage Abraham Lincoln, his wife, Mary Todd, and their son Tad to come on Saturday evening to see Jones "repeat, by special request, her CELEBRATED IMPERSONATION OF LEAH, in the famous play of LEAH, THE FORSAKEN."[6]

The emphasis on the wonders of "impersonation" here would likely have been as much to Brecht's modernist taste as the inflated publicity that nineteenth-century theater managers used to market touring stars as great tragic actresses. For the Lincolns and the other spectators who came to witness Jones give her impersonation of Leah, however, it was the spectacle of a virtu-

Figure 30. Avonia Jones, carte-de-visite photograph. By permission of the Folger Shakespeare Library, Washington, DC.

oso performance that was at stake. Experiencing Jones become Leah on stage obviously depended on the theatergoers' willingness to suspend disbelief. Yet it also went hand in hand with their keen sense of Jones's artistry bringing this, her latest impersonation, to life—much as one might marvel at the wonders of a circus act or the special effects of a sensation drama.

The audience at Grover's Theatre in 1865 did not consist of quiet, seemingly passive, spectators sitting in the dark, their attention focused on a well-lit stage, with displays of emotion limited to rituals of clapping at a finite number of well-defined moments. Nineteenth-century spectators, indeed, had yet to embrace the norms of audience behavior that theatrical modernism sought to institute around 1900 and that Brecht takes for granted. The technology to darken the auditorium while lighting the stage did not even emerge until the late nineteenth century, and theatergoers during this period often bore a closer resemblance to spectators at sporting events today than to the restrained, well-disciplined audiences that emerge as an ideal in the early twentieth century.[7] To be sure, new expectations about spectator behavior in the theater developed gradually, and nineteenth-century audiences themselves were hardly uniform.[8] Yet even at upscale theaters that might be attended by presidents, audiences were far less outwardly passive than their twentieth-century counterparts whom Brecht wanted to rouse from their trance.

When Fanny Janauschek made her English-language debut performing *Deborah* at the New York Academy of Music in October 1870, for instance, audience applause forced Janauschek to make three or four curtain calls after each of the play's five acts, and every time she made an appearance on stage, she was greeted with boisterous cheers of "bravo" [sic].[9] When critics heralded Janauschek's "impersonation of the wild, passionate nature of the Jewess" as a "masterpiece of poetic conception and dramatic art," then, they were expressing an opinion that Janauschek's fans had made audible throughout the performance.[10] Reports of nineteenth-century performances of *Deborah* and *Leah* on both sides of the Atlantic are full of tales of seemingly endless curtain calls and demands for encores, particularly after the curse scene. When Kate Bateman returned to New York from England in January 1866 and revived the role of Leah at Niblo's Garden, her initial appearance in Act I provoked seemingly boundless applause. As Bateman rushed onto the stage chased by a mob of peasants seeking to stone her and drag her into the river, she was greeted by the waving of handkerchiefs and animated cheers from a New York theatergoing public giving the international star an enthusiastic homecoming.[11] Oakland, California, native Nance O'Neil played Leah in *The Jewess* in her hometown in the late 1890s to similar effect. When O'Neil hurried onto the stage, "wild and hunted, down through the forest to the feet of her savior, the priest, pursued by a maddened mob," it was as if "Oakland held breath for one long minute" before "burst[ing] into a perfect storm of applause" for an actress whom Oakland theatergoers hailed as the "Sarah Bernhardt of the West."[12]

As much as they may have relished experiencing quasi-magical impersonations where leading ladies became Deborah and Leah on stage, nineteenth-century audiences were hardly set into a trance or rendered passive by witnessing actors who fully identified with their roles. They were aware of and applauded the theatricality of these performances. Bernhardt was an obvious point of reference here not only because she herself played Leah in a new version of the drama on her 1892 American tour and was famously photographed in the role by Napoleon Sarony, the leading theatrical photographer of the day. (See Figures 44–49.) Bernhardt's unparalleled international celebrity hinged on nineteenth-century audiences' dual desire to experience the emotional roller-coasters of her various roles while also observing her as an artist. As Willmar Sauter has pointed out, spectators of Bernhardt were at times no longer "capable of—or interested in—distinguishing the artist from her role. Yet, paradoxically, spectators also remained entranced by her stage personality and always enjoyed watching her perform."[13]

The paradox that Sauter describes was not limited to Bernhardt; it proved central to the pleasures that theatergoers took in performances of *Deborah* and *Leah* throughout the nineteenth century. A London theatergoer in 1865, for instance, noted that the most "touching scene" of *Leah* was Bateman's death scene: "We can almost fancy that she is really dying, and we wonder how any acting can be so natural. As the curtain falls, we feel for a moment that we have been looking at a real tragedy—that the beautiful pale face we have just lost sight of is really the face of the dead Jewess *Leah*. But we are soon recalled to the actual: there is around us a sound of vociferous applause, and our last illusion respecting the reality of what we have seen vanishes, when *Leah* comes on, led by the smiling *Rudolf*." Realizing that Bateman is not dead but "*alive* and *well*"— and likely ready to "go back to her Hotel, and probably eat an excellent supper after the fatigues of the evening"—obviously destroys the illusion that she just died on stage.[14] It is precisely this realization, however, that enables spectators to appreciate and recognize the wonder they felt over Bateman's "natural" acting. To cast this in Brecht's terms, it is not the trance but the interruption of the trance that gives spectators pleasure. Through the ritual of "vociferous applause," theatergoers participate in the performance, disrupting the illusion as they acknowledge their enjoyment of it.

Of course, this sort of toggling back and forth between an absorption in a role and a sense of the theatricality of performance is arguably constitutive of all spectating in the theater. Theater scholars drawing on cognitive studies speak here of a constant "conceptual blending" that rips the rug out from under Brecht's assumption of a clear-cut opposition between passive identification with characters and the model of active, detached spectating that epic theater wishes to institute.[15] As Bruce McConachie notes, all spectating involves empathy, and indeed, in the theater and in everyday life, empathy is "natural, easy, ubiquitous and mostly unconscious" and always productive of emotion. Rather than following Samuel Taylor Coleridge's famous phrase and speaking of spectators "suspending disbelief," McConachie's insistence on conceptual blending underscores the active role that spectators take on combining actors and characters into an image that makes their own affective investment in the performance possible in the first place.[16]

Actresses performing *Deborah* and *Leah* were routinely praised by critics for the "natural acting" that made their emotional pyrotechnics on stage so appealing to their audiences. Never, though, was this celebration of the emotional impact of impersonation divorced from a keen sense of its theatricality. In this regard, performances of *Deborah* and *Leah* give us a window less into spectating in general than into the unique ways in which nineteenth-century audiences interacted with the new model of the star actress that dominated the theatrical culture of the era. Brecht's polemics against audience absorption in theatrical illusion and actors' identification with their roles undeniably had a transformative impact on both twentieth-century theater and thinking about theater more generally. But this model of theatrical modernism also hinges on and perpetuates a caricature of nineteenth-century theater, obscuring the ways in which impersonations of Deborah or Leah thrived at the crossroads of audiences' self-consciousness about theatricality and their absorption in theatrical illusion. For nineteenth-century theatergoers, enjoying the wonders of impersonation and the stage personality of the female artist simultaneously did not constitute a paradox. Rather, to return to the example of Jones playing Leah, this mode of enjoyment was presumably what brought theatergoers like Abraham Lincoln into the theater in the first place.

To some extent, *Deborah* does not differ from other plays that touring actresses used to make a splash, whether *Camille*, *East Lynne*, or *Oliver Twist* in the United States or *Maria Stuart*, *Macbeth*, or Grillparzer's *Medea* in the German-speaking world. All these plays provided female actors occasions for grandiose displays of emotion, encouraging spectators to lose themselves in performances while developing a special appreciation for the performers able to master such demanding roles. The unique niche that *Deborah* occupied in this market was its exotic Jewish content. Indeed, the Boston theater critic Charles Wingate noted in the 1890s that *Deborah* was "the only play with a Jewish woman as the heroine which has survived to the present day."[17] Whether playing Deborah in

Europe or the U.S., for instance, Janauschek was not just praised for the way her performance brought to life a spectacular vision of "womanhood," with its "unfathomable depth of feeling, the wonderful power of the soul, and the all-overcoming power of passion."[18] For many critics, the "irresistible force" of her performance lay in her ability to overcome an audience unable to defend itself against the onset of tears and sympathy for the "passionate, proud Jewess" whom she brought to life so effectively on the stage.[19]

Nineteenth-century spectators experienced the Jewishness performed on stage in this manner, accordingly, as both theatrical and authentic. In recent cultural theory, it has sometimes become fashionable to celebrate theatricality for its potential to disrupt claims to authenticity. Nineteenth-century culture, however, often regarded theatricality and authenticity less as fixed terms in a binary opposition than as concepts that complemented each other. For Lynn M. Voskuil, the idea of "natural acting" promulgated by Victorian critics such as William Hazlitt and George Henry Lewes foregrounds the dual insistence on "spectacle and genuineness, art and artlessness" that captures nineteenth-century culture's characteristic vision of theatricality.[20] The sensation dramas full of special effects that became the novelty of the British and American stage in the 1860s depended on precisely this sort of cooperation between the semblance of authenticity of the spectacles orchestrated on stage and the spectator's awe over their patent theatricality.[21] Performances of *Deborah* and *Leah* provided spectators a similar thrill, even if their plots did not hinge on the technological wonders that helped make Dion Boucicault's *The Colleen Bawn* (1860) or Augustin Daly's *Under the Gaslight* (1867) such commercial successes. Our understanding of the *Deborah* phenomenon will thus gain little by repeatedly calling attention to the ways in which performances of this role trafficked in exotic stereotypes or promoted a vision of Jewishness that lacked authenticity. To be sure, as we noted earlier, and as we shall see again in Chapter 4, Mosenthal's melodrama did perpetuate stereotypes, provoking occasional complaints among Jews about its "un-Jewish" portrayal of Jews. But audiences, for the most part, relished the heartfelt tears they wept over the Jewish suffering that star actresses impersonated for them so powerfully on stage, and this tended to be as true for Jewish audiences as it was for non-Jews.

"Natural acting" brought Jewishness to life on stage not despite but because of its theatricality. This chapter focuses on the interaction between theatricality and authenticity by studying some of the most prominent actresses who made the role of Deborah or Leah their own. In some cases, as we shall see in the next section, actresses performed this role so convincingly that audiences were determined to believe that the artists were themselves Jewish. Nineteenth-century accounts of performances of *Deborah*, nevertheless, routinely emphasized the wonders of impersonation, repeatedly expressing awe over the virtuoso actresses able to master this difficult role. In this sense, the sources we will examine all provide insight into the role that spectators played in helping to create a model of Jewishness on stage that could be perceived as both theatrical and authentic. Repeatedly, we shall see, the experience of Jewishness produced in this manner could be entrusted to elicit authentic tears at the same time as audiences admired the leading ladies whose spectacular performances of raw emotion in the theater could appear so natural—and so Jewish. In many cases, critics and audiences moved by these performances insisted that Mosenthal's drama was much more than a tearjerker or a melodrama. In the hands of the proper artist able to demonstrate her virtuosity in natural acting, indeed, *Deborah* could rise above its shortcomings and become a true work of art.

Rachel's Progeny

In the United States, where she eventually came to settle permanently, Fanny Janauschek continued to perform *Deborah* well into the 1880s, when she was in her mid-fifties. In her final years playing the role, she fueled the urban myth of a special connection with the part, alleging in promotional materials that Mosenthal had originally written *Deborah* for her.[22] Some fans also speculated that the Czech-Austrian actress was herself of Jewish descent. During Sarah Bernhardt's 1892 American tour, indeed, press coverage of Bernhardt's new version of *Leah* routinely mentioned that Janauschek's Deborah was so convincing that the German public "insisted" at the time of *Deborah*'s premiere that Janauschek "must be a Jewess, but the actress denied the statement."[23] These allegations about Janauschek's Jewish roots in the 1890s were unfounded; it is not clear that anyone in the 1850s maintained that the actress christened in Prague as Francesca Romana Magdalena Janauschek was of Jewish descent. Undoubtedly, these speculations about Janauschek's secret Jewish background reflect the way in which Bernhardt's own Jewish heritage was used to underscore her personal connection with the role of Leah during her 1892 American tour.[24] But they also play into much broader associations in the nineteenth-century cultural imagination between Jews and actors, and between Jewish women and actresses in particular.

As noted in the Introduction, some contemporaries regarded Jews' rapid assimilation of Western modes of speech and behavior in the nineteenth century as a theatrical phenomenon akin to acting (or aping), a form of pretense and dissimulation to be approached with the same level of suspicion traditionally reserved for the theater. The role that Jews themselves sometimes played in the nineteenth-century theater world only reinforced these associations. The most famous European actress before Bernhardt, the international celebrity Elisabeth-Rachel Félix (1821–1858), often known simply as "Rachel," was not just herself Jewish; her Jewishness was very much in the public eye for much of her illustrious career in France and on her many tours abroad.[25] When Janauschek first performed *Deborah*, in Frankfurt in October 1849, she was immediately hailed as the "German Rachel," and this epithet was frequently used in relation to her as she rose to fame in the 1850s performing *Deborah* and other plays throughout the German-speaking world.[26] The memory of Rachel's 1855 American tour was still strong when theater manager H. L. Bateman sought to convince the public in the early 1860s that his former child-prodigy daughter Kate should be taken seriously as an adult actress. Much of the early publicity for *Leah*, accordingly, introduced Bateman to the American and English public as a "distinguished young tragedienne" ready to be welcomed as the "Rachel of America." Indeed, Augustin Daly began the anonymously published "memoir" he wrote for Bateman in 1862 by comparing himself to Jules Janin, the author of an early memoir for Rachel. Throughout the 1860s, fans of Bateman on both sides of the Atlantic celebrated the star of *Leah* as the "American Rachel."[27]

Such references to Rachel may have been intended to evoke images of the great actress's international fame and her passionate acting rather than her Jewishness; publicity for up-and-coming actresses often drew comparisons to the Italian star Adelaide Ristori as well. But particularly in the case of the era's most

Figure 31. Elisabeth-Rachel Félix, carte-de-visite photograph. Hess private collection.

popular drama about a Jewish woman, invocations of Rachel inevitably also called attention to the elective affinity between the figure of the actress and the figure of the Jewess. As Kim Marra has noted, the Jewess as portrayed in *Leah* as a figure "living in the forest outside the pale of civilization became an allegory as well as vehicle for the thrilling actress who, regardless of her actual religious affiliation, was morally unchristian by dint of her profession and thus in need of conversion to respectability."[28] In this context, spectators often found it difficult to resist fantasizing about the Jewishness of the actresses offering up such riveting impersonations of the persecuted and wronged Jewess. While the Irish actress Augusta Dargon was playing *Deborah* in Galveston, Texas, in 1877, an enthusiastic fan wrote to the *Galveston Daily News* to share the knowledge that Mosenthal originally wrote the play for Antonie Wilhelmi, "a young, beautiful Jewish actress" from the Thalia Theater in Hamburg.[29] Wilhelmi did create the role in Hamburg at the play's first performance, as we shall see in the following section. Mosenthal, nevertheless, did not write *Deborah* expressly for her (or for anyone else, for that matter); the play was performed at the Stadttheater, not the Thalia Theater; and, most importantly, like Janauschek, Wilhelmi was not Jewish.

Facts rarely got in the way of an audience's fantasies about the Jewishness of actresses who brought Mosenthal's beautiful and exotic character to life on the stage. Lucille Western was the first American actress after Kate Bateman to adopt *Leah, the Forsaken* into her repertoire, and she played the role throughout the country, until her death in 1877. Like Bateman, Western was not Jewish. Several days before she performed the role in Washington, DC, in November 1863, however, a puff piece in the *Daily National Republican* noted that "Miss Lucille Western enjoys, in the character which she plays in this drama, a peculiar advantage, from the very decided Jewish cast of her features; in fact, we have heard it hinted that such was her origin; consequently we may expect the part of the Jewish maiden, Leah, to receive full justice at her hands."[30] The "Jewish" looks of this dark-haired actress often provoked comment. In 1872, a reviewer in the *Chicago Tribune* noted that Western's "features are those of a Jewess, and the Oriental modes and colors of the stage dress suit her complexion and figure admirably."[31] An article published on the occasion of her death similarly recollected that Western's "appearance as she stood in defiance of the peasantry" in Act I of *Leah* was "poetry itself. Her features were somewhat of a Jewish cast and the highly-colored stripes of her dress set off her hair and eyes to great advantage."[32]

For fans of Western, Janauschek, Bernhardt, and others, the fact that the form of Jewishness produced on stage was a theatrical spectacle did not mean that it lacked authenticity. Indeed, its authenticity was linked fundamentally to its theatricality, and Jewish audiences often responded just as enthusiastically

Figure 32. Lucille Western, carte-de-visite photograph. Hess private collection.

Figure 33. Lucille Western as Leah, carte-de-visite photograph. Harvard Theatre Collection, THE GEN TCS 19, theatrical cartes-de-visite photographs of women, ca. 1854–1879, Lucille Western folder, Houghton Library, Harvard University.

to performances of *Deborah* as did non-Jews. In 1892, after Bernhardt left the U.S. and performed her new version of *Leah* in London, the London correspondent of the *American Israelite* expressed tremendous pride that the "greatest actress in the world, Sarah Bernhardt, the Jewess, has been delighting London," performing the "beautiful Jewish tragedy" by the "Jewish dramatist" Mosenthal. "There is no one like Sarah Bernhardt, who could adequately mirror the sufferings, the anguish of the poets' [sic] heroine, with such truth and force."[33] Tellingly, the excitement that this American Jewish newspaper shared over the forceful performance of Mosenthal by "Sarah Bernhardt, the Jewess" in 1892 differs little from what we encounter three decades earlier in response to non-Jewish actresses who took on the role. Reviewing Bateman's *Leah* in January 1863, the New York *Jewish Record* praised Bateman for the "fire and spirit" of her "personation," which is "done in such a perfectly natural manner, that it stirs within her audience their most hidden feelings and forces them to rise to the surface." Not only was there apparently "scarcely a dry eye visible" in the "crowded houses" that gathered "at Niblo's nightly" to witness Bateman's "natural" "personation" of a Jewess. The *Jewish Record* made clear to its readers that "among the audiences the majority are of the Jewish persuasion."[34]

It is impossible, of course, to know the exact makeup of the audiences at early performances of *Leah*. From the early nineteenth century on, moreover, there was a long history of commenting on Jews' overrepresentation in theater audiences.[35] Both the Jewish and the general press make clear, however, that Jews were often both present and perceived to be present in audiences attending performances of *Deborah* and *Leah*. The *Philadelphia Inquirer*, for instance, noted in April 1863 that "numbers of the peculiar faith to which the heroine of the tragedy was attached" were a regular fixture in the audiences coming out to see Bateman's *Leah* at the Chestnut Street Theatre, with even the "most fastidious" Jews finding nothing offensive in the drama.[36] In 1868, when Janauschek performed *Deborah*, in German, in Cincinnati, the *Israelite* noted that Mozart Hall's "immense auditorium was fully occupied," with the "parquette [parquet] ... densely taken up with a crowd of ladies and gentlemen, nearly all Israelites, whose partiality toward Deborah is easily accounted for."[37] When Janauschek made her American debut performing German drama the year before, she began with Grillparzer's *Medea* on a Thursday evening before playing *Deborah* on Saturday night. The timing was wise, since, as a Viennese review journal pointed out, her performance of *Medea* fell on Yom Kippur; as a result, her audience was smaller than usual.[38] Two days later, she played *Deborah* to a packed house.[39]

Outside of major metropolitan centers, Jews took a similar interest in performances of the play. The first time the Austrian Jewish writer Karl Emil Franzos visited the theater in his native Czortków (Chortkiv, in western Ukraine today) at age nine, he saw a German-language production of *Deborah* by a traveling theater troupe that was heavily attended by both Jews and Polish-speaking Christians.[40] In 1870, a commentator at a series of performances of *Leah* in Shreveport, Louisiana, noted that the majority of those who sat "spell-bound" in the crowded theater were "composed of our Hebrew population."[41] Two years earlier, in 1868, a Memphis, Tennessee, newspaper anticipated that that evening's performance of *Leah, the Forsaken*, starring Charlotte Thompson, would yield a house "crammed with the *crème de la crème* of Hebrew society to witness her rendition."[42] In 1892, Margaret Mather performed *Leah, the Forsaken* in Nashville to an audience that the Nashville *Daily American* reported was largely Jewish.[43]

For Jews, impersonations of Deborah or Leah on stage could be every bit as appealing as for non-Jews. In 1864, a Hungarian Jewish newspaper expressed unbridled pride that a production of Mosenthal's *Deborah* had finally made it to the Burgtheater in Vienna, fifteen years after the play's premiere. "After years of begging," we are told, "a simple black-eyed Jewish girl with black locks and with a heart of inexhaustible love and almost unusual hatred has now finally been permitted to enter into the temple of the muses." The Burgtheater premiere of *Deborah* marks a great day for the Jews, only made better by the fact that Deborah's Christian love interest, Joseph, was portrayed magnificently by "our co-religionist, the artist [Adolf] Sonnenthal." Like most of the actresses who played Deborah over the years, the Burgtheater's star Charlotte Wolter was not Jewish. But Wolter earned tremendous praise for her portrayal of the "loyal and steadfast love" of which a Jewish woman is capable. She demonstrated to the Christian world, indeed, how "familial peace and familial bliss are more sacred to the Jewish woman than anything else."[44]

As the author and readers of this article were no doubt aware, the authentic Jewishness that Wolter and Sonnenthal helped bring to life in the Viennese "temple of the muses" differed from modes of Jewishness experienced in other realms. Indeed, the fact that this discussion of *Deborah* appeared in a journal for Jewish theology edited by Leopold Löw, chief rabbi of Szeged and a leading figure in Hungarian Jewish life, highlighted these differences even as it embraced the authenticity of Wolter's rendition of Deborah. In Chapter 4, we shall explore Jewish reactions to the play in detail, considering the criticism that Mosenthal's play sometimes provoked among the Jewish elite. For Jews and non-Jews alike, however, the Jewishness produced in the theater commanded authority; the theater became a place where Jews and non-Jews alike could experience authentic forms of Jewishness. Rarely do audiences attending performances of *Deborah* and *Leah* seem to have been caught up in a trance where they were unable to separate actors from their roles. Indeed, the frequent speculation over the Jewishness of women playing the part underscores a fascination with

Figure 34. Viennese Burgtheater actors Charlotte Wolter and Adolf Sonnenthal, nineteenth-century postcard. In the 1864 Burgtheater premiere of *Deborah*, Wolter played Deborah and Sonnenthal played Joseph. Hess private collection.

the connection between actress and role, one that speaks to an ongoing interest in the process of impersonation that made performances of the drama so powerful. As absorbing as performances of the play were, and as focused as spectators were on the lead actresses who played the part of Mosenthal's Jewess, *Deborah* and *Leah* were clearly enjoyed as spectacular performances where virtuoso actresses became Jewesses on the stage.

In Chapter 1, we explored the sophisticated poetics of compassion that Mosenthal wrote into the drama from the beginning, bringing to light a level of formal complexity lost on nineteenth-century critics who complained that Mosenthal lacked a sense for the grandeur of tragedy. Our task for the remainder of this chapter is to explore how the poetics of impersonation functioned at actual performances of *Deborah* in greater detail. We will begin by examining some of the German and Austrian actresses whose performances made the play such a success following its 1849 premiere. Particularly in the European context, praise for performances at times went hand in hand with criticism of Mosenthal's play. Rarely did nineteenth-century theatergoers reflect explicitly on the sophisticated way in which the script was set up to elicit their tears. But accounts of performances of *Deborah* often stressed the brilliant way in which the play functioned as a star vehicle. In the hands of the right actress, indeed, Mosenthal's Jewess could be brought to life in such a way as to eclipse the alleged aesthetic shortcomings of the script, making an authentic impersonation of Mosenthal's Jewess in the theater appear the epitome of great art.

The Birth of a Star Vehicle

The Hamburg production that premiered on January 15, 1849, called itself *Deborah, die Jüdin* (Deborah, the Jewess), a title that drew special attention to the play's Jewish content and cast *Deborah* in the shadow of Fromental Halévy's *La Juive* (The Jewess, 1835), the enormously popular grand opera that was performed in Mosenthal's Vienna and elsewhere in the German-speaking world under the title *Die Jüdin*.[45] In a roundabout way, then, Rachel herself co-officiated at the premiere. It was in part the popularity of Halévy's opera and its heroine Rachel that enabled Rachel Félix to brand herself Rachel when she began performing in 1836.[46] Whether or not Hamburg theatergoers made the connection to Rachel, the initial press coverage prominently placed the play's value as a star vehicle into the public eye. Critics at the premiere protested that Mosenthal's plot was dominated by intrigue, and they objected that the play's concern with the topical issue of Christian-Jewish relations constituted an affront to "true poetry." Indeed, a Hamburg correspondent for a Viennese paper noted that if Mosenthal would simply select less topical material for future plays, this "undoubtedly gifted poet" would gain "the complete freedom to allow the tragic element to take center stage."[47] The remarkable performance by leading lady Antonie Wilhelmi at the Hamburg premiere, however, ultimately rendered such quibbles over the shortcomings of Mosenthal's script beside the point.

For Wilhelmi, *Deborah, die Jüdin* was not just another incarnation of the literary type of the beautiful Jewess that Halévy's opera had helped make so popular. Nor was it merely a topical drama of the type common on the Hamburg stage in the 1840s.[48] As even the reviewer quoted above was forced to concede, *Deborah* played brilliantly with the public because it offered the perfect "master role" for Wilhelmi: "How beautifully she portrayed the [Jewish] nationality in her speech rushing with passion and in her quick and rich gestures. Truly, only indefatigable diligence, the most vital internal spark, true inspiration for art and poetry and—anxious and modest listening to experienced advice have brought her to this point. Must I add that a storm of applause, curtain calls, and wreaths crowned her achievement?"[49] Another reviewer noted that the play and Wilhelmi, in particular, earned an extraordinary show of appreciation on the part of the audience. Wilhelmi received frequent curtain calls at the end of acts and spontaneously throughout the play, and one of her monologues was apparently interrupted by "unremitting acclamations."[50] The evening concluded with an auditorium full of fans crying out, "*Hierbleiben!*" (Stay here!) to an actress rumored to be considering leaving the Hamburg Stadttheater.[51]

Anxieties over Wilhelmi's imminent departure may have been exacerbated by the sudden death of the theater's director, Maurice Baison, just two days before the premiere. The immediate occasion for these cries, however, was Wilhelmi's extraordinary impersonation of a Jewess overflowing with passionate speech and grand gestures. The reviewer above attributes her masterful performance as much to careful study and rehearsal as to the "vital, internal spark" that she brought to the role. Wilhelmi brought a Jewess to life on stage that transformed *Deborah* into something greater than itself, a vehicle for her own "true inspiration for art and poetry" that rendered objections to Mosenthal's topical play irrelevant. In the hands of an actress able to identify properly with this exotic role, *Deborah* was thus not an affront to "true poetry." It became an exemplary work of art.

At the Berlin premiere of *Deborah* several months later, Wilhelmi's erstwhile Hamburg rival Bertha Thomas surpassed Wilhelmi, giving a performance that generated even more enthusiasm for the aesthetic grandeur that an actress could achieve working with Mosenthal's material. In March, Karl Theodor von Küster, director of the Königliches Schauspielhaus in Berlin, invited Thomas to Berlin for a series of guest performances after a special trip to Hamburg to see her perform Schiller's *Maria Stuart* there. Experiencing the audience applause at her performance of *Maria Stuart* in Berlin, von Küster immediately offered Thomas a permanent job and persuaded her to break her contract in Hamburg.[52] By April, Thomas had settled into her new position in Berlin and was rapidly emerging as the darling of the theater world there. When she began performing *Deborah* in May, she played Mosenthal's Jewess with such fervor that she caused a twenty-nine-year-old apothecary-turned-journalist named Theodor Fontane to "weep streams of tears" over this "splendid play" and its "passionate main character."[53] For von Küster, the "passion and deep feeling" that Thomas produced in *Deborah* made this one of her best roles.[54] At the Berlin premiere, Thomas did not just receive an enthusiastic standing ovation at the end of the performance; at numerous times in the middle of the play, she was called back to the stage by thunderous applause.[55]

Like Wilhelmi in Hamburg, Thomas appeared to identify completely with the exotic role of the Jewess, and the result, here as well, was a performance that towered over Mosenthal's script. Years later, Mosenthal recalled sitting through the dress rehearsal and being shaken to the core by Thomas's passionate acting.[56] A report that was widely circulated in the press made clear that his reaction at the premiere was even more intense. Thomas apparently took the role to places that he himself could not have imagined:

Figure 35. Bertha Thomas, portrait. F. N. Manskopf Collection, Universitäts-Bibliothek Johann Christian Senckenberg, Frankfurt am Main.

The dramatist Mosenthal, who was at the premiere at the Royal Theatre, remarked that he himself was surprised by the heights of dramatic expression that Thomas brought to this role. The author of this article himself saw Thomas perform the role of Deborah out of the vital depths of her soul and mind. Thomas brought Deborah to life amid her banished, wandering religious comrades with a singular, national, Oriental hue. Upon learning of the infidelity of the simple Styrian countryman who was not her equal, she expressed southern passion and the deepest pain. Later, once she had regained her composure [in the final act], she displayed the noblest resignation, a heavenly forgiveness that burst forth in the blessings she pronounced on him and his family. Her departing words of mercy produced the deepest impression and the most heartfelt emotion in every feeling person present—incontrovertible proof that the truth and depth of her acting was the reason behind the manifold repeat performances of the play.[57]

Deborah owes its glory thus not to Mosenthal but to the actress for whom the play provides such a spectacular star vehicle. Thomas here does not merely play Deborah. In a performance that masterfully moves from pain and rage to reconciliation and forgiveness, she appears to bring forth the passions and sufferings of this southern, Oriental woman from the innermost depths of her soul, pronouncing farewell blessings on the Christian couple that trigger the most heartfelt emotions of all the members of the audience—including the playwright. Seemingly moved herself by the "singular, national, Oriental hue" that she brings to her complete identification with role of Deborah, Thomas moves everyone present, surprising Mosenthal with the possibilities of his play.

Through this grand emotional performance, the actress surpasses the playwright, establishing herself as the true artist to be revered. For fans in Berlin, Thomas's impersonation proved far more significant than the play that Mosenthal wrote; Mosenthal was properly recognized at the premiere, but for all intents and purposes, this was Thomas's evening, not his. The *Vossische Zeitung*, a leading daily newspaper in Berlin, published a poem soon after the premiere that idealized this explicit subordination of playwright to actress. It was clearly Thomas's Jewess and not Mosenthal the Jewish writer who was the star of the day:

> The rustling applause that you earned,
> It even flew past the poet's head.
> If we forget him experiencing his work,
> You have robbed him—involuntarily.
>
> You may quarrel with him over his laurel,
> But it was no acting that your genius offered us—
> It was a silver tone from David's harp,
> A beam of light from the dawning of Zion!
>
> And if this image dispelled, even just for a few minutes,
> The mists of the present day,
> It enabled to swell forth from its floods
> A redemptive image of a temple in a heathen age.[58]

Thomas thus rightfully robs Mosenthal of his laurels, stealing the fire of the Jewish writer to pronounce a new dawn for Zion and a vision of redemption for the present era. Through acting that seems not to be acting at all, this non-Jewish actress provides her audience with the ultimate theatrical spectacle, enabling theatergoers to experience the emotional highs and lows of Jewish suffering while transforming Mosenthal's *Deborah*—once again—into something much more than a topical drama.

The Jewishness that Thomas produced on stage commanded authority not despite but because of its theatricality. Between 1849, when she first created the role of Deborah in Berlin, and her untimely death three years later, Thomas increasingly came to define her professional persona in relation to Mosenthal's exotic Jewess. In early 1852, the distinguished actor Emil Devrient at the court theater in Dresden invited Thomas to join him in a mission that summer to London, where he and other leading German artists would demonstrate to Shakespeare's countrymen the grandeur of the contemporary German theater. Thomas made her participation in this effort contingent on her opening the tour by playing Deborah, a condition that Devrient had to refuse, given that he had committed to performing only classic German drama before introducing the public, on a subsequent tour, to more contemporary fare.[59] Instead of traveling to London, Thomas used her summer vacation for guest performances from Cologne to the Prussian city of Königsberg (modern-day Kaliningrad). After playing Lady Macbeth in Königsberg, she gave in to the request of the theater director in Thorn in Posen/Posznań (known today as the Polish city of Toruń) to stop and perform Deborah there on her way back to Berlin. Soon after playing Deborah in Thorn to great acclaim, however, Thomas came down with rheumatic fever. She not only continued to recite lines from *Deborah* in her delirium;[60] she also died in character, as a contemporary account makes clear: "Thus Deborah's final words, 'I bless you, all of you, all of you,' which Thomas had pronounced just days before, became the swan song with which this magnificent artist bade farewell to her theatrical and earthly career. She was buried in Thorn. The sympathy that the population of Thorn showed for the artist whom they had only known from this one role is almost without parallel. The secondary school was closed early on the day of her burial, as the teachers and, to some extent, the students as well were attending the funeral."[61] Thomas did not just die a tragic death at the age of thirty-three. As von Küster pointed out, she "died in the role of Deborah," bidding farewell to fans near and far with the same blessing she used to forgive and bless the Christian world that had wronged her on stage.[62] Local fans in Thorn, inspired by the performance of the actress whom they had known only as Deborah, demonstrated their sympathy in unprecedented ways, and this story continued to be cultivated for decades—at times, prominently by Mosenthal himself.[63]

The fact that Thomas's offstage persona drew so much of its energy from her impersonation of Deborah hardly indicates a trance-induced blurring of the distinction between actor and role. It underscores, rather, the keen sense of the theatricality of performance that was as inspiring to spectators at the Berlin premiere as it was to the small-town theatergoers who came out in droves for her funeral. Despite the extraordinary conditions of her death—a parallel might be drawn to the Viennese Burgtheater star Charlotte Wolter, who was famously buried in costume as Goethe's Iphigenie in 1897—the spectacular nature of Thomas's identification with the role of Deborah was typical for many actresses during the 1850s. For Thomas, Deborah defined the premature end to

Figure 36. Marie Straßmann-Damböck, portrait. F. N. Manskopf Collection, Universitäts-Bibliothek Johann Christian Senckenberg, Frankfurt am Main.

an illustrious career. For Marie Damböck, a struggling twenty-three-year-old Austrian actress at the court theater in Hannover, Mosenthal's play provided the breakthrough role that catapulted her to star status and caught the attention of critics and audiences alike. After playing Deborah in Hannover and on tour, Damböck received invitations to join prestigious theaters in Berlin, Stuttgart, Munich, and Vienna. By 1850, she had settled into what became an illustrious career at the Munich court theater.[64]

Deborah remained a fixture in Damböck's repertoire for much of her career. In 1857, long after she was established as the lead actress in Munich, Damböck opened a series of guest performances in the northern Bavarian town of Ansbach with *Deborah*, with unusually high ticket prices. In the eyes of the individuals who wrote to the local paper to report on the performance, Damböck's "genius" rendition of Deborah was well worth the inflated price for seats. Damböck did not just use Mosenthal's drama as a "showpiece." Skillfully avoiding melodramatic excess, she performed the role with tremendous moderation, giving even "the most passionate scenes the consecration of true art." Nowhere was this more apparent than in her performance of the curse scene: "There was no hollow pathos audible here; this was the outcry of a fatally wounded heart in its horrific truth. The actress was called back to the stage twice by enormous applause at the end of the third act [i.e., following the curse scene], which proves just how much the entire public recognized this genuine artistic achievement." Damböck earned seemingly constant applause, indeed, throughout the entire performance. The reason supplied for this was her "natural acting": "Fräulein Damböck's conception and performance of Deborah was so brilliant that it may perhaps never be surpassed. Indeed, it was not acting. It was pure nature, and that is why she exerted such captivating power over the audience that did not tire of expressing its appreciation with tempestuous applause."[65]

In captivating her audience with acting that appeared to be nature itself, Damböck hardly set spectators into a trance. Rather, her spectators' tempestuous applause spoke to their sense that she had transformed Mosenthal's melodramatic script into a great work of art, one that for this reviewer promised to be equaled—but not surpassed—by Damböck's forthcoming appearance in Schiller's *Maria Stuart*. As was the case with Wilhelmi and Thomas, *Deborah* became in Damböck's hands something greater than Mosenthal's drama. Indeed, an 1851 article in a Munich newspaper already commented on Damböck's unique ability to make Mosenthal's drama rise above its "exaggerated situations" to give a vivid portrait of "the noble Jewish soul" that ascended into the spheres of the spirit: "We are the declared enemies of the 'very popular' topical literature with its declaiming heroism. Fräulein Damböck, however, brought a vision to life that was full of ideal truth, spirit, and high, rich coloring. Indeed, this almost made us forgive the morbid nature of this type of literature."[66] As a Munich reviewer noted in 1850, Damböck's extraordinary Deborah gave contemporary German audiences the much needed opportunity to experience something approaching the grandeur of Greek tragedy.[67] As spectators inevitably realized, of course, Deborah was neither a Greek heroine nor the Scottish queen executed by Elizabeth I. She was a "dame full of spirit, mind, and universal, Oriental culture," an "Oriental woman struggling with prejudices against her tribe and her faith."[68] It was Damböck's brilliant combination of "the deep national conception of this role and the captivating fire of her performance" that enabled her to triumph as Deborah.[69] Her performance elevated the exotic otherness of the Jewess into the realm of high culture, healing Mosenthal's script from the sickness of topical literature to render his moving plea for acceptance of Jews the epitome of great contemporary drama.

Even in cases where the disparity between Mosenthal's script and the performances it occasioned was perceived to be acute, Damböck routinely earned praise for the artistry of her rendition. A Dresden critic in 1853, for instance, began his review of a performance of *Deborah* by protesting that Damböck had chosen to open her series of guest appearances with a "tasteless and unnatural" drama that

Figure 37. Fanny Janauschek as Deborah, in Germany, likely 1850s, photograph. F. N. Manskopf Collection, Universitäts-Bibliothek Johann Christian Senckenberg, Frankfurt am Main.

simply "does not resonate with our educated public." But even this reviewer eventually recognized the grandeur of Damböck's *Deborah*. He registered the "lively signs of acclamation" that Damböck received during the first act and increasingly throughout the play, complaining about the repeated curtain calls that constituted an "abuse of applause" and a breach of "good taste"; clearly, the "educated public" seems to have enjoyed itself watching this allegedly "tasteless and unnatural drama." On a more unequivocally positive note, the reviewer recognized and celebrated the aesthetic merits and the "great success" of Damböck's rendition of Deborah. He did so by comparing her to "Rachel," the "French Oriental woman."[70]

The German Rachel and the Queen of American Tragedy

The "natural acting" that enabled actresses to transform Mosenthal's drama into a great work of art was key to the success of the most famous of all German-speaking Deborahs, and an actress who performed this role longer than anyone else on either side of the Atlantic: the great "German Rachel" Fanny Janauschek. Janauschek created the role at its Frankfurt am Main premiere in

1849, at age nineteen, and she played Deborah across the German-speaking world in the 1850s and 1860s. By the mid-1860s, Janauschek had dissolved her affiliations with both the Frankfurter Stadttheater, where she was the lead actress from 1849 to 1861, and the Dresden Court Theatre, where she worked for a brief stint afterward, and she had established herself as one of the most prominent exemplars of a novel phenomenon in the German theater world: the star who made a career solely from touring.[71] *Deborah* was a fixture in Janauschek's standard European touring repertoire, along with *Macbeth*, *Maria Stuart*, and Grillparzer's *Medea*, and it was also among the small group of plays she performed (in German) on her initial American tours in the late 1860s.

Performing *Deborah* at the New York Academy of Music, Janauschek caught the attention of Augustin Daly, who, in the aftermath of his *Under the Gaslight*, was quickly emerging as a major force in American theatrical life. The adapter of *Leah, the Forsaken* took Janauschek under his wing, encouraging her to perform in English. Following her second American tour, in 1868–1869, Janauschek devoted a year to studying English; legend has it that she worked fifteen hours a day. In October 1870, Daly arranged for Janauschek to make her much awaited English-language debut, at the New York Academy of Music. She did so, performing her own version of Mosenthal's play, earning generally rave reviews, and critics praised her English as miraculous.[72] Much to the dismay of some of her German and German American fans, Janauschek eventually made America—and the English-language stage—her permanent home. She continued to perform *Deborah* on tours throughout the United States. When she finally abandoned the role, at age fifty-five, it was not simply because she was getting on in years. In 1884, she overhauled her entire repertoire, jettisoning not just *Deborah* but also *Maria Stuart*, *Medea*, *Macbeth*, and *Chesney Wold* (a dramatization of Charles Dickens's *Bleak House*) in an effort to try new plays that might ensure her ongoing popularity with the American public.[73]

One of Janauschek's final performances of *Deborah*, in 1883, encouraged a Salt Lake City critic to echo a familiar theme, noting with awe that Janauschek "transcends the character itself," making it "greater than the author does."[74] Indeed, throughout her career playing Deborah, critics in Europe and America heralded her performance as a work of genius superior to Mosenthal's script. An enthusiastic critic at the Frankfurt premiere in October 1849, for instance, was one of the most generous when it came to judging Mosenthal's play. Indeed, Gustav Heckenast, Mosenthal's publisher, quoted extensively from this review in marketing the print edition of *Deborah*.[75] The Frankfurt reviewer placed *Deborah* alongside *The Merchant of Venice*, Lessing's *Nathan der Weise*, and Richard Cumberland's *The Jew* as a grand exposition of the theme of Jewish suffering and celebrated the applause that Mosenthal's topical play was provoking

CHESTNUT ST. Theatre
PHILADELPHIA.
CONSTELLATION

Edw. L. Davenport,_____Lessee and Manager

P. E. Abel,_____Business Agen

No. 8.   PROGRAMME.   Vol. 2.

FANNY JANAUSCHEK,
For the Sixth and Sevent Time on any Stage in
ENGLISH TRAGEDY,
UNDER THE MANAGEMENT OF
AUGUSTIN DALY.

STAGE MANAGER _____ Mr. GEORGE DE VERE
TREASURER _____ A. APPLETON
BUSINESS MANAGER _____ W. H. BOWDITCH

For the First Time, will be produced a New and Original Adaption, in Five Acts, of MOSENTHAL'S Famous Play, entitled

DEBORA!

DEBORA, the Jewish Maiden.................................M'LLE JANAUSCHEK
JOSEPH, her Recreant Lover...........................Mr. FREDERIC ROBINSON
THE SHOOL MASTER......................................Mr. GEORGE DE VERE
Farmer Lorenz...Mr. A. Fisher
The Doctor..Mr. Rendle
Hanna, the Pastor's Niece....................................Mrs. Winter
The Pastor..Mr. T. Taylor
Old Abraham..Mr. J. Dunn
Reuben..Mr. Egbert
Jacob...Mr. Dovey
Rosel, a village girl..Miss Amy Ames
The Landlady..Miss Nellie Mortimer
Old Elsie...Mad. De Lesdernier

Villagers, Hebrews, &c.

Doors Open at 7.15 o'clock.   Commence at 8 o'clock.

Mrs. M. A. BINDER, N. W. cor. of 11th and Chestnut Sts. Dress and Cloak Making Fans, Gloves, Trimmings, Laces, Ribbons, Velvets, Bridal Veils, Flowers, Fine Jewelry and Trimmed Paper Patterns.

Figure 38. Program for Philadelphia performance of Janauschek's *Debora* in 1870. Hess private collection.

across the German-speaking world. But even this critic praised Janauschek's rendition of the "beautiful Oriental woman" in Frankfurt as something greater than Mosenthal's topical drama: "Fräulein Janauschek played the title role with all the fervor of southern passion and all the truth of human feeling. Her acting was reminiscent of Rachel, yet she was not a copy, she was burning with inspiration."[76] In her performance of Deborah, the German Rachel was not an imitation of the great French Jewish tragedienne. She was an original in her own right, Rachel's very able German successor. By the 1860s, German newspapers routinely noted that no other actress could equal the German Rachel in this role,[77] and it was Janauschek's Deborah that established her claim to Rachel's legacy. After a performance of *Deborah* in Bremen in 1861, several years after Rachel's death, one critic was inspired to proclaim: "Italy has its Ristori; France had its Rachel, and Germany can be proud to call a Janauschek its own."[78]

As a critic at a high-profile guest performance in Vienna in 1863 noted, in the hands of other artists, the "sensational" role of Deborah typically gave rise to "excesses of all type," particularly in the curse scene. But Janauschek, guided as she was by "the most proper principles of art," restored the role to its "true artistic measure," and it was the "true feeling" and "the psychologically proper recognition of emotion" that her measured, aesthetic performance brought to life that were responsible for the "great chorus of tears that took hold of man and woman alike."[79] The grandeur of Janauschek's art lay in the spectacular yet restrained manner in which she brought the emotional richness of Mosenthal's Jewess to life. During her first American tour, Max Maretzek, director of the New York Academy of Music, who served as her manager, promoted Janauschek in advertisements throughout the U.S. as the "Greatest Living Tragedienne."[80] For a critic in Chicago, it was precisely Janauschek's natural acting that made her Deborah "one of the most wonderful productions of dramatic art we have ever seen on the stage, the like[s] of which we may never see again": "We use the term 'artistic' [to describe Janauschek's Deborah,] and yet it is not applicable, for art was concealed. It was nature. There was no atmosphere of the stage, no declamation, no elocution. It was the veritableness of life, the sufferings and misery of nature, the language of nature."[81] As the *New York Times* noted on several occasions, the brilliant, natural acting of Janauschek's performance lent Mosenthal's play with its "superficial love story" and its "verbose conversations" nothing short of the "majesty of tragedy."[82]

By all accounts, spectators typically were riveted and brought to tears by Janauschek's Deborah at the same time as they recognized her majesty as an actor. A Bremen reviewer at an 1861 performance noted that Janauschek's Deborah made the audience "nearly forget everything and everyone else; we could turn neither our eyes nor our ears away from her. Normally we find the long

Figure 39. American publicity poster praising Janauschek as Rachel's successor. Hess private collection.

monologues [in this play] boring, but at her performance we would not have grumbled had the entire play consisted of a single long monologue. The sounds of her words awakened such wonderful feelings in us, and she enabled us to see such beautiful images as she, with a sacred hand, lifted the veil to reveal what the poet saw—and what he could only suspect."[83] As an actress, Janauschek did not just "completely sink her individuality and fascinate her audiences with the character" of Deborah, as the *New York Herald* noted in 1867.[84] A Louisville, Kentucky, critic observed several months later that her "identity is wholly lost" in the role.[85] As a Cleveland paper put it, "The great secret of the power of Janauschek . . . is the complete identification of self with character. . . . We do not see nor hear Janauschek, but 'Deborah,' the unhappy Jewess[,] is before us in all her love, her hate, and her final forgiveness."[86] After Janauschek's English-language debut in 1870, the drama critic of the *New York Herald* pronounced her triumph "complete and unquestionable." Her Deborah was "startling in its life-like photograph of a woman's heart," and what made her performance possible was "a spontaneity of feeling, a complete absorption in the *role*, [and] a grandeur of conception throughout."[87]

Despite the tears it provoked and the theatrical illusion it engendered, Janauschek's lifelike rendition of Deborah drew its power as much from its theatricality as from Janauschek's apparent absorption in the role. A German American newspaper, reviewing Janauschek's first performance of Mosenthal's drama in the U.S., noted that her "acting was in the main scenes of the play—the abandonment, the curse scene, the act of reconciliation—so full of overpowering beauty, so intimate, so captivating and yet so measured, so grandiose and shattering, so well-thought-out and electrifying that the audience's appreciation ascended into tempestuous enthusiasm with one curtain call after the next."[88] Indeed, an American journalist reporting on the same performance noted that Germans in the theater were "so carried away with their enthusiasm that they sometimes compelled her to stop in the middle of the most impassioned scenes, while they shouted and stamped and waved hats and handkerchiefs until want of breath brought them to a standstill."[89] Performing Deborah on her second American tour yielded similar results, with audiences constantly alternating between seeming "at times spellbound and then again burst[ing] out in enthusiastic plaudits."[90]

As was the case with other performances of the play, audiences took pleasure in toggling back and forth between their own absorption in Janauschek's complete identification with the role and their vocal expressions of admiration for the ways in which this theatrical illusion was being constructed for them on stage. Reviews of Janauschek are full of comments about "her gestures, her movements, the play of her features"; the way she used her mouth, eyes, and nostrils; and her "flashing eyes."[91] In Milwaukee, Janauschek's Deborah "electrified" her audiences "as if by magic," drawing "involuntary tears," as "cheer by cheer shook the house" and "greeted [Janauschek] with storms of applause."[92] In New York, her "impersonation of the wild, passionate nature of the Jewess" was "presented to the audience with thrilling truthfulness and grandeur" in such a way as "to touch any manly heart and soften it with pity."[93] In Cleveland, she "carrie[d] her audience with her," and "many of her audience shrank and trembled while they listened spell bound by her powers of fascination."[94] Playing Deborah in Chicago in the mid-1870s, Janauschek delivered her audience "a degree of tragic intensity such as one sees but once in a generation": "We hear of 'emotional' acting. If there was a dry eye in the house last night during that scene between Deborah and her child, it must have belonged to some being not connected with our common humanity."[95]

The rich paper trail that Janauschek's performances of *Deborah* left behind on both sides of the Atlantic provides a window on a theatrical culture where audiences shrank, trembled, and wept at the same time as they were keenly aware of Janauschek's stage personality. In this context, it makes little sense to set absorption in opposition to theatricality or to imagine a rational, detached, self-conscious spectator as the antithesis of an emotionally involved audience member riveted by an actress who appeared to identify completely with her role. For audiences attending Janauschek's performances of *Deborah* from 1849 to 1883, there was nothing paradoxical about a self-conscious enjoyment of Janauschek's "natural acting" going hand in hand with an intense identification with the suffering young Jewess whom she brought to life on the stage. Natural acting, indeed, hinged on this triangular relationship between actor, role, and spectators. If the result was a once-in-a-generation feeling of connection with "common humanity" cemented by tears shed by men and women alike, this was an experience of identification with Jewish suffering that was no less powerful for being produced in the theater. On the contrary, it was precisely the theatricality of the experience of Janauschek's Deborah that enabled her spectators to feel that they were in touch with their inmost sentiments in such a seemingly authentic manner—whether she played this part at age nineteen or age fifty-three.

Becoming the American Rachel

Of all the actresses who played Deborah or Leah, there was none whose career was more closely linked to the role than Baltimore native Kate Josephine Bateman. The daughter of Sidney Frances Bateman, an actress, and H. L. Bateman, an actor and theater manager, Kate grew up in the theater and enjoyed an illustrious career as a child actress. Indeed, by the time she "retired" from the stage several months before her fourteenth birthday, in 1856, she had already become

Figure 40. *The Bateman Children*, *Gleason's Pictorials*, October 15, 1853. Hess private collection.

an international celebrity with over a decade of experience under her belt. Along with her sister Ellen, Kate had toured England and appeared in theaters from New York to California, performing varied fare, including scenes from *Richard III*, *The Merchant of Venice*, and *Macbeth* and the Bateman sisters' standard piece, a one-act comedy called *The Young Couple*.[96] As touring child stars on display in adult roles, the Bateman sisters were not just the most successful example of what contemporaries termed the "infant phenomenon"; they were also the last. After the 1850s, children tended to appear on stage only in supporting roles, playing children. When Kate Bateman's daughter Sidney Crowe made her debut at age five in 1876, she did so playing young Leah, alongside her mother.[97]

It was the role of Leah that established Kate as an adult star, and this happened after almost four years of essaying a number of other parts. After her initial retirement, Kate spent several years in school, allegedly "bringing to her tasks the energy of the vigorous child artiste, and the aptitude acquired by the mental efforts on the stage."[98] Managed by her father, she then made her *rentrée* in March 1860. She appeared as Evangeline in her mother's dramatic adaptation of Henry Wadsworth Longfellow's poem; she played Julia in Sheridan

Knowles's *The Hunchback*; and she appeared as Juliet alongside future Lincoln assassin John Wilkes Booth as Romeo. When German American actress Marie Methua-Scheller suggested to H. L. Bateman that Mosenthal's *Deborah* might be the perfect star vehicle for his daughter, Kate's father pounced on the idea. He quickly arranged for the relatively unknown drama critic Augustin Daly, a friend of Methua-Scheller and her scene-painter husband J. Guido Methua, to produce a version of the play suited to enable his daughter to make a splash.[99] *Leah* turned out to be a brilliant choice. It remained Bateman's bread and butter for twenty-six years, until 1888, surviving numerous announcements that she would be retiring from the stage. Bateman repeatedly played Leah in New York and London, where she settled after marrying an Englishman in 1866, and she frequently took the play on tour throughout the eastern United States and the British Isles. At several points, it was even rumored that she would be traveling to Germany and Vienna to perform the play there.[100]

Occasionally, Bateman made efforts to add other plays to her repertoire. In 1868, for instance, John Oxenford, the drama critic of the London *Times* who reworked Daly's *Leah* prior to its London premiere, translated Mosenthal's *Pietra* especially for her. The following year, Tom Taylor worked off William Gilbert's novel *Margaret Meadows* to write *Mary Warner* for her. In 1872, W. G. Willis created a new version of *Medea* as a star vehicle for Bateman, and in 1875, she performed in a high-profile London production of *Macbeth* alongside Henry Irving at the Lyceum Theatre. Apart from *Mary Warner*, which Bateman performed along with *Leah* for several months on both sides of the Atlantic in 1869–1870 and intermittently thereafter, none of these efforts met with lasting popular success. In the eyes of both her fans and her detractors, Bateman the adult actress was a one-hit wonder.

Like other actresses playing Deborah and Leah, Bateman was often praised for perfecting the type of "natural acting" that elevated Mosenthal's drama to the heights of great tragedy. At a performance in Washington, DC, in January 1870 that was attended by President Ulysses Grant and his family, for instance, Bateman was commended for achieving "the matchless art which conceals all trace of artifice" as she delivered a rendition of Leah that was "most natural and unaffected, free from the stage rant that mars some of our best actresses, and yet was given with a power and effect that was truly grand."[101] Arguing along similar lines, a New Orleans paper claimed that, particularly in the final scene with the young Leah, Bateman's acting became "something more than mere acting. It is a touch of nature that surrounds the suffering of the elder *Leah* with the halo of womanly tears. And those tears find their counterpart in front of the footlights."[102] For many, the intense power of Bateman's rendition of Leah was clear evidence of her genius. As a New Orleans critic wrote in February 1870, "Miss Bateman's 'Leah' is perfect itself, as she conceals the art under the extraordinary naturalness of her representation. . . . A spell is cast around the audience, uncomfortable and unaccountable; and when she reaches the footlights, we tremblingly acknowledge ourselves in the presence of one whose genius, like a halo, sheds a light that awakens awe and reverence. She is the greatest of all American actresses; perhaps the greatest of all living artists. . . . She is the personification of living, moving, all-absorbing genius, and her merits can only be known by those who see her."[103]

Despite the favorable judgments she earned in the press at times, Bateman never inspired the level of critical regard as Janauschek and the European stars who took on the role of Deborah. Indeed, the "natural acting" celebrated by one critic was often rejected by another as the work of artifice, written off as a "clumsy parody on human feelings" or a mode of "forcible acting" that "degenerates too often into rant and vulgarity."[104] Reviewers on both sides of the Atlantic derided this former child prodigy as a product of the star system, characterizing the most distinctive aspects of her rendition of Leah as weaknesses rather than strengths. Some critics praised her "statuesque" poses, her "statuary" and "picturesque" form, and the pantomimic, nonverbal acting central to her creation of Leah as evidence of artistic genius. Others decried precisely these traits—typical for melodramatic acting—as unpardonable examples of star actresses playing for effects.[105] From the beginning, moreover, the enthusiasm that audiences and some critics expressed for the richness of Bateman's emotional acting was undercut by persistent complaints that she lacked tenderness in the play's romantic scenes with Rudolph.[106] The international fame that Bateman achieved as Leah was not without its downside. In England, reviewers complained about Bateman's "transatlantic accent";[107] after she returned from England, American critics grumbled about the affected speech patterns that she developed during her time abroad.[108]

Yet however they dissected her rendition of Leah, critics typically traced the power of Bateman's performance to her acting in the final moments of the play, particularly the tear-jerking encounter with Rudolph and Madalena's daughter Leah that follows the scene where Leah eavesdrops on the couple's reunion. When it came to making spectators weep, even Mosenthal recognized that Bateman's Leah had no equal. In 1865, Mosenthal accepted Bateman's invitation to travel to London to see *Leah*. Initially alienated by the sensationalism of British acting styles, the playwright was surprised by Bateman's costume and her "Oriental turban." Indeed, until the curse scene, he remained unimpressed. But once the play was over, he was able to marvel at the way the entire play started slowly and built up to culminate in the final scene, where Bateman truly demonstrated "her great artistry." For Mosenthal, Bateman in her encounter with young Leah produced "tones of the heart such as I had never before seen

Figure 41. James Edgell Collin's *Leah*, a portrait of Bateman as Leah, Harvard Theatre Collection, THE PF TCS 43, theatrical portrait prints, Kate Bateman Folder, Houghton Library, Harvard University.

in the theater" as "a stream of tears bathed her face and the handkerchiefs in all the boxes made the theater appear remarkably like a large bleachery."[109]

Even those who decried Bateman as a product of the star system tended to concede the power of Bateman's tears in the final scene. The same year as Mosenthal traveled to London to see *Leah*, a Viennese review journal offered its readers a detailed description and analysis of the wonders of Bateman's performance in the final scene:

> Bateman's pantomimic acting, the way she expresses her emotions while others speak, is one of her great assets. She accompanies the speeches of the other characters with accelerated breathing, the shivering and shuddering of limbs, interjections, and inarticulate sounds. All this makes the artist the central point of scenes in which she speaks no lines. We must call Deborah's scene with the child of her unfaithful lover virtually unsurpassable, and it is this scene that is behind the success of the play in England. Leah departs without hatred, without anger, resolved, apathetic. Only one last ephemeral wish seems fleetingly to touch the soul of this woman who is ready to renounce everything: she would like

to see his child. She turns, she sees the child, and a bright ray of light shines on her apathetic face. She approaches, creeping fearfully, and we believe to hear her heart throbbing. Conflicting feelings quiver through her pale face, as she grasps the child and examines her. She exclaims, "His image!" and the old love emerges again, with passion. She does not know whether to hug the child or to push her away. She breathes deeply and rapidly, as if burning with fever, and her arms quiver up and down the child's body. She asks for the child's name and hears her own. She believes she is dreaming, and then she learns that the child and her parents pray for her and remember her with love. Here her whole being collapses, as it were, into a stream of tears. This is no theatrical crying; it is a natural, almost elementary eruption of the deepest agony, the highest joy. The sobbing robs her of language, and her next words are inarticulate sounds that melt together with tears and kisses. The entire auditorium is magically forced to cry and sob along with her, and enjoys this emotion with truly thirsty zeal.

How can an artist produce this same shocking effect every evening for a year, making it seem that she herself is experiencing these feelings, and how does she manage to generate the spirit and the strength to do so without losing stamina? Someone else will have to explain this phenomenon. For us it is a physiological and a psychological rarity.[110]

Like much nineteenth-century theatrical journalism, this review does not merely report on a performance. It seeks to capture, for its German readers, the thrill of Bateman's spectacular acting and the primal power it holds over her London audience. The formidable, raw emotion that Bateman brings to her performance of Leah forces audience after audience to partake in her intense suffering and to enjoy the experience of doing so. In transforming the theater into a magical arena where night after night, she *becomes* Leah and overwhelms her audience in doing so, Bateman does not just play the Jewess. She forces her audiences to delight in their empathy with Jewish suffering, delivering a performance that has a parallel even as it defies the laws of physiology and psychology. Echoing advertisements used in New York in 1863, this article refers to Bateman explicitly as the "American Rachel."

Bateman's magical performance—"this is no theatrical crying"—brings Leah to life, appearing once again to elevate melodrama into the realm of great art. Bateman creates a theatrical experience in which the theater disappears at the same time as the audience becomes keenly aware of her skills in making this happen. In this way, she establishes herself not just as a great artist and perhaps "the most popular actress of our time"; the young Episcopalian from Baltimore becomes a great Jewish actress as well, establishing her credentials to the title of the American Rachel.[111] To be sure, not everyone responded so positively to this type of spectacle and the tears it produced. After seeing Bateman's *Leah* in February 1864, for instance, Victorian critic George Henry Lewes and his partner, novelist George Eliot, wondered at both the "badness of the piece and the success it has with the playgoing public." Yet even Lewes, the great theorist of natural acting, perceived the power of Bateman's performance. He and Eliot immediately started scheming how they might create a play like *Leah*, perhaps for the great British actress Helen Faucit.[112] These plans never came to fruition, but as Michael Ragussis has pointed out, the abandoned Jewish maiden that Lewes and Eliot experienced in Bateman's *Leah* left its mark on Eliot's oeuvre. The forsaken Leah became a central paradigm for Eliot's *Daniel Deronda* (1876), a novel that performs a powerful reversal of Mosenthal's material to grant its Jewish maiden Mira a husband while rendering Eliot's Christian heroine Gwendolen the forsaken one.[113]

Beyond Rachel: The Divine Sarah and the Legacy of Leah

Bateman's performance of Leah set the tone for an entire generation of actresses who took on the role, many of whom ended up being praised and condemned in the same terms that reviewers used for Bateman. Avonia Jones, for instance, was frequently celebrated for the depths, the good taste, and the "natural genius" of her emotional acting. Others, however, took Jones to task for overdoing her "statuesque poses," for showing "exaggerated energy" and for her "disposition of retaining a picturesque or appropriate attitude so long as to induce a suspicion that she is thinking more of the audience than of the character."[114] Lucille Western was also extolled for her natural acting, her rendition of high emotion, and the "absolutely Hebraic" way she played Leah; others complained of "boisterous declamation and excessive demonstration."[115] For many theatergoers, authenticity and theatricality clearly reinforced each other. Precisely this model of emotional acting, nevertheless, opened itself up to the charge of reveling in melodramatic excess; natural acting could easily appear overly theatrical.

The scores of American and British actresses who achieved popular success playing Deborah or Leah in the 1860s, 1870s, and 1880s—Elizabeth Crocker Bowers, Sara Conway, Augusta Dargon, Fanny Davenport, Susan Denin, Mary Gladstane, Julia Dean Hayne, Fanny Herring, Emily Jordan, Margaret Mather, Fanny B. Price, Cecile Rush, Charlotte Thompson, and Emma Waller, to name but the most prominent—typically provoked similar responses. Obviously, there were differences in the way these stars played Deborah or Leah (or Clysbia, Lysiah, Miriam, or Naomi) and the scripts they used. But these actresses all

Figure 42. Italian actress Adelaide Ristori, carte-de-visite photograph. Hess private collection.

met the same fate: they were all heralded for the authenticity of their emotional impersonations but vilified at times for overacting and playing for effects.

Tellingly, even the international celebrity Adelaide Ristori ran up against the same problem. In the 1850s and 1860s, Ristori performed *Deborah*, in Italian, from Moscow to Barcelona; in 1866, after having performed the play in London with Bateman in the audience three years earlier, she also included the play on her first American tour.[116] In 1858, the King of Prussia was so inspired by Ristori's performance of *Deborah* that he awarded her a special Order of Merit.[117] In Dresden that same year, however, a critic complained that Ristori's performance of *Deborah* was "more powerful than the subject allows," clear evidence that constant touring had ruined the Italian actress, encouraging her to develop "virtuoso" habits of overacting and seeking out grandiose stage effects.[118] When Ristori played Deborah on her first American tour, there were those who praised her for giving an "infinitely more natural portrait of the unfortunate Jewess" than any of her precursors, portraying a Deborah that was much "closer to real life" and "freer from the purely sensational" than what American actresses typically offered.[119] Others, though, complained about Ristori's well-orchestrated tour and the publicity machine behind it, ridiculing the pretentious American theatergoers who sat through an Italian-language *Deborah* looking "as if some dire calamity were impending over each one of them individually."[120]

Until Sarah Bernhardt performed her new version of *Leah* on her 1892 American tour, the frequent productions of *Deborah* and *Leah* that became a staple of American theatrical life did little to distinguish themselves and break free from these critical parameters. Actresses who included the role in their touring repertoires or played the part at home typically earned enthusiastic but generic praise, eliciting special interest often more because of their status as celebrities than because of artistic innovation. Jones, for instance, gained attention in the press after her dog Nero, a Newfoundlander, repeatedly interrupted dress rehearsals of *Leah*; when the mob pursued Leah in Act I, Nero developed the habit of abandoning his post near the prompter's table to come to his mistress's defense.[121] Like many others, the American actress Susan Denin was celebrated during her lifetime as the "best delineator of the character [of Leah] that has ever been introduced to the public."[122] Denin's real claim to fame in the role, however, came from the circumstances of her death. In 1875, Denin made national news when she died from injuries sustained when the bridge in an Indianapolis theater collapsed during her performance of *Leah*.[123]

In this context, Bernhardt's performance of *Leah* on her 1892 American tour commanded special attention. As the most famous international actress of her era, the divine Sarah embodied nineteenth-century star culture like no one else, and in her performance of *Leah*, her personality as a celebrity came together with the role of the persecuted Jewish maiden in unique and unprecedented ways.[124] *Leah* never occupied a permanent place in Bernhardt's repertoire. Indeed, most biographers of Bernhardt pay minimal attention to *Leah*, and for good reason. Bernhardt performed *Leah* only in the first half of 1892, in Boston, Chicago, New Orleans, New York, Philadelphia, and Washington, DC, and briefly in London as well. The fact that she even added this role to her repertoire at all at this point—when she was almost forty-eight, and already a grandmother—requires explanation.

Born to a Jewish mother but raised and baptized as Catholic, Bernhardt was frequently the subject of antisemitic typecasting in the press. In 1890, in fact, her much awaited performance in the title role of Jules Barbier's *Joan of Arc* outraged right-wing French newspapers, which were not shy in expressing their indignation that a "Jewish actress, whose scandalous adventures currently fill the gossip columns in the Boulevard press," was playing a "sublimely Christian figure on stage."[125] As Mary Louise Roberts has argued, Bernhardt proudly defended her right, as a French woman and one of the most prominent symbols of France at home and abroad, to play this French national heroine who eventually became a Catholic saint, and she did so in both Paris and London in 1890. Against this backdrop, Bernhardt's choice two years later to add the most popular nineteenth-century drama featuring a Jewish heroine to her touring repertoire appears stra-

Figure 43. *Sarah Bernhardt as Joan of Arc, at Her Majesty's Theatre*, Illustrated London News, June 28, 1890. Hess private collection.

tegic, an attempt to use the stage to play with the category of Jewishness in a manner that would prove similarly unsettling to her antisemitic opponents.

Whatever Bernhardt's exact intentions may have been, American critics were keyed into this dynamic as they claimed that Joan of Arc and Leah deserved to be celebrated together as Bernhardt's two most triumphant roles.[126] Aware that Bernhardt was reviving Mosenthal's *Deborah* in an era that witnessed unprecedented Jewish suffering in Eastern Europe, reviewers noted that Bernhardt was performing the play for political reasons related to its Jewish content. Discussions in the press routinely mentioned Bernhardt's own Jewish ancestry in this context.[127] Whether her Leah was celebrated as the "best pathetic bit of acting that I have ever known her to display" or written off by the occasional cynic as an "unworthy piece of sensationalism" by "a mistress of stage effects" and the "goddess of the trivial," the connection between Bernhardt's Jewishness and the Jewishness of the material was very much in the public eye.[128] Reviewing Bernhardt's *Leah* in April 1892, for instance, a Philadelphia critic cited Bernhardt's Jewish background as part of the reason that the play was so successful: "No artist of this day so completely envelops herself in her part and makes the scenic stage a real page from life." In the curse scene, in particular, Bernhardt "seemed to feel every word that she spoke, for she is herself of the race that is made the subject of many taunts and jibes in the play. The discarded Jewess arose to the heights of dramatic fervor and not only vindicated herself but her race."[129]

Audiences attending Bernhardt's *Leah*, then, had the pleasure of imagining that the great star was both playing Leah and somehow playing herself, that she was using the theater to create a more authentic and more spectacular mode of Jewishness than had ever been experienced before. The fact that the great Sarah Bernhardt was performing in her native French helped make *Leah* a theatrical event of an entirely different order from previous renditions of the role, particularly in an era where the curse scene had become a staple in acting schools and a typical "test for young lady amateurs" on both sides of the Atlantic.[130] Over and over again, Bernhardt's *Leah* was heralded, on the one hand, as being both natural and genuine—a Washington, DC, critic marveled at her "poses" and "pictures that seldom or never sin with the stiffness of tableaux"—and praised, on the other, for offering a riveting and masterful performance full of "tragic force" comparable only to the greatest accomplishments of Rachel or Edmund Kean.[131] It was hardly unique for Bernhardt fans to be in awe of her acting at the same time as they immersed themselves in the roles she brought to life on stage. The difference here was that, analogous to Rachel's celebrated performance of Racine's *Esther* back in 1839, Bernhardt was putting herself on display as a Jewess at the same time as she was playing Leah.[132]

The version of the play that Bernhardt commissioned Albert Darmont to create for her, accordingly, updated Mosenthal's material for an era that had witnessed new levels of anti-Jewish violence in Eastern Europe and the beginnings of mass Jewish immigration to the United States. Despite the claim that it was based largely on Mosenthal, Darmont's version of *Leah* borrowed roughly two-thirds of its material from Daly's adaptation, taking occasional elements from Charles Smith Cheltnam's *Deborah; or, the Jewish Maiden's Wrong!* as well.[133] Working off the two versions of the play that American audiences were most familiar with, Darmont nevertheless made numerous strategic changes. He resituated the action of the play almost 200 miles toward the east, moving it from Mosenthal's unnamed village near Graz, in the Austrian province of Styria, to the small city of Komárom, located today on the border between Hungary and Slovakia. Darmont may have been taking his lead here from other American versions of the play; several years earlier, Margaret Mather had sought to render *Leah* more up-to-date by moving the action to Galicia, in Austrian Poland.[134] For Darmont and Bernhardt, however, setting the drama in an Eastern European milieu was part of a larger, systematic plan. Darmont introduced several new scenes to focus the action less on the love story between Leah and

Rudolph and more on the struggle between Leah and the melodramatic villain Nathan the schoolmaster, who, in this version, becomes Leah's cousin, the nephew of her father, Abraham, whom Nathan murders. Rudolph does not even appear in the play's final scene of reconciliation. In Bernhardt's version, when Leah returns in Act V, she is no longer hardened by hatred and in need of the conversion experience that she gains from witnessing Rudolph and his wife's reunion and the tearful scene with their child. Bernhardt's Leah returns to the village already with the intent of forgiveness, motivated by her desire to seek justice for Nathan, whom she calls "the author of my grief and my tears."[135] Most importantly, in a scene that gives a nod to Mosenthal's original, in Bernhardt's version Leah does not die on stage or go off feebly. Instead, she heads off proudly with her people, with a large group of Jewish emigrants visible on stage through a window in the play's final scene.

Bateman's *Leah* concluded with the emotional embrace between a feeble Leah and her namesake before Leah unmasks the schoolmaster and then dies on stage in Rudolph's arms. As Bernhardt's play comes to a close, Nathan confesses and stabs himself with Leah's knife, and Leah then takes leave of Rudolph's wife, Madeleine, and young Leah, disappearing "*in the midst of the emigrants, who pass at the back.*"[136] Bernhardt's Leah thus does what even Mosenthal's Deborah does not: she joins a Jewish collective visible on stage, one headed off for America, which Leah herself celebrated earlier in the play as "that great land of Liberty."[137] Bernhardt challenged her antisemitic critics, then, not just by insisting on her right to play a Roman Catholic and French national heroine. Her adaptation of Mosenthal staged her own Jewishness in a French drama that celebrated Jewish solidarity and hailed America as the Promised Land for victims of anti-Jewish persecution.

As Janis Bergman-Carton has pointed out, despite the relatively short time Bernhardt spent playing Leah, the photographs that Napoleon Sarony produced of her in the role took on a life of their own in subsequent decades, shaping Bernhardt's legacy as an international celebrity long after she abandoned the drama.[138] Bernhardt may have performed Leah for only six months, but the images of her as Leah circulated for decades, as postcards, on magazines, and in other publicity material. Of the more than ten images that Sarony created in his New York atelier, four came to be particularly widely disseminated: a shot of Bernhardt as Leah barefoot that was widely discussed in the press (Figure 44); a sexualized image of Bernhardt's upper body (Figure 45) that was republished on the June 1906 covers of *Theatre Magazine*, the *Burr McIntosh-Monthly*, and elsewhere (Figure 46); and, most iconically, the images of Bernhardt as Leah standing before a cross (Figure 47) and an image of her on the ground in a pose forming a cross with her own body (Figure 48).

Figure 44. Sarah Bernhardt as Leah, postcard. Hess private collection.

Figure 45. Publicity photograph of Sarah Bernhardt in the role of Leah. Billy Rose Theatre Division, New York Public Library for the Performing Arts, Astor, Lenox and Tilden Foundations.

Figure 46. Sarah Bernhardt as Leah on the cover of the June 1906 issue of the *Burr McIntosh-Monthly*, fourteen years after she featured the role on her 1892 North American tour. Hess private collection.

In both Mosenthal and Daly, the cross figured importantly in the scene where the heroine and her Christian lover met in the woods outside of town, where it was explicitly invoked as a symbol of Christianity that gave Jews a painful reminder of Christian persecution. Indeed, Charlotte Wolter in Vienna and Margaret Mather in the U.S. had also posed for photographs as Deborah along with the cross, occasionally in highly dramatic ways (Figures 49 and 50). As she moved from playing a Catholic saint to a persecuted Jewish maiden, Bernhardt made the cross the central prop in her play, cleverly foregrounding what one

Figure 47. Sarah Bernhardt as Leah, postcard. Hess private collection.

Figure 48. Sarah Bernhardt as Leah, cabinet photograph. Billy Rose Theatre Division, New York Public Library for the Performing Arts, Astor, Lenox and Tilden Foundations.

Figure 49. Charlotte Wolter as Leah, cabinet photograph. Hess private collection.

Boston critic noted was a deeply ambivalent symbol representing "the emancipation of one race and the enslavement of another."[139] Not only did Bernhardt use a large stone cross on stage—the simpler, wooden cross in the Sarony photograph was a studio prop—and give the cross much more stage time than in previous versions of the play. Her Leah featured three different moments where she stood in front of the cross, using her arms to perform a second cross on stage just as she did in the widely circulated images.[140] Critics, indeed, often hailed the "magnificent" way in which Bernhardt stood "on the stone pedestal of the cross, reached her arms up toward heaven, and formed, as it were, a second cross under the larger one of stone."[141] The fact that her production of *Leah* apparently made liberal use of a dark and gloomy stage set these scenes of Bernhardt-qua-cross in even starker relief.[142] To be sure, there were some who complained about this iconic attitude and the way Bernhardt used her body to "extend her arms and throw her head back and stand in an agonized pose" to suggest the way the cross symbolized the "persecution of cruelty to the Jews."[143] But for theater audiences in 1892 and Bernhardt fans in years to come, it was

Figure 50. Margaret Mather as Leah, cabinet photograph. Harvard Theatre Collection, theatrical cabinet photographs of women, ca. 1866–1929, TCS 2, Box 348, Houghton Library, Harvard University.

this image that often defined both *Leah* and the disruptive Jewishness of Bernhardt herself. Fourteen years later, long after she had ceased performing *Leah*, Bernhardt used publicity materials that ostentatiously made her Leah pose the centerpiece of a crucifixion triptych (Figure 51).

Taken to task for daring to play a French Catholic heroine, Bernhardt staged *Leah* in such a way as to render her own body a symbol of Jewish persecution, a supplement to and replacement for the crucifix. Later that year, in a much more whimsical shot produced in England that has little to do with the play, Bernhardt posed in her Leah costume lying down with her dog in front of a cross (Figure 52). In its playfulness, this image underscores the subversive manner in which Bernhardt staged her own Jewishness and the figure of Leah, flaunting both the role of the *belle juive* and her own play with Jewishness as a serious challenge to her antisemitic opponents. By all accounts, Bernhardt's *Leah* seems to have often provoked the same sort of intermingling of heartfelt tears with thun-

Figure 51. Resembling a crucifixion triptych, this 1906 postcard featured Bernhardt in her Leah pose in front of the cross alongside Bernhardt in two of her other roles. Hess private collection.

derous applause that had been the hallmark of performances of *Deborah* from mid-century on.[144] But as her use of the cross indicates, Bernhardt's *Leah* also provided audiences a different sort of spectacle, one that forced at least some spectators to move beyond the comforts of identification. As a New York critic noted, Bateman, like Margaret Mather, "moved us to sympathy for the outcast." Bernhardt's *Leah*, however, is "tragic rather than pathetic and inclines us to awe instead of tears.... Miss Bateman and Miss Mather made the Jewess conscious of the spectators, artfully arranged to catch their visual approval and solicitous for their sympathy. Sarah Bernhardt comes before us in repellant guise, remains wholly oblivious of the audience, and is from first to finale an outcast, her hand against every one and every one's hand against her." After the curse scene, for instance, there was "trembling silence" and "no sound in front of the house. Then such a thunderburst of cheers and hand clapping broke forth that the big house appeared a second Bedlam and Mme. Sarah was called out eight times to receive the applause of the spectators of one of the most impressive bits of tragedy that has even been witnessed in this country."[145]

Figure 52. Sarah Bernhardt as Leah, in front of a cross, with dog, cabinet photograph. Bibliothèque nationale de France.

For at least this reviewer, the spectacle of Bernhardt's performance of Leah fundamentally altered the model of tearful sympathy that had been the motor behind Mosenthal's *Deborah* since 1849. Spectators here were not invited in to feel Bernhardt's pain as Leah, to identify with Leah while admiring Bernhardt as the actress whose magic brought Mosenthal's heroine to life. Bernhardt's *Leah* made for a much more uncomfortable evening at the theater, one that both repelled and attracted its audience. The double spectacle of Bernhardt's and Leah's Jewishness was experienced not as a reassuring reminder of a common humanity but as a source of terror. Despite the play's hopeful ending and its invocation of emigration to America as the solution to Jewish persecution in Eastern Europe, Bernhardt's *Leah* ultimately created an unsettling image of the persecuted Jewish maiden, one whose reenactment and subversion of the cross left no room for easy tears of compassion.

Whether the sublime experience of witnessing Bernhardt as Leah helped reform any antisemites is difficult to know. The New York *Jewish Messenger*, for instance, welcomed the way Bernhardt used *Leah* to express "her sympathy for her unfortunate sisters still under the ban in Eastern Europe." Extolling Bernhardt's performance in *Leah* as "thrilling," "tremendous," and "intensely natural," the paper nevertheless also expressed skepticism about the impact of "the great success that she has made as the loving Jewess"; after all, this is a character whose "woes have made a million weep without effecting any special reduction in the amount of prejudice that has been vented against the race in actuality."[146] We should be careful not to attribute too much direct agency to the transgressive way in which Bernhardt performed the role of Leah. Within the history of performances of Mosenthal's *Deborah*, nevertheless, Bernhardt's *Leah* does mark a milestone. Foregrounding her own Jewishness and her stature as an international celebrity playing the role, Bernhardt as Leah was not merely a second Rachel—and not simply because her star image, fame, and international celebrity surpassed anything anyone could have imagined when Rachel Félix came onto the boards in the aftermath of Halévy's *La Juive* in the 1830s. In performing *Leah*, Bernhardt gave an extravagant dramatization of her own exotic status as a Jewess. Linking the mob pursuing Leah to anti-Jewish violence in Eastern Europe, she used the stage to present her own Jewishness as a provocation to both contemporary antisemites and the long tradition of finding comfort in Leah's woes.

After the Divine Sarah: *Deborah*, *Leah*, and the Fate of Natural Acting

Bernhardt ended up being the last actress to be recognized for any significant artistic innovation in the role of Deborah or Leah. The American stage and silent film star Nance O'Neil performed *The Jewess*, her version of the Mosenthal material, from 1897 well into the second decade of the twentieth century. O'Neil often earned enthusiastic reviews for her extravagant emotional acting. Critics also took note of the renewed relevance of the play in the wake of pogroms in Russia and the Dreyfus affair in France and occasionally compared her to Bernhardt, as we mentioned earlier.[147] Yet even during this period, O'Neil often appeared as an anachronism, touring with a repertoire reminiscent of the fare offered by actresses such as Lucille Western in the 1860s and 1870s. O'Neil's old-fashioned repertoire—she performed *The Jewess* alongside other nineteenth-century warhorses such as *East Lynne*, *Camille*, and *Oliver Twist*—was often perceived as the niche that helped her become a "popular idol."[148] Like some of her nineteenth-century forebears, not surprisingly, O'Neil was often taken to task for "overacting and melodramatic effects"; the fact that she performed a shorter, vaudeville version of *The Jewess* on several occasions in 1907 indicates a level of self-consciousness about the dated nature of both the play and her acting style that one would have been hard-pressed to find among the stars who created the role fifty years earlier.[149] Bateman's *Leah*, to be sure, yielded burlesques and even a famous caricature in the 1860s. Bateman herself, however,

Figure 53. Nance O'Neil as Leah, cabinet photograph. Harvard Theatre Collection, theatrical cabinet photographs of women, ca. 1866–1929, TCS 2, Box 370, Houghton Library, Harvard University.

Figure 54. Nance O'Neil as Leah, cabinet photograph. Harvard Theatre Collection, theatrical cabinet photographs of women, ca. 1866–1929, TCS 2, Box 370, Houghton Library, Harvard University.

never subjected her performance in *Leah* to parody or created a short skit of it for a variety show.

With the emergence and entrenchment of new models of theater that stressed ensemble acting and the artistic vision of the director rather than the spectacle of the virtuoso actor, the great emotional plays of the nineteenth century lost much of the cultural cachet that they held during their heyday.[150] When O'Neil first took on the role of Leah in 1897, the rise of naturalist theater and the advent of modernism had already begun to drive out the types of star vehicles that O'Neil favored from the prestigious theaters where they had often been performed in the mid- to late nineteenth century. In Vienna, the last performance of *Deborah* at the Burgtheater took place in 1893, and by the 1890s, most Austrian and German court theaters had dropped *Deborah* from their standing repertoires. In the late 1880s, a Berlin newspaper noted that despite the scorn of critics, the "wandering Jewess *Deborah*" was unrelenting in its ability to return from the past like a "pale ghost," "sitting at the waters of Babylon, crying, cursing, and praying."[151] A decade or so later, though, *Deborah* began to lose some of its appeal. When the play was revived in Vienna in the second decade of the twentieth century, in the wake of a wave of refugees flooding in from Poland, many of whom were Jewish, it was performed at the Lustspieltheater, a venue for lighter fare.[152] In both Europe and North America, performances of *Deborah* and *Leah* in the early twentieth century generally tended to take place either in urban theaters that lacked the prestige of many of the places where Mosenthal's drama had been performed during its first half-century on the boards, in smaller venues outside the cultural center, or in amateur playhouses. O'Neil, to be sure, continued to star in *The Jewess* at the Freemont Theatre and the Majestic Theatre in Boston, the Grand Opera House in San Francisco, the Mason Opera House in Los Angeles, the Shaftesbury Theatre in London, and similar venues. And Adele Sandröck, in the German-speaking world, continued to include *Deborah* on her high-profile tours at the same time, much to the dismay of her critics.[153] Yet these performances of Mosenthal's material were an exception, the last gasp of a sixty-five-year-old tradition.

An anecdote about a touring European star in the early twentieth century proves instructive here. When Agathe Bârsescu set off for an American tour in 1905, this former Burgtheater actress from Bucharest harbored aspirations to perform in the prestigious German-language Irving Place Theatre in New York. Bârsescu's engagements were apparently so poorly managed, however, that she ended up performing in a more downtown venue instead, starring in productions of *Deborah* and *Camille* at the Yiddish Theater on the Bowery. *Deborah* had been popular among Yiddish-speaking theatergoers in the United States since Keni Liptsin created the role at the Roumania Opera House in New York in

1884. For decades, *Deborah* could be counted on to generate enthusiasm among Yiddish-speaking theatergoers.[154] For Bârsescu, however, the great acclaim that she received performing *Deborah* on the Bowery hardly met her expectations. Indeed, a decade earlier in Berlin, Bârsescu refused to open her series of guest performances at the Königliches Schauspielhaus with *Deborah*, claiming that this role was not "literary enough" for her.[155] In the German press, her story became a cautionary tale about the way American impresarios were ready to exploit the European artists they claimed to be representing.[156]

Despite the enthusiasm that audiences continued to experience, performances of *Deborah* and *Leah* in the early twentieth century lacked both the prestige and the cultural authority that they had commanded decades earlier. During the era when *Leah* was performed at Niblo's Garden and *Deborah* was on the boards at the Königliches Schauspielhaus in Berlin, the play was performed in a wide range of venues, including small municipal theaters in Europe, makeshift stages in mining communities in Australia and the American West, and scaffolds used by wandering troupes on several continents. But by the early twentieth century, Mosenthal's play had become almost exclusively the property of theaters that mounted no claims to be watering holes for the cultural elite. For the most part, the unique coordination of theatricality with authenticity constitutive of nineteenth-century modes of natural acting and central to the appeal of *Deborah* and *Leah* from the beginning did not survive the 1890s. The play continued to be performed well into the 1920s, and the curse scene lived on in the curricula of German and American acting schools. But the dynamic interaction between actress, role, and spectator so central to the celebration of "natural acting" that enabled nineteenth-century audiences to celebrate performances of *Deborah* and *Leah* as the epitome of great art had long since been consigned to the past by this point. *Deborah* no longer functioned as a brilliant star vehicle. It became, instead, a simple melodrama.

During O'Neil's final years of performing *The Jewess*, Mosenthal's material did not just move downtown; it also made an easy transition from the stage to a more dubious aesthetic medium: the screen. Indeed, three separate filmic treatments of the material were released between 1908 and 1914: *Leah, the Forsaken* (1908), starring Mary Fuller; a second *Leah* (1912), featuring Vivian Prescott; and a third film, *Deborah, the Jewish Maiden* (1914), based on the Cheltnam version and starring Maud Fealy. Like many early silent pictures, these filmic treatments of the Mosenthal material have, for the most part, not survived. All that is available for viewing today, indeed, is a sequence of eleven short clips of Mary Fuller playing Leah in the 1908 film, a little over a minute from a feature film that was likely ten to twelve minutes long.[157] Silent film was famous for making liberal use of the pantomimic, nonverbal acting styles in which nineteenth-century stars like Bateman distinguished themselves. Not surprisingly, the fragments that have been preserved of the 1908 film feature precisely the grand melodramatic poses and gestures for which stage actresses playing the role were sometimes taken to task. Even a positive review of the 1914 film in *Moving Picture World* chastised *Deborah* for its "mawkish sentimentality," which "carries the clear earmarks of the stage melodramas of the last period."[158]

The fact that *Deborah* inspired three different film adaptations that were shown widely in North America, Europe, and elsewhere underscores not merely the popularity of the material but the particular ways it lent itself to the performance of melodramatic excess.[159] In this sense, twentieth-century adaptations and performances of *Deborah* bring to light less the ongoing relevance of Mosenthal's tale of the forsaken Jewess than the way changing aesthetic norms in the theater had rendered its mode of performance a caricature of itself. With the exception of positive reviews of O'Neil's *The Jewess*, few fans in the twentieth century celebrated the aesthetic grandeur of performances of *Deborah* or *Leah*. Rarely did twentieth-century spectators feel that they were in the presence of an artistic genius able to move her audiences to tears while impressing them with her skills in the realm of natural acting. In the nineteenth century, the spectacle of impersonating a Jewess on stage was often celebrated as the epitome of great art, as a cultural phenomenon where theatricality and authenticity worked in tandem to produce heightened levels of aesthetic feeling that enabled spectators to experience their common humanity. By the second decade of the twentieth century, few spectators seem to have reveled in the "authenticity" of portrayals of Deborah's or Leah's sufferings. With the advent of the silent film versions of the material, indeed, Deborah's woes became a mass-produced affect as never before.

The three known productions of the play in its entirety in the postwar period offer an illuminating commentary on this process. In 1966, a production of *Leah, the Forsaken* at a summer theater in Park City, Utah, advertised itself not as a masterpiece or a vehicle for a great tragic actress but simply as an appealing melodrama—one given the additional subtitle "Alone in the World," lest potential ticket-buyers not pick up on the meaning of the term "forsaken."[160] In 2004, a student and community theater company connected with the University of Göttingen in Germany gave its production of *Deborah* a more serious inflection, emphasizing the largely historical reasons for putting on the play. Publicity material for the play introduced *Deborah* as "one of the most hybrid and most confusing stage plays of its era," noting that it took all of Europe by storm, ceding its enormous popularity only with the rise of antisemitism in the late nineteenth century. While acknowledging the play's alienating mix of generic features—"romantic-mythological" exaggeration of character, "sensational melodrama," elements of both comedy and domestic tragedy—this statement ultimately attributed *Deborah*'s fall from critical grace to political factors. In a post-Holocaust world, this play set "in Styria, in 1780" was expected to help its spectators enter a world destroyed by the antisemitism that culminated in the Nazi genocide and that was apparently the reason for the play's disappearance in the late nineteenth century.[161]

For all their differences, these two productions of the play are striking for their blindness to the unique nineteenth-century features that rendered *Deborah* and *Leah* so popular. In this respect, they differ considerably from the well-received 2017 production of *Leah, the Forsaken* directed by Francis X. Kuhn at the Metropolitan Playhouse in New York City, a theater dedicated to excavating seldom-performed American plays from the past.[162] The rise of antisemitism, as we have seen, hardly rendered the play marginal; if anything, antisemitic incidents were often cited as reasons for the continued relevance of Mosenthal's material. From the very beginning, the play was seen as a powerful argument for tolerance and against anti-Jewish prejudice. *Deborah*'s loss of popularity around 1900 had less to do with the rise of antisemitism than with new models of the theater. Complaints about melodrama and sensationalism, we have seen, plagued Mosenthal's *Deborah* from the beginning. Yet, as we have repeatedly seen, in the hands of the right actress, *Deborah* had little difficulty rising above the register of melodrama, giving actresses a star vehicle that enabled them to give performances that held their audiences spellbound at the same time that their spectators developed a keen appreciation of their own powers of impersonation. The 2017 production of *Leah* in New York was hailed for its contemporary relevance, tellingly, at the same time that its director and cast were praised for achieving a "heightened realism" that "undercuts the play's sensationalism and treats it naturalistically."[163]

Returning to Brecht's polemics that we explored at the beginning of this chapter, it bears emphasizing that nineteenth-century spectators were anything but passive as they watched *Deborah* and *Leah*. Rarely were audiences lulled into trances as they experienced the thrills of virtuoso performances on stage. Quite to the contrary, spectators experiencing the excitements of feeling Deborah's or Leah's sufferings in the theater were self-conscious about their own theatrical pleasures, experiencing absorption and theatricality not as polar opposites but as flip sides of the same coin. The fact that it was Jewishness that was constructed through this dynamic interaction between star actresses and their spectators does not just shed light on the central role of the theater in nineteenth-century life; as we shall see in the following chapter, it also opens up a fascinating window on Jewish history. Contrary to the expectations harbored in Göttingen in 2004, the content of Mosenthal's play may not give us any deep insights into the historical realities of European Jewish life before the rise of political antisemitism in the late nineteenth century. But repeatedly, performances of *Deborah* and *Leah* created spaces where Jews and non-Jews came together to experience highly theatrical modes of Jewishness. The importance of these encounters for understanding non-Jews' views of Jews as well as Jews' changing ideas about themselves in the nineteenth century has yet to be fully appreciated. Performances of *Deborah* and *Leah*, we shall see, gave rise to a type of philosemitic liberalism that was frequently a Jewish and non-Jewish coproduction and, as such, arguably one of the most significant Jewish cultural events of the nineteenth century.

Chapter 4

Shylock and the Jewish Schiller: Jews, Non-Jews, and the Making of Philosemitism

Shylock Bateman's Pound of Flesh

On April 20, 1866, A. Oakey Hall, the New York County district attorney who would be elected the city's mayor two years later, delivered a dramatic closing statement in a civil case that made news across the country. Invoking the language of class warfare, Hall railed against the power and privilege of "rich, theatrical managers" and "theatrical monopolists" seeking to "reap the benefit" of the "labor" of poor, struggling artists. Defending the "claims of the poor man against the rich," Hall sang the praises of his friend and client Augustin Daly, who was suing H. L. Bateman for "literary services" rendered at the time of the premiere of *Leah, the Forsaken* in 1863.[1] After adapting Mosenthal's *Deborah* for the Batemans, Daly wrote a memoir for Kate Bateman that was sold in theater lobbies, and during *Leah*'s three-week run in Philadelphia in April 1863, he traveled with Kate and her father to manage the press there, wining and dining critics to ensure positive reviews and writing the occasional puff piece himself. Claiming that he had never been properly compensated for this public-relations work three years earlier, Daly initiated legal proceedings in January 1866, on the day that Kate returned from England to open in a revival of *Leah* at Niblo's Garden.

In suing first Kate (who had the case dismissed, pleading that she was a still a minor at the time of *Leah*'s premiere) and then her father, Daly had his eye on more than the $410 that he alleged the Batemans owed him. As H. L. Bateman pointed out in a letter he published in the *New York Saturday Press*, he himself had had numerous interactions with Daly during the six months he spent in New York prior to his daughter's return, and at no point did Daly approach him for fees, submit an invoice, or even mention the allegedly uncompensated literary services.[2] Indeed, the lawsuit was only peripherally related to fees. Before

Kate returned from England, Daly had asked her father for permission to print and sell his edition of *Leah* at Niblo's Garden during Kate's upcoming run there. Bateman refused, citing the differences between the *Leah* that his daughter had been performing in England and Daly's original script. Starting in early January, advertisements for Kate's "grand reappearance" noted that she would be performing not Daly's play but "her celebrated rôle of LEAH in Mosenthal's beautiful tragedy of that name"; after *Leah* opened, programs similarly made no mention of the play's original American adapter.[3] Against this backdrop, the lawsuit against Bateman gave Daly a chance to assert—in court and even more so in the press—his role in creating the play that had enabled Bateman to become an international celebrity.

From February 1866 until October 1867, when the case was finally settled, the Bateman-Daly lawsuit was frequently reported on in the press, and not always to Daly's advantage. To be sure, many articles invoked the image of the poor struggling playwright taken advantage of by the Batemans that was the centerpiece of Hall's closing statement, occasionally alleging that the version of *Leah* that Bateman was performing differed only superficially from Daly's.[4] Others, however, were unrelenting in their criticism of the way Daly had used oyster dinners and alcohol to obtain positive responses to Bateman and *Leah* in Philadelphia, using this case to rail against the "brazen effrontery" and "disgrace to journalism and literature" typical for this all too widespread practice of manipulating the press.[5] Daly's reputation was certainly not helped by an additional lawsuit that his (former) friend Emile Beneville filed and won against him amid his legal battles with Bateman. In a much publicized trial where H. L. Bateman appeared as a witness, Beneville revealed that Daly had never properly compensated him for the initial, rough translation of *Deborah* that Daly used as the basis for *Leah*.[6] In his closing statement, Hall set up Daly to rise above all such criticism. He not only emphasized the "genius" of Daly's work adapting *Deborah* and "breathing the breath of life" into a "dead, soulless translation." He likened Daly to Shakespeare, whose "plays were but adaptations" as well.[7]

Proclaiming Daly a nineteenth-century Shakespeare set the stage for an even more remarkable moment in Hall's closing statement. In 1863, a piece in the *Philadelphia Press*—written most likely by one of the critics Daly bought off or by Daly himself—celebrated the way Daly's *Leah* was revisiting the "theme that tempted the prejudiced genius" of the author of *The Merchant of Venice*. Daly's *Leah* improved on Shakespeare to expose "bigotry and fanaticism" and put forth a powerful "argument in behalf of the general equality of man."[8] Hall's closing statement echoed and amplified this understanding of *Leah* as the great successor to *The Merchant of Venice*. Turning to the Jews sitting in the courtroom, Hall defended Daly by dubbing Kate's father "Shylock Bateman": "What sort of creature is this Bateman? Gentlemen, I see among you several of my friends who belong to the Israelite nation. You know how for centuries it has been customary for every obloquy to be heaped upon that race, and it has passed into a proverb—'As mean as a Jew.' But now let this be altered; let future Shakspers [sic] take for the butt of scorn this Southern-Yankee Bateman; let us henceforth express our contempt by saying, not 'As mean as a Jew,' but 'As mean as Shylock Bateman.' Shylock Bateman, who says to this poor author, struggling for fame and fortune, 'You have made no contract! I agreed to give you nothing! It is not nominated in the bond! I claim the pound of flesh!'"[9]

In his brazen exploitation of Daly's work, Hall insists, Bateman has given future dramatists the prototype of a new Shylock, one who is a non-Jew seeking to profit from the labors of those, like Daly, who write plays that generate sympathy for Jews. In representing the creator of *Leah* in court, Hall thus decouples the figure of Shylock from the troubling anti-Jewish stereotypes in Shakespeare's play, putting "Shylock Bateman" on trial in a court scene that builds on and seeks to surpass the famous court scene in *The Merchant of Venice*. In this way, Hall celebrates his own speech as a dramatic event of the first order, one that initiates a revision of *The Merchant of Venice* that he expects his Jewish

Figure 55. Augustin Daly, photograph. Hess private collection.

friends in the courtroom to applaud just as they welcomed Daly's *Leah*. Hall's closing statement thus finishes the job that Daly began when adapting the "dead, soulless translation" of *Deborah* years before. If Daly's *Leah* surpasses and supersedes *The Merchant of Venice*, Hall's vision of a new, non-Jewish Shylock Bateman finally enables the prejudices that tainted *The Merchant of Venice* to find their proper place in the dustbin of history.

Hall's remarks are quoted here not from the court record, which no longer exists, but from the re-creation of Hall's speech that Daly produced and placed first in the *New York Herald*, and subsequently in the *New York Clipper*, the Philadelphia *Daily Evening Telegraph*, and elsewhere. After he read his closing statement in the *Herald*, in fact, an enthusiastic Hall wrote Daly to congratulate him on his work, telling him that his "report of the speech" was "ten times better than the original."[10] With its outlandish defense of the author of *Leah* as a modern-day Shakespeare victimized by a non-Jewish Shylock, the published version of Hall's closing statement helped transform the Bateman-Daly case into a media spectacle that overshadowed Daly's quest for compensation for his public-relations work or anything that actually happened in the Manhattan courtroom. Indeed, the legal case itself was eventually settled out of court, after numerous trials and appeals. In future years, Daly maintained good relations with both Kate and her family, even after another flare-up of legal trouble in 1875, when Kate sought an injunction to prevent Daly from putting on his play *The New Leah*, starring Clara Morris as Esther.[11] What requires our attention are less Daly's legal claims than the rhetorical gestures he used to celebrate himself in the press as the unrecognized true author of *Leah*. At its dramatic climax, Daly's creative reconstruction of Hall's closing statement hinges on the connections between the ideologically fraught representation of Jews on stage and the real Jews living in the nineteenth century, whether the members of the "Israelite nation" allegedly sitting in the Manhattan courtroom whom he has Hall enlist as friends or the sympathetic Jews assumed to be reading his account of Hall's speech in the press, the venue where Daly ultimately sought to have his lawsuit tried. Jews, indeed, are as crucial to the persona that Daly seeks to create for himself as is *The Merchant of Venice*, the drama that he claims to have improved on when adapting Mosenthal's *Deborah* for the English-speaking world.

As we mentioned in the Introduction, scholarship on philosemitism has often studied the idealization of Jews and Judaism among non-Jews as a largely non-Jewish affair, one that Jews themselves have historically approached with discomfort and suspicion. For many, philosemitism past and present often serves as a mask either for anti-Jewish sentiments or, at the very least, for visions of Jews and Judaism typically at odds with the way Jews perceive of themselves. With its dramatic flair, Daly's rendition of Hall's closing statement is important not only because of the explicit connections it draws between Jewish figures on stage and real-life Jews, whether they be sitting in a New York city courtroom, attending a performance of *Leah*, or reading about Daly in the newspapers. For us in this chapter, it opens a window on a broader phenomenon that studying the *Deborah* craze puts on our radar: the ways idealizations of Jews and Judaism often emerged in the nineteenth century as a product of interactions between Jews and non-Jews. In both Europe and North America, the sentimental vision of Jewishness central to the history of *Deborah* was hardly peripheral to Jewish life. Rather, starting with Mosenthal's original script, this was a phenomenon that Jews decisively helped mold, working together with non-Jews in a variety of settings to create images of Jewishness for Jews and non-Jews alike that shaped the relations between them. Particularly in the German-speaking world, the exotic performances of Jewishness promoted by performances of Mosenthal's play rarely won the endorsement of the Jewish elite; in many cases, we shall see, German rabbis singled out *Deborah* for particularly harsh criticism. But the popular fascination with Jewishness on stage that Mosenthal's drama launched is important because it was hardly the product of Christian fantasies about Jews and Judaism. We shall encounter in this chapter, rather, a rich tradition of philosemitic liberalism that was produced by Jews and non-Jews alike, and often without the stamp of approval of central institutions of nineteenth-century Jewish life.

The legacy of *The Merchant of Venice* looms large here, in Europe, North America, and elsewhere. But there is more at stake than the revision of a theatrical tradition that yielded more liberal attitudes toward Jews and Judaism. The theater repeatedly served as a place where Jews and non-Jews came together to produce and experience idealized modes of Jewishness. In this sense, the performance history of *Deborah* and *Leah* offers us insight not just into theater history but into the social role that the theater played in mediating between Jews and non-Jews in the nineteenth century. The Jews whose sympathies Daly counts on as he has Hall brand Bateman as the new Shylock in the Manhattan courtroom may have been fictional, created for the purposes of the published version of Hall's speech. But the sphere of shared interests that Daly imagines between Jews and non-Jews through a revision of Shakespeare was hardly peripheral to the *Deborah* craze. It was, from the very beginning, one of its defining characteristics, yielding a popular mode of experiencing Jewishness that came to take on a significant role in Jewish life, alongside other, more official, expressions.

From Shylock to Leah: Superseding *The Merchant of Venice*

According to an enthusiastic 1870 review of Bateman's *Leah* in New Orleans, Mosenthal pursued one key aim in writing a drama that presented Christians as marked by the "wrong of prejudice" and gave "the persecuted Jewess to the sympathy of those who do not believe in creed with her." He apparently sought to "put himself forward as a foil to Shakespeare," writing a drama appropriate for an era in which "narrow legislation" no longer drives "the Israelites from Ghetto to Judenstrasse, and back again from Judenstrasse to Ghetto."[12] Like other statements in the American press about Mosenthal and the original context of *Deborah*, it is unclear what source, if any, the author of this review may have been using. Indeed, as we saw in Chapter 1, when struggling to establish himself as a playwright in Vienna in his twenties, Mosenthal hardly harbored grand fantasies of taking Shakespeare off his pedestal. As a drama about a suffering Jewess, indeed, *Deborah* drew on a well-established literary tradition. In the aftermath of Walter Scott's best-selling novel *Ivanhoe* (1820) and Fromental Halévy's popular grand opera *La Juive* (1835), the figure of the "beautiful Jewess" had become a staple of nineteenth-century culture, and one that often inverted the plotlines of *The Merchant of Venice*. Rebecca in *Ivanhoe* and Rachel in *La Juive* both reject the path taken by Shylock's daughter Jessica. They do not abandon their fathers and convert to Christianity. Rather, like Deborah and Leah a generation later, they remain Jewesses, eliciting sympathy for Jews as Jews.

Journalists who were well disposed to *Deborah* and *Leah*, nevertheless, rarely concerned themselves with such academic details of the play's genesis or its precise position in literary history. At Fanny Janauschek's first performance of *Deborah* in Frankfurt in 1849, an enthusiastic German critic took the same approach as the New Orleans reviewer two decades later, celebrating Mosenthal's play as a successor to *The Merchant of Venice* appropriate for the "modern era," with its characteristic commitment to "justice, education, and humanity." For this reviewer, the "beautiful Oriental woman" and the sympathy she generated in Mosenthal's play provided the perfect antipode to Shylock's "dehumanized malice." As figures, both Shylock and Deborah derived their dramatic energy from the "injustice" of the "great world sin" of the persecution of the Jews, but in keeping with the liberal spirit of the nineteenth century, Mosenthal's play had the ability to promote reconciliation.[13] Mosenthal's publisher Gustav Heckenast marketed the print version of *Deborah* by quoting extensively from this review, advertising *Deborah* in good company alongside Gotthold Ephraim Lessing's *Nathan der Weise* (1779) and Richard Cumberland's *The Jew* (1792) as a modern alternative to *The Merchant of Venice*.[14]

Writing in the same year that *Deborah* had its premiere in Hamburg, Brünn (Brno), Vienna, Berlin, Prague, Frankfurt, Munich, and elsewhere, the distinguished German literary historian Julian Schmidt also drew parallels to Shylock, using *The Merchant of Venice* not to celebrate but to critique Mosenthal's newly popular play. Writing in the prominent cultural review *Die Grenzboten*,

Schmidt deplored the sentimental idealizations of Jews that he claimed had become a cliché in the seventy years since Lessing's *Nathan*. Rejecting *Deborah* as a sentimental melodrama that lacked coherence as a tragedy, he called for a return to *The Merchant of Venice*. Contemporary literature, Schmidt insisted, "is simply too good-natured when it comes to the genuine representation of Jews and Judaism. Who would dare today to portray a Shylock? If one regards the Jews in our poetry today, indeed, it is absolutely incomprehensible how the contempt for this tribe could ever have become so universal in public opinion. Nothing but heroes, nothing but suffering angels!"[15]

Whatever else one might say about Schmidt's misgivings about *Deborah* and his longing for a return to the allegedly "genuine" figure of the Venetian moneylender, his contrast between Shylock and the rise of romantic idealizations of Jews on stage is misleading. It fails to capture the extent to which nineteenth-century audiences experienced Shylock and Deborah not as polar opposites but as flip sides of the same phenomenon. For nineteenth-century theatergoers in German-speaking Europe and the Anglo American cultural orbit, indeed, *The Merchant of Venice* was not a relic from Elizabethan England. Whether in German or English, Shakespeare experienced unprecedented popularity on the nineteenth-century stage, and *The Merchant of Venice* was among the most widely performed Shakespeare plays. Nineteenth-century productions of *The Merchant of Venice* in Germany, England, and North America, moreover, were famous for interpreting Shylock as a tragic and sometimes a sympathetic figure.

Early in the nineteenth century, August Wilhelm Iffland, the celebrated actor, prolific playwright, and director of the Berlin court theater, performed Shylock as a Jewish caricature and a villain, with the same exaggerated Yiddish accent he used to play Sheva, the benevolent protagonist of Cumberland's *The Jew*. But starting with Ludwig Devrient's Shylock in 1815, many German actors began to transform Shylock into a noble, tragic figure.[16] In England, Edmund Kean inaugurated a parallel tradition with his celebrated debut in *The Merchant of Venice* a year earlier.[17]

Starting with Jacob Adler's *Shylock* in 1901, *The Merchant of Venice* earned a secure place in the repertoire of the American Yiddish stage.[18] But the Jewish involvement in this novel reinterpretation of Shylock goes back much further. During the latter half of the nineteenth century, a number of prominent Jewish actors also sought to create a sympathetic Shylock, often as a polemical challenge to rising antisemitism. By far the most famous of these was the Polish Jewish celebrity actor Bogumil Dawison. Starting in the mid-1850s, Dawison created an idealized, heroic Shylock on the German stage, often performing *The Merchant of Venice* without its final act so that it would end as a tragedy, and one that was fundamentally about Shylock rather than Antonio, the merchant of Venice referenced in

Figure 56. Herbert König, *Bogumil Dawison in verschiedenen Rollen* (Bogumil Dawison in various roles), *Die Gartenlaube* (1864). Shylock is role 7, second to right in the second row from the top. Hess private collection.

Shakespeare's title.[19] In Shakespeare, Shylock's wife is named Leah, and whatever Daly and the Batemans' intentions may have been in giving *Deborah* a new title, calling the play *Leah* reinforced the connection to *The Merchant of Venice*.[20]

The circumstances surrounding *Leah*'s American premiere also set the relationship between *Deborah* and *The Merchant of Venice* into particularly sharp relief. Three days before Bateman opened in *Leah* at Niblo's Garden, the twenty-five-year-old actor Daniel E. Bandmann made his much awaited English-language debut at Niblo's, launching his own version of the sympathetic Shylock. By 1863, Bandmann had emerged as one of the stars of New York's German-language theater, where his powerful performances of Shakespeare elicited notice in the mainstream press (and where, on at least one occasion in the late 1850s, he was also cast as Joseph in *Deborah*).[21] Born, like Mosenthal, to a Jewish family in Kassel, Bandmann had immigrated with his parents as a teenager to New York, where his father, Solomon, established himself as a liquor dealer.[22] Following his debut in *The Merchant of Venice* at Niblo's, Bandmann quickly rose to fame, becoming an international celebrity in the English-speaking world, known for the brilliance of his Shakespearean roles. Like Dawison, who performed *The Merchant of Venice* on his 1866 American tour, in German, Bandmann transformed Shylock into a noble and sympathetic character, making at least one critic reviewing his English-language debut wonder whether Shakespeare's goal was in fact "to satirize Christian justice rather than Jewish greed."[23]

In 1863, as Bandmann was emerging as one of the bright lights of the English-language stage, his Shylock was frequently discussed alongside

Figure 57. Daniel E. Bandmann as Shylock, carte-de-visite photograph. Harvard Theatre Collection, THE GEN TCS 18, theatrical cartes-de-visite photographs of men, ca. 1854–1879, Houghton Library, Harvard University.

Bateman's *Leah*, and the Jewish press routinely claimed Bandmann as a fellow Jew.[24] Bandmann's Jewishness, indeed, was very much in the public eye. By the fall of that year, he had become so well known that he was received by First Lady Mary Todd Lincoln.[25] That September, his refusal to perform on Kol Nidre out of respect for his coreligionists also provoked notice—and respect—in the press.[26] Later in life, Bandmann did not cultivate connections to Jewish communities, and none of the women he married was Jewish. (Incidentally, Bandmann's second wife, the American actress Millicent Palmer-Bandmann, often played Leah; in the Lotus-Eaters episode of *Ulysses*, James Joyce's protagonist, Leopold Bloom, fondly remembers her in the role.)[27] Nevertheless, for both Jewish and non-Jewish fans and supporters, Bandmann's Jewishness continued to define his persona as an actor and a celebrity. In the early 1880s, while performing *The Merchant of Venice*, among other plays, on his Australian tours, Bandmann's Jewish background was frequently reported on in the press, often linked to his grand project to restore dignity and humanity to the depictions of Jews on stage.[28]

In January 1863, New York newspapers advertised Bateman's *Leah* and Bandmann's *Merchant of Venice* side by side, reporting on them in the same articles and often comparing the two plays explicitly in terms of their message. One critic noted that "the great lesson" of *Leah* was "that of tolerance toward mankind in general and Jews in particular," and, in this sense, the critic remarked, Bateman's new play differed considerably from *The Merchant of Venice*, "which we all had so recently seen."[29] As we observed in the previous chapter, Jewish newspapers welcomed Bateman's *Leah* with open arms, occasionally reporting on the overrepresentation of Jews in audiences attending the play. Niblo's Garden, in fact, made special efforts to court Jewish theatergoers. William Wheatley, the manager at Niblo's, took out special advertisements in the New York *Jewish Messenger*, calling "special attention of the Hebrew residents of New York . . . to the faithful manner in which the historical minutiae of this favorite work has [*sic*] been attended to" and noting the "special attractiveness" of this drama "to a large class of our refined and cultivated Jewish citizens."[30] In the American context, tellingly, the notion that *Leah* was exceptionally well situated to displace *The Merchant of Venice* had its earliest formulations not in Daly's puff pieces but in the Jewish press, as a Jewish reaction to the two dramas that played back-to-back at Niblo's Garden.

Writing about Bandmann in February 1863, the *Jewish Messenger* applauded its "co-religionist" for imagining an "ideal" Shylock, "of noble nature, goaded by persecution, humiliated, tortured, but not broken, seizing with not unnatural avidity on an opportunity for retaliation upon his bitter reviler Antonio." Bandmann's Shylock was certainly preferable to more traditional renderings of the role. Yet "for the sake of the sensibilities of the Jewish community," the *Jewish Messenger* continued, *The Merchant of Venice* should nevertheless still be "banned" from the stage. Even when performed sympathetically, as Bandmann did so well, the figure of Shylock cannot do enough to encourage those who "come to the theatre with an innate prejudice against the Jewish race" to cast aside their anti-Jewish sentiments.[31] In this context, the critic turned to Bateman's *Leah* with tremendous enthusiasm, praising a drama that the *Jewish Messenger* had heralded two weeks earlier as a refreshing "contrast to the stern and unyielding character of Shylock."[32] The American adaptation of *Deborah* found praise in the *Jewish Messenger* not just for its "truthful" portrayal of "that dreadful prejudice against the Jewish race" but for the powerful "effect of the drama" on "the audience that usually assemble at our places of amusement." The conclusion was unequivocal: "'Leah, the Forsaken,' should supersede 'Shylock.'"[33]

Daly, then, was thus not just pandering to Jewish fans when he celebrated *Leah* as a response to *The Merchant of Venice* and introduced H. L. Bateman as a new prototype of a non-Jewish Shylock appropriate for the nineteenth century. He was building in part on a Jewish line of argument, one that found its earliest American articulation in the Jewish press. Tellingly, the memoir that Daly wrote for Bateman in late 1862 never once compared *Leah* to anything in Shakespeare. As we recall from Chapter 2, Daly here compared *Leah*'s comprehensive "picture of German village life, as it existed two centuries ago" not to *The Merchant of Venice* but to Nathaniel Hawthorne's *The Scarlet Letter*.[34] In the American context, celebrating *Leah* as the drama destined to supersede *The Merchant of Venice* was a Jewish intervention in the reception of Mosenthal, and one that experienced a considerable afterlife among critics and fans well disposed toward the play. Of course, *The Merchant of Venice* ultimately survived the nineteenth century in ways that *Leah* did not. Yet for many in the latter half of the nineteenth century, it could be invoked as a given that *Leah* was superior to Shakespeare's portrait of the vengeful Venetian moneylender. On purely aesthetic grounds, this view may have been misguided. Nevertheless, when Daly arranged for Philadelphia theater critics to celebrate *Leah* in print as "the noblest appeal for the Hebrew ever penned," he was not just engaging in cynical public-relations work.[35] He was giving voice to a mode of perception that Jews shared self-consciously with non-Jews—and vice versa.

Hebrew Switzerland and the Jewish Schiller: Jewish and Non-Jewish Coproductions from Kostel to Idaho City

Over and over again, and on both sides of the Atlantic, performances of *Deborah* and *Leah* emerged as the product of Jews interacting with non-Jews. This phenomenon was not limited to the shared modes of perception formulated in print that that gave rise to the notion that *The Merchant of Venice* had found its true rival in Mosenthal's drama. Performances of *Deborah* and *Leah* frequently brought Jews and non-Jews together more concretely on the ground as well. Eduard Kulke, a Jewish writer in Vienna, saw *Deborah* numerous times in Vienna and Dresden. As he commented in an article he published in 1865, however, his favorite performance was one that he himself occasioned during his student days during an 1851 visit to his hometown of Kostel (Podivin), in southern Moravia, located today in the Czech Republic some sixty miles from Vienna. Kulke here tells the story of a wandering theater troupe that found that its usual fare of farces and plays about knights and robbers was not playing as well with the locals as expected. Frustrated by playing to empty houses, the desperate couple in charge of the theater troupe encountered Kulke at one of their performances and approached him for advice. When Kulke asked whether the troupe ever performed *Deborah*, his question unleashed great enthusiasm: "'Oh, the Jewish play [*Judenstück*] by the Jewish Schiller?' the director's wife responded. 'What troupe doesn't have that in its repertoire? I play Deborah myself, just as you see me here, with my blond hair, for I don't wear wigs, and my husband plays Joseph.'"[36]

Inspired by the blond actress's comparison between Mosenthal and the classical German dramatist Friedrich Schiller, Kulke asked whether the troupe might be in a position to perform *Deborah* the next day. When he received an emphatic yes as the answer, Kulke single-handedly took on the task of arranging for publicity. He composed cheesy advertisements in iambic pentameter praising the play for its commitment to "fraternity and equality, human rights and human dignity," and he drafted a public invitation—also in verse—addressed to both the Christians and the Jews of Kostel, speaking in glowing terms of the wonders they should all expect to experience in the theater that night. Thanks to Kulke's efforts, the "Jewish play by the Jewish Schiller" was performed to a full house. According to his account, no one was disappointed, even though the script had to be changed to accommodate the blond actress.[37]

In 1891, when Harper's Theatre in Rock Island, Illinois, repeatedly advertised "Rosenthal's [*sic*] Celebrated Tragedy *Leah, the Forsaken*" as a play of "interest to both Jew and Gentile,"[38] this small-town theater was thus hardly engaging in a unique or unusual business strategy. Giving the author of *Deborah* the more traditionally Jewish-sounding name Rosenthal may well have been an honest mistake; American newspapers had been making this error on occasion for almost four decades.[39] But casting *Deborah* and *Leah* as a drama that naturally appealed to both Jews and non-Jews and brought them together to enjoy an evening of experiencing Jewish suffering on stage was part of a tried-and-true

Figure 58. The Jewish Schiller? This oft-reproduced image of Mosenthal was published in the mass-market journal *Über Land und Meer* after his death in 1877. Hess private collection.

marketing practice, one that spoke to the well-established appeal to both Jews and Gentiles of this play by "Rosenthal."

Whether in Moravia or on the Mississippi, Mosenthal's Jewishness was often part of the play's appeal, and indeed, in the English-speaking world, the fact that Mosenthal was a "German Hebrew" was often noted in the press.[40] In the German world, dubbing Mosenthal the Jewish Schiller was hardly unique to the theater troupe touring through Moravia in the summer of 1851. Less off the beaten path, in the Saxon city of Chemnitz, a theater program introducing Mosenthal as the Jewish Schiller attracted notice as far away as Vienna.[41] The exact origin of this moniker is difficult to determine, but it may have begun to take off with an 1852 article that circulated widely throughout the German and Austrian press. Reporting on a performance of *Deborah* in the Rhineland resort town of Bad Kreuznach, 500 miles from Kostel, a Frankfurt newspaper noted that "a traveling theater troupe visiting Kreuznach during the resort season recently performed Mosenthal's thrilling play *Deborah* there. Kreuznach has many Jewish inhabitants, and the play's director thus found it wise to make the following remark under the title: 'On account of his great talent, the author of this tragedy, an Israelite, is universally known as the Jewish Schiller.'"[42] Like the publicity materials Kulke prepared or the advertisements that Niblo's Garden

Figure 59. Zerline Gabillon, carte-de-visite photograph. Hess private collection.

took out in the Jewish press, this over-the-top celebration of Mosenthal as the Jewish Schiller obviously sought to do what was good for business. But we need not approach this understanding of Mosenthal as a great Jewish writer of an immensely popular German play with unnecessary skepticism. *Deborah* was performed and enjoyed as a Jewish play, and like their peers in Kostel and Rock Island, this theater troupe expected that the local Jewish community would greet the performance of the Jewish Schiller's masterpiece with enthusiasm. Just as importantly, the fact that this anecdote was reproduced in mainstream newspapers from Frankfurt to Vienna indicates an expectation that this charming story of local lore would be of wide interest to non-Jews as well. Regardless of whether one accepted that Mosenthal deserved to be celebrated as the Jewish Schiller, there were certainly theatergoers for whom this appellation both made sense and translated into ticket sales. The fact that a critic for the *Neue Freie Presse* in Vienna declared this appellation preposterous in 1864—at the moment that *Deborah* finally had its long-awaited premiere at the Burgtheater in Vienna— only underscores the power that it had come to wield.[43]

Philosemitism, then, was not merely part of the play's content. *Deborah* helped create social spaces where Jews and Christians came together, sitting side by side to enjoy a Jewish play. In most cases, as we saw in Chapter 3, actors performing in the play tended not to be Jewish. At some points, however—and not just in the case of Sarah Bernhardt or the Yiddish theater—Jewish actors did play prominent roles in productions of *Deborah*. In 1864, when *Deborah* enjoyed its premiere at the Burgtheater, the most prestigious stage in the German-speaking world, Jewish newspapers did not neglect to point out that Adolf von Sonnenthal, the actor playing Joseph, was a coreligionist.[44] Many prominent Jewish actresses in the German-speaking world also included the role in their repertoire. Zerline Gabillon, née Würzburg (Figure 59), came from a Jewish family in the northern German city of Güstrow, where her father had a store in the center of town trading in "clothes and various other things" and where, as a child, she found herself fascinated by the theater. Gabillon spent her childhood, indeed, dreaming of following in the footsteps of the French Jewish celebrity actress Rachel Félix.[45] In the early 1850s, Gabillon made a name for herself playing Deborah—among other roles—in Prague, Dresden, Vienna, and elsewhere before receiving an invitation to join the company of the Burgtheater, where she was generally cast in supporting roles and became a close friend of Mosenthal as well.[46] The Austrian Jewish actress Kathi Frank (Figure 60), celebrated at one time as Burgtheater star Charlotte Wolter's greatest rival, made her debut in 1867, at age twenty, performing the role of Deborah at Vienna's Thalia-Theater.[47] Gabillon's Jewish background was well known, even after her conversion and marriage to her actor-husband Ludwig, but reviews of Gabillon in *Deborah* tended not to grant it importance. Frank, in contrast, herself cultivated the notion of a special connection to the role. Born Katharina Frankl in the Hungarian town of Bazin, or Bösing, near Pressburg (Pezikok, near Bratislava, located in Slovakia today), Frank often told the story of how she came to make her grand debut not at twenty playing Mosenthal's Jewish maiden in Vienna but at age seven playing young Deborah in the provinces.[48]

During a visit to her grandmother in Stomfa (Stampfen in German; Stupava in Slovak), a town just north of Pressburg that had a significant Jewish community in the nineteenth century, Frank heard that a traveling theater troupe was in need of a child actress for "Mosenthal's famous Jewish play [*Judenstück*] *Deborah*," the drama it had chosen to open a series of guest performances. "Despite my youth," Frank recollected, "I had heard quite a bit about *Deborah*." When she presented herself to the director and was asked whether she was serious about taking on the role of Joseph and Hanna's daughter, Frank explained, "I'll get beaten by my grandmother if I do it, but if I can play the child of the man who likes the Jews so much, then I'll do it, even if I get beaten by my grandmother." Impressed by the young girl's tenacity, the director gave in, under the condition that Frank secretly bring from her grandmother's house a Jewish prayer shawl that the adult actress playing Deborah could drape herself with during the performance. When Frank showed up on the night of the performance, prayer shawl in hand, the director rewarded her with sweets, and her performance in the final act went well—that is, until her grandmother showed up. Indeed, as soon as Frank appeared on stage and began to speak her lines, her grandmother interrupted the performance, calling for her to get down off the stage and return home. Boldly ignoring her grandmother, Frank continued to perform until she had completed her scenes, only then responding, "Grandmother, I'm done now, I'll be right there." At that point, she "saw her grandmother's powerful figure rise up from her chair and leave the auditorium in a hurry." (It is unclear whether the prayer shawl ever made it back to her grandmother's house.)

As Frank told the story later in life, she may not have earned recognition from her grandmother, but the director gave her a necklace made of pink glass that she treasured for years, and she cherished the notion that she had been given the opportunity to "be of service to the cause of art in Stampfen." By telling this story as an adult, Frank framed her entry into the world of the theater

Figure 60. Kathi Frank, photograph. F. N. Manskopf Collection, Universitäts-Bibliothek Johann Christian Senckenberg, Frankfurt am Main.

as a struggle between her traditionally minded provincial Jewish grandmother who felt that young Katharina had no place on stage and the liberating spirit of the philosemitism of Mosenthal's *Deborah*. Even as a seven-year-old, this future star of the stage wanted to be part of the world of Mosenthal's *Deborah*, playing the daughter of the "man who likes the Jews so much." For both Katharina the child and Kathi Frank the adult actress, stealing the tallit from her grandmother's house so that the actress starring Deborah might have an "authentic" Jewish costume represents neither a childhood act of transgression nor a violation of Jewish ritual practice; prayer shawls were traditionally worn only by men, not women, and certainly never intended to serve as props in the theater. For Frank, rather, borrowing the prayer shawl marks yet another way in which Jews could contribute to the success of the performance of *Deborah*, another way in which Jews and non-Jews worked together to portray Jewishness on stage.

The performance of *Deborah* in Stomfa, incidentally, seems to have been one of many in which actresses playing Deborah draped themselves in Jewish prayer shawls. In an 1874 essay commemorating the twenty-fifth anniversary of *Deborah*'s career on the stage published in *Die Gegenwart*, a prominent Berlin weekly cultural review, Mosenthal reported on performances of *Deborah* in southern Germany where an unnamed actress similarly wore a tallit.[49] In this context, it is likely no accident that when she created the role of Deborah at the Burgtheater premiere in 1864, Charlotte Wolter also wore a shawl with broad stripes that bore a resemblance to a traditional Jewish prayer shawl.[50] For Mosenthal, as for Frank, at any rate, the unorthodox use of the Jewish prayer shawl on stage did not provide occasion for criticism. Rather, it served as yet another unproblematic example of the positive reception of his drama, yet more proof of the spectacular way that his "daughter" *Deborah*—like the "wandering Jew"—had been traveling from stage to stage in the German-speaking world and abroad for the last quarter-century.[51]

Jews occasionally played roles writing and performing the incidental music for *Deborah* and *Leah* as well. The music for the Prague premiere of *Deborah* in 1849, for instance, was written by Jewish composer Eduard Tauwitz, who conducted the orchestra at the German theater there.[52] Playbills and advertisements indicate instances where numerous conductors from Jewish backgrounds conducted the orchestra or composed music.[53] In Baltimore in 1864, Jacob H. Rosewald, a prominent musician who was active in Jewish community life, composed and conducted original music for the production of *Leah, the Forsaken* at Ford's Holliday Street Theatre, starring Mrs. D. P. Bowers.[54] Jews were no doubt frequently involved as members of the orchestra as well. In most of these cases, nevertheless, few sources remain to gauge the significance of this participation. Indeed, with the exception of Robert Stoepel's *Reminiscences of Leah* (1863), which featured selections from the incidental music that the German American composer wrote for Bateman's *Leah*, none of the music used in performances of *Deborah* or *Leah* was published. With very few exceptions—sections of Stoepel's music, a score for a performance of *Deborah* in the Bavarian city of Coburg in 1849, and the incidental music that Lawrence Barrett used for *Leah, the Jewess* in the last quarter of the nineteenth century in the United States—none of this music has survived in archives, either.[55] What is significant is that, like Stoepel's music and the competing versions of "Leah's Song," which we discussed in Chapter 2, the music that has survived manifests little in the way of Jewish content. Unlike, say, Jerry Bock's music for *Fiddler on the Roof* (1964), the music for *Deborah* and *Leah* never makes use of the augmented seconds or the mournful melodies in minor keys that defined clichés about Jewish music in the twentieth century. In one prominent case, nevertheless, Jewish exoticism was strategically put to use in music used at performances of Mosenthal's drama. As was the case with the prayer shawl in Stomfa, moreover, here Jewish exoticism emerged as the product of Jews working together with non-Jews.

Despite Mosenthal's best efforts, as we have mentioned, the powers that be at the Burgtheater in Vienna refused to consider performing what they dismissed as Mosenthal's *Judenstück* for the first fifteen years of its existence.[56] It was only in September 1864—after *Leah* had established itself as a showstopper in New York and London—that *Deborah* had its Burgtheater premiere. Mosenthal chose to mark the arrival of his play at this bastion of German high culture by arranging for special music foregrounding the play's Jewish content and themes. As newspapers reported, he himself supplied the (non-Jewish) composer Robert von Hornstein "ancient Hebrew melodies," or at least "some motifs from the synagogue that are supposed to be ancient Hebrew in origin."[57] Advertisements for Deborah at the Burgtheater in Viennese newspapers routinely highlighted the "ancient Hebrew music" that von Hornstein integrated into the overture and entr'acte that continued to be used in performances of *Deborah* for almost four decades.[58] The score for von Hornstein's music has unfortunately not survived.[59] Reactions to von Hornstein's music in the Viennese press, however, indicate that there was nothing subtle about its Jewish exoticism. The Austrian Jewish writer Emil Kuh noted that von Hornstein's Hebrew melodies "were reminiscent of the jewels of Heinrich Heine's savage 'Princess Sabbath.'"[60] Ludwig Speidel, a preeminent Viennese music and theater critic, wrote less generously that the music that the "amicable song-composer and vaudevillian" produced sounded about "as idyllic as cows performing round dances in Hebrew Switzerland." All in all, he concluded, in an equally cynical tone, von Hornstein's "Hebrew melodies" met the needs of Mosenthal's drama in an exemplary manner.[61]

In one prominent instance in the United States, the aura of Jewish exoticism came from the pen of the translator-adaptor. The American actress Julia Dean Hayne, known after her divorce in 1866 as Julia Dean, frequently performed *Leah* from 1864 until she died in childbirth in 1868. As a Louisville, Kentucky, newspaper noted in 1867, her version of *Leah* was special, as it was created by Dr. H. M. Bien, "the rabbi of San Francisco" and a "writer whose culture rendered him capable of treating with vigor and judgment Mosenthal's sublime perception of the fanaticism evinced in earlier ages by the persecutions of the Jews."[62] Herman Milton Bien, a native of Naumburg, near Kassel, and an unusual character who had neither a doctorate nor a rabbinic ordination, spent several years at Temple Emanu-El in San Francisco, where he also edited a Jewish newspaper and wrote widely for the theater.[63] In March 1864, Bien produced what he presented as an original translation of *Deborah* for a production starring Emily Jordan at the Metropolitan Theatre in San Francisco.[64] Building on the success of Bateman's *Leah* on the East Coast and in London, Bien gave his version the title *Leah, the Forsaken*, and his *Leah* was a curious mix of Daly's adaptation and Mosenthal's original. In Bien's version, as in Daly's, Nathan the schoolmaster returns in the final act and tries to kill Leah; the figure of Ruben is deleted; and the play is divided into five acts. Following Mosenthal, however, Bien's Leah does not die but rejoins her people, and Bien retained Joseph's and Hanna's names from the German original.

Bien left California weeks after the premiere of *Leah*,[65] but his version of the play continued to be used in San Francisco, where Julia Dean Hayne served briefly as the joint manager of the Metropolitan Theatre and herself took on the role that July. Bien relocated initially to Nevada, where he edited the German-language *Nevada Staats-Zeitung*, continued to serve as a rabbi, opened a Jewish school, and was elected to the legislature. As early as April 1864, just one month after *Leah* premiered in San Francisco, he also arranged for the performance of "his" original play, *Leah, the Forsaken*, in Nevada, at the Virginia City Opera House.[66] (After a series of rabbinical positions in New York and Dallas, Bien eventually ended up in Vicksburg, Mississippi, where continued to write prolifically and was known as the "Rabbi-Poet." He ended his life with a dramatic suicide in 1895 after a job offer for a rabbinic post in Birmingham, Alabama, was rescinded.[67])

The play that Julia Dean advertised in Louisville as the product of a special rabbi-translator served her well. From 1864 on, she performed *Leah* frequently on tour, making it as far as New York and Boston, where she gave the play the title *Leah, the Outcast*.[68] In Salt Lake City, where she was a local celebrity in 1865–1866 and a favorite of Brigham Young, she frequently performed Bien's translation of "Mosenthal's great play of *Leah, the Forsaken*" to great acclaim to a mixed audience of Jews, Mormons, and other Gentiles.[69] Perhaps the most interesting of Dean's performances of Bien's *Leah*, however, was in Idaho City, a mining town founded in 1862 that boasted a population of 6,000 by 1863. Hayne's first Idaho City performance of *Leah*, in September 1864, was so spectacular that 350 local residents published an open letter to the actress in a Boise City paper days later, begging her to come back and perform Leah once again that month. Touched by her fans, Hayne agreed and returned to Idaho City two weeks later.[70] The venue where she performed Bien's version of *Leah*, the Forrest Theatre, was not just a Jewish-owned business. It was also the place where Idaho City Jews held their first High Holy Day services in 1865.[71]

It is difficult to know, of course, what sort of connections Idaho City theatergoers may have made between this performance of Rabbi Bien's play, the Jewish-owned theater in their mining town, and the growing Jewish community that used the venue where *Leah* had been performed one year later as a place of worship. Nor will we ever be likely to determine what sort of connections theatergoers in Petroleum Centre, Pennsylvania—a boomtown during the Pennsylvania Oil Rush of the 1860s—made between the Jewish content of the production of *Leah, the Forsaken* they saw in 1870 and the Jewish family that owned both the local dry-goods store and the adjacent opera house where the play was presented.[72] Whether in London, New Orleans, Salt Lake City, Memphis, or Central City, Colorado, moreover, advertisements for *Leah* and *Deborah* in the Anglo American world frequently appeared alongside advertisements for Jewish businesses, forging a link, once again, between the representation of Jews on stage and Jews living in the nineteenth century.[73] What is clear from the examples we have been studying in this section is that performances of Mosenthal's drama hardly took place as part of an abstract culture of philosemitism where Jews played no role. Indeed, part of the appeal of Mosenthal's drama in its various incarnations was that it launched a type of philosemitism that Jews helped shape, a type of philosemitism where Jews and non-Jews came together to enjoy the pleasures of experiencing the trials and tribulations of Mosenthal's Jewish maiden.

The Jewish Schiller's Last Hurrah?

Of course, not every performance of *Deborah* and *Leah* created spaces where Jews and non-Jews sat together in peace and harmony. When he was a well-established writer living in Berlin in his forties, Karl Emil Franzos recalled his first visit to the theater, at age nine, in 1858, in his native Czortków in eastern Galicia (Chortkiv, in western Ukraine today). The play that Franzos saw was *Deborah*, performed in German before a mixed audience of Jews and non-Jews.

Like Kathi Frank several years earlier on the other side of the Austro-Hungarian Empire, this future writer of tales about Eastern European Jewry was delighted that he would be seeing a play about Jews. But Czortków proved to be different from Stomfa. For when the schoolmaster in Act II expressed his desire to rid his land of Jews, many non-Jews in the audience spontaneously began to applaud, including the classmate with whom Franzos had gone to the theater. Franzos, enraged, started to attack his friend physically, his behavior causing the Jews and the Christians in the theater alike to break out in laughter. His friend's father responded by grabbing Franzos and dragging him out of the theater. Feeling like a "martyr for his faith," Franzos was left to his own devices to figure out how the fascinating play by Mosenthal ended.[74]

In his posthumously published novel *Der Pojaz* (The Clown, 1905), Franzos concocted an even more elaborate story about Mosenthal's *Deborah* generating strife and multiethnic conflict. A masterpiece of literary modernism that Franzos completed in 1893, *Der Pojaz* drew its energy from the way it wedded a satiric view of Eastern European Jewish life to a humorous reworking of Johann Wolfgang von Goethe's celebrated bildungsroman *Wilhelm Meisters Lehrjahre* (Wilhelm Meister's Apprenticeship, 1795–1796). Franzos's novel tells the story not of a German bourgeois young man named Wilhelm but of a Yiddish-speaking son of a schnorrer (beggar or sponger) whose peers among the Polish Hasidim call him a clown. Wilhelm Meister famously plays Hamlet in a production of Shakespeare. Sender Glatteis, Franzos's protagonist, also dreams of Shakespeare and a life on the stage, but his model is Bogumil Dawison's Shylock, and Dawison himself makes a cameo in the novel. At a key moment in *Der Pojaz*, Sender attends a performance of *Deborah* by a touring theater troupe from Czernowitz in the Galician town of Zaleszcycki (located today, like Franzos's native Czortków, in western Ukraine).

Cynically, the theater troupe creates a "bilingual" playbill for *Deborah*, in Hebrew letters for Jews (transliterated for Franzos's readers) and in German letters for Christians. The ridiculously long playbill—it spans several pages in the novel—addresses two audiences at once, framing the play in two different ways for two discrete sets of theatergoers. *Deborah* is advertised to Jews as a great Jewish play written by the pious coreligionist "Schlome Hirsch Mosenthal," who hails not from Kassel via Vienna but from Tarnow in Galicia. Non-Jews are told that the author of *Deborah*, the world-famous dramatic poet from Berlin, "Dr. Professor Ritter Sigmund Heinrich Mosenthal," was born a Catholic but is rumored to have had a Jewish great-great-grandfather.[75] In Hebrew letters, the play's full title is given as *"Deborah, the most noble and most beautiful Israelite maiden in the entire world!!! Or: You honest Jewish child, do not get involved with a Christian!! It will turn out poorly!!! Or: The great victory of the Israelites over all their enemies, who will have to bless them in the end."* Non-Jews are served up different fare: *"Deborah, the cursed and accursed Jewess! Or: Christian and Jewish love and what becomes of it! Or: The curse of the Jews and the blessing of the Christians."*

Writing in the 1890s, after *Deborah* had enjoyed more than four decades of popularity in the German-speaking world and abroad, Franzos thus serves up a brilliant parody of the very notion that performances of *Deborah* might enable Jews and non-Jews to come together in the theater in meaningful ways. Like the show that he reports seeing at age nine, the performance of *Deborah* in *Der Pojaz* does anything but bring Jews and non-Jews together to partake of the pleasures of philosemitism. At the end of the third act, many non-Jews react to Deborah's famous curse scene with loud noises calling for the Jews to leave. Unlike the nine-year-old Franzos, the Jewish theatergoers in the novel respond by sitting in their seats and applauding even more forcefully. This behavior, in turn, prompts one of the Austrian army officers present to cry out, facetiously, "Three cheers for Mosenthal, the Jewish Schiller!"[76] Faced with this preposterous scene, the rest of the officers break out in hearty laughter, ridiculing the "Jewish Schiller" at precisely the moment in *Deborah*—the curse scene—when audiences typically found themselves spellbound and electrified. To be sure, the scene in which Deborah reconciles with the Christian world in the final act ends up "satisfying all parties, Christians and Jews alike."[77] This happens, however, only after an evening where the masterpiece of the "Jewish Schiller" has repeatedly given rise to tensions between Jews and non-Jews unlike anything reported at actual nineteenth-century performances of the play.

Of course, the fact that Franzos, writing toward the end of the century, singled out *Deborah* for parody in *Der Pojaz* only serves to underscore the crucial role that performances of Mosenthal's drama played in creating social spaces where Jews and non-Jews came together to enjoy the pleasures of sympathy with Jewish suffering. By the 1890s, as we recall from Chapter 3, *Deborah*'s and *Leah*'s popularity had begun to recede. Sender Glatteis's fictional experience of *Deborah* in Zaleszcycki in the 1850s no doubt reflects an era where Mosenthal's melodrama had lost its broad appeal, particularly in urban centers like Berlin, where Franzos had been living since the mid-1880s. In the world that Franzos creates, *Deborah* has hardly superseded *The Merchant of Venice*. Indeed, Dawison's Shylock maintains a level of power and allure in *Der Pojaz* that the provincial performance of *Deborah* cannot even begin to match. Nevertheless, the fact that more than four decades after its premiere, *Deborah* becomes the focal point of a fictional scene of multiethnic strife between Jews and non-Jews also bears testimony to the tremendous power that this drama held for decades as a cultural force that brought Jews and non-Jews together. Without this backdrop, Franzos's ingenious parody would have made little sense.

Jews, Jewishness, and Popular Culture

The scenarios of Jews and non-Jews coming together to produce and enjoy the pleasures of liberal philosemitism we have encountered both in this chapter and throughout this book illuminate a cultural phenomenon that has typically not made it onto the radar of those who study nineteenth-century Jewish history or those who work in the field of Jewish literature. To be sure, work on the emergence of Jewish "ghetto fiction" in the mid-nineteenth century has stressed the dual appeal of this novel genre of literature, exploring how sentimental tales of ghetto life generated a sense of shared community among the Jews and non-Jews who enjoyed reading this type of fiction.[78] As we noted in the Introduction, Moritz Daniel Oppenheim's celebrated prints of traditional Jewish family life were similarly marketed to both Jews and non-Jews in the latter half of the nineteenth century, launching a romanticized vision of traditional Jewish folkways that achieved cultural currency among a wide segment of the general public as well as among Jews. For Mosenthal, moreover, both of these developments came together with his posthumously published *Erzählungen aus dem jüdischen Familienleben* (Tales of Jewish Family Life, 1878), a frequently reprinted collection of tales of Jewish life in his native Kassel. Many of the stories in the collection originally appeared in the years before Mosenthal's death in mainstream illustrated magazines such as *Die Gartenlaube* and *Über Land und Meer*, accompanied by illustrations by Oppenheim. But there is a difference between the virtual communities produced by fiction enjoyed privately in the domestic sphere of the home or mass-produced images that might end up on the coffee table and the experience of going to the theater to enjoy a live performance of a play that friends and foes alike regarded as a *Judenstück*. As popular as ghetto tales and Oppenheim's prints may have been, and as important as they are as cultural-historical phenomena, they pale in comparison to this drama that millions of theatergoers came together to see performed for decades, in fifteen languages, across Europe, North America, and the British Empire.

The pleasures that *Deborah* and *Leah* afforded Jews and non-Jews alike were public pleasures, pleasures enjoyed in social spaces where Jews encountered Jewishness produced on stage for an audience that was almost always mixed. What this means for the way Jews experienced their own Jewish identity is the final question to be explored in this chapter, and here, too, we will be investigating a phenomenon that has typically not captured the attention of Jewish historians. Before we can address the significance of the play for Jews, accordingly, we need to consider some of the reasons that the *Deborah* craze has eluded the gaze of historians.

Jewish historians have traditionally relied heavily on the Jewish press, and as Klaus Hödl has argued, when it comes to Jews' consumption of and involvement with popular culture, the use of Jewish newspapers as source material has at times created a distorted image of the past. As Hödl points out, focusing on turn-of-the-century Vienna, Jewish newspapers—with their natural interests in Jewish community life, religious affairs, and other specifically Jewish concerns—rarely address contemporary urban forms of popular culture. In the mainstream Viennese press during the same period, however, one frequently encounters advertisements for music halls and lowbrow forms of entertainment that publicize the availability of kosher food for their patrons, signaling a significant Jewish involvement with popular culture that has largely gone unnoticed by Jewish historians.[79]

Using the German-language Jewish press or statements by official Jewish community leaders to gauge the significance of Mosenthal's *Deborah* can yield a similarly misleading account of the historical record. Particularly in the play's early years, the popularity that it enjoyed among Jews and non-Jews was a phenomenon that unfolded largely without the authority or the blessings of traditional organs of Jewish communal life. At times, the play unleashed particularly harsh criticism in the Jewish press. Of course, the fact that Jews used the Jewish press to rail against Mosenthal's *Deborah* underscores indirectly the play's broad appeal. An examination of the criticism that Jewish community leaders typically leveled at Mosenthal will thus help illuminate the contours of the unique experience of Jewishness that *Deborah* and *Leah* engendered among Jewish theatergoers.

Ludwig Philippson's *Allgemeine Zeitung des Judenthums*, the most widely circulated Jewish newspaper in the world in the mid-nineteenth century, reacted with alarm to the tremendous popularity that *Deborah* experienced in the German theater world, explicitly calling on its readers to resist the *Deborah* craze. This review deserves to be quoted at length, precisely because it flies in the face of much of what we have seen in this chapter:

> It is very strange indeed. The entire world is captivated by "Mosenthal's *Deborah*," the entire world leaves the theater very pleased, and I—truly I am beginning to doubt myself—I am almost outraged. This drama was written by a Jew? . . . The poet has allotted everything in the play that is bad and displeasing, repulsive and nasty, to the Jews and assigned everything that is noble, inviting, peaceful, and affectionate to the Christians.

From the lips of the Jews we hear cursing, passion, and baseness; from the lips of the Christian we are served up blessing, benevolence, and reassurance. Even when we see the Christian mob flaring up and raging against the Jews without reason, it turns out that the instigation of a baptized Jew was behind it all. Peace and happiness in love are the lot of the Christians, particularly once they keep away from the Jews; even the baptized Jew finds peace at the end. The Jews themselves, however, collectively wander around a bit like Gypsies and then set off for America. This is the work of a Jew!

In truth! Here we have again the sort of pandering to Christians that has been the sin so many Jews commit against the genius of Judaism and the genius of truth! This flirtation with Christians goes so far, in fact, that the flirter does not refrain from attacking his coreligionists and his religion in order to gain entry into Christian society. . . .

The Jew who leaves the theater pleased with *Deborah* is the Jew who is easy to please, the Jew who is pleased when a Christian says hello or extends an invitation to him. But the Jew who demands something higher, who is conscious of his 4,000-year lineage and his world-overcoming religion, the Jew who can imagine something other than the ghetto Jew of the last decades—this Jew will turn away from *Deborah* in disgust.[80]

For the reviewer in the *Allgemeine Zeitung des Judenthums*, *Deborah* does little more than pander to its non-Jewish audience; there is nothing that is authentically Jewish in the drama. The reviewer recognizes, of course, that Jews, like non-Jews, are going to the theater to see Mosenthal's blockbuster drama and not actually turning away from *Deborah* in disgust, as he suggests. It is against this backdrop, however, that the critic seeks to shame these Jews and expose their sinful ignorance of their history and religion. The rejection of Mosenthal's drama becomes in this way a litmus test for Jews' commitments to Judaism.

This spirited denunciation of Mosenthal's drama did not come out of nowhere. Philippson himself was a prolific writer of fiction, one of the prominent rabbi-novelists of the era. When it came to promoting new forms of Jewish literature and culture for the nineteenth century, the *Allgemeine Zeitung des Judenthums* pursued a strategic agenda that left little room for the sentimental ways in which Mosenthal's drama sought to forge common ground between Jews and non-Jews. Philippson, in particular, routinely sang the praises of his own preferred genre of heroic historical fiction, frequently singling out Leopold Kompert's popular ghetto tales for criticism that was almost as harsh as the vitriol reserved for Mosenthal.[81]

The disparaging view of *Deborah* in 1850 set the tone for the newspaper's ongoing criticism of *Deborah* in subsequent decades.[82] It also found itself echoed in equally polemical statements by other Jewish luminaries. The Viennese journalist Wilhelm Goldbaum wrote thirty years later that, like Mosenthal's *Erzählungen aus dem jüdischen Familienleben*, *Deborah* lacked any true Jewish specificity and pandered to non-Jews: "Mosenthal, after all, was always thirsty for applause, perhaps from Christians most of all."[83] In the orthodox world, *Deborah* provoked bitter criticism as well. Isaak Hirsch, son of Rabbi Samson Raphael Hirsch, the most prominent modern orthodox rabbi of the century, commented in 1859 in a journal edited by his father that *Deborah* lacked any Jewish authenticity, offering little more than a caricature of Judaism, Jewish customs, and Jewish religious practices.[84] Marcus Lehmann, an orthodox rabbi and novelist in Mainz and the editor of the premier orthodox newspaper *Der Israelit: Ein Centralorgan für das orthodoxe Judenthum* (The Israelite: A Central Organ for Orthodox Judaism), wrote in 1863 that Mosenthal was completely out of touch with authentic Judaism. *Deborah* was certainly a "drama with Jewish figures" but it was one "written in a supremely un-Jewish spirit."[85]

In the German-speaking world, the theatrical experience of Jewishness that Mosenthal gave rise to in *Deborah* often did not earn the stamp of rabbinic authority or the approval of Jewish community leaders. Much to Mosenthal's dismay, the leaders of the Viennese Jewish community were appalled at *Deborah*'s Viennese premiere in 1849. Disturbed by the play's graphic portrayal of anti-Jewish persecution in Act I and the scheming of the villagers against Deborah in Act II, they expressed their displeasure to an unnerved Mosenthal in no uncertain terms: "May God forgive you for what you have done to us," Mosenthal was told, immediately after the premiere. "If Austria never emancipates the Jews, it will be the fault of this play."[86]

In many cases, it was not just Mosenthal's sensational interreligious love story but his persona as a public figure that provoked concern among members of the German Jewish elite. To be sure, Mosenthal boasted impeccable Jewish credentials. His uncle Moses Büdiger ran a highly regarded Jewish school in Kassel,[87] and another uncle, Karl Weil, the father of his wife (and first cousin), Lina, held an important post in the Austrian imperial government and was a highly respected figure in the Jewish community.[88] When Mosenthal originally came to Vienna in 1842, it was to serve as a tutor in the home of Moritz Goldschmidt, the senior representative for the House of Rothschild in Vienna.[89] In later years, after he became an established writer in Vienna, Mosenthal was famous among non-Jews for his fastidious observance of Yom Kippur.[90] He played an active role in Jewish community life as well, serving on the board of the Israelitischer Taubstummenverein (Israelite Association for the Deaf and

Dumb). At Mosenthal's funeral in 1877, in fact, one of the pupils from the Taubstummenverein recited kaddish, following a psalm sung by the celebrated cantor Salomon Sulzer and the eulogy by Adolf Jellinek, the prominent rabbi and famed orator of the Leopoldstädter Tempel in Vienna.[91]

But Mosenthal's commitments to Judaism often took on unconventional forms that earned reprimand in the Jewish press. Mosenthal took particular pride in the many medals and awards he earned for his contribution to the arts, and in his final years he often had himself photographed wearing his many decorations.[92] Much to the dismay of the Jewish authorities, it became known the day after Mosenthal's death that he had requested in his will that all his medals and awards be placed in the synagogue in his native Kassel, next to the medals of Jewish soldiers who fell in battle during the Franco-Prussian war. This demand provoked censure from the *Allgemeine Zeitung des Judenthums*, *Der Israelit*, other Jewish newspapers, and the Hessian rabbinate, all of which agreed that Mosenthal's request was in violation of Jewish law; some critics went further, noting that Mosenthal had demonstrated poor taste, providing yet more evidence of the author's vanity.[93] Another unusual bequest, to provide care for indigent new mothers in the Viennese Jewish hospital under the condition that these women name their daughters Lina—after Mosenthal's late wife— also triggered consternation in the Jewish press.[94]

The fact that *Deborah* came to experience such popularity among Jews in the absence of the approval of Jewish community leaders in the German-speaking world thus speaks volumes about the disconnect between the Jewish elite's vision of Judaism and the ways Jews on the ground sometimes experienced their Jewishness. To be sure, outside major urban centers, Mosenthal sometimes earned greater recognition from the Jewish authorities. When the Jewish community of Graz was founded in 1869, *Deborah* was on people's minds, Graz being the capital of the Austrian province where the action of *Deborah* was set. At the event marking the official creation of the small, new congregation—a synagogue was not even built until 1892—the board of directors gave a festive toast where they explicitly thanked Mosenthal. The author of *Deborah* figured here not as a Jewish writer pandering to a Christian audience but as a true pioneer, "the individual who first blazed the trail for this new homeland of the Jews in Styria."[95] For much of *Deborah*'s career in the German-speaking world, however, the scenarios we have examined in this chapter in which Jews and non-Jews came together to enjoy the pleasures of sentimental identification with Jewishness in the theater made up a cultural phenomenon that took place outside the boundaries of the official Jewish community, and sometimes without its approval.

Contrary to Philippson's hopes, then, Jews did not turn away from *Deborah* in disgust to embrace more institutionally valid forms of experiencing their Jewishness. In the decades following its premiere, *Deborah* came to enjoy unprecedented popularity among Jews, whether performed in German, English, Yiddish, or Hebrew.[96] By the late nineteenth century, moreover, many German Jewish luminaries had begun to celebrate Mosenthal for his sense of Jewish solidarity, occasionally expressing disbelief that Jewish leaders of his day had given him and the play such a hard time.[97] The American rabbi Henry Samuel Morais, the founding editor of the *Jewish Exponent*, also praised Mosenthal as an "Israelite whose heart beats in unison with the oppressed of his race" and whose *Deborah* thus "forcibly carries away all who listen," whether Jew or Gentile.[98] The further one moves away from domains where the German Jewish elite exercised authority, the more frequently one encounters a phenomenon that would have horrified the rabbinate in German-speaking Europe: in numerous cases in the late nineteenth and early twentieth centuries, *Deborah* came to play an important role in Jewish institutional life as well.

In April 1869, several weeks before the community in Graz was founded, Austrian actress Fanny Janauschek concluded her second major American tour with two high-profile benefit performances at the New York Academy of Music. Janauschek was rumored at that time to be studying English in preparation for her next American tour but was still performing exclusively in German. As we noted in Chapter 3, Janauschek enjoyed particular popularity among German-speaking Jews in America. Commentators at her American debut in October 1867 noted what a significant portion of her fans were Jews. When she opened with Grillparzer's *Medea* on Yom Kippur, she played to a small audience; her performance of *Deborah* two days later was extremely well attended.[99] At the first benefit in 1869, on Wednesday, April 21, Janauschek performed Schiller's *Die Braut von Messina* (The Bride of Messina) as a fund-raiser for New York's German Hospital (known today as Lenox Hill Hospital). The following Saturday evening, she gave a second benefit performance, for the Hebrew Free School Association, performing *Deborah* to raise funds for a prominent Jewish organization that sought to provide free-of-cost religious education to Jewish immigrant children.[100]

As the *Jewish Messenger* noted in its review of the benefit performance, Janauschek performed *Deborah* with her "usual force," delivering a performance that was both "fascinating and effective," and her rendition of the curse scene at the end of Act III was full of such "grandeur" that she earned three curtain calls. After the second curtain call following the curse scene, Abraham Oettinger and M. S. Isaacs, the president and secretary of the association, presented

Janauschek with a letter thanking her profusely for using one of her greatest roles to help the association in its "benevolent labor of importing a free Hebrew education to the Israelitish youth of this city."[101] The event netted $1,000 (more than $17,000 today), clear proof that, contrary to Philippson's expectations two decades earlier, performances of *Deborah* could make tangible contributions to Jewish communities and to institutions promoting Jewish religious life. Indeed, precisely the extravagant performance of Old Testament vengeance that Philippson felt was in poor taste served here to bolster Jewish community life, becoming the backdrop for an alliance between the touring Austrian actress and American Jewish community leaders that benefited immigrant children who would otherwise not have been able to receive a Jewish education.

Janauschek's performance of *Deborah* in 1869 was not the only time a Jewish organization used Mosenthal's play to raise money for Jewish causes. In the 1920s, the Viola Wilson Stock Company in the summer resort town of Monticello, New York, in the Catskills, presented a performance of *Leah* as a benefit for the local Jewish General Aid Society.[102] In 1911, one year after hosting the annual convention of the Federation of American Zionists, the Zionist Council of Pittsburgh was inspired by Yiddish actress Bertha Kalich's success with *Deborah* to choose Daly's *Leah, the Forsaken* for an all-Jewish cast to perform at a high-profile fund-raising benefit that was widely reported on in the general press.[103] As the Zionist Council noted, "those who have followed the tribulations of the Jewish people during the last century" will find both the "theme and locale of the drama" familiar, and this amateur production of one "of the most celebrated old plays in the history of the stage" sought to give a performance that would "in every detail equal any ever presented in this country."[104] For the Zionists in western Pennsylvania, Mosenthal's vivid portrayal of Jewish suffering hardly pandered to Christian audiences. *Leah* was, rather, the perfect drama to perform in the name of the Jewish nationalist cause. (Clearly, it proved convenient for the amateur actors in Pittsburgh that both the character of Ruben and his unequivocal pronouncement that "the old city of Zion is dead and will never be resurrected" never made their way into Daly's version of the play.)

Part of the reason that the Pittsburgh Zionist council could turn to *Leah* so easily was that Mosenthal, *Deborah*, and *Leah* had all become fixtures in American Jewish life by the second decade of the twentieth century. Six months after Mosenthal's death in 1877, a new B'nai Brith Lodge in Boston was named the "Mosenthal Lodge" to commemorate the "author of 'Deborah,' and numerous Jewish tales," with the hope that the charter members of this new chapter of B'nai Brith would "do honor to the name the Lodge has chosen."[105] As we have mentioned earlier, scenes from *Deborah* and *Leah* were frequently reprinted in acting manuals and selections of materials for dramatic recitals. The curse

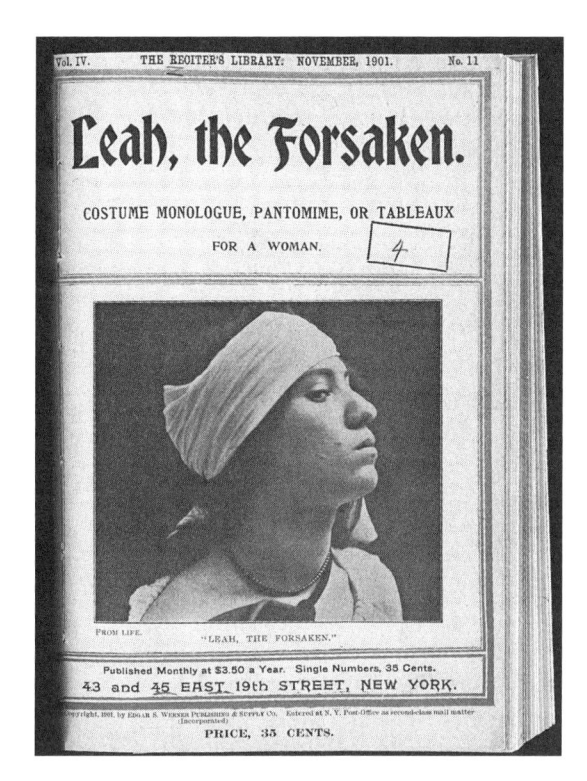

Figure 61. This costume monologue version of *Leah*, a set of eleven illustrative poses with photographs, originally appeared in *Werner's Magazine* in 1901, with photographs by Otto Sarony, son of the celebrated theatrical photographer Napoleon Sarony. General Research Division, New York Public Library, Astor, Lenox and Tilden Foundations.

scene, in particular, was a favorite among established actresses and amateurs well into the early twentieth century. Aspiring Jewish actresses did not just participate in this phenomenon; in a development that German Jewish leaders could not have foreseen, young Jewish women in the United States frequently performed selections from *Deborah* and *Leah* in Jewish community settings and as part of Jewish communal events.

In 1879, for instance, a certain Josephine Koch gave a moving rendition of selections from *Leah* at a high-profile evening of entertainment at the Maimonides Library Association in New York. Koch's selections from *Leah* were sandwiched between a German-language lecture on the relationship between religion, art, and science; piano and violin solos; and dramatic recitations, all of which were followed by a reception and dance.[106] In Philadelphia in 1891, Miss Emma M. Silberman presented a scene from *Leah* in costume at a variety show to raise funds for Herman Solomon, a young Jewish band leader who had lost all his money in the Keystone Bank failure. Silberman's "powerful" performance of the scene from *Leah*—she apparently played both Leah and Rudolph—was presented alongside vocal solos by members of Philadelphia's Adath Jeshurun congregation, performances by Solomon's band, in his absence, and a violin solo by the well-known Jewish violinist Max Weil.[107] In 1890, the Manette Club, a new organization consisting of prominent Jewish citizens of Pittsburgh and Allegheny (a city annexed by Pittsburgh in the early twentieth century), gathered at Cyclorama Hall for a promenade concert and ball. The concert portion of the evening included musical and dramatic selections performed by Jewish teenagers, including Miss Lillian Burkhart's rendition of the curse scene from *Leah*.[108] In Providence, Rhode Island, in 1908, the First Grand Concert and Ball given by the Silverman Brothers Mutual Relief Association opened with five numbers performed largely by members of the Goldberg family, with Miss Laura Goldberg giving a performance of the curse scene from *Leah*.[109] Even as late as 1932, the Young Israel All Star Dramatic Night in Roxbury, Massachusetts, gave second prize to the drama club from a Jewish girls' school that had entered the competition performing *Leah, the Forsaken* with two of its female pupils, Cella Magnet and Ida Sklar, in the main roles.[110]

* * *

Despite the initial reproaches of the German Jewish elite, then, the figure of Mosenthal's Jewess proved captivating to Jews, continuing to command attention well into the early twentieth century, long after Mosenthal's play had fallen out of fashion. This chapter, indeed, has given us a window on a mode of experiencing Jewishness that differs considerably from what emanated from the synagogue or other central institutions of Jewish life in the nineteenth and early twentieth centuries. In its formative years, the type of Jewishness that *Deborah* and its various incarnations set into play was not one produced by Jews primarily for Jews. It emerged, rather, as the product of encounters between Jews and non-Jews, in social spaces where Jews and non-Jews interacted with each other in a variety of roles—as actors, writers, composers, orchestra conductors, musicians, set painters, advertisers, theater managers, and, not least of all, audience members. In all these cases, the melodramatic, sentimental model of Jewishness enacted on stage was, like all theatrical performances, obviously situated at a remove from the exigencies of real life. But the relative autonomy of the theater was important precisely because of its abilities to make connections between the depictions of Jews on stage and the bustling forms of Jewish life outside the theater. Mosenthal's *Deborah*, to be sure, neither simply reflected real forms of Jewishness outside the theater nor did it somehow establish models of Jewish behavior that Jews might choose to imitate in real life after the curtain fell. Indeed, wherever it was performed and in whatever version, *Deborah* was a highly stylized theatrical event. But productions of *Deborah* hardly unfolded in a sphere abstracted from the world of nineteenth-century Jewish life. As it rendered the performance of Jewishness a mode of entertainment for Jews and non-Jews alike, *Deborah* forged connections between Jews and non-Jews, both on and off stage, and both inside and outside the theater.

Daly's invocation of a shared sphere between Jews and non-Jews as he had Hall brand H. L. Bateman a modern Shylock was thus much more than a scene in a courtroom drama engineered to get Daly recognized as a great playwright on par with Shakespeare. It reflected a key element of the *Deborah* craze from the moment that Mosenthal sought to get his *Judenstück* performed on the German stage in the late 1840s. Over and over again, performances of Mosenthal's *Deborah* converted the theater into a place where Jews and non-Jews came together to indulge in a good cry, congratulating themselves on their own liberal sentiments as they wept together to feel the joys of Jewish pain and suffering. In this sense, the *Deborah* craze needs to be recognized, from the perspective of Jewish history, as one of the most significant cultural events in nineteenth-century Jewish life. Obviously, from the perspective of some Jewish elites, *Deborah* may have unleashed an uncomfortable cultural phenomenon. The popularity of the play among Jews from the moment of its premiere through the early twentieth century, however, speaks volumes about its significance as a factor shaping the way Jews thought and felt about themselves and their relations to the non-Jewish world. The *Deborah* craze played a key role in creating affective communities that rendered liberal affect synonymous with sympathy with Jewish suffering, giving generations of theatergoers the sense that tears shed in identification with Jewish suffering meant something. For Jews, participating in this popular cultural phenomenon meant being a part of a transnational community of sentimental compassion that they themselves decisively helped form, a community they helped shape as both subjects and objects.

Concluding Remarks

Jewishness, Theatricality, and the Legacy of *Deborah*

Mosenthal Contra Wagner, or, the Virtues of Philosemitism

In his antisemitic rant "Das Judenthum in der Musik" (Judaism in Music, 1850), the celebrated composer Richard Wagner famously turned his back on the liberalism of the 1848 revolution and its vision of extending equal rights to Jews. Claiming that the liberal principles of the failed revolutions of 1848 ultimately amounted to a "not very clairvoyant mental game," Wagner directed his energies at vindicating the "instinctive dislike" and "involuntary repellence" that Jews allegedly provoked in non-Jews. For Wagner, any appeal to grant Jews rights in the name of a universal humanity was doomed to fail because of the impossibility of developing "genuine sympathy" with Jews. It was not the Jews' religion that made liberal ideals of universalism difficult to sustain in practice. It was, rather, what Wagner termed *jüdisches Wesen*, that is, the Jews' essence, their very being. Arguing along these lines, Wagner emphasized the Jews' alien, unaesthetic looks, their unpleasant, foreign-sounding speech, and their inability to create art. Grafting these proto-racial arguments onto anxieties about capitalism and the commercialization of culture, he cited the power of Jewish money and the Jews' addiction to turning culture into a commodity to be bought and sold as further evidence to justify the "aversion" that non-Jews naturally and justifiably feel in the presence of Jews.[1]

Particularly after Wagner reissued his anonymously published essay under his own name as a pamphlet in 1869, the vision of German culture under siege by Jewishness that his essay fueled gained traction, especially in the music world.[2] Wagner's controversial polemics never became mainstream in the nineteenth century, but in the German-speaking world, they were ubiquitous, whether in the daily press or in writings by elites. Not surprisingly, as we noted in Chapter 1, polemics against Mosenthal's *Deborah*, with its obvious effort to elicit sympathy for Jewish suffering, often echoed Wagner's diatribes. Some critics reacted to the play's commercial success and its power to generate liberal feelings of identification with Jews by invoking Wagner's insistence on the unnatural power that Jews were wielding over German culture as a whole. Whether *Deborah* was praised for promoting a sentimental mode of liberalism that helped consign Jew-hatred to the past or denounced for epitomizing the problems that Wagner's critique of Jewishness in contemporary culture sought to bring to the surface, the philosemitism of Mosenthal's play was often defined in relation to Wagner's distinctly modern form of antisemitism.

From Otto Nicolai's *Die lustigen Weiber von Windsor* (The Merry Wives of Windsor, 1849) to Karl Goldmark's *Die Königin von Saba* (The Queen of Sheba, 1875) and Ignaz Brüll's *Das goldene Kreuz* (The Golden Cross, 1875), Mosenthal composed more opera libretti than any other German-language playwright of his generation. While he and Wagner crossed paths at times, Wagner never deigned to mention either Mosenthal or *Deborah* directly in any of his writings.[3] "Das Judenthum in der Musik," nevertheless, first appeared just one year after *Deborah* had begun enthralling theater audiences in the German-speaking world. At one key moment, Wagner's essay on contemporary music indulged in telling comments about the propriety of representing Jews on stage: "It is inconceivable for us that this [unattractive Jewish] exterior should ever be the subject of the arts of representation. When visual art represents Jews, it takes its models mostly from fantasy, wisely ennobling or completely omitting everything that characterizes the Jews' appearance for us in common life. Never, though, does the Jew wander onto the theatrical stage. The exceptions here are so rare and unusual that they only confirm the general rule. It is impossible for us to imagine a Jew representing an ancient or a modern character on stage—be it a hero or a lover—without instinctively sensing the absurd incongruity of such an idea."[4]

In 1850, when Wagner first published these lines, Rachel Félix was arguably the most famous actress in the world, and *Deborah* had already begun to take the German theater world by storm. Claiming in this context that Jews "never wander onto the theatrical stage"—whether as actors or as characters represented by non-Jews—was thus patently counterfactual. Wagner's essay on "Judaism in music" offered up an outright denial of the extent to which mid-nineteenth-century theater audiences were, in fact, not repelled by but singularly attracted to experiencing Jews and Jewishness in the theater.

"What good actor today is *not*—a Jew?" Friedrich Nietzsche asked several decades later, equating Jewishness with theatricality.[5] As we mentioned in the Introduction, Nietzsche's provocative question invoked a long tradition of regarding the Jews' integration into the modern world as a phenomenon akin to acting (or aping)—a form of pretense to be approached with the same level of suspicion traditionally reserved for the theater. Writing at a moment when

Mosenthal's play was rendering compassion with Jewish suffering as the ultimate theatrical pleasure, Wagner took a different approach from that of Nietzsche. As theater audiences were reveling in the joys of feeling Deborah's Jewish pain and suffering, Wagner declared such pleasures paradoxical, writing as if the deep connections between theatricality and Jewishness that we have seen come to light in the *Deborah* craze simply did not exist. Our investigation into the transnational performance history of Mosenthal's drama in its many incarnations has shed light on a world in which Jewishness and theatricality were deeply intertwined with each other, and without the negative inflection that Nietzsche forced on this relationship. Mosenthal's philosemitism here was not just defined in relation to Wagner by critics who rejected it. Wagner's antisemitism itself also emerged in part, indirectly, as a reaction to the *Deborah* craze. "Das Judenthum in der Musik" was not just attacking the perceived power of Jews in German culture. Wagner's fantasy of a theater devoid of Jewishness was also reacting to the ways Jews and non-Jews alike were coming together in the theater to produce and experience idealized forms of Jewishness.

How are we ultimately to understand the relationship between the positive connections between Jewishness and theatricality that we have been exploring over the course of this book and the negative configurations of this same relationship that rear their heads in Nietzsche's and Wagner's polemics? Mosenthal's play, to be sure, was neither written nor performed with the principal goal of combating antisemitism. Similarly, the antisemitic polemics of Wagner's "Das Judenthum in der Musik" were hardly directed primarily or even explicitly at Mosenthal. Yet for many in the nineteenth century, these two phenomena functioned as inverted images of each other. Indirectly, Wagner's antisemitism and the *Deborah* craze were cultural phenomena responding to each other. What, then, are we to make of the structural similarity between the philosemitism of the *Deborah* phenomenon and the form of antisemitism that we find spelled out with such passion and venom in Wagner's treatise?

In an oft-cited essay, sociologist Zygmunt Bauman used the term "allosemitism"—a term coined by the Polish Jewish literary critic Artur Sandauer—to describe what antisemitism and philosemitism have in common at their core: the practice of "setting Jews apart as people radically different from all the others" and along with this profound insistence on Jewish difference, a "radically *ambivalent* attitude" toward Jews. For Bauman, both antisemitism and philosemitism hinge on a notion of "the Jew as such," that is, an abstract vision of Jews that is "located at secure distance from experience and immune to whatever emotions may be aroused by daily intercourse." In and of itself, Bauman stresses, allosemitism is neutral, neither positive nor negative in the way it evaluates the radical Jewish difference whose existence it posits. For Bauman, understanding the fundamental connections between allosemitism's manifestations as philosemitism and antisemitism sheds light on the fundamental ambivalence toward Jews that is at the very heart of Western culture; this, in turn, ultimately helps us grasp how antisemitism could gain such a stronghold in the twentieth century.[6]

As we have commented at several junctures, ambivalence toward Jews played a pivotal role in the thrills offered by *Deborah*. Starting with Mosenthal's original script, with its reveling in Jewish exoticism and its call for the extravagant performance of Old Testament vengeance, the *Deborah* craze was inextricable from a hypostatized vision of Jewish difference. For so many of its adapters, as we saw in Chapter 2, it was precisely this ambivalence that made Deborah's and Leah's Jewishness so alluring. But to what extent is it illuminating to insist on the structural similarity of this ambivalence to a form of antisemitism that clearly functioned as the antithesis of Mosenthal's sentimental liberalism? Like some of the other scholars we discussed in the Introduction, Bauman ultimately presents philosemitism as inherently problematic, a phenomenon necessarily related, via allosemitism, to antisemitism. To be sure, Mosenthal's *Deborah*, in its various incarnations, did promote an abstract vision of the Jew or the Jewess as such at the same time as it sought to promote the sympathy with Jews that Wagner deemed a contradiction in terms. Even as a melodrama, however, Mosenthal's *Deborah* was not "located at secure distance from experience and immune to whatever emotions may be aroused by daily intercourse." The *Deborah* craze was hardly a product of abstract fantasies that non-Jews held about Jews. It was, rather, as we saw particularly in Chapter 4, produced, sustained, and enjoyed by Jews and non-Jews working together in tandem. It was a mode of Jewishness—however abstract and ambivalent—that was nevertheless enjoyed and sometimes coproduced on the ground by empirical Jews, generating emotions in daily life that often brought Jews and non-Jews together.

In this context, it is telling that Wagner expends so much energy delineating the forms of aversion and repellence that real-life Jews allegedly incite in non-Jews. Following Bauman to situate the philosemitism of the *Deborah* craze on a spectrum of allosemitic phenomena that includes Wagner, however, blinds us to the fundamental difference between the dynamic interactions between Jews and non-Jews that produced this alluring model of theatrical Jewishness and Wagner's fantasy of banning Jews and Jewishness from the theater. As one of the nineteenth-century German theater's most commercially successful dramas, *Deborah*, in its various forms, reached millions of theatergoers, far more people than likely ever sat down to read through Wagner's antisemitic rant from beginning to end. Is it really appropriate to regard these two phenomena as flip sides of the same coin?

As we saw when analyzing Mosenthal's original script and its many adaptations in Chapters 1 and 2, the compassion with Jewish suffering that the *Deborah* craze sought to engender was, to some extent, inseparable from lingering ambivalence about Jews. The sources about the drama's performance and reception that we examined in Chapters 3 and 4 admittedly did little to reveal how performances of Old Testament vengeance may have helped reinforce stereotypes about Jews. Particularly given that the curse scene was a central aspect of the allure of performances of Mosenthal's material, it certainly stands to reason that *Deborah* or *Leah* may have promoted notions about Jews and vengeance that might make some people today uncomfortable. Yet both amid and through this ambivalence, performances of Mosenthal's play generated sympathy for Jews, calling on Jews and non-Jews alike to identify with Jewish suffering. In understanding the affective work that the drama performed in its historical context, it makes little sense to emphasize what may make us uncomfortable today at the expense of grasping the comforting sense of compassion with Jewish suffering that the drama afforded both Jewish and non-Jewish spectators in the nineteenth century.

Generating feelings of goodwill within the theater, of course, is not the same as political intervention. In many instances, as we have commented, this theatrical "Jewess whose woes have made a million weep" may have indeed promoted complacency and self-congratulatory sentiments among theatergoers who found themselves moved by the play.[7] The liberal pleasures that *Deborah* and *Leah* produced worked so well, indeed, precisely because they were not directly political, because they rarely took theatergoers outside their comfort zones. We make a grave error, nevertheless, if we insist on rejecting the affective communities of compassion with Jewish suffering that this play helped generate in theaters across Europe and North America for decades as insignificant for this reason. For a good part of the nineteenth century, millions of Jews and non-Jews came together in theaters to enjoy the pleasures of Jewish suffering, giving rise to a unique experience of Jewishness that was neither simply an abstract fantasy of the Gentile imagination nor necessarily in sync with the more institutionally sanctioned forms of Judaism that were promoted in synagogues, institutions of Jewish learning, or the numerous newspapers that addressed themselves toward a primarily Jewish readership. Reducing this phenomenon to an expression of philosemitism that we should regard as inextricable from the forms of antisemitism that it so obviously unsettles blinds us to the tremendous appeal that this play held and continued to hold for decades as it repeatedly performed Jewishness on stage for an eager audience of Jewish and non-Jewish spectators.

Part of the reason that this phenomenon has receded from our radar has to do with the way Jewish literature and culture are often still studied today, namely, as a discrete body of texts and cultural artifacts often set in relation to a well-defined body of Jews, typically accompanied by normative assumptions about what constitutes authentic Jewish experience. Ruth Wisse, in her award-winning book *The Modern Jewish Canon* (2000), defined modern Jewish literature as the "repository of modern Jewish experience" and thus the "most complete way of knowing the inner life of the Jews." The "concept of modern Jewish literature," Wisse insisted, "would have no value whatsoever if one were not prepared to respect the autonomy of Jewishness, and respect for that autonomy would have to be implicit in any work of Jewish literature."[8] In recent years, scholars such as Jonathan Freedman, Lisa Silverman, and Benjamin Schreier have put forth new and more productive models, insisting on the value of studying literary and cultural constructions of Jewishness and Jewish difference without necessarily anchoring them in the study of those who identify as Jews.[9] *Deborah*, not surprisingly, does not make it into Wisse's canon of Jewish texts worthy of study. The *Deborah* craze commands our interest here precisely because it did not respect Wisse's "autonomy of Jewishness." Indeed, as Rabbi Ludwig Philippson and other German Jewish luminaries recognized as they rejected *Deborah* in the mid-nineteenth century, the Jewishness of Mosenthal's drama took on a life of its own outside the influence they exerted in houses of worship or the Jewish press. The Jewishness of *Deborah* was created not by Jews but by Jews and non-Jews coming together to produce and enjoy both the theatrical pleasures of Jewishness and the Jewish pleasures of the theater. When confronted by this, one of the most prominent transnational Jewish cultural phenomena of the nineteenth century, Wisse's model of Jewish literature concedes its limits.

The problem here, nevertheless, is not just that the field of modern Jewish literary studies has often lacked a conceptual apparatus to recognize and appreciate the significance of *Deborah* and its distinctive mode of Jewishness. As one of the preeminent theatrical star vehicles from the heyday of stage melodrama, *Deborah* itself was ill equipped to survive the nineteenth century. It is telling, in this context, that Mosenthal's material yielded three silent films in the first decades of the twentieth century but never a feature-length sound film nor any significant stage revivals after the 1920s. Indeed, the romantic figure of the suffering beautiful Jewess so central to *Deborah*'s phenomenal success never truly made the transition to modernism. Later, in the German-speaking world, Mosenthal's works were banned by the Nazis, along with those by all other Jewish authors. In postwar Germany, theaters often used Gotthold Ephraim Lessing's classic Enlightenment drama *Nathan der Weise* (Nathan the Wise, 1779) to reconnect with a repressed liberal tradition of tolerance and goodwill toward Jews, sometimes casting prominent Jewish actors in the title role.[10] For the last seventy years, Lessing's *Nathan* and its abstract humanism have served this function well, proving more useful than the once far more popular *Deborah*, with its deeply ambivalent Jewish heroine and its extravagant performances of Jewish difference. For both political and aesthetic reasons, it is hard to imagine the melodramatic excesses of the curse scene making a comeback anytime soon, whether on Broadway, in acting manuals, or at the Burgtheater in Mosenthal's Vienna.

The Return of the Jewess

The "Jewess whose woes have made a million weep" as she took nineteenth-century stages by storm has not disappeared entirely from contemporary culture. If Sandra Goldbacher's British period film *The Governess* (1998) had been a nineteenth-century novel, it could just as easily have been called *The Jewess*.[11] Set in England in the 1830s, *The Governess* tells the story of Rosina da Silva (Minnie Driver), a beautiful, dark-haired Jewish woman who grows up in the Sephardic community in London. Goldbacher enhances the exoticism of her heroine and her milieu by foregrounding the luxurious exteriors and bright colors of Rosina's home and clothing and by using a soundtrack of Ladino and Middle Eastern music sung by Israeli Yemenite singer Ofra Haza. After Rosina's father is murdered on the streets because of unpaid debts—he turns out to have been more like Shylock than Lessing's Nathan, it seems—Rosina seeks to support her family. Leaving London behind and making a secret of her Jewish background, she reinvents herself as Mary Blackchurch, a Protestant governess whose mother's partial Italian ancestry explains her dark looks, and she takes a position in the Hebrides on the Isle of Skye. Here she develops a romantic relationship with her married employer, Charles Cavendish (Tom Wilkinson), and also provokes the interest of his Oxford dropout son Henry (Jonathan Rhys Meyers), who eventually discovers her true identity and becomes consumed by, and overjoyed at, his attraction to the exotic Jewess.

On the surface, *The Governess* seems as if it could be yet another lush adaptation of a nineteenth-century novel rather than a film with an original screenplay that Goldbacher developed out of the fictional diary that she originally wrote for Rosina. The opening sequence of *The Governess* follows Rosina leaving synagogue heading home, where she stops to admire a poster for the premier appearance of Rachel Félix, advertised here not just as "La Grande Tragedienne" but as a "Jewess" and the "Jewel of Paris." Indeed, as we find out minutes later, Rosina dreams of becoming an actress like Rachel, and she also has a role model in her own family, her unmarried aunt Sofka da Silva, a renowned opera singer. Sure enough, as Rosina encounters the poster advertising

Rachel's upcoming appearances on stage, a prostitute approaches her, bares her breast, and asks, "Jew girl, Jew girl, want some lessons?" *The Governess* thus opens by foregrounding the same connections between Jewesses, prostitutes, and actresses that we saw in Annie Lewis's impromptu rendition of Leah at the Memphis police station in the Introduction. The fact that the name of Goldbacher's protagonist is reminiscent of Sarah Bernhardt's original first name, Rosine, is certainly no accident in this context. Nor will readers of this book be surprised to encounter numerous moments where Rosina—like Deborah and Leah before her—experiences and visibly expresses great discomfort in the presence of crosses. Goldbacher even includes a scene where Rosina, secretly celebrating a Passover seder by herself in her room on the Isle of Skye, drapes herself in a male prayer shawl just as actresses playing Deborah did on occasion.

In *The Governess*, then, the nineteenth-century figure of the beautiful Jewess returns with a vengeance. Particularly in the context of the conclusion to this book, *The Governess* is important for the systematic way in which it both revives and subverts the figure of the beautiful Jewess at the core of the popularity of Mosenthal's material. Rosina is far less passive and submissive and far feistier and more sexually aware than her nineteenth-century precursors. The film also includes a level of open discussion and expression of sexuality that one would be hard-pressed to find in any adaptation of *Deborah* or *Leah*. It is, however, the alternative history for the invention of photography that the plot of *The Governess* hinges on that ultimately grants the figure of the Jewess a radically different function from anything that we have seen over the course of this book. Rosina's employer, Charles Cavendish, devotes all his time to scientific experiments to capture images on paper, and it is by assisting Cavendish in these efforts and his race with Louis Daguerre—the inventor of the daguerreotype—and others that Rosina first gets to know her employer and enters into an affair with him.[12] Ultimately, it is not Cavendish but Rosina who discovers the missing link in their process and figures out how to fix photographic images on paper. She does so thanks to an accident during her private seder, spilling the ceremonial saltwater onto a photograph.

Cavendish does not just fail to give Rosina credit for her discovery when presenting their work to a visiting member of the Scottish Royal Society. He also insists on being the one behind the camera at all times, allowing Rosina to be only his assistant or his subject. Rosina, though knowledgeable about botany, finds Cavendish's predilections for photographing fossils and natural historical specimens dull. She eventually persuades him to attempt to create works of beauty featuring the human form. While playing Mary Blackchurch on the Isle of Skye, Rosina continues her passion for acting by dressing up as classic beautiful Jewesses—Salomé and Queen Esther—for erotic photo shoots in Cavendish's studio. Ultimately, however, she abandons acting to take a place behind the camera. It is this move—along with Cavendish's refusal to give her credit for her discovery—that causes their relationship to unravel. At one point after their lovemaking, Rosina quietly stations herself behind the camera. She takes a photograph of Cavendish sleeping, entirely naked, positioning his limbs to create an image of her Gentile lover as both erotic and vulnerable.[13] Cavendish is infuriated when he discovers that he has been recorded as the erotic object of Rosina's photographic gaze. He promptly ends the relationship.

At this point in the plot, *The Governess* refuses to follow in the footsteps of *Deborah* and morph into *Rosina, the Forsaken*. Rather than indulging in a theatrical performance of Old Testament vengeance and cursing her lover, Rosina forsakes acting entirely to take a more creative form of revenge. She quietly enters the dining room, and with the entire family present, she delivers the vapid Mrs. Cavendish a copy of her photographic study of her husband naked. Rosina then abandons the persona of Mary Blackchurch and gives up her plain-Jane governess garb. Dressed again as a Jewess, she leaves the Cavendish home and returns to London. As in *Deborah* and *Leah*, the final sequence of *The Governess* takes place several years later, to present a scene of reconciliation between the Jewess and the Christian world that wronged her. Reconciliation here, however, transpires not just in an entirely Jewish milieu but entirely according to Rosina's terms. We find Rosina back in the Sephardic community in London, established as a prominent professional photographer known and admired for the images that she creates "captur[ing] the beauty of my father's people." Rosina, then, becomes a sort of Anglo Jewish Moritz Daniel Oppenheim, with the difference that the photographs she takes that we see hanging in her studio clearly individualize their subjects rather than create patriarchal family scenes such as the Oppenheim seder painting that we considered in the Introduction. In many ways, indeed, Rosina appears more like a Jewish Lady Clementina Hawarden. The final sequence of the film opens with Rosina performing a photo shoot of two adolescent girls, reminiscent of the costume tableau of Hawarden's two daughters, dressed as Leah, that we considered in the opening pages of this book. The fact that the Cavendish girl whom she is hired to educate is named Clementina certainly invites this association as well. We learn from the voiceover that concludes the film that Rosina is not just admired as a Jewish photographer. Her photographs have crossover appeal as well, and she is scheduled to give a lecture at the Royal Society on her work.

In the final scene of *The Governess*, Rosina—unlike Deborah or Leah—neither forgives those who wronged her nor does she express regret over the way she acted several years earlier. Instead, Cavendish shows up in her home studio to be photographed, now fully submitting to the authority she exercises behind the camera in her visibly Jewish studio: "I'm in your hands, Miss Da Silva. Do with me what you will." While visibly unsettled by the encounter, Rosina tells Cavendish after the sitting that they are "quite done" and simply sends him on his way. Before the film concludes, we hear a voiceover, with Rosina telling the viewers repeatedly that she hardly thinks of her days as Mary Blackchurch on the Isle of Skye. "Work is a wonderful restorative," Rosina tells us, as she proceeds to sit for a photographic self-portrait, occupying the dual position of the eye behind the camera and the subject to be photographed.

Like Deborah and Leah, Rosina sublimates her desire. But unlike her nineteenth-century precursors, Rosina does not die, disappear, or wander off with her people, channeling her love for Joseph/Rudolf into a love of all humanity. Goldbacher's film patently refuses any melodramatic spectacle of suffering Jewish femininity. Rather, Rosina renounces acting and her dreams of the theater and comes to occupy a position of power behind the camera. Like Deborah and Leah, she occupies a familiar position of relative isolation, but she is not the object of pity and compassion at the end of the film. Spectators here are not encouraged to feel good about how bad they feel about her suffering. Rather, in *The Governess*, the Jewess emerges triumphant, photographing herself as the film celebrates her own artistic voice as a modern portraitist of contemporary Jewish life. In nineteenth-century burlesques of *Leah*, Leah often managed to live happily ever after, whether embracing the fortunate prospect of living rent-free with Rudolf and Madalena or finding unlikely love in the arms of Nathan the schoolmaster or the village priest. The laughter that these comic recastings of Mosenthal's material provoked served as a clear inversion of, and commentary on, the tears that the conclusion of *Leah* generally produced. Using the figure of the beautiful Jewess to displace this entire tradition, Goldbacher's film disrupts the connections between Jewishness and theatricality that sustained the *Deborah* craze from the moment of the drama's premiere in 1849 well into the early part of the twentieth century. In their place, she offers us an indirect model of herself as an Anglo Jewish filmmaker, empowering herself through a brilliant rewriting of the theatrical figure of the beautiful Jewess.

When it was released in 1998, *The Governess* played in art-house movie theaters in major metropolitan centers. Although never widely released, Goldbacher's film earned generally positive reviews in both the Jewish and the general press. In this sense as well, *The Governess* differs considerably from the theatrical tradition of *Deborah* and *Leah* that it creatively reconfigures. As we have seen throughout this book, the allure of *Deborah* and *Leah* was not a cultural phenomenon of or for the elite. *Deborah* and *Leah*, rather, were part and parcel of nineteenth-century popular culture, often achieving widespread acceptance and commercial success without highbrow critics' stamp of approval. For decades, millions of nineteenth-century theatergoers felt sympathy with Mosenthal's forsaken Jewess, experiencing their common humanity by indulging in a good cry over Deborah's or Leah's woes. With its unequivocal celebration of the power of film and the camera, Goldbacher's film maintains no trace whatsoever of the significance of these tears.

Lachrymose History Revisited

For much of the latter half of the nineteenth century, *Deborah* and *Leah* brought Jews and non-Jews together in the relatively unauthorized space of popular culture and gave them an important collective experience that has been systematically overlooked by Jewish historians: the pleasure of a good cry. In the early twentieth century, the pioneering historian Salo Baron helped create the field of modern Jewish history by railing against what he famously termed the "lachrymose conception of Jewish history," that is, a bleak vision of the Jewish past as defined by suffering, persecution, and victimhood, on the one hand; and great moments of scholarly achievement, on the other.[14] The image of the premodern past that *Deborah* created certainly conforms to the paradigm that Baron challenged. Indeed, with its vision of an epochal shift from a world of medieval persecution and victimhood to the more liberal and tolerant political order that becomes visible by the end of the play, Mosenthal's drama itself contributed to a lachrymose conception of Jewish history. Our investigation into the *Deborah* craze is important, however, because it has laid bare the dynamic and productive functions that such lachrymose visions of the Jewish past took on in the nineteenth century, particularly when it came to forms of popular culture that mediated between Jews and non-Jews. Whatever its merits as a mode of studying the Jewish past, the lachrymose conception of Jewish history did not just promote a vision of premodern Jews as victims of oppression and persecution. It also helped create a space where experiencing sympathy with Jewish suffering in the theater emerged as the ultimate liberal pleasure, a pleasure shared by Jews and non-Jews alike as they looked forward to a brighter day by weeping together over Deborah's and Leah's woes.

In and of themselves, of course, these tears of sympathy may not have done anything tangible to create a more liberal political order. Indeed, as we have seen repeatedly over the course of this book, the powerlessness that they promoted along with their fantasies of a better future was part of their appeal, part of what made these tears such an exemplary expression of liberal feeling in all its contradictions and ambivalence. Yet for us today, looking back at the nineteenth century, it makes a tremendous difference that the affective communities forged through crying celebrated identification with Jewishness as the ultimate liberal experience. Performances of *Deborah* and *Leah* bound Jews and non-Jews together at precisely the same time as new forms of antisemitism challenging this mode of liberal community were beginning to rear their head in an effort to drive them apart. Today, more than seventy years after the Holocaust, there are undoubtedly still those who would insist on regarding this shared experience of melodramatic Jewishness with suspicion, stressing its inauthenticity and forcing it into the shadow of the antisemitism that it challenged. In following this path, we make a grievous error. We render ourselves blind to the tremendous power that the theater wielded in shaping how our Jewish and non-Jewish forebears thought and felt about Jewish difference. We ignore the powerful ways that grand theatrical performances of Jewishness helped create a shared culture of compassion with Jewish suffering that could function as the epitome of and foundation for liberal feeling.

Notes

Introduction

1. "Theatrical Nymph du Pave," *Public Ledger* (Memphis), June 29, 1866.

2. I quote *Leah* here according to the print edition that first appeared in the 1870s: Augustin Daly, *Leah, the Forsaken: A Play in Five Acts* (New York: Samuel French, n.d.), 35. Cf., e.g., "The Jewess's Curse," in H. M. Dickson, ed., *The Elocutionist* (Chicago, 1882), 9–11; "Scene from 'Leah,'" in Phineas Garrett, ed., *The Speaker's Garland: Comprising 100 Choice Selections* (Philadelphia: Penn, 1890), 7:194–197; "Scene from Leah, the Forsaken," in Frank H. Fenno, ed., *The Speaker's Favorite, or, Best Things for Entertainments for Home, Church and School, Consisting of Recitals, Dialogues and Dramas* (Philadelphia: John E. Potter, 1893), 176–180; and "Scene from 'Leah,'" in Delbert Moyer Staley, *Psychology of the Spoken Word* (Boston: Richard G. Badger, 1914), 127–130.

3. "Theatrical Nymph du Pave."

4. For context, see Kirsten Pullen, *Actresses and Whores: On Stage and in Society* (Cambridge: Cambridge University Press, 2005).

5. Friedrich Nietzsche, *The Gay Science*, trans. Walter Kaufmann (New York: Vintage, 1974), 317. For context, see Steven E. Aschheim, "Reflections on Theatricality, Identity, and the Modern Jewish Experience," in Jeanette R. Malkin and Freddie Rokem, eds., *Jews and the Making of Modern German Theatre* (Iowa City: University of Iowa Press, 2010), 21–38; and Jonas Barish, *The Antitheatrical Prejudice* (Berkeley: University of California Press, 1981), 464–469. Nietzsche's statement here is significant because of how ubiquitous this notion of Jews as inveterate actors was in nineteenth-century culture. Within the context of *The Gay Science*, Nietzsche uses this statement less to promote stereotypes about Jews than to disrupt the opposition between Hellenism and Hebraism that was such a crucial organizing force in nineteenth-century intellectual culture; he actually charges the ancient Greeks with inaugurating a type of theatricality that modern Jews continue. For context on Nietzsche and antisemitism, see Robert C. Holub, *Nietzsche's Jewish Problem: Between Anti-Semitism and Anti-Judaism* (Princeton, NJ: Princeton University Press, 2015).

6. See Rachel M. Brownstein, *Tragic Muse: Rachel of the Comédie Française* (New York: Knopf, 1993); and Maurice Samuels, *The Right to Difference: French Universalism and the Jews* (Chicago: University of Chicago Press, 2016), chap. 2, "France's Jewish Star."

7. For background information, see Carol Mavor, *Becoming: The Photographs of Clementina, Viscountess Hawarden* (Durham, NC: Duke University Press, 1999).

8. Scott's narrator in *Ivanhoe* famously highlights Rebecca's "Eastern dress" following the "fashion of the females of her nation" as well as her "turban of yellow silk" that complements the "darkness of her complexion." Walter Scott, *Ivanhoe: A Romance* (New York: Modern Library, 2001), 78. On the iconographic tradition of representing Jews with turbans, see Ivan Davidson Kalmar, "Jesus Did Not Wear a Turban: Orientalism, the Jews, and Christian Art," in Ivan Davidson Kalmar and Derek J. Penslar, eds., *Orientalism and the Jews* (Waltham, MA: Brandeis University Press, 2005).

9. See, esp., "Aus der Theaterwelt," *Fremden-Blatt* (Vienna), January 6, 1918; and "Wie Kathi Frank zur Bühne kam," *Prager Tagblatt, Abend-Ausgabe*, October 14, 1917. I discuss this incident in greater detail in Chapter 4.

10. See, e.g., "Kreuz- und Querzüge: Von der Saale, 26. Dezember," *Allgemeine Zeitung des Judenthums*, January 1, 1850; Isaak Hirsch, "Der Jude in der Literatur," *Jeschurun* 5, no. 4 (January 1859): 203–207; "Literarischer Wochenbericht," *Allgemeine Zeitung des Judenthums*, May 17, 1864; and "Neuere Dramen mit jüdischen Stoffen," *Allgemeine Zeitung des Judenthums*, February 1, 1876.

11. [Julian Schmidt,] "Deborah von Mosenthal," *Die Grenzboten* 8, no. 4 (1849): 139–143; Heinrich Theodor Rötscher, "Deborah, Volks-Schauspiel in 4 Akten von S. H. Mosenthal," *Jahrbücher für dramatische Kunst und Literatur* 3 (1849): 220–225; and Hermann Marggraf, "Deutsches Drama und Deutsches Theater," *Blätter für literarische Unterhaltung*, March 9, 1854, 189–193.

12. See, e.g., A. E. Schönbach, "S. H. Mosenthal," *Allgemeine Deutsche Biographie* (Leipzig, 1885), 22:368–371; Leopold Sacher-Masoch, *Harmlose Geschichten aus der Bühnenwelt* (Leipzig: Hartknoch, 1878), 41; and S. Heller, "S. H. Mosenthal, eine literarische Skizze," *Neue Monatshefte für Dichtkunst und Kritik* (1877): 334–345.

13. On *Deborah* in Yiddish, see Leonard Prager, *Yiddish Culture in Britain* (Frankfurt am Main: Peter Lang, 1990), 196; Michael Charles Steinlauf, "Polish-Jewish Theater: The Case of Mark Arnshteyn" (diss., Brandeis University, 1988), 85n124; and Brigitte Dalinger, *Trauerspiel mit Gesang und Tanz: Zur Ästhetik und Dramaturgie jüdischer Theatertexte* (Vienna: Böhlau, 2010), 175. See also Jacob Adler, *A Life on the Stage: A Memoir*, trans. Lulla Rosenfeld (New York: Applause, 2001), 308–309. David Radner's Hebrew translation appeared in print as early as 1884; see S. H. Mosenthal, *Devorah: ḥizayon: yesodato be-ḥaye ha-'am, be-arba'ah maḥazot*, trans. David ben Yirmiyahu Radner (Vilna, 1884). In the early twentieth century, Richard Davey, the London *Times* correspondent in Istanbul, recalled seeing a Hebrew-language performance of *Deborah* by a touring group from Pest decades earlier. See Davey, *The Sultan and His Subjects* (London: Chatto & Windus, 1907), 251.

14. "Amusements: Academy of Music," *Inter Ocean* (Chicago), February 17, 1875.

15. "Schneider Sees Leah: Written for the *New York Clipper*, by the 'Modest Quencher,'" *New York Clipper*, December 18, 1869.

16. See Andrew G. Bonnell, *Shylock in Germany: Antisemitism and the German Theatre from the Enlightenment to the Nazis* (London: Tauris, 2008); Judith W. Page, "'Hath Not a Jew Eyes?' Edmund Kean and the Sympathetic Shylock," *Wordsworth Circle* 34, no. 2 (2013): 116–119; Peter W. Marx, *Ein theatralisches Zeitalter: Bürgerliche Selbstinszenierungen um 1900* (Tübingen: A. Francke, 2008), esp. 121–164; and Nicole Anae, "'The Majestic Hebrew Ideal': Herr Daniel E. Bandmann's Shylock on the Australian Stage, 1880–1883," *Shakespeare Jahrbuch* 150 (2014): 128–145.

17. Joel Berkowitz, *Shakespeare on the American Yiddish Stage* (Iowa City: University of Iowa Press, 2010), 172–205.

18. "Theaterschau: Theater an der Wien," *Blätter für Musik, Theater und Kunst* (Vienna), April 17, 1863.

19. The following databases have been instrumental in the research for this book: American Broadsides and Ephemera (Readex); American Periodicals Series Online (ProQuest); America's Historical Newspapers (Treadex); Chronicling America (Library of Congress); ANNO-Austrian Newspapers Online (Austrian National Library); California Digital Newspaper Collection (Center for Bibliographical Studies and Research, University of California at Riverside); Europeana Newspapers (Staatsbibliothek zu Berlin Preußischer Kulturbesitz); Gale NewsVault (Cengage Learning); Illinois Digital Newspaper Collections (University of Illinois Library); Illustrated Civil War Newspapers and Magazines (Alexander Street); ProQuest Historical Newspapers; Papers Past New Zealand Newspapers (National Library of New Zealand); Nineteenth-Century MasterFile (Paratext); Nineteenth-Century US Newspapers (Gale Cengage Learning); Periodicals Index Online (ProQuest); Readers' Guide Retrospective (EBSCOhost); and ZEFYS Zeitungsinformationssystem (Staatsbibliothek zu Berlin Preußischer Kulturbesitz). The wealth of print material that Google Books, the Hathi Trust Digital Library, and the Internet Archive now make available digitally deserves to be mentioned here as well. I owe a special debt to Robert Dalton and Libby Chenault of the University of North Carolina Library for helping me learn to navigate my way around these resources.

20. Daniel Goldhagen, *Hitler's Willing Executioners: Ordinary Germans and the Holocaust* (New York: Vintage, 1997), 58.

21. See Lars Fischer, "Anti-'Philosemitism' and Anti-Antisemitism in Imperial Germany," in Jonathan Karp and Adam Sutcliffe, eds., *Philosemitism in History* (Cambridge: Cambridge University Press, 2011), 170–189.

22. See, e.g., Karp and Sutcliffe, *Philosemitism in History*; Yaakov Ariel, *An Unusual Relationship: Evangelical Christians and Jews* (New York: New York University Press, 2013); Gertrude Himmelfarb, *The People of the Book: Philosemitism in England from Cromwell to Churchill* (New York: Encounter, 2011); Jacques Berlinerblau, "On Philo-Semitism," *Occasional Papers on Jewish Civilization, Jewish Thought and Philosophy* (Winter 2007), Georgetown University Program for Jewish Civilization; Lisa Moses Leff, *Sacred Bonds of Solidarity: The Rise of Jewish Internationalism in Nineteenth-Century France* (Stanford, CA: Stanford University Press, 2006), 81–116; Alan T. Levenson, *Between Philosemitism and Antisemitism: Defenses of Jews and Judaism in Germany, 1871-1932* (Lincoln: University of Nebraska Press, 2004); and William D. and Hilary L. Rubenstein, *Philosemitism: Admiration and Support in the English-Speaking World for Jews, 1840–1939* (New York: St. Martin's, 1999).

23. Karp and Sutcliffe, *Philosemitism in History*, 2.

24. "Music and Drama: Sarah Bernhardt in 'Leah,'" *Jewish Messenger*, April 22, 1892.

25. "Theater," *Laibacher Zeitung* (Ljubljana), April 4, 1884.

26. Wilhelm Marr, *Der Sieg des Judenthums über das Germanenthum: Vom nicht confessionellen Standpunkt aus betrachtet* (Berlin, 1879), 20.

27. Adolf Bartels, *Geschichte der deutschen Literatur* (Leipzig: Eduard Avenarius, 1905), 2:267.

28. See Hans-Joachim Neubauer, *Judenfiguren: Drama und Theater im frühen 19. Jahrhundert* (Frankfurt am Main: Campus, 1994); Harley Erdman, *Staging the Jew: The Performance of an American Ethnicity, 1869–1920* (New Brunswick, NJ: Rutgers University Press, 1997), 17–39; and Katrin Sieg, *Ethnic Drag: Performing Race, Nation, Sexuality in West Germany* (Ann Arbor: University of Michigan Press, 2002), esp. 29–72. Edna Nahshon offers a succinct overview of the phenomenon of the stage Jew in her introductory essay to *From the Ghetto to the Melting Pot: Israel Zangwill's Jewish Plays* (Detroit: Wayne State University Press, 2006), 49–57. For general context, see Edna Nahshon, ed., *Jewish Theatre: A Global View* (Leiden: Brill, 2009).

29. See Jonathan M. Hess, "Lessing and German-Jewish Culture: A Reappraisal," in Ritchie Robertson, ed., *Lessing and the German Enlightenment* (Oxford: Voltaire Foundation, 2013), 179–204.

30. See, esp., Sieg, *Ethnic Drag*, 29–72; and Neubauer, *Judenfiguren*.

31. There is a rich literature on this topic. See, esp., Nadia Valman, *The Jewess in Nineteenth-Century British Literary Culture* (Cambridge: Cambridge University Press, 2007). See also Valman, "Bad Jew / Good Jewess: Gender and Semitic Discourse in Nineteenth-Century England," in Karp and Sutcliffe, *Philosemitism in History*; Eric Fournier, *La belle Juive: d'Ivanhoé à la Shoah* (Seyssel: Camp Vallon, 2011); Elvira Grözinger, *Die schöne Jüdin: Klischees, Mythen und Vorurtheile über Juden in der Literatur* (Berlin: Philo, 2003); and Florian Krobb, *Die schöne Jüdin: Jüdische Frauengestalten in der deutschsprachigen Erzählliteratur vom 17. Jahrhundert bis zum Ersten Weltkrieg* (Tübingen: Niemeyer, 1993).

32. See Valman, *The Jewess*, 20, also 2–4.

33. On *La Juive*, see Diana R. Hallman, *Opera, Liberalism, and Antisemitism in Nineteenth-Century France: The Politics of Halévy's* La Juive (Cambridge: Cambridge University Press, 2007); F. Scott Lerner, "Jewish Identity and French Opera: Stage and Politics, 1831–60," *Historical Reflections / Réflexions historiques* 30, no. 2 (2004): 255–281; and Ruth Hacohen, *The Music Libel Against the Jews* (New Haven, CT: Yale University Press, 2011), 179–238.

34. Michael Jahn, "Jacques Fromental Halévy (1799–1862): Gedanken zu seinen Opern und deren Rezeption in Wien," in Michael Jahn and Clemens Höslinger, eds., *Vergessen: Vier Opernkomponisten des 19. Jahrhunderts. J. F. Halévy, A. Rubinstein, K. Goldmark und J. J. Albert* (Vienna: Der Apfel, 2008), 9–28. The German libretto makes numerous changes, primarily to work around the censors and avoid having high-church officials on stage: *Die Jüdin: Oper in fünf Aufzügen von Scribe. Musik von Halévy*, trans. Friederike Ellmenreich (Leipzig: Sturm und Koppe [1840?]). As in most versions performed in the German-speaking world, the Cardinal here is downgraded to a Knight Templar.

35. See, e.g., the ads in the *Börsen-Halle: Hamburgische Abend-Zeitung für Handel, Schifffahrt und Politik*, January 19, 1849, January 24, 1849, and October 31, 1849.

36. Meyer does so as an explicit mode of resistance to the figure of the beautiful Jewess. See Jonathan M. Hess, *Middlebrow Literature and the Making of German-Jewish Identity* (Stanford, CA: Stanford University Press, 2010), 139–154.

37. See texts collected in Jonathan M. Hess, Maurice Samuels, and Nadia Valman, eds., *Nineteenth-Century Jewish Literature: A Reader* (Stanford, CA: Stanford University Press, 2013); and Maurice Samuels, *Inventing the Israelite: Jewish Fiction in Nineteenth-Century France* (Stanford, CA: Stanford University Press, 2009).

38. See Hess, *Middlebrow Literature*, 54–61.

39. See Hess, *Middlebrow Literature*; and Samuels, *Inventing the Israelite*. See, more generally, Richard I. Cohen's seminal essay "Nostalgia and 'Return to the Ghetto': A Cultural Phenomenon in Western and Central Europe," in Jonathan Frankel and Steven J. Zipperstein, eds., *Assimilation and Community: The Jews in Nineteenth-Century Europe* (Cambridge: Cambridge University Press, 1992).

40. Mosenthal's *Erzählungen aus dem jüdischen Familienleben* appeared for the first time as a set in Mosenthal's *Gesammelte Werke* (Stuttgart: Eduard Hallberger, 1878), vol. 1. In German, the *Erzählungen* appeared in book form in 1908 and 1911 and twice in 1912. They appeared in English in 1907 as *Stories of Jewish Home Life* (Philadelphia: Jewish Publication Society, 1907), republished in 1971. Many of the individual tales were published in Hebrew, Dutch, and Polish as well. See Hans Otto Horch and Gabriele von Glasenapp, eds., *Ghettoliteratur: Eine Dokumentation zur deutsch-jüdischen Literaturgeschichte des 19. und frühen 20. Jahrhunderts* (Tübingen: Niemeyer, 2005), 3:989–992.

41. Ismar Schorsch, "Art as Social History: Oppenheim and the German Jewish Vision of Emancipation," in *Moritz Oppenheim: The First Jewish Painter* (Jerusalem: Israel Museum, 1983), 31–61. On Oppenheim, see Georg Heuberger and Anton Merk, eds., *Moritz Daniel Oppenheim: Die Entdeckung des jüdischen Selbstbewusstseins in der Kunst / Jewish Identity in 19th Century Art* (Cologne: Wienand, 1999), as well as my essays "Lesewut unter dem Volk des Buches? Reflexionen über die jüdische Unterhaltungskultur im 19. Jahrhundert," in Klaus Hödl, ed., *Nicht nur Bildung, nicht nur Bürger: Juden in der Populärkultur* (Innsbruck: Studienverlag, 2013), 21–44, and "Reading and the Writing of German-Jewish History," in Richard V. Benson, Eric Downing, and Jonathan M. Hess, eds., *Literary Studies and the Pursuits of Reading* (Rochester, NY: Camden House, 2012), 105–129.

42. See Andreas Gotzmann, "Traditional Jewish Life Revived: Moritz Daniel Oppenheim's Vision of Modern Jewry," in Heuberger and Merk, *Moritz Daniel Oppenheim*, 232–250.

43. See Shalom Sabar, "In the Footsteps of Moritz Oppenheim: Hermann Junker's Postcard Series of Scenes of Traditional Jewish Life," in Heuberger and Merk, *Moritz Daniel Oppenheim*, 259–271.

44. Exact figures on the numbers of theatergoers who saw a performance of *Deborah* or *Leah* are elusive. But considering that even during her initial run in London in 1863–1864, Kate Bateman performed *Leah* 210 times to packed houses in a theater that seated 2,500, it seems safe to assume a figure well into the multiple millions.

45. Charles E. L. Wingate, "A Notable Night: Bernhardt's First Appearance as Leah, the Forsaken," *Boston Journal*, January 9, 1892.

46. See David Kertzer, *The Kidnapping of Edgardo Mortara* (New York: Vintage, 1998); Victor Séjour, *The Fortune-Teller*, trans. Norman R. Shapiro, intro. M. Lynn Weiss (Urbana: University of Illinois Press, 2002); and Elèna Mortara, *Writing for Justice: Victor Séjour, the Kidnapping of Edgardo Mortara, and the Age of Transatlantic Emancipations* (Hanover, NH: Dartmouth College Press, 2015). A German script for *La Tireuse de cartes* was published within a year of the play's premiere in Paris: *Die Kartenlegerin: Drama in 4 Akten*, trans. Emil Neumann (Berlin: Guthschmidt, 1860).

47. *The Woman in Red* (London: Ward and Lock, 1864).

48. See Seth L. Wolitz, "Translations of Karl Gutzkow's *Uriel Acosta* as Iconic Moments in Yiddish Theatre," in Joel Berkowitz and Barbara Henry, eds., *Inventing the Modern Yiddish Stage: Essays in Drama, Performance, and Show Business* (Detroit: Wayne State University Press, 2012), 87–115.

49. See Marvin Felheim, *The Theatre of Augustin Daly: An Account of the Late Nineteenth Century American Stage* (New York: Greenwood, 1956), 164–166; and Jonathan D. Sarna and Benjamin Shapell, *Lincoln and the Jews: A History* (New York: St. Martin's, 2015), 189–190.

50. Steven E. Aschheim, *In Times of Crisis: Essays on European Culture, Germans, and Jews* (Madison: University of Wisconsin Press, 2001), 89.

51. See Malkin and Rokem, *Jews and the Making of Modern German Theatre*.

52. Marline Otte, *Jewish Identities in German Popular Entertainment, 1890–1933* (Cambridge: Cambridge University Press, 2006), 5. See Klaus Hödl, *Wiener Juden, jüdische Wiener: Identität, Gedächtnis und Performanz im 19. Jahrhundert* (Innsbruck: Studienverlag, 2006); Klaus Hödl, "'Jüdische Differenz' in der Wiener Populärkultur," *Medaon* 11 (2001): 1–11; and Hödl, *Zwischen Wienerlied und Klabrias: Juden in der populären Wiener Kultur um 1900* (forthcoming). In terms of reconceptualizing the relationship between Jewish and general history, Till van Rahden's work has been particularly influential. See van Rahden, *Jews and Other Germans: Civil Society, Religious Diversity, and Urban Politics in Breslau, 1860–1925*, trans. Marcus Brainard (Madison: University of Wisconsin Press, 2008). Lisa Silverman's *Becoming Austrians: Jews and Culture Between the World Wars* (Oxford: Oxford University Press, 2012) deserves special attention here as well.

53. Andrea Most, *Theatrical Liberalism: Jews and Popular Entertainment in America* (New York: New York University Press, 2013).

54. Henry Bial, *Acting Jewish: Negotiating Ethnicity on the American Stage and Screen* (Ann Arbor: University of Michigan Press, 2005).

55. Karl von Thaler, "Der Dichter der 'Deborah': Ein Erinnerungsblatt," *Die Gartenlaube*, no. 11 (1877): 183.

56. See "Aus Mähren," *Der Orient*, July 21, 1849; *Konstitutionelles Blatt aus Steiermark*, June 28, 1849; and *Deutsche Zeitung* (Frankfurt am Main), June 30, 1849, supplement. Karl Schug's 1966 dissertation on Mosenthal does not mention the breast pin but does include a list of the thirteen major awards and accolades that Mosenthal earned during his lifetime. See Schug, "Salomon Hermann Mosenthal: Leben und Werk in der Zeit. Ein Beitrag zur Problematik der literarischen Geschmacksbildung" (diss., University of Vienna, 1966), 41–42.

57. The photographs of Mosenthal with his medals were often singled out for ridicule in the press. See, e.g., Franz Dingelstedt, "Mosenthal, ein Stammbuchblatt," *Die Gegenwart*, April 14, 1877, repr. in Dingelstedt, *Literarisches Bilderbuch* (Berlin: A. Hofmann, 1879), 165–186; and Daniel Spitzer's 1876 essay "Der Vesuv, Mosenthal, Weilen und sonstige Ursachen der Langeweile," and his 1878 essay "Rückblick auf das Jahr 1877," both repr. in Spitzer, *Wiener Spaziergänge* (Leipzig: Julius Klinkhardt, 1879).

58. See Fontane's letters to Bernhard von Lepel of June 19, 1849, and May 15, 1852, in Fontane, *Der Briefwechsel: Kritische Ausgabe* (Berlin: De Gruyter, 2006), 133–134, 330–331. Later in life, Fontane recalled his enthusiasm for Bertha Thomas's June 18, 1849, performance of *Deborah* in a review in the *Vossische Zeitung*, October 12, 1880, repr. in Fontane, *Ausgewaählte Schriften und Kritiken* (Munich: Hanser, 1969), 2:470–473.

59. Ruth Klüger, the most prominent exception here, offered a discussion of Mosenthal in *Katastrophen: Über deutsche Literatur* (Göttingen: Wallstein, 1994) and created a new edition of Mosenthal's *Erzählungen aus dem jüdischen Familienleben* (Göttingen: Wallstein, 2001). See also Jeffrey L. Sammons, "Sender Glatteis Reads Lessing and Comes to a Sad End: Some Thoughts on Karl Emil Franzos's *Der Pojaz* and the Problem of Jewish Reading," in Benson, Downing, and Hess, *Literary Studies and the Pursuits of Reading*, 168–186; Karlheinz Rossbacher, *Literatur und Liberalismus: Zur Kultur der Ringstrassenzeit in Wien* (Vienna: Edition Wien, 1992), 392–399; and Charlene A. Lea, *Emancipation, Assimilation and Stereotype: The Image of the Jew in German and Austrian Drama (1800–1850)* (Bonn: Bouvier, 1978), 65–68.

60. See Erdman, *Staging the Jew*, esp. 40–60; Valman, *The Jewess*, 34–43; Kim Marra, *Strange Duets: Impresarios and Actresses in the American Theatre, 1865–1914* (Iowa City: University of Iowa Press, 2006), 13–14; Stefanie Halpern, "Kate Bateman: Sanitizing the Beautiful Jewess," *TDR: The Drama Review* 55, no. 3 (2011): 72–79; and, most recently, Stephen Watt, "Something Dreadful and

Grand": American and the Jewish-Irish Unconscious (Oxford: Oxford University Press, 2015), 81–99.

61. In studying adaptation, I follow Linda Hutcheon's seminal study *A Theory of Adaptation*, 2nd ed. (London: Routledge, 2012), particularly as it has been reinterpreted for theater and performance studies by Henry Bial. See Bial, *Playing God: The Bible on the Broadway Stage* (Ann Arbor: University of Michigan Press, 2015), 18–23. In terms of thinking about cultural mobility, the essays collected in Stephen Greenblatt, ed., *Cultural Mobility: A Manifesto* (Cambridge: Cambridge University Press, 2009) represent an important resource. David Reynolds's *Mightier than the Sword: Uncle Tom's Cabin and the Battle for America* (New York: W. W. Norton, 2012) offers a fascinating example of the power of scholarship that places the study of adaptation at its center, focusing—like the present book—on the adaptability of a major work of nineteenth-century popular culture.

62. See Christopher B. Balme, *The Theatrical Public Sphere* (Cambridge: Cambridge University Press, 2014); Henry Bial and Scott Magelssen, eds., *Theatre Historiography: Critical Interventions* (Ann Arbor: University of Michigan Press, 2010); Charlotte M. Canning and Thomas Postlewait, eds., *Representing the Past: Essays in Performance Historiography* (Iowa City: University of Iowa Press, 2010); W. E. Wilmer, ed., *Writing and Rewriting National Theatre Histories* (Iowa City: University of Iowa Press, 2004); Willmar Sauter, *The Theatrical Event: Dynamics of Performance and Perception* (Iowa City: University of Iowa Press, 2000); Erika Fischer-Lichte, *The Transformative Power of Performance: A New Aesthetics*, trans. Saskya Jain (London: Routledge, 2008); and Thomas Postlewait and Bruce A. McConachie, *Interpreting the Theatrical Past: Essays in the Historiography of Performance* (Iowa City: University of Iowa Press, 1989).

63. See Most, *Theatrical Liberalism*, 15–38, as well as Jeremy Dauber, "Between Two Worlds: Antitheatricality and the Beginnings of Modern Yiddish Theatre," in Berkowitz and Henry, *Inventing the Modern Yiddish Stage*, 27–39.

64. This is, in fact, the approach that Halpern takes in "Kate Bateman," concluding that Bateman's *Leah* ultimately helps "enact" "antisemitic sentiments" (78).

Chapter 1

1. "Schneider Sees Leah: Written for the *New York Clipper*, by the 'Modest Quencher,'" *New York Clipper*, December 18, 1869. The noted elocutionist Alfred Post Burbank began performing "Schneider Sees Leah" under a variety of different titles in 1873, occasionally attributing it to [Charles M.] Connolly, a well-known composer of popular songs and dance melodies whose authorship of the Uncle Schneider sketches came to light in the 1870s. See "The Disguises of Authorship," *New York Clipper*, March 24, 1877. When Burbank later included the sketch in *A Collection of Humorous, Dramatic, and Dialect Selections, Edited and Arranged for Public Reading or Recitation* (New York: Dick & Fitzgerald, 1878), 23–26, however, he mentioned neither Connolly nor the *New York Clipper*. Jacob W. Shoemaker, founder of the National School of Elocution and Oratory in Philadelphia, published "Schneider Sees Leah" earlier, also with no mention of its source, in *The Elocutionist's Annual* 2 (1873): 185–188. The sketch was frequently reprinted in anthologies well into the twentieth century, both in collections of American "dialect" readings and in volumes designed for students of elocution, usually marked as anonymous in origin.

2. See, e.g., ads in the *New York Herald*, January 12 and January 17, 1863; *Daily National Intelligencer* (Washington, DC), November 24, 1863; and *Sun* (Baltimore), March 12, 1864.

3. Mosenthal, "Aus den 'Memoiren' der Deborah," *Die Gegenwart* 6, no. 46 (November 14, 1874): 312; and Felix Theilhaber, "Salomon Hermann Mosenthal," *Hamburgisches Israelitisches Familienblatt* 23, no. 2 (January 13, 1921): 2.

4. See ad for the premiere of *Leah* on the backside of the playbill for the December 5, 1862, performance of *Macbeth* at the Howard Athenaeum, Boston, Harvard Theatre Collection, playbills and programs concerning female "stars," THE BPF TCS 72, Houghton Library, Harvard University. *Leah* played for two weeks in Boston in December 1862 before opening on January 19, 1863, at Niblo's

Garden in New York. The same language is used in [Augustin Daly,] "A Memoir of Miss Bateman: Being a Brief Chronicle of the Early Successes and Later Triumphs of the Great American Tragic Artiste. Together with a Condensation of the Incidents and Some Extracts from the Book of the Play of 'Leah, the Forsaken,' as Played by Miss Bateman" (New York: Wynkoop, Hallenbeck & Thomas, 1863), 14.

5. Undated 1863 review of *Leah, the Forsaken* at Niblo's Garden, in *Correspondence of Augustin Daly and Joseph F. Daly and Documents Serving for Memoirs, 1858–1899* [hereafter, Daly, *Correspondence and Documents*], 9 vols., New York Public Library for the Performing Arts, T-Mss 2011-251, vol. 1; also in Harvard Theatre Collection, Clippings 13, Folder: Leah, the Forsaken, Houghton Library, Harvard University.

6. On the differences in the endings of the various versions of *Deborah* and *Leah*—in neither Mosenthal's original script nor Daly's published script for *Leah* does the title figure die—see my discussion in Chapter 2.

7. There is a rich literature on this topic, starting with Hans-Jürgen Schings's classic 1980 *Der mitleidigste Mensch ist der beste Mensch: Poetik des Mitleids von Lessing bis Büchner*, 2nd ed. (Würzburg: Königshausen & Neumann, 2012). See, esp., Dorothea von Mücke, *Virtue and the Veil of Illusion: Generic Innovation and the Pedagogical Project in Eighteenth-Century Literature* (Stanford, CA: Stanford University Press, 1991); and Paul Fleming, *Exemplarity and Mediocrity: The Art of the Average from Bourgeois Tragedy to Realism* (Stanford, CA: Stanford University Press, 2009).

8. On German theater in New York, see John Koegel, *Music in German Immigrant Theater: New York City, 1840–1940* (Rochester, NY: University of Rochester Press, 2009); Sabine Haenni, *The Immigrant Scene: Ethnic Amusements in New York, 1880–1920* (Minneapolis: University of Minnesota Press, 2008); and Fritz A. H. Leuchs, *The Early German Theatre in New York, 1840–1872* (New York: Columbia University Press, 1928).

9. Schiller, *Ueber das Pathetische*, in *Schillers Werke* (Stuttgart: Cotta, 1867), 11:298.

10. See Fleming, *Exemplarity and Mediocrity*, 67.

11. Letter from Kate Bateman to Augustin Daly, London, October 6, 1863, Folger Shakespeare Library, Y.c. 2673 (1–3).

12. "Theatres," *Orchestra* (London) 2, no. 37 (June 11, 1864): 582.

13. See, e.g., "Liverpool (from Our Own Correspondent)," *Musical World* (London) 42, no. 44 (October 29, 1864): 700; *Sun* (Baltimore), January 10, 1865; and "In General," *Boston Daily Advertiser*, January 21, 1865.

14. "Personal Intelligence," *Republican Banner* (Nashville, TN), November 18, 1869. The fact of Bateman's ownership of the silk mill was widely reported on in the press. See *New-York Tribune*, November 12, 1869; "In General," *Boston Daily Advertiser*, November 15, 1869; *Bangor Daily Whig & Courier*, November 17, 1869; "Why," *Fun* (London) 10 (December 25, 1869): 155; and "Personal," *Harper's Bazaar* 3, no. 6 (February 5, 1870): 83.

15. See "Nance O'Neil's Best Offering" (n.d.) and "The Theaters Last Night: Nance O'Neil Again Appears as Leah at the Grand Opera House," *San Francisco Chronicle*, December 30, 1902, Billy Rose Theatre Collection, New York Public Library for the Performing Arts, Nance O'Neil Scrapbooks 8-MWEZ+n.c. 19, 872.

16. Indeed, the description of Leah falling into Rudolf's arms refers to a unique feature of Bateman's script that departs from Daly's original.

17. See fm. [Fritz Mauthner], "Feuilleton," *Berliner Tageblatt*, May 8, 1897; and Josef Weilen, "S. H. Mosenthal: Ein Lebensbild," originally published in the *Wiener Abendpost* and subsequently reprinted in *S. H. Mosenthal's gesammelte Werke* (Stuttgart: Eduard Hallberger, 1878), 6:60.

18. See, e.g., *Mnemosyne: Beiblatt zur neuen Würzburger Zeitung*, December 23, 1855; *Theater-Pfeile, ein Beiblatt zum Münchener Punsch*, July 7, 1850; and *Ansbacher Morgenblatt*, March 19, 1862.

19. Charles Lamb Kenney, "The New Actress and the New Play at the Adelphi Theatre" (London: W. S. Johnson, 1863), 7–8.

20. See, e.g., review of the Prague premiere of *Deborah* in *Bohemia: Unterhaltungsblätter für gebildete Stände*, June 2, 1849, and June 5, 1849; "Miss Bateman as 'Leah,'" clipping from an unnamed

New York newspaper, January 25, 1863, Daly, *Correspondence and Documents*, vol. 1; "The Idler About Town," *Frank Leslie's Illustrated Newspaper*, February 7, 1863; ad for Lucille Western in *Leah, the Forsaken*, *Sun* (Baltimore), March 14, 1864; "Miss Cecile Rush," *Milwaukee Daily Sentinel*, December 19, 1866; "Fanny Janauschek as Deborah," *Milwaukee Daily Sentinel*, March 7, 1868; "Music and the Drama," *Spirit of the Times* (New York), March 7, 1874; and "Miss Mather at the Boston," clipping from Boston newspaper, December 26, 1888, Harvard Theatre Collection, Clippings 13, Folder: Leah, the Forsaken (performances by Margaret Mather), Houghton Library, Harvard University.

21. Salomon Hermann Mosenthal, *Deborah: Volks-Schauspiel in vier Akten* (Pest: Gustav Heckenast, 1850), 118 (IV.viii). I quote *Deborah* according to this edition throughout, indicating act and scene numbers parenthetically in the body of the text. Translations are my own. We find a similar dynamic in Daly's version of the play, even though it is not echoed as forcefully in Deborah's/Leah's lines here: "I will wander on with my people, but the hate that I have nourished has departed. I may not love, but I forgive" (Daly, *Leah*, 43).

22. "Letter from Tycoon, Idaho City, September 4, 1864," *Idaho Tri-Weekly Statesman* (Boise City), September 6, 1864; *Idaho Tri-Weekly Statesman*, July 29, 1865; and W. S., "Theater," *Znaimer Wochenblatt*, October 31, 1869.

23. See, e.g., Anne Vincent-Buffault, *The History of Tears: Sensibility and Sentimentality in France*, trans. Teresa Bridgeman (New York: St. Martin's, 1991).

24. See Franco Moretti, "Kindergarten," in Moretti, *Signs Taken for Wonders: Essays in the Sociology of Literary Forms*, trans. Susan Fischer, David Forgacs, and David Miller, 2nd ed. (London: Verso, 1988), 157–181. For examples of more recent scholarship that takes crying seriously, see literature on melodrama cited below. See also Gertrud Koch, "Zu Tränen gerührt: Zur Erschütterung im Kino," in Klaus Herding and Bernhard Stumpfhaus, eds., *Pathos, Affekt, Gefühl: Die Emotionen in den Künsten* (Berlin: De Gruyter, 2004), 562–574; Tom Lutz, *Crying: A Natural and Cultural History of Tears* (New York: Norton, 2001); Hermann Kappelhoff, *Matrix der Gefühle: Das Kino, das Melodrama und das Theater der Empfindsamkeit* (Berlin: Vorwerk, 2004); and Elina Gertsman, *Crying in the Middle Ages: Tears of History* (New York: Routledge, 2012). Within the field of cognitive studies, some recent literature is beginning to take crying seriously as well. See Michael Trimble, *Why Humans Like to Cry: Tragedy, Evolution, and the Brain* (Oxford: Oxford University Press, 2012); and A J. J. M. Vingerhoets, *Why Only Humans Weep: Unravelling the Mysteries of Tears* (Oxford: Oxford University Press, 2013).

25. Peter Bauland, *The Hooded Eagle: Modern German Drama on the New York Stage* (Syracuse, NY: Syracuse University Press, 1968), 25.

26. Emil Müller-Samswegen, "Das bürgerliche Drama," in Franz Brendel and Richard Pohl, eds., *Anregungen für Kunst, Leben und Wissenschaft* (Leipzig: C. Merseburger, 1858), 3:161–168, 201–213, here 210.

27. "Musical and Theatrical Notes," *New York Herald*, October 11, 1868.

28. "Theaterschau: Theater an der Wien," *Blätter für Musik, Theater und Kunst* (Vienna), April 17, 1863.

29. George Augustus Sala, *The Life and Adventures of George Augustus Sala, Written by Himself* (New York: C. Scribner, 1896), 2:37.

30. The examples are too many to list. See, e.g., ads for Bateman's *Leah* in the *New York Times* and the *New-York Daily Tribune* on January 31, 1863; for Lucille Western's *Leah* in the *Daily National Intelligencer* (Washington, DC), November 25, 1863; the review of Fanny B. Price in *Leah* in the *Daily Union and American* (Nashville, TN), September 1, 1866; "Mrs. Breslau's Benefit," *Daily State Register* (Des Moines, IA), July 1, 1867; and "Janauschek," *Cleveland Morning Herald*, November 25, 1871.

31. Peter Brooks, *The Melodramatic Imagination: Balzac, Henry James, and the Mode of Excess*, 2nd ed. (New Haven, CT: Yale University Press, 1995), 4–5.

32. Steve Neale, "Melodrama and Tears," *Screen* 27, no. 6 (1986): 6–23. In his emphasis on fantasy, Neale builds on and self-consciously revises Moretti's "Kindergarten," cited above.

33. Linda Williams, "Melodrama Revised," in Nick Browne, ed., *Refiguring American Film Genres* (Berkeley: University of California Press, 1998), 47–48, 62. See Christine Gledhill, "The Melodramatic Field: An Investigation," in Gledhill, ed., *Home Is Where the Heart Is: Studies in Melodrama and the Woman's Film* (London: British Film Institute, 1987); Linda Williams, "Film Bodies: Gender, Genre, and Excess," *Film Quarterly* 44, no. 4 (1991): 2–13; and Linda Williams, *Playing the Race Card: Melodramas of Black and White from Uncle Tom to O. J. Simpson* (Princeton, NJ: Princeton University Press, 2002). Other important studies that have informed my thinking about melodrama include Jacky Bratton, Jim Cook, and Christine Gledhill, eds., *Melodrama: Stage, Picture, Screen* (London: British Film Institute, 1994); Michael Hays and Anastasia Nikolopoulou, eds., *Melodrama: The Cultural Emergence of a Genre* (New York: St. Martin's, 1996); Ben Singer, *Melodrama and Modernity: Early Sensational Cinema and Its Contexts* (New York: Columbia University Press, 2001); and Kappelhoff, *Matrix der Gefühle*, cited above. John Mercer and Martin Shingler, *Melodrama: Genre, Style, Sensibility* (New York: Columbia University Press, 2004), offers a helpful overview of the emergence of serious scholarship on melodrama within the field of film studies.

34. In an 1885 article in the *Allgemeine Deutsche Biographie*, Anton Schönbach called *Deborah* the "most popular drama of the century." See Schönbach, "S. H. Mosenthal," *Allgemeine Deutsche Biographie* (Leipzig, 1885), 22:368–371. The Austrian writer Leopold Sacher-Masoch celebrated *Deborah* as the only German play of its era that became a true international sensation. See Sacher-Masoch, *Harmlose Geschichten aus der Bühnenwelt* (Leipzig: Hartknoch, 1878), 41.

35. Julian Schmidt, "Deborah von Mosenthal," *Die Grenzboten* 8, no. 4 (1849): 139–143.

36. Fleming, *Exemplarity and Mediocrity*, 57.

37. Lessing, *Hamburgische Dramaturgie, 14. Stück*, in idem, *Werke in drei Bänden* (Munich: Hanser, 1982), 2:93.

38. See Martha Woodmansee, *The Author, Art and the Market: Rereading the History of Aesthetics* (New York: Columbia University Press, 1994); Daniel L. Purdy, *The Tyranny of Elegance: Consumer Cosmopolitanism in the Era of Goethe* (Baltimore: Johns Hopkins University Press, 1998), 22–50; Karin Wurst, *Fabricating Pleasure: Fashion, Entertainment and Cultural Consumption in Germany, 1780–1830* (Detroit: Wayne State University Press, 2005); and Matt Erlin, *Necessary Luxuries: Books, Literature, and the Culture of Consumption in Germany, 1770–1815* (Ithaca, NY: Cornell University Press, 2014).

39. See, e.g., George Williamson, "What Killed August von Kotzebue? The Temptations of Virtue and the Political Theology of German Nationalism, 1789–1819," *Journal of Modern History* (2000): 890–943; and Birgit Pargner, *Zwischen Tränen und Kommerz: Das Rührtheater Charlotte Birch-Pfeiffers (1800–1868) in seiner künstlerischen und kommerziellen Verwertung* (Bielefeld: Aisthesis, 1999).

40. Schmidt, "Deborah von Mosenthal." This piece was published anonymously, but the similarity to Schmidt's later *Geschichte der deutschen Literatur seit Lessing's Tod*, 4th ed. (Leipzig: Friedrich Ludwig Herbig, 1858), vol. 3, indicates Schmidt as the author.

41. Schmidt, "Deborah von Mosenthal," 142; Heinrich Theodor Rötscher, "Deborah: Volks-Schauspiel in 4 Akten von S. H. Mosenthal," *Jahrbücher für dramatische Kunst und Literatur* 3 (1849): 220. See also Hermann Marggraf, "Deutsches Drama und Deutsches Theater," *Blätter für literarische Unterhaltung* 11 (March 9, 1854): 189–193; and the critical article in *Europa* (1849): 632.

42. See, e.g., Rötscher, "Deborah"; Rudolph Gottschall, *Die deutsche Nationalliteratur in der ersten Hälfte des neunzehnten Jahrhunderts*, 2nd ed. (Breslau: Eduard Trewendt, 1860), 3:457; and Gerhard Zillgenz, *Aristoteles und das deutsche Drama* (Würzburg: Ernst Thein, 1865), 29–31. This particular criticism of the play appears in some of the earliest reviews. See, e.g., the January 15, 1849, report on the Hamburg premiere, repr. in *Wiener Zeitschrift*, February 8, 1849.

43. Zillgenz, *Aristoteles und das deutsche Drama*, 29–31.

44. See, e.g., Lessing's letter of December 18, 1756, in Gotthold Ephraim Lessing, Moses Mendelssohn, and Friedrich Nicolai, *Briefwechsel über das Trauerspiel*, ed. Jochen Schulte-Sasse (Munich: Winkler, 1972), 76–85.

45. "Dr. Mosenthal," *Theatre* (London) 1, no. 5 (February 27, 1877): 53.

46. S. H. Mosenthal, "Eine Skizze meines Lebens," *Die Gegenwart* 6, no. 30 (August 22, 1874): 117–119, continued in no. 31 (August 29, 1874): 134–136; and Mosenthal, "Aus den 'Memoiren' der Deborah." Mosenthal's brief service in the civil militia is substantiated by contemporary reporting on the 1848 revolution; see *Der Humorist* (Vienna), May 26, 1848.

47. See the notice of the Viennese premiere of *Deborah* on March 10, 1849, *Der Humorist*, March 10, 1849; "Theater-Revue," *Das freie Oesterreich: Journal für alle Stände*, March 14, 1849; and "Nationaltheater an der Wien," *Wiener Zeitschrift*, March 13, 1849.

48. *Konstitutionelles Blatt aus Steiermark*, June 28, 1849; and *Deutsche Zeitung* (Frankfurt am Main), June 30, 1849, supplement. For a critical account of the tokenism involved with Mosenthal's appointment to a government post, see Wilhelm Goldbaum, *Literarische Physiognomien* (Vienna: Karl Proschaska, 1884), 192. In his 1874 essay "Eine Skizze meines Lebens," Mosenthal acknowledges that he was appointed symbolically as a Jew, adding that his superior Count Leo Thun made it difficult for him to advance.

49. Weilen, "S. H. Mosenthal," 42; and Mosenthal, "Eine Skizze meines Lebens" and "S. H. Mosenthal," *Neue Freie Presse*, February 18, 1877, 5–6.

50. "S. H. Mosenthal," *Neue Freie Presse*, February 18, 1877.

51. Weilen, "S. H. Mosenthal," 31.

52. See *Wiener Zeitschrift für Kunst, Literatur, Theater und Mode*, May 1, 1847; and *Der Humorist*, May 1, 1847.

53. Weilen, "S. H. Mosenthal," 33–34. See Otto Prechtler, *Mara: Romantische Oper mit Tanz in drei Akten* (Prague: Berra und Hoffmann, 1843). The music for *Mara* was composed by Josef Netzer, and following its premiere at the Viennese court opera in March 1842, *Mara* saw several performances throughout the German-speaking world in the 1840s. Critics often blamed Prechtler's libretto for the opera's lackluster success. See, e.g., *Revue et gazette musicale de Paris*, May 8, 1842; Bernhard Glutt, *Bohemia: Ein Unterhaltungsblatt*, November 12, 1843; *Allgemeine musikalische Zeitung*, December 6, 1843, 885–887; *Zeitung für die elegante Welt*, July 31, 1844; and "Theater in Leipzig," *Illustrierte Zeitung* (Leipzig), November 9, 1844.

54. Carmen appeared in German in *Prosper Mérimée's gesammelte Werke* (Stuttgart: Adolph Becher, 1846), 6:69–150.

55. In the German context, Prechtler's libretto, with its love affair between a gypsy woman and a Christian man, stood in a tradition that went back to Pius Alexander Wolff's drama *Preciosa* (1821), itself a reworking of Cervantes's *La gitanilla* (1613). For context, see Klaus-Michael Bogdal, *Europa erfindet die Zigeuner: Eine Geschichte von Faszination und Verachtung* (Frankfurt am Main: Suhrkamp, 2011); Nicholas Saul, *Gypsies and Orientalism in German Literature and Anthropology of the Long Nineteenth Century* (London: Legenda, 2007); Lou Charnon-Deutsch, *The Spanish Gypsy: The History of a European Obsession* (University Park: Pennsylvania State University Press, 2004); and Rudolf Angermüller, "Zigeuner und Zigeunerisches in der Oper des 19. Jahrhunderts," in *Die "Couleur locale" in der Oper des 19. Jahrhunderts*, ed. Heinz Becker (Regensburg: Gustav Bosse, 1976).

56. Mosenthal, "Miniaturbilder: Grillparzer," in Mosenthal, *Gesammelte Werke*, 1:280. Mosenthal's series of *Miniaturbilder* first appeared in *Über Land und Meer*.

57. See, e.g., J. W., "Deborah: Volks-Schauspiel in 4 Abth. von S. Mosenthal," *Didaskalia*, October 10, 1849; and "Frankfurt am Main," *Morgenblatt für gebildete Leser*, November 2, 1849. See also the lengthy review of *Leah, the Forsaken*, in *Times* (London), October 2, 1863; "Zur Tagesgeschichte: Wien, 17. October," *Wiener Zeitung*, October 18, 1863; and E. Bürde, "Dresdner Hoftheater," *Wissenschaftliche Beilage der Leipziger Zeitung*, November 6, 1879, continued on November 9, 1879.

58. Heckenast's ads included a long quotation from the October 10, 1849, review in *Didaskalia*. See, e.g., ads in *Wiener Zeitung*, April 20, 1850; and *Die Presse* (Brünn/Brno), May 26, 1850.

59. See Jonathan M. Hess, "Lessing and German-Jewish Culture: A Reappraisal," in Ritchie Robertson, ed., *Lessing and the German Enlightenment* (Oxford: Voltaire Foundation, 2013), 179–204.

60. See, on this issue, Hess, "Lessing and German-Jewish Culture."

61. See the exemplary study by Nadia Valman, *The Jewess in Nineteenth-Century British Literary Culture* (Cambridge: Cambridge University Press, 2007), as well as the other literature on the figure of the Jewess cited in the Introduction.

62. On the reaction of the leaders of the Viennese Jewish community to this and other depictions of anti-Jewish violence in the play, see Mosenthal, "Aus den 'Memoiren' der Deborah," 312.

63. Olive Logan, *Before the Footlights and Behind the Scenes: A Book About "The Show Business" in All Its Branches* (Philadelphia: Parmalee, 1870), 52–53. Daly's *Leah, the Forsaken* follows Mosenthal to the letter when it comes to Deborah's/Leah's entrance here. See *Leah*, 9.

64. As Eva Lezzi argues, such invocations of a "religion of love" were a staple in representations of romantic relationships between Jews and Christians in nineteenth-century literature, where such interfaith unions tend more often than not to end tragically. See Lezzi, *"Liebe ist meine Religion!" Eros und Ehe zwischen Juden und Christen in der Literatur des 19. Jahrhunderts* (Göttingen: Wallstein, 2013).

65. Daly, *Leah, the Forsaken,* 14–15. Emphasis in original.

66. Neale, "Melodrama and Tears," 6–23. Neale builds here on Moretti's "Kindergarten," stressing, however, not just the powerlessness of the spectator in melodrama but the way melodrama encourages its spectators to indulge in the pleasures of fantasy.

67. Stephen Watt, *"Something Dreadful and Grand": American Literature and the Irish-Jewish Unconscious* (Oxford: Oxford University Press, 2015), 89–96.

68. Daly, *Leah, the Forsaken*, 29.

69. Hermann Hettner, *Das moderne Drama: Aesthetische Untersuchungen* (Braunschweig, 1852), 123–124.

70. Oscar Teuber, *Geschichte des Prager Theaters von den Anfängen des Schauspielwesens bis auf die neueste Zeit* (Prague, 1888), 3:593.

71. "Provincial," *Orchestra* (London) 9, no. 218 (November 30, 1867): 147.

72. "Table Talk," *Musical Standard* (London) 2, no. 38 (February 13, 1864): 224.

73. J. M., *Die Presse* (Vienna), March 18, 1849.

74. Williams, "Melodrama Revised," 49.

75. See, e.g. "Kreuz- und Querzüge: Von der Saale, 26. Dezember," *Allgemeine Zeitung des Judenthums* 14, no. 1 (January 1, 1850): 2–3.

76. *Abdias* was discussed in Viennese intellectual circles widely during the period when Mosenthal was seeking to establish himself as a force in Austrian literary life. Mosenthal and Stifter used the same publisher, Gustav Heckenast, who sometimes advertised *Abdias* and *Deborah* together. See, e.g., ad in *Allgemeine Zeitung* (Munich), July 29, 1853. Mosenthal's *Deborah* is hardly the only work by a nineteenth-century Jewish author who sought to rewrite Stifter's *Abdias*. See Ludwig Philippson's 1854 novella *Drei Brüder*, in English, in Jonathan M. Hess, Maurice Samuels, and Nadia Valman, eds., *Nineteenth-Century Jewish Literature: A Reader* (Stanford, CA: Stanford University Press, 2013), 210–247. On *Abdias*, see Martha Helfer, *The Word Unheard: Legacies of Anti-Semitism in German Literature and Culture* (Evanston, IL: Northwestern University Press, 2011), 113–142; and Joseph Metz, "The Jew as Sign in Stifter's *Abdias*," *Germanic Review* 77 (2002): 219–232. Abdias's wife is also named Deborah.

77. See Leopold Kompert, "Auf nach Amerika," *Oesterreichisches Central-Organ für Glaubensfreiheit, Cultur, Geschichte und Literatur der Juden* 1 (1848): 77–78, 88–89; and Rudolf Glanz, "Source Materials on the History of Jewish Immigration to the United States," *YIVO Annual of Jewish Social Science* 6 (1951): 73–156, 97–101. Ruben's path from Austria to America presents the antithesis of Abdias's journey in Stifter from North Africa to Austria.

78. Richard Wagner, "Das Judenthum in der Musik" (Leipzig: J. J. Weber, 1869), 9–10; English: Wagner, "Judaism in Music," in *Judaism in Music and Other Essays*, trans. William Ashton Ellis (Lincoln: University of Nebraska Press, 1995), 80–81.

79. Cosima Wagner does mention, in her diary, Mosenthal and gatherings in Wagner's honor where Mosenthal was present. See Cosima Wagner, *Die Tagebücher*, ed. Martin Gregor-Dellin and Dietrich Mack (Zurich: Piper, 1976), 1:900, 947. Her reaction to Goldmark's *Die Königin von Saba*,

which she saw with her husband, is legendary. "Abends mit R[ichard] in: 'Die Königin von Saba' von Goldmark und Mosenthal, kein Gold, noch Mark, aber viel Mosenthal!"

80. Gottfried Keller, "Jeremias Gotthelf," *Blätter für literarische Unterhaltung*, March 1, 1855, 163. Keller makes these comments as a critique of Mosenthal's 1854 drama *Der Sonnwendhof*, which allegedly pilfered from Gotthelf's 1843 novella *Elsi, die seltsame Magd*.

81. Gottfried Keller, June 26, 1854, letter to Hermann Hettner, in Keller, *Sämtliche Werke: Historisch-Kritische Ausgabe* (Frankfurt am Main: Stroemfeld, 1996–), http://www.gottfriedkeller.ch/briefe.

82. Ferdinand Kürnberger, "Von uns und unsern Dichtern. 28. Jänner 1872," *Literarische Herzenssachen: Reflexionen und Kritiken* (Vienna: L. Rosner, 1877), 298–302. See also Kürnberger, "Wien im Spiegel eines Sarges: 8. Februar 1872," 303–310.

83. Franz Dingelstedt, "Mosenthal, ein Stammbuchblatt," in Dingelstedt, *Literarisches Bilderbuch*, 2nd ed. (Berlin: A. Hofmann, 1879), 165–186, originally published in *Die Gegenwart* in 1877. An even more explicitly antisemitic attack on Mosenthal echoing Wagner's vocabulary is found in Skaldafpilli, "Unsere Zeit- und Streitfragen: S. H. Mosenthal. Eine Charakterskizze," *Deutsche Monatsblätter: Centralorgan für das literarische Leben der Gegenwart* 2 (October 1878): 70–75.

84. Wilhelm Marr, *Der Sieg des Judenthums über das Germanenthum: Vom nicht confessionellen Standpunkt aus betrachtet* (Berlin, 1879), 20.

85. Adolf Bartels, *Geschichte der deutschen Literatur* (Leipzig: Eduard Avenarius, 1905), 2:267. The only dissertation written on Mosenthal in the postwar period uncritically relies on these types of sources to present its subject as a "Jewish speculator on the theater" (*Theaterspekulant*) bent on commodifying the world of high culture. Karl Schug, "Salomon Hermann Mosenthal: Leben und Werk in der Zeit. Ein Beitrag zur Problematik der literarischen Geschmacksbildung" (diss., University of Vienna, 1966), 152.

Chapter 2

1. "Leah," *Harper's Weekly* 7, no. 323 (March 7, 1863): 146. All further references to this article will simply be cited in the text.

2. Lincoln saw Avonia Jones in *Leah*, referenced in Kushner's screenplay near the beginning of the film when Tad tells his brother Robert that his parents "went to see Avonia Jones last night in a play about Israelites" (Tony Kushner, *Lincoln*, final shooting script, http://www.imsdb.com/scripts/Lincoln.html). On Lincoln's attendance at the play, see "Lincoln and the Lively Arts," *Lincoln Lore* no. 1508 (October 1963): 4; Thomas A. Bogar, *American Presidents Attend the Theatre: The Playgoing Experiences of Each Chief Executive* (Jefferson, NC: McFarland, 2006), 110–111; and Jonathan D. Sarna and Benjamin Shapell, *Lincoln and the Jews: A History* (New York: St. Martin's, 2015), 189–190. In a February 17, 1864, letter to Augustin Daly, Jones mentions offering a repeat performance of *Leah* in Nashville, at General Grant's special request. See Avonia Jones, February 17, 1864, letter to Augustin Daly, Folger Shakespeare Library, Y.c. 4198 (1–8), #7. As president, Grant later saw Bateman perform *Leah* as well; see "National Theater," *National Republican* (Washington, DC), January 11, 1870.

3. For context, see David Reynolds's fascinating study *Mightier than the Sword: Uncle Tom's Cabin and the Battle for America* (New York: W. W. Norton, 2012).

4. See, e.g., "Amusements. The Drama: New Richmond Theatre," *Southern Punch* (Richmond, VA), August 29, 1864; and "The Drama: Critics and Criticism," *Southern Punch*, September 12, 1864.

5. Leopold Sacher-Masoch, *Harmlose Geschichten aus der Bühnenwelt* (Leipzig: Hartknoch, 1878), 41.

6. See, e.g., S. Heller, "S. H. Mosenthal, eine literarische Skizze," *Neue Monatshefte für Dichtkunst und Kritik* 5 (1877): 334–345.

7. See, e.g., W. Th., "Londoner Theaterschau," *Recensionen und Mittheilungen über Theater und Musik*, February 27, 1864; and "'Deborah' in England," *Recensionen und Mittheilungen über Theater und Musik*, September 16, 1864.

8. In addition to the various versions I discuss in this chapter and throughout this study, see "Statistisches über Mosenthal's 'Deborah,'" *Münchener Abendzeitung*, September 23, 1864; Constantin von Wurzbach, "Mosenthal," in *Biographisches Lexikon des Kaiserthums Oesterreich* (Vienna: C. Zamarski, 1868), 19:137–143; Mosenthal, "Eine Skizze meines Lebens," *Die Gegenwart* 6, no. 30 (August 22, 1874): 117–119, continued in no. 31 (August 29, 1874): 134–136; Mosenthal, "Aus den 'Memoiren' der Deborah," *Die Gegenwart* 6, no. 46 (November 14, 1874): 311–313; Leonard Prager, *Yiddish Culture in Britain* (Frankfurt am Main: Peter Lang, 1990), 196; and Michael Charles Steinlauf, "Polish-Jewish Theater: The Case of Mark Arnshteyn" (diss., Brandeis University, 1988), 105.

9. The reference to performances in Calcutta comes from Daniel E. Bandmann, *An Actor's Tour, or Seventy Thousand Miles with Shakespeare*, ed. Bernard Gisby (Boston: Cupples, Upham, 1885), 141–145. Actresses often performed *Leah* in Hawaii when traveling between California and Australia. See, e.g., ad, *Pacific Commercial Advertiser* (Honolulu), April 23, 1870; "Sandwich Islands," *North American and United States Gazette* (Philadelphia), May 31, 1870; and "The Theatre," *Pacific Commercial Advertiser*, January 10, 1880. In the early twentieth century, Richard Davey, the London *Times* correspondent in Istanbul, recalled seeing a Hebrew-language performance of Deborah by a touring group from Pest decades earlier, in *The Sultan and His Subjects* (London: Chatto & Windus, 1907), 251. For Jamaica, see Errol Hill, *Jamaican Stage, 1655–1900: Profile of a Colonial Theatre* (Amherst: University of Massachusetts Press, 1992), 80.

10. Only the libretto remains. See *Lia: Dramma lirico in 5 atti dei M. Marcello. Musica del maestro Cav. Francesco Schira da rappresentarsi al Teatro la Fenice di Venezia* (Milan: Tito di Gio, 1876). For early reports on Schira's work on *Lia*, see *Musical World* (London), October 31, 1863; *Orchestra* (London), January 16, 1864; and *Reader* (London), January 23, 1864.

11. The score for *Debora* has never been published. See, however, the piano reduction for Josef Bohuslav Foerster, *Debora: Zpěvohra o 3 jednáních. Libreto napsal dle motivů Rosenthalovy* [sic] *činohry Jaroslav Kvapil* (Prague: Foersterova Společnost, 1919); and the 1959 archival recording of *Debora*, issued on CD in 2009 (Prague: Radioservis, 2009), with an English translation of Kvapil's Czech libretto. For background, see Foerster's autobiography, *Der Pilger: Erinnerungen eines Musikers*, trans. Pavel Eisner (Prague: Artia, 1955), as well as Annemarie Fischer, "Die 'schöne Jüdin' in Oper und Schauspiel: Heinrich Marschners *Der Templer und die Jüdin*, Salomon Hermann Mosenthals und Josef Bohuslav Foersters *Debora(h)*," in Hans-Peter Bayerdörfer, Jens Malte Fischer, and Frank Halbach, eds., *Judenrollen: Darstellungformen im europäischen Theater von der Restauration bis zur Zwischenkriegszeit* (Tübingen: Niemeyer, 2008), 57–76.

12. For background, see Laurence Senelick, "Melodramatic Gesture in Carte-de-Visite Photographs," *Theatre* 18, no. 2 (1987): 5–13.

13. Robert Stoepel, "Reminiscences of Leah" (New York: William Pond, 1863). For background, see Michael V. Pisani's fascinating study *Music for the Melodramatic Theatre in Nineteenth-Century London and New York* (Iowa City: University of Iowa Press, 2014), 115–116.

14. Brinley Richards (music) and Henry Farnie (lyrics), "Leah's Song" (London: Cramer, 1864); and A[ugustus] Greville (music) and W[ellington] Guernsey (lyrics), "It Is the Hour: Leah's Song" (London: Hutchings & Romer, 1864).

15. Edward W. Price, *Leah: Ecce Homo, and Other Poems* (London: Dalton and Lucy, 1864); *London Review*, June 25, 1864; and "New Poetry: Leah, Ecce Homo, and Other Poems. By Edward W. Price," *Athenaeum*, July 16, 1864.

16. "Literary Notices," *Godey's Lady's Book and Magazine* 77 (November 1868): 451.

17. For positive reviews, see "Literary Notices," *North American and United States Gazette* (Philadelphia), December 30, 1869; "Review of New Books," *Philadelphia Inquirer*, January 3, 1870; "New Publications," *American Israelite*, January 26, 1877; *Jewish Messenger*, February 23, 1877; "Peterson's Series," *Jewish Exponent*, July 1, 1892; "Recent Publications," *Morning Call* (San Francisco), July 24, 1892; "The Review Table," *Bismarck (ND) Daily Tribune*, October 9, 1892; and "Notes on New Books," *North American* (Philadelphia), August 6, 1892. The British edition of *Leah, the Jewish Maiden* (London: Ward and Lock, 1864) was republished in 1865 and 1870, with the second edition bearing

the subtitle *A Romance of the Forsaken*; the American edition, first released in 1868 with a somewhat different title (see below), was republished in 1876 and 1892.

18. *Leah; or, the Forsaken: A Romance of a Jewish Maiden by Dr. Mosenthal* (Philadelphia: T. B. Peterson & Brothers, [1868]). The promotional blurb printed on the cover was frequently echoed in ads and the reviews quoted above.

19. As mentioned in the Introduction, in stressing the creative dimensions of adaptation, I follow Linda Hutcheon, *A Theory of Adaptation*, 2nd ed. (New York: Routledge, 2012).

20. See, e.g., *Album österreichischer Dichter*, n.s. (Vienna: Pfautsch & Voss, 1858), 254.

21. The 1850 print edition of *Deborah* referred theater managers to Mosenthal's agent Hermann Michaelson, one of the most prominent theatrical agents of his era; see Salomon Hermann Mosenthal, *Deborah: Volks-Schauspiel in vier Akten* (Pest: Gustav Heckenast, 1850), 6. Josef Weilen reports that after the Berlin premiere in May 1849, Mosenthal sold the rights to *Deborah* for all German stages—with the exception of those in Berlin and Vienna—to Michaelson for the relatively large sum of 100 thaler; see Weilen, "S. H. Mosenthal: Ein Lebensbild," originally published in the *Wiener Abendpost* and subsequently repr. in *S. H. Mosenthal's gesammelte Werke* (Stuttgart: Eduard Hallberger, 1878), 6:40. On Michaelson, see "Nekrologie," *Almanach der Genossenschaft deutscher Bühnen-Angehöriger* 4 (1876): 98; Susanne Jährig-Ostertag, "Zur Geschichte der Theaterverlage in Deutschland bis zum Ende des Dritten Reiches," *Archiv für Geschichte des Buchwesens* 16 (1976): 143–290, esp. 176ff.; and Birgit Pargner, *Zwischen Tränen und Kommerz: Das Rührtheater Charlotte Birch-Pfeiffers (1800–1868) in seiner künstlerischen und kommerziellen Verwertung* (Bielefeld: Aisthesis, 1999), 282–302. Mosenthal himself points out that the French and Italian versions of the play yielded him profits, in his December 23, 1863, letter to Augustin Daly, Folger Shakespeare Library, Y.c. 4601 (1).

22. Mosenthal, December 23, 1863, letter to Augustin Daly, Folger Shakespeare Library, Y.c. 4601 (1).

23. See "Theaterschau," *Blätter für Musik, Theater und Kunst* (Vienna) February 12, 1864; *Morgenblatt der Bayerischen Zeitung*, March 8, 1864; and "Literarischer Wochenbericht," *Allgemeine Zeitung des Judenthums*, May 17, 1864. The fact that Bateman thought that Mosenthal was dead is mentioned in Mosenthal's "Aus den 'Memoiren' der Deborah," where he notes that she sent him fifty British pounds, half of her earnings on the hundredth performance in London, along with a letter. Bateman's father reports a similar story; see H. L. Bateman, "To the Editors of the N. Y. Express," *New York Saturday Press*, April 28, 1866.

24. The copyright was registered in the name of "Miss Bateman," even in the initial edition of the play that Daly had printed privately. See *Leah, the Forsaken: A Play in Five Acts by Augustin Daly. Arranged from the "Deborah" of Mosenthal Expressly for Miss Bateman*, Billy Rose Theatre Collection 9-NCOF+p.v.498, New York Public Library for the Performing Arts, 2. We shall see in Chapter 4 that at numerous times in the coming years, Daly, who arranged for the copyright, alleged that it had been issued in his name.

25. The performance that Mosenthal attended on May 28, 1865, was given in his honor. See the article in *Der Sammler: Ein Blatt zur Unterhaltung und Belehrung. Beilage zur Augsburger Abendzeitung*, June 7, 1865.

26. See Mosenthal, "Aus den 'Memoiren' der Deborah," 311–313. Mosenthal makes numerous mistakes with the information that he does include in this essay. He claims that Bateman played *Leah* for an entire year in New York before taking the play to London; he notes that she performed *Leah* for a run of 500 performances at the Adelphi with the same troupe she used in New York; and he speculates that Ristori's performance of Deborah in New York encouraged H. L. Bateman to have Daly adapt the play for his daughter. (Ristori first performed the play in New York in 1866, four years after Daly created *Leah* for Kate Bateman.)

27. The version of *Deborah* that Fanny Janauschek used when performing *Deborah* in German in the United States, for instance, trims lines throughout, but without changing anything substantial. See *Classic Dramas as Performed by Fanny Janauschek: Deborah* (New York, Wynkoop & Hallenbeck, 1867), which reproduces Janauschek's version of the play and supplies a crude English

translation. Ristori's version of the play follows a similar principle, with the exception of the change to the ending noted below. See *Debora: Drame en 4 actes de S. B.* [sic] *Mosenthal*, Italian translation by Gaetano Cerri, published alongside the French translation of the Italian text by Constanzo Ferrari (Paris: Morris, 1860); and *Deborah: A Drama in Four Acts by S. B.* [sic] *Mosenthal . . . the Italian Translation by Sig. Gaetano Cerri* (New York: Sanford, Harround, 1866), which also includes an English translation by Isaac C. Pray. The Spanish version follows Mosenthal almost to the letter, with the only difference being that the entire drama is set in Castilian verse, including the sections among the villagers that are in prose in the German original. See *Débora: Drama en cuatro actos, escrito en alemán por Mosenthal, y arreglado en verso castellano por D. Fidel de Sagarminaga* (Bilbao: Juan E. Delmas 1872).

28. See S. H. Mosenthal, *Deborah: Narodna igra v štirih dejanjih*, trans. Fr. Cegnar (Ljubljana: Natisnila "Národna, tiskarna," 1883).

29. See S. H. Mosenthal, *Devorah: ḥizayon: yesodato be-ḥaye ha-'am, be-arba'ah maḥazot*, trans. David ben Yirmiyahu Radner (Vilna, 1884); for bibliography, William Zeitlin, *Kiriat Sefer. Bibliotheca Hebraica Post-Mendelssohniana. Bibliographisches Handbuch der neuhebräischen Litteratur* (Leipzig: Koehler's Antiquarium, 1891), 2:286.

30. S. H. Mosenthal, *Debora* (Warsaw: Jozef Unger, 1858). Wurzbach mentions an earlier Polish translation by the actor Siegmund Anczyc, who played Father Abraham in his final years and who died in 1855. *Deborah* was performed in Polish as early as 1851; see *Der Humorist* (Vienna), January 15, 1851, regarding a performance in Lwów.

31. See the prefatory note to *Deborah: A Drama in Four Acts by S. B.* [sic] *Mosenthal*, 1.

32. Mosenthal, *Debora* [Polish], 116–117. Cf. *Debora: Drame en 4 actes de S. B.* [sic] *Mosenthal*, 42; and *Deborah: A Drama in Four Acts by S. B.* [sic] *Mosenthal . . . the Italian Translation by Sig. Gaetano Cerri*, 45.

33. On Kenney's involvement with the Ristori performance of *Deborah*, see *Saturday Review*, July 11, 1863. On Bateman's response to Ristori's *Deborah*, see the letter from Kate Bateman to Augustin Daly, Paris, August 8, 1863, Folger Shakespeare Library, Y.c. 2673 (1–3).

34. The libretto distributed at the London performance of Ristori's *Deborah* is lost. Manuscripts for Conquest's *Deborah*, *Rebecca*, and *Ruth*, however, have survived in the collection of *Lord Chamberlain's Plays and Day-Books* in the British Library. See *Deborah: A Drama in Four Acts Adapted from Mosenthal's Drama by Geo. Conquest* (MS 53029 S), [Fanny Garthwaite,] *Rebecca, the Jewish Wanderer* (MS 53031 O), and [R. Moore,] *Ruth, the Jewess* (MS 53069 R). Each of these plays concludes, following Ristori, with its heroine making a final speech of forgiveness and reconciliation. Conquest uses the original character names. Apart from that, there is no evidence that Conquest, Garthwaite, or Moore made use of the German text of *Deborah* in preparing their versions of the material. The attribution of *Rebecca* to Garthwaite comes from the British Library catalog. A 1868 playbill indicates that *Ruth* was "adapted by R. Moore, Esq. from Mosenthal's pastoral play of *Deborah*, from which was derived the play of *Leah*"; see playbill, Princess Theatre, London, week of July 20, 1868, Harvard Theatre Collection, playbills and programs, London theaters, ca. 1700–1930, TCS, Princess Theatre, 1867–1896, Houghton Library, Harvard University.

35. The information about Beneville's role in preparing the initial translation of *Deborah* and several other plays for Daly became public in 1866, as part of a series of lawsuits between Daly and the Batemans and between Beneville and Daly over Daly's fees. I return to this issue in Chapter 4. Marvin Felheim erroneously notes: "From all accounts, H. L. Bateman originally gave the play to Daly to adapt in a translation prepared by W. Benneux." See Felheim, *The Theater of Augustin Daly: An Account of the Late Nineteenth Century American Stage* (Cambridge, MA: Harvard University Press, 1956), 158. This misinformation likely comes from a note in a New York Public Library Bulletin on a prompter's copy of the 1890 edition of *Leah*. In contrast, Joseph Daly, in a biography of his brother, notes that a "German friend mentioned this play to Bateman, and he suggested it to Daly, who procured a copy, had it hastily and roughly translated, perceived at once its theatrical value, and adapted it for performance in English." See Joseph Francis Daly, *The Life of Augustin Daly* (New York: Macmillan, 1917), 48. By all accounts, this German friend was the actress Marie Methua-Scheller, who was,

along with her husband, J. Guido Methua, a friend of both the Batemans and Daly. See H. L. Bateman, "To the Editors of the N.Y. Express," *New York Saturday Press*, April 28, 1866.

36. See the playbill for the second performance of *Leah* in Boston, Howard Athenaeum, December 9, 1862, Harvard Theatre Collection, playbills and programs concerning female "stars," THE BPF TCS 72, Houghton Library, Harvard University; and "Local Matters," *Boston Daily Advertiser*, December 10, 1862. Numerous other changes took place between the Boston premiere and the first two weeks of *Leah*'s run in New York. A so-called carpenter scene, a comic interlude between a barber-doctor and a peasant that Bateman's mother had introduced in Boston, was also cut after the *New York Herald* pronounced it "silly." See "The Theatres: Miss Bateman at Niblo's Garden," *New York Herald*, January 20, 1863; "Theatrical," *New York Herald*, February 16, 1863; "Theatrical," *New York Herald*, January 26, 1863; and "Wishing Daly Success: Starting on His Third Foreign Tour," *New York Times*, April 22, 1888.

37. Augustin Daly, *Leah, the Forsaken: A Play, in Five Acts* (New York: Samuel French, 1890), 44. All references to Daly's version are to this edition.

38. See *Leah: A Drama in 5 Acts*, manuscript copy submitted to W. B. Donne at the Lord Chamberlain's Office on September 23, 1863, and approved on September 28, included in *The Lord Chamberlain's Plays and Day-Books*, British Library, MSS 53025 R; and *Leah: A Drama in Five Acts. Property of Miss Bateman*, in Stephen Venner, *Scrapbook on Kate Josephine Bateman and Family*, Robert E. and Jean R. Mahn Center for Archives and Special Collections, MSS397, Ohio University, Athens, Ohio. Stephen Venner, a friend and admirer of Bateman's granddaughter, the actress Valerie Skardon, included the original script in a scrapbook dedicated to Bateman, her daughter the actress Sidney Crowe, Skardon, and other members of the Bateman family who made careers in the theater.

39. Ad for *Deborah of Steinmark*, *New York Herald*, May 30, 1863; "Theaters," *New York Daily Tribune*, May 30, 1863; and "Drama," *Albion*, June 6, 1863. Despite rendering "Steiermark" (Styria) in English as "Steinmark," it stands to reason that Pray knew German and went back to the original to prepare *Deborah of Steinmark*. In 1866, he later prepared the bilingual libretto for Ristori's American production of *Deborah*, placing an English translation of Mosenthal's original alongside Cerri's Italian translation.

40. See "Theatrical," *New York Herald*, May 31, 1863; "Musical and Dramatic," *Jewish Messenger*, June 5, 1863; "Drama," *Albion*, June 6, 1863; "Amusements," *New York Times*, June 8, 1863; and "The Drama," *Knickerbocker Monthly: A National Magazine of Literature, Art, Politics, and Society* 62, no. 7 (July 1863): 93–95.

41. Ad, *Sun* (Baltimore), October 14, 1863. This ad was reprinted on subsequent days, presenting *Miriam, the Deserted* as George Marlowe's translation of the original, four-act play by Mosenthal that was also the basis of *Leah, the Forsaken*. Gladstane continued to perform *Miriam* for several years. Ristori did not perform *Deborah* in the U.S. until 1866; there is no surviving manuscript for Marlowe's version, which may indeed be an original translation from the German.

42. "Dramatic and Musical," *Boston Daily Advertiser*, December 14, 1863; "Theatrical and Musical Items," *Sacramento Daily Union*, January 30, 1864; ad, *Daily National Republican* (Washington, DC), January 9, 1864, and January 13, 1864; "Amusements," *Chicago Tribune*, January 27, 1864; "New Memphis Theatre," *Public Ledger* (Memphis, TN), October 20, 1866; and *Public Ledger* (Memphis, TN), October 20, 1866.

43. Ad, *New York Herald*, January 3, 1864, addressed to managers, lessees, and proprietors of theaters. Daly's correspondence from this period contains numerous references to him and his brother Joseph scanning newspapers from across the country to track down theater managers who owed him money for performing his play and seeking to determine which actresses secured unauthorized copies of his script. See Augustin Daly, letter to Joseph, Nashville, October 3, 1864; Joseph Daly to Augustin (calling him "Johannes"), October 15, 1864; Augustin Daly, letter to Joseph, November 12, 1864; Augustin Daly, letter to Joseph, January 1, 1865, from DC, in *Correspondence of Augustin Daly and Joseph F. Daly and Documents Serving for Memoirs, 1858–1899* [hereafter, Daly, *Correspondence and Documents*], New York Public Library for the Performing Arts, T-Mss 2011-251, vol. 1.

44. I discuss both these adaptations in detail below.

45. I discuss Herman M. Bien and his adaptation of *Leah* in Chapter 4.

46. *Naomi* was created for Emma Waller but also performed later by Fanny B. Price as well. See, e.g., ad, *Sun* (Baltimore), February 25, 1864; "Amusements," *Chicago Tribune*, March 17, 1864; "Opera House, Mrs. Waller as Naomi," *Daily Ohio Statesman* (Columbus), December 14, 1864; ad for *Naomi*, *New York Herald*, October 20, 1867; and "Amusements," *New York Times*, October 22, 1867. See also the playbill for the October 23, 1867, performance of *Naomi, the Jewish Maiden* at the Worrell Sisters' New York Theatre, Harvard Theatre Collection, playbills and programs, New York City theaters, ca. 1800–1930, TCS 65, Folder: Broadway Athenaeum, Houghton Library, Harvard University.

47. See "Provincial," *Orchestra* (London), July 2, 1864.

48. See "Manchester," *Orchestra*, October 15, 1864, 37.

49. Playbills, Fox's Old Bowery Theatre, New York, October 14–15, 1864, October 21, 1864, May 17, 1865, January 26, 1866, Harvard Theatre Collection, playbills and programs from New York City theaters, TCS 65, Folder: Bowery Theatre, 1864–1866, Houghton Library, Harvard University. See also the ads in *Spirit of the Times* (New York), October 15, October 22, October 29, 1864; *Daily Ohio Statesman* (Columbus), June 16, 1865; and New *York Herald*, December 18, 1868.

50. See ad and "Dramatic and Musical," *Boston Daily Advertiser*, February 13, 1865.

51. "Amusements," *New York Herald*, August 29, 1866; and "Miss Lacoste at the French Theatre," *New York Herald*, August 31, 1866.

52. See ad, *New York Herald*, February 26, 1867; and "Park Theatre—Brooklyn," *New York Herald*, March 1, 1867.

53. Playbill, *Leah, the Outcast*, September 5, 1867, Whitman's Continental Theatre, Boston, Harvard Theatre Collection, playbills and programs, Boston theaters, ca. 1800–1930, THE GEN TCS 66, Folder: Continental Theatre, Houghton Library, Harvard University; and "Dramatic and Musical," *Boston Daily Advertiser*, September 5 and 7, 1867.

54. *Era*, July 11, 1869.

55. "Amusements," *New York Times*, November 23, 1875; "Music and the Drama: The New Leah," *Jewish Messenger*, November 26, 1875; and "Fifth Avenue [Theater]—Miss Morris as Leah," *Spirit of the Times*, November 27, 1875.

56. Charles Smith Cheltnam, *Deborah; or, the Jewish Maiden's Wrong! A Drama in Three Acts* (London: Lacy, n.d.), *Lacy's Acting Edition*. In the U.S., Cheltnam's drama appeared in *De Witt's Acting Plays* as *Deborah; [Leah,] or, the Jewish Maiden's Wrong. A Drama in Three Acts* (New York: De Witt, n.d.).

57. "Preacher-Dramatist Is Here: Rev. Mr. Booth Will Conduct Rehearsals of 'Leah, the Forsaken,'" *New York Telegraph*, October 24, 1898; and "New Theatrical Matter: The Jewess in 'Leah' Weds the Christian in Harlem," *Sun* (New York), October 13, 1898; "Columbus—Leah," clipping dated October 15, 1898, unknown paper, Harvard Theatre Collection, Clippings 13, Leah, the Forsaken, Houghton Library, Harvard University; and *New York Dramatic Mirror*, October 15, 1898. For background on Booth, see "A Reverend's Downfall," *Deseret Evening News*, July 14, 1890, repr. from *New York World*, July 13, 1890; "Too Much Wine," *Wheeling Daily Intelligencer*, July 14, 1890; "Rector Booth Assaulted: Attacked in a Railroad Car by an Angry Husband," *New York Times*, January 7, 1887; "Telegraphic Brevities," *Sacramento Daily Record-Union*, February 15, 1887; and "Rev. Mr. Booth Resigns," *Evening Star* (Washington, DC), January 25, 1887.

58. "Miss Nance O'Neil's Matinee," British newspaper (unnamed), June 27, 1899; and Harvard Theatre Collection, Clippings 13, The Jewess.

59. See my discussion of the films in Chapter 3.

60. See, e.g., promptbook for unidentified production of *Leah, the Forsaken*, bound together with *Frou Frou*, Harvard Theatre Collection, THE TS 22445.101; and promptbook for *Leah, the Forsaken*, Harvard Theatre Collection, THE TS 2378.30, Houghton Library, Harvard University.

61. *Leah, the Forsaken*, handwritten script belonging to the actress Ada Lawrence, State Library of Victoria, Australia, Box 1867/5, Ms 11683.

62. Helen D'Este, for instance, performed a three-act version of *Leah* that reviews make clear has to have been an unacknowledged version of Cheltnam's play; see ad, *Atlanta Constitution*, February 16, 1872; and "Theatrical Notes," *Daily Phoenix* (Columbia, SC), April 13, 1872. The *Leah* that Katherine Rogers performed in San Francisco and Chicago seems to have been using the Cheltnam script as well; see "Amusements," *Daily Evening Bulletin* (San Francisco), February 7, 1874; and "Amusements," *Chicago Daily Tribune*, April 9, 1874. Augusta Dargon performed Daly's play with Cheltnam's title in both Wheeling, WV, and Galveston, TX; see "Deborah," *Wheeling Daily Intelligencer*, November 8, 1876; and "Miss Dargon Took Her Leave of Galveston Last Night in Her Great Play of Deborah," *Galveston Daily News*, January 20, 1877.

63. Playbills and reviews for Fanny B. Price's *Naomi, the Jewish Maiden*, for instance, indicate a play that differed little from the *Leah* that Price performed in other cities. Mary Gladstane, who created the role of Miriam in *Miriam, the Deserted*, occasionally performed the same play, billing it as *Deborah* or *Leah*. See playbill for Price in *Naomi, the Jewish Maiden*, Worrell Sisters' New York Theatre, October 23, 1867, Harvard Theatre Collection, playbills and programs, New York City theaters, ca. 1800–1930, TCS 65, Folder: Broadway Athenaeum, Houghton Library, Harvard Theatre Collection; and "Amusements," *New York Times*, October 22, 1867. Price began performing *Leah* in early 1866 and performed it regularly until the mid-1870s. For Gladstane performances of *Deborah* and *Leah* that bear a striking resemblance to her *Miriam*, see "Amusements: Academy of Music," *Daily Cleveland Herald*, April 23, 1868; "Amusements," *Chicago Tribune*, April 8, 1869; "St. Charles Theatre," *New-Orleans Times*, February 2, 1870; and the broadside for a July 15, 1878, performance of *Leah, the Forsaken* at the Theatre Royal in Dublin, Billy Rose Theatre Collection, New York Public Library for the Performing Arts, MWEZ+n.c. 20, 329 Programs file.

64. "Amusements," *New York Herald*, October 22, 1867.

65. See, e.g., "Kate Josefine Bateman und die 'Leah' auf der englischen Bühne," *Recensionen und Mittheilungen über Theater und Musik*, July 29, 1865.

66. See Nicholas Daly, *Sensation and Modernity in the 1860s* (Cambridge: Cambridge University Press, 2013); and Michael Diamond, *Victorian Sensation, or, the Spectacular, the Shocking and the Scandalous in Nineteenth-Century Britain* (London: Anthem, 2003).

67. See, e.g., "Kate Josefine Bateman und die 'Leah' auf der englischen Bühne"; and "Deborah," *Fränkischer Kurier (Mittelfränkische Zeitung)*, July 11, 1850.

68. Daly, *Leah, the Forsaken*, 38, 42.

69. Daly's decision to call his drama *Leah* rather than *Deborah* was the subject of numerous urban legends in the nineteenth century. H. L. Bateman, Kate's father, claimed that his daughter "rebaptized" the play *Leah* after finding this "beautiful Jewish name" on a set of wedding cards that she encountered by chance on the evening that he agreed to purchase the play from Daly. See H. L. Bateman, "To the Editors of the N.Y. Express," *New York Saturday Press*, April 28, 1866. In an 1896 interview, however, Kate Bateman recalled that her mother—not her father—first put the play into her hands, at which point she immediately recognized "that in America, where all the black cooks, then to be found in almost every house, were called Deborah, its title would be a great mistake. The name of Leah instantly occurred to me, and *Leah* the title became." See "Memories of the Stage: Interview with Miss Bateman," *Black and White*, April 25, 1896; this argument was echoed earlier in "The London Theatres," *London Review*, October 17, 1863. The German American press in the 1860s assumed that Daly called the play *Leah* to avoid the unpleasant way Americans pronounced the name Deborah, with the accent on the first rather than the second syllable. See clipping from the *New Yorker Staatszeitung*, in Daly, *Correspondence and Documents*, vol. 1. A Viennese review journal, finally, similarly noted that given that Deborah was too difficult to pronounce in English, Daly simply selected the name of the first Jewish bride announced in the *New York Herald* for the title of his play. See "Kate Josefine Bateman und die 'Leah' auf der englischen Bühne." This tale has little basis in fact. A review of James P. Maher's *Index to Marriages and Deaths in the New York Herald, 1856–1863* (Alexandria, VA, 1991) reveals that there was only one Leah whose marriage was reported in the *New York Herald*, and she does not seem to have been Jewish. The fact that Leah was such a

rare name in North America during this period does speak to an Old Testament exoticism that set it apart from Deborah and made it appealing.

70. Daly, *Leah, the Forsaken*, 1. This is also the case in the privately printed script.

71. See, e.g., the ad for the premiere of *Leah* on the backside of the playbill for the December 5, 1862, performance of *Macbeth* at the Howard Athenaeum, Boston, Harvard Theatre Collection, playbills and programs concerning female "stars," THE BPF TCS 72, Houghton Library, Harvard University; "Niblo's Garden" [review of *Leah*, in an unnamed New York newspaper, from late January 1863], Daly, *Correspondence and Documents*, vol. 1; "Musical and Dramatic," *Jewish Messenger*, January 23, 1863; "Miss Bateman as Leah," *Philadelphia Press*, April 14, 1863; and broadside poster for *Leah* at the Chesnut [sic] Street Theatre, Philadelphia, both in *Daly Theatre Scrapbooks*, New York Public Library for the Performing Arts, 8-MWED+, vol. 1.

72. "Music and the Drama," *Spirit of the Times*, January 24, 1863. This review, rare for its familiarity with the reception of *Deborah* in the German-speaking world, also contains numerous inaccuracies, claiming that the censors at the Burgtheater in Vienna rejected the play because of its subversive nature.

73. "Musical and Dramatic," *Jewish Messenger*, January 23, 1863.

74. See (one example among many) ad for *Leah* in the *New York Herald*, January 18, 1863.

75. For background, see Jonathan D. Sarna, *When Grant Expelled the Jews* (New York: Schocken, 2012). General Grant, as we noted at the beginning of the chapter, saw *Leah* on more than one occasion and seems to have been particularly enamored of Avonia Jones's performance as Leah.

76. [Augustin Daly,] "A Memoir of Miss Bateman: Being a Brief Chronicle of the Early Successes and Later Triumphs of the Great American Tragic Artiste. Together with a Condensation of the Incidents and Some Extracts from the Book of the Play of 'Leah, the Forsaken,' as Played by Miss Bateman" (New York: Wynkoop, Hallenbeck & Thomas, 1863), 14–15.

77. [Daly,] "Memoir," 15. The language is used elsewhere. See, e.g., the ad for the premiere of *Leah* on the backside of the playbill for the December 5, 1862, performance of *Macbeth* at the Howard Athenaeum, Boston, Harvard Theatre Collection, playbills and programs concerning female "stars," THE BPF TCS 72, Houghton Library, Harvard University.

78. *Leah, the Forsaken*, 44.

79. *Leah, the Forsaken*, 44.

80. See, e.g., Bryan Cheyette and Nadia Valman, eds., *The Image of the Jew in European Liberal Culture, 1789–1914* (London: Vallentine Mitchell, 2004).

81. For background, see Daly, *Sensation and Modernity in the 1860s*; Diamond, *Victorian Sensation*; and George Pate, "'Totally Original': Daly, Boucicault, and Commercial Art in Late Nineteenth Century Drama," *Theatre Symposium* 22 (2014): 9–21.

82. See *Jewish Record* (New York), January 31, 1863, quoted according to Daly, *Correspondence and Documents*, vol. 1; *Philadelphia Inquirer*, April 22, 1863; "Mozart Hall—Janauschek," *Israelite*, December 25, 1868; "Mrs. Crisp's 'Leah,'" *Dallas Herald*, February 3, 1870; and "New Memphis Theater," *Public Ledger* (Memphis), October 28, 1868.

83. The New York *Jewish Messenger*, e.g., celebrated *Leah* for its ability to "disabuse" the "minds of the masses" of "the unfounded prejudice they have formed against the Hebrew race." See "Leah, the Forsaken," *Jewish Messenger*, February 6, 1863. The New York *Jewish Record* singled out Bateman for the way she elicited sympathy for Jewish suffering, pronouncing *Leah* a drama "intensely interesting to our co-religionists, as it is founded on the persecutions endured by our nation throughout Europe during the eighteenth century." *Jewish Record*, January 31, 1863, quoted according to Daly, *Correspondence and Documents*, vol. 1.

84. "Musical and Dramatic," *Jewish Messenger*, January 23, 1863.

85. See the review of *Leah* in the New York *Jewish Record*, January 31, 1863; and Daly, *Correspondence and Documents*, vol. 1. A similar point is made in "Leah, the Forsaken," *Jewish Messenger*, February 6, 1863.

86. "Feuilleton: Aus London. 20. Jänner," *Die Presse* (Vienna), January 25, 1865.

87. "Kate Josefine Bateman und die 'Leah' auf der englischen Bühne."

88. See the November 14, 1862, letter from Sidney Frances Crowell Bateman to Augustin Daly and the December 3, 1862, letter from Hezekiah Linthicum Bateman to Augustin Daly, Folger Shakespeare Library, Y.c. 2674 (1–7), #1 and Y.c. 2671 (1).

89. See, e.g., "Local Matters," *Boston Daily Advertiser*, December 8, 1862; "Dramatic and Musical," *Boston Daily Advertiser*, December 15, 1862; ad for premiere of *Leah* on the backside of playbill for the December 5, 1862, performance of *Macbeth* at the Howard Athenaeum, Boston, Harvard Theatre Collection, playbills and programs concerning female "stars," THE BPF TCS 72, Houghton Library, Harvard University; and ad for *Leah*, *Jewish Messenger*, January 23, 1863.

90. By the end of the first week of Bateman's initial run of *Leah* in New York, newspapers were already venturing the speculation that Daly was the author. See "Leah," *Evening Courier* (New York), January 24, 1863, in Daly, *Correspondence and Documents*, vol. 1.

91. See, e.g., "The Theatres: Miss Bateman at Niblo's Garden," *New York Herald*, January 20, 1863; "Theatrical," *New York Herald*, January 26, 1863; "The Footlights: Niblo's," *New-York Illustrated News*, February 7, 1863; and reviews of *Leah* included in Daly, *Correspondence and Documents*, vol. 1.

92. For clear attributions of Daly's authorship, see playbill, Bateman in *Leah*, May 21, 1863, Niblo's Garden, New York, Harvard Theatre Collection, playbills and programs, New York City theaters, ca. 1800–1930, TCS 65, Folder: Niblo's Garden, 1861–1864, Houghton Library, Harvard University; and the ad for the Daly benefit performance of *Leah*, *New York Herald*, May 23, 1863.

93. Ads for Daly's other plays of the 1860s, *Taming a Butterfly* (1864), *Griffith Gaunt* (1866), and *Under the Gaslight* (1867), all listed Daly as the "author of *Leah, the Forsaken*."

94. Charles Lamb Kenney, "The New Actress and the New Play at the Adelphi Theatre" (London: W. S. Johnson, 1863).

95. "Leah," *Times* (London), October 2, 1863, in *Daly Theatre Scrapbooks*, vol. 1, New York Public Library.

96. See, e.g., "Drama: 'Leah' at Niblo's Garden," *Round Table* 3, no. 21 (January 27, 1866): 55; and "Theater and Things Theatrical," *Spirit of the Times*, January 27, 1866.

97. The official manuscript submitted to the Lord Chamberlain's Office for licensing in September 1863 differs at points from Bateman's personal handwritten copy of the script. Bateman's script includes copious stage directions, as well as detailed directions regarding props and music. It also includes additional dialogue, integrating a small amount of material from Daly's *Leah* that does not appear in the 1863 script produced by Oxenford. The dialogue from Daly that Bateman's script restored, nevertheless, was subjected to the same level and type of rigorous stylistic rewriting as Oxenford's script, giving one reason to speculate that the surviving copy of Bateman's script is simply a later version of Oxenford's rewriting of Daly's text. Differences between these two scripts will be noted below, as relevant. I cite Bateman's personal copy of the script below as Bateman, *Leah*, referring to the manuscript copy in the British Library as Oxenford, *Leah*.

98. Mosenthal had actually offered *Pietra* to Daly first, as part of an exchange for royalties. See Mosenthal, December 23, 1863, letter to Augustin Daly. Mosenthal's later letter to Bateman about *Pietra* and her right to perform it was reproduced in the press. See, e.g., "Mrs. Typeset's Diary," *Harper's Bazaar* 1, no. 6 (December 7, 1867): 87. *Helvellyn* premiered at Covent Garden in November 1864. See the vocal score and piano reduction, G. A. Macfarren and John Oxenford, *Helvellyn: An Opera in Four Acts* (London: Cramer, [187?]).

99. Bateman, *Leah*, Act II.viii; and Oxenford, *Leah*, 21. In Bateman's personal copy of the script, each act is separately paginated.

100. Bateman, *Leah*, Act V.vi. Oxenford, *Leah*, 63, retains the reference to a "tribe of Jews . . . afraid of our villagers" but not the invocation of their plans to emigrate to America.

101. Bateman, *Leah*, Act V.xx. The final sentence, "Madalena + child too," is added in, in Bateman's handwriting, as are numerous other minor revisions throughout the script. The dialogue in the Oxenford manuscript is practically identical. The earlier manuscript, however, does not yet integrate all the changes in staging that became characteristic of Bateman's *Leah*. In the Oxenford

manuscript, Leah simply "draws a knife," as in Daly, and she does not die in Rudolf's arms; rather, she "is caught by Rudolf+Madelina [sic], falls into their arms—and dies." Oxenford, *Leah*, 75–76. Both "Schneider Sees Leah" and the 1869 illustration in *Frank Leslie's Illustrated Newspaper* (see Chapter 1) indicate that Bateman had revised the original stage directions of the Oxenford manuscript by the late 1860s, at the latest.

102. Bateman, *Leah*, Act I.i. Bateman's script actually includes only the first verse but mentions that the curtain rises at the beginning of the second verse and that the villagers leave the church when the hymn is complete. The Oxenford manuscript does not include the hymn. Given that Stoepel's music was used in London, it stands to reason that the hymn was used at the initial performances of *Leah* there as well. Mosenthal's original text mentions a hymn that is sung in church but does not include a text for one.

103. Bateman, *Leah*, Act I.ii. The Oxenford manuscript gives this a slightly different phrasing. Madelina [sic] here refers to the Jewess she has encountered outside of town as a "child of Adam+therefore a sister" (Oxenford, *Leah*, 2).

104. "'Deborah' in England," *Musical World* (London), October 1, 1864. This comment is included in an article that offered a translation of an article in a Viennese review journal that made precisely this point: "'Deborah' in England," *Recensionen und Mittheilungen über Theater und Musik*, September 16, 1864. Baffled by *Leah*'s success in London, the Austrian reviewer speculated that it was the final scene, with Leah's death performing the "victory of Christ over Jehova," that ensured its success among the English, with their "addiction" to missionary activity and their "massive piety." *Musical World* appended the following comment to its translation of the German article: "Miss Bateman would not quite agree with the writer of the above as to the cause of the great run of *Leah*."

105. Kenney, "The New Actress and the New Play at the Adelphi Theatre," 6.

106. Apart from invoking the moon and reflecting on mortality and the afterlife in vague terms, the lyrics to "It Is the Hour: Leah's Song" have nothing to do with *Leah*. There is no mention of the persecution of the Jews—or indeed, of Jews at all—or of the tortured love affair between Leah and Rudolf.

107. See, e.g., ad for "Leah's Song," *Illustrated London News*, June 18, 1864.

108. *Orchestra* (London), January 16, 1864.

109. Richards/Farnie, "Leah's Song," 4–5.

110. Richards/Farnie, "Leah's Song," 2.

111. Price, *Leah: Ecce Homo, and Other Poems*, 129, 145.

112. *Leah, the Jewish Maiden*, 316.

113. I quote here following the published libretto from the Venice premiere in 1876: *Lia: Dramma lirico in 5 atti dei M. Marcello*, 52.

114. Ad, *Tages-Post* (Linz), April 21, 1865.

115. The short-lived production of *Ruth*, an 1868 adaptation based on Ristori's version, actually brings a Jewish collective onto stage in the final scene, an innovation that later became a hallmark of Sarah Bernhardt's version of *Leah*. See *Ruth, the Jewess*, 53. I discuss Bernhardt in detail in Chapter 3.

116. Playbill, Edith Heraud in *Deborah*, Great National Standard Theatre, June 4, 1866, East London Theater Archive, http://www.elta-project.org/browse.html?recordId=2923.

117. Conquest shortens Ristori's version considerably, deleting the character of Ruben and the scene with the group of Jewish emigrants at the beginning of Act IV. He also trims back the dialogue of the play at many junctures, introduces a small amount of new material, and folds several minor figures into one another. Following Bateman's *Leah*, he also has the schoolmaster eavesdrop on Deborah and Joseph during their romantic scene in the woods.

118. "Music and the Drama," *Athenaeum*, February 20, 1864. "Muttoniana," *Musical World*, June 18, 1864, notes the similarities between Conquest's *Deborah* and Ristori's version, setting both in contrast to Bateman's *Leah*. See also "The Drama," *Reader*, February 11, 1865. "Music and the Drama," *Athenaeum* (London), February 25, 1865, makes clear that the punctuation of sentiments

regarding religious tolerance with applause was an ongoing feature of performances of Conquest's *Deborah*.

119. See *Rebecca, the Jewish Wanderer*, 27–28. One highly critical review of Marian Ferris's performance of *Rebecca* at the Marylebone Theatre does concede that the play "appeared to gratify the audience to the highest extent"; see "Theatres," *Orchestra* (London), August 13, 1864, 725. Sophia Miles apparently performed *Rebecca* at the Queen's Theatre in Dublin the following month as well; see "Dublin," *Orchestra* (London), September 17, 1864, 807.

120. See "Princess's," *Athenaeum* (London), July 11, 1868; "The Theatres," *Orchestra* (London), July 11, 1868; "Theater- und Kunstnachrichten," *Neue Freie Presse* (Vienna), July 14, 1868; "Ruin Seize Thee, Ruthless," *Fun* (London), July 25, 1868; and "Eine Bearbeitung der Deborah auf der englischen Bühne," *Blätter für literarische Unterhaltung*, August 20, 1868. These negative judgments were not universal, however. See "The Drama: Princess's Theatre," *Examiner* (London), July 11, 1868. According to a note in the *London Review*, September 26, 1868, Kate Saville, who created the role of Ruth in London, also performed the play that summer in Edinburgh.

121. I quote Cheltnam according to the print version of *Deborah; or, the Jewish Maiden's Wrong!* 29–30. The manuscript of Cheltnam's *Deborah* in *Lord Chamberlain's Plays and Day-Books* at the British Library manifests only minor differences. Cf. Cheltnam, *Deborah: A New Drama*, MSS 53033 E.

122. Cheltnam, *Deborah*, 2.

123. Cheltnam, *Deborah*, 2.

124. Cheltnam, *Deborah*, 26.

125. Cheltnam, *Deborah*, 27.

126. In the original manuscript version of Cheltnam's *Deborah*, the scene between Deborah and Reuben is the third rather than the second scene in the act, following a dialogue between Rose and Peter that follows it in the print version of Cheltnam.

127. Cheltnam, *Deborah*, 38. The dialogue for this scene is identical in the manuscript version of the play. Like other copies of scripts submitted to the British licensing commission, the manuscript version of *Deborah* contains only minimal stage directions.

128. For other examples of biting satire directed toward Mosenthal and *Deborah*, see "Auf nach Rom!," *Figaro* (Vienna), March 20, 1869; and "Mosenthalia," *Der Floh* (Vienna), March 21, 1869.

129. The same issue of *Figaro* that published this cartoon also included a poem poking fun of Cerri's dedication to Ristori. See "Sign. Cajetano der Dichter der Iris an die Ristori." Cerri, the son of an Austrian official in Cremona (Austrian Lombardy), learned German as a young man and wrote in both German and Italian.

130. "Grand Masquerade Ball Given by Mr. Maretzek at the Academy of Music, April 4, 1866," *Harper's Weekly*, April 14, 1866, 232–233.

131. "The Bal d'Opera," *New York Times*, April 6, 1866. Oversize heads on dwarf-like bodies have been typical of caricature since the late sixteenth century. See E. H. Gombrich (with Ernst Kris), "The Principles of Caricature," *British Journal of Medical Psychology* 17 (1938): 319–342.

132. The title for the image is mentioned in "The Bal d'Opera," *New York Times*, April 4, 1866.

133. On Setchell's biography, see William Winter, "Daniel E. Setchell," in *Brief Chronicles* (New York: Dunlap Society, 1889), 255–257; and the editorial preface to Mark Twain's sketch "A Voice for Setchell," in Mark Twain, *Early Tales and Sketches, Vol. 2, 1864–65*, ed. Edgar Marquess Branch and Hobert H. Hirst (Berkeley: University of California Press, 1981), 169–171.

134. For examples of Burbank's performance of "Leah the Forsook," see "Readings," *Lowell Daily Citizen*, November 26, 1878; and ad, *Sun* (Baltimore), September 30, 1879.

135. For references to performances of Howard's burlesque on *Leah* in New York, Philadelphia, and Buffalo, see "First Time on Any Stage, LEAH THE SHOOK," *Buffalo Courier*, October 7, 1876; ad, *New York Clipper*, October 14, 1876; "Theatrical Record," *New York Clipper*, November 4, 1876; and ad, *New York Clipper*, August 18, 1877. For references to the copy of *Leah the Forsook* that was for sale, see ad, *New York Clipper*, February 26, 1881. While some of the scripts and ballads for Howard's minstrel routines are available in libraries and archives, none of the materials from his *Leah the Forsook* seem

to have survived. Rollins did not actually write "Shoo Fly" but was listed as the arranger on the original 1869 publication of "Shew Fly! Comic Song and Dance, or Walk Round," words by Billy Reeves, music by Frank Campbell, arranged by Rollin Howard (Boston: White, Smith & Perry, 1869).

136. William Routledge, *Leah, a Hearty Joke in a Cab Age* (1869), bound with *Mrs. Beflat's Blunder*, 34–76, Harvard Theatre Collection, TS Promptbook, Houghton Library, Harvard University. For the New York performance, see "Amusements," *New York Times*, April 27, 1871. The nineteenth-century press makes references to several other burlesques on *Leah* and *Deborah* for which there seems to be little in the way of further information. An article in the March 24, 1866, edition of the *Boston Daily Advertiser* mentions a burlesque *Leah* "now being performed by negro minstrels" that foregrounded the peculiarity of Bateman's acting, with her vacantly staring eyes. The English actor Edward Righton performed a short minstrel burlesque on *Leah* at Wood's Museum in New York in February 1870; see "New-Yorkisms," *Daily Evening Telegraph* (Philadelphia), February 10, 1870. Bateman's *Leah* also made a cameo in H. J. Byron's burlesque revue, *1863; or, the Sensations of the Past Season*, repr. in Richard W. Schoch, ed., *Victorian Theatrical Burlesques* (Burlington, VT: Ashgate, 2003), 53–94.

137. *New York Herald*, July 13, 1863; "Academy of Music," *Milwaukee Daily Sentinel*, December 15, 1864; and "Our Gossip," *Jewish Messenger*, March 3, 1876.

138. See, e.g., "Miss Bateman as 'Leah,'" *Spirit of the Times*, January 31, 1863; and the running column, "Music and the Drama: Theaters and Things Theatrical, by 'Bayard,'" *Spirit of the Times*, February 7, February 14, February 21, May 16, and May 23, 1863. For biographical background on Wood, see "Literary Notes," *Round Table* 1, no. 16 (April 2, 1864): 249; and William Winter, "Frank Wood," *Brief Chronicles* (New York: Dunlap Society, 1889), 337–338.

139. On Wood's relationship to Daly, see Joseph Francis Daly, *The Life of Augustin Daly* (New York: Macmillan, 1917), 55–56.

140. Ad, *New York Herald*, February 21, 1864. On Beneville's involvement in preparing the original rough translation from the French, see "Things Theatrical," *Public Ledger* (Memphis), May 8, 1866; and "The Play of 'Leah' Again in Court—How It Was Translated and What It Cost. Emile Benville [*sic*] vs. Augustine [*sic*] J. Daly," *New York Herald*, November 20, 1866.

141. [Mark Twain,] "A Voice for Setchell," *Californian*, May 27, 1865, repr. in Twain, *Early Tales and Sketches, Vol. 2, 1864–65*, 172–173.

142. See, e.g., "Winter Garden," *New York Times*, July 15, 1863; "Drama," *Albion*, July 25, 1863; *New York Clipper*, July 25, 1863; "The Idler About Town," *Frank Leslie's Illustrated Newspaper*, August 1, 1863; and "Dramatic and Musical," *Boston Daily Advertiser*, August 12, 1863.

143. "Amusements," *Daily Evening Bulletin* (San Francisco), August 21 and August 22, 1865. Heron was, incidentally, married to Robert Stoepel, who composed the music for Bateman's *Leah*.

144. "The Idler About Town," *Frank Leslie's Illustrated Newspaper*, August 1, 1863; and "Dramatic and Musical," *Boston Daily Advertiser*, August 12, 1863. There is no surviving script of *Leah the Forsook*. My reconstruction comes from the reviews and discussions listed above, in addition to "Theaters and Things Theatrical," *Spirit of the Times*, July 25, 1863, and the detailed playbills for the August 5, 1863, and August 19, 1863, performances of *Leah the Forsook* in New York and Boston, respectively: Harvard Theatre Collection, J. S. Hagan, *Records of the New York Stage, 1860–1870, Extended and Illustrated for Augustin Daly by Augustus Toedteberg*, vol. 3, *New York Dispatch*, 85, THE pf TS 939.5.3; and Harvard Theatre Collection, playbills and programs from Boston theaters, THE GEN TCS 66, Folder: Howard Athenaeum, Houghton Library, Harvard University.

145. "Theatrical," *New York Herald*, July 14, 1863; and "Theatrical. WINTER GARDEN," *New York Herald*, July 23, 1863.

146. Performing the play in San Francisco, Setchell seems to have moved the action there; see "Amusements," *Daily Evening Bulletin* (San Francisco), August 22, 1865.

147. Playbills for the August 5, 1863, and August 19, 1863, performances of *Leah the Forsook*, quoted above.

148. Playbills for the August 5, 1863, and August 19, 1863, performances of *Leah the Forsook*, quoted above.

149. See Jacqueline L. Romeo, "Comic Coolie: Charles T. Parsloe and Nineteenth-Century American Frontier Melodrama" (diss., Tufts University, 2008).

150. "Drama," *Albion*, July 25, 1863.

151. "Drama," *Albion*, July 18, 1863.

152. Classified ads, *Israelite*, February 17, 1865.

153. Pike was born in Baden, in Germany, where his original surname was Hecht (the German word for "pike"). See Jacob Rader Marcus, *United States Jewry, 1776–1985* (Detroit: Wayne State University Press, 1993), 229, 326, 334.

154. "Our Gossip," *Jewish Messenger*, March 3, 1876.

155. *New-York Illustrated News*, August 1, 1863.

156. *New York Clipper*, August 1, 1863. Apparently, the management of the Winter Garden Theatre felt that Setchell's extemporizing was "not well taken"; in subsequent performances, he did not repeat this remark.

157. "Amusements," *New York Times*, April 27, 1871, reviewing an April 26, 1871, performance at the Union League Theatre.

158. Routledge, *Leah*, 35.

159. Routledge, *Leah*, 39.

160. Routledge, *Leah*, 35.

161. See, e.g., *Examiner* (London), April 2, 1864. For background, see Adam D. Mendelsohn, *The Rag Race: How Jews Sewed Their Way to Success in America and the British Empire* (New York: New York University Press, 2014).

162. Routledge, *Leah*, 70.

163. Routledge, *Leah*, 71.

164. C. H. Hazlewood, *Burlesque Entitled Debo-Leah*, in *Lord Chamberlain's Plays and Day-Books*, in the British Library, MS 53031 R. *Debo-Leah* was performed in London at the Britannia Theatre Hoxton in April 1864, two months after Conquest's *Deborah* had premiered at the Grecian Theatre and just after Bateman's *Leah* closed its initial run at the Adelphi. *Debo-Leah* makes far fewer jokes about Jews than *Leah the Forsook* or Routledge's *Leah*. Colin Henry Hazlewood, well known for his 1863 stage adaptation of Mary Elizabeth Braddon's 1862 sensation novel *Lady Audley's Secret*, was the resident dramatist for the Britannia Theatre.

Chapter 3

Note to epigraph 1: Avonia Jones, January 11, 1863, letter to Augustin Daly, Folger Shakespeare Library, Y.c. 4198 (1–8), #1. Note to epigraph 2: Quoted according to William Archer, *Masks or Faces? A Study in the Psychology of Acting* (London: Longmans, Green, 1888), 65–66.

1. Brecht, "A Short Organon for the Theatre," *Brecht on Theatre: The Development of an Aesthetic*, ed. and trans. John Willett (New York: Hill and Wang, 1964), 193–194; German in Brecht, *Schriften zum Theater: Über eine nicht-aristotelische Dramatik* (Frankfurt: Suhrkamp, 1957), 152–154.

2. Archer, *Masks or Faces?*, 4–5.

3. See Robert Gordon, *The Purpose of Playing: Modern Acting Theories in Perspective* (Ann Arbor: University of Michigan Press, 2006), 8–36.

4. Ad, *Evening Star* (Washington, DC), January 2, 1865.

5. Ad, *Evening Star* (Washington, DC), January 3, 1865; and "Amusements To-Night," *Evening Star* (Washington, DC), January 3, 1865. The reference to Jones as the "high priestess of tragedy" is in "Miss Avonia Jones," *Evening Star* (Washington, DC), December 28, 1864. The review in the *Daily National Intelligencer* (Washington, DC), January 4, 1865, is far more critical of Jones's "melodramatic" acting.

6. Ad, *Daily National Intelligencer*, January 7, 1865. On the Lincolns' attendance at the play, see "Lincoln and the Lively Arts," *Lincoln Lore* no. 1508 (October 1963): 4; Thomas A. Bogar, *American Presidents Attend the Theatre: The Playgoing Experiences of Each Chief Executive* (Jefferson, NC:

McFarland, 2006), 110–111; and Jonathan D. Sarna and Benjamin Shapell, *Lincoln and the Jews: A History* (New York: St. Martin's, 2015), 189–190.

7. See Dennis Kennedy, *The Spectator and the Spectacle: Audiences in Modernity and Postmodernity* (Cambridge: Cambridge University Press, 2009); and Willmar Sauter, "The Audience," in David Wiles and Christine Dymkowski, eds., *The Cambridge Companion to Theatre History* (Cambridge: Cambridge University Press, 2013), 169–183.

8. See Bruce A. McConachie, *Melodramatic Formations: American Theatre and Society, 1820–1870* (Iowa City: University of Iowa Press, 1992).

9. "The Janauschek," *Daily Evening Bulletin* (San Francisco), October 20, 1870; and "Janauschek—Her Debut in English Tragedy," *New York Herald*, October 11, 1870. When performing *Deborah* in English, Janauschek followed Daly and divided the play into five acts.

10. "Theatrical and Musical," *Spirit of the Times* (New York), October 15, 1870.

11. "Theater and Things Theatrical," *Spirit of the Times*, January 27, 1866.

12. "As the Jewess: Nance O'Neil in One of Her Best Characters," *Pacific Commercial Advertiser* (Honolulu), November 17, 1898. The original report referenced in this article appeared in the *Oakland Tribune*.

13. Willmar Sauter, *The Theatrical Event: Dynamics of Performance and Perception* (Iowa City: University of Iowa Press, 2000), 138–139.

14. "A Night at the Adelphi and Haymarket Theatres," *S. G. Sharpe's London Magazine of Entertainment and Instruction for General Reading* (February 1865): 102.

15. See Bruce McConachie, *Engaging Audiences: A Cognitive Approach to Spectating in the Theatre* (New York: Palgrave Macmillan, 2008); and idem, "A Cognitive Approach to Brechtian Theatre," *Theatre Symposium* 14 (2006): 9–24. The notion of conceptual blending is elaborated by Gilles Fauconnier and Mark Turner, *The Way We Think: Conceptual Blending and the Mind's Hidden Complexities* (New York: Basic Books, 2002).

16. McConachie, "A Cognitive Approach to Brechtian Theatre," 15–16; and idem, *Engaging Audiences*, 40–47.

17. Charles E. L. Wingate, "A Notable Night: Bernhardt's First Appearance as Leah, the Forsaken," *Boston Journal*, January 9, 1892.

18. *Deutsches Theater-Album* (Munich), May 5, 1861.

19. *Morgenblatt der Bayerischen Zeitung*, January 20, 1863. A similar point is made in the *Deutsches Theater-Album* review discussed above.

20. Lynn M. Voskuil, *Acting Naturally: Victorian Theatricality and Authenticity* (Charlottesville: University of Virginia Press, 2004), 22.

21. See Lynn M. Voskuil, "Feeling Public: Sensation Theatre, Commodity Culture, and the Victorian Public Sphere," *Victorian Studies* 44, no. 2 (2002): 245–274; and idem, *Acting Naturally*, 62–94. Voskuil draws a productive parallel to the "vacillation between belief and incredulity" that Tom Gunning has identified in early film spectatorship. See Tom Gunning, "An Aesthetic of Astonishment: Early Film and the (In)Credulous Spectator," in Linda Williams, ed., *Viewing Positions: Ways of Seeing Film* (New Brunswick, NJ: Rutgers University Press, 1994), 114–133.

22. See, e.g., the program for a performance of *Deborah* at the Park Theatre in Boston on February 10, 1883, which notes that Mosenthal "conceived and wrote" the role of the "wronged Jewess" for Janauschek; Harvard Theatre Collection, playbills and programs concerning female "stars," THE BPF TCS 72, Fanny Janauschek folder, Houghton Library, Harvard University. Similar claims were promoted in Washington, DC, and elsewhere the year before. See ad, *Evening Star* (Washington, DC), January 26, 1882, and January 27, 1882; "Amusements: Janauschek at Ford's," *Washington Post*, January 28, 1882; and ad, *Rocky Mountain Post* (Denver), April 22, 1882. This rumor had begun to appear already in the mid-1870s. See, e.g., "Fifth Avenue [Theater]—Miss Morris as Leah," *Spirit of the Times*, November 27, 1875.

23. Wingate, "A Notable Night"; and idem, "Bernhardt: Her Reappearance of Leah, the Forsaken," unnamed newspaper, Harvard Theatre Collection, Clippings 13, Folder: Leah, the Forsaken (performances by Sarah Bernhardt), Houghton Library, Harvard University.

24. See, e.g., "The Theatres Last Night," *Philadelphia Inquirer*, April 5, 1892; "Music and Drama: Sarah Bernhardt in 'Leah,'" *Jewish Messenger*, April 22, 1892; Isidore, "London Jottings," *American Israelite*, July 21, 1892; and Wingate, "Bernhardt: Her Reappearance of Leah, the Forsaken." When Janauschek first began to perform in English in 1870, her Czech background was widely reported on in the press. See, e.g., "Janauschek—Her Debut in English Tragedy," *New York Herald*, October 11, 1870; "Janauschek in English Drama," *Frank Leslie's Illustrated Newspaper*, November 5, 1870; and "Janauschek as Deborah at the Academy," *Israelite*, November 11, 1870.

25. See Rachel M. Brownstein, *Tragic Muse: Rachel of the Comédie Française* (New York: Knopf, 1993); and Maurice Samuels, "France's Jewish Star," in *The Right to Difference: French Universalism and the Jews* (Chicago: University of Chicago Press, 2016), chap. 2.

26. See, e.g., J. W., "Deborah: Volks-Schauspiel in 4 Abth. von S. Mosenthal," *Didaskalia*, October 10, 1849; and *Deutsches Theater-Album* (Munich), May 5, 1861.

27. See, e.g., [Augustin Daly,] "A Memoir of Miss Bateman: Being a Brief Chronicle of the Early Successes and Later Triumphs of the Great American Tragic Artiste. Together with a Condensation of the Incidents and Some Extracts from the Book of the Play of 'Leah, the Forsaken,' as Played by Miss Bateman" (New York: Wynkoop, Hallenbeck & Thomas, 1863); ad for *Leah*, *New York Herald*, February 20, 1863; "Miss Bateman as Leah," *Philadelphia Press*, April 14, 1863, in *Daly Theatre Scrapbooks*, New York Public Library for the Performing Arts, 8-MWED+, vol. 1; Charles Lamb Kenney, "The New Actress and the New Play at the Adelphi Theatre," (London: W. S. Johnson, 1863); "Kate Josefine Bateman und die 'Leah' auf der englischen Bühne," *Recensionen und Mittheilungen über Theater und Musik* (Vienna), July 29, 1865; "Drama," *Albion*, January 20, 1866; "Theater," *Belletristisches Journal*, April 20, 1866; and "Amusements," *New York Herald*, September 21, 1869.

28. Kim Marra, *Strange Duets: Impresarios and Actresses in the American Theatre, 1865–1914* (Iowa City: University of Iowa Press, 2006), 14.

29. "The Play of Deborah," *Galveston Daily News*, January 24, 1877. See also "Miss Dargon Took Her Leave of Galveston Last Night in Her Great Play of Deborah," *Galveston Daily News*, January 20, 1877.

30. "Amusements," *Daily National Republican*, November 23, 1863.

31. "Amusements: Academy of Music," *Chicago Tribune*, February 13, 1872.

32. "Recollections of Lucille Western," *Theatre*, undated, Harvard Theatre Collection, Clippings 14, Lucille Western Folder, Houghton Library, Harvard University.

33. Isidore, "London Jottings," *American Israelite*, July 21, 1892.

34. *Jewish Record*, January 31, 1863, quoted according to *Correspondence of Augustin Daly and Joseph F. Daly and Documents Serving for Memoirs, 1858–1899* [hereafter, Daly, *Correspondence and Documents*], New York Public Library for the Performing Arts, T-Mss 2011-251, vol. 1.

35. See, e.g., Karl Wilhelm Friedrich Grattenauer, *Erster Nachtrag zu seiner Erklärung über seine Schrift: Wider die Juden* (Berlin: Schmidt, 1803), 71. See John Koegel, *Music in German Immigrant Theater* (Rochester, NY: University of Rochester Press, 2009), 265–269.

36. "Chesnut [sic] Street Theatre," *Philadelphia Inquirer*, April 22, 1863.

37. "Mozart Hall—Janauschek," *Israelite*, December 25, 1868.

38. "Ausländische Bühnen," *Blätter für Musik, Theater und Kunst* (Vienna), October 29, 1867.

39. "New-Yorker Bühnenschau," *Belletristisches Journal*, October 18, 1867.

40. Karl Emil Franzos, "Mein Erstlingswerk: 'Die Juden von Barnouw,'" in idem, ed., *Die Geschichte des Erstlingswerks: Selbstbiographische Aufsätze* (Berlin: Concordia Deutsche Verlags-Anstalt, 1894), 227–228.

41. "Mrs. Crisp's 'Leah,'" *Dallas Herald*, February 3, 1870. The *Dallas Herald* reprinted this article from the January 22, 1870, edition of the *Shreveport South-Western*.

42. "New Memphis Theater," *Public Ledger* (Memphis), October 28, 1868.

43. "Amusements," *Daily American* (Nashville), January 23, 1892.

44. "Korrespondenz," *Ben-Chananja: Wochenblatt für jüdische Theologie*, September 21, 1864.

45. See, e.g., ads in the *Börsen-Halle: Hamburgische Abend-Zeitung für Handel, Schifffahrt und Politik*, January 19, 1849; January 24, 1849; and October 31, 1849.

46. On the connection between Rachel Félix and *La Juive*, see Brownstein, *Tragic Muse*, 47–51; and F. Scott Lerner, "Jewish Identity and French Opera, Stage and Politics, 1831–60," *Historical Reflections / Réflexions Historiques* 30, no. 2 (2004): 255–281.

47. "Bericht aus der Ferne," *Wiener Zeitschrift*, February 8, 1849.

48. For context, see Hermann Uhde, *Das Stadttheater in Hamburg, 1827–1877: Ein Beitrag zur deutschen Kulturgeschichte* (Stuttgart: Cotta, 1879), esp. 189–198, 292–294.

49. "Bericht aus der Ferne."

50. "Theatersaal," *Österreichischer Courier*, January 26, 1849. This article includes a report from a Hamburg correspondent on the premiere.

51. "Bericht aus der Ferne."

52. "Bertha Thomas, geb. Hausmann," *Album des königlichen Schauspiels und der königlichen Oper zu Berlin* (Berlin: Gustav Schauer, 1858), 139. An earlier version of this widely reproduced biographical sketch was published in the *Spenerische Zeitung* (Berlin) and ran as well in the *Frankfurter Conversationsblatt*, September 23–24, 1852.

53. By the end of the century, Fontane had emerged as one of Germany's preeminent novelists. See Fontane's letters to Bernhard von Lepel from June 19, 1849, and May 15, 1852, in Fontane, *Der Briefwechsel: Kritische Ausgabe* (Berlin: De Gruyter, 2006), 133–134, 330–331. Later in life, he recalled his enthusiasm for Thomas's June 18, 1849, performance of *Deborah* in a review in the *Vossische Zeitung*, October 12, 1880, repr. in Fontane, *Ausgewählte Schriften und Kritiken* (Munich: Hanser, 1969), 2:470–473.

54. Karl Theodor von Küster, *Vierunddreißig Jahre meiner Theaterleitung in Leipzig, Darmstadt, München und Berlin* (Leipzig: Brockhaus, 1853), 250.

55. See Feodor Wehl's review of the May 26 Berlin premiere, "Neue Dramen," *Europa: Chronik der gebildeten Welt* 23 (1849): 325.

56. Mosenthal, "Aus den 'Memoiren' der Deborah," *Die Gegenwart* 6, no. 46 (November 14, 1874): 312.

57. "Bertha Thomas, geb. Hausmann," 140.

58. "Deborah, an Frau Thomas," quoted according to the report on the Berlin premiere of *Deborah*, *Allgemeine Zeitung des Judenthums*, June 4, 1849. The *Vossische Zeitung* labels this twelve-line poem a sonnet, strangely enough.

59. Heinrich Hubert Houben, *Emil Devrient: Sein Leben, sein Wirken, sein Nachlass* (Frankfurt am Main, 1903), 121; and Karl Gutzkow, "Die deutschen Schauspieler in London," *Unterhaltungen am häuslichen Herd* 47 (1853): 47.

60. Weilen, "S. Mosenthal: Ein Lebensbild," in *S. H. Mosenthal's gesammelte Werke* (Stuttgart: Eduard Hallberger, 1878), 6:37.

61. "Bertha Thomas, geb. Hausmann," 140.

62. Von Küster, *Vierunddreißig Jahre meiner Theaterleitung*, 251.

63. Mosenthal, "Aus den 'Memoiren' der Deborah," 312.

64. On Damböck's biography, see the articles on "Damböck" in Constant von Wurzbach, *Biographisches Lexikon des Kaiserthums Oesterreich* (Vienna, 1858), 3:138–140; and Franz Steger, *Ergänzung-Conversationslexikon* (Leipzig, 1853), 8:703–704.

65. *Ansbacher Morgenblatt*, March 22 and March 25, 1857.

66. "Vereinigte Kunstnotizen von W.," *Der Bayerische Landbote*, January 23, 1851.

67. *Theater-Pfeile, ein Beiblatt zum Münchener Punsch*, July 7, 1850.

68. "Deborah," *Fränkischer Kurier (Mittelfränkische Zeitung)*, July 11, 1850; and "Vereinigte Kunstnotizen von W.," *Der Bayerische Landbote* (Munich), January 23, 1851.

69. *Ansbacher Morgenblatt*, March 24, 1857.

70. "Feuilleton," *Deutsche Allgemeine Zeitung* (Leipzig), April 6, 1853.

71. For context, see Anna Stettner, "'Wer ist ein Virtuose in der Schauspielkunst?': Das Phänomen des Virtuosentums im deutschen Sprechtheater des 19. Jahrhundert" (diss., Ludwig Maximilians-Universität Munich, 1998). On Janauschek's break with the Frankfurter Stadttheater,

see Janauschek's own pamphlet, *Illustrationen zur neuesten Geschichte des Frankfurter Theaters unter der Leitung des Herrn Dr. von Guaita* (Frankfurt am Main, 1861).

72. Daly's management of Janauschek was made explicit in the program. See "The Season," New York, October 10, 1870, theater program, Theatre Collection, Museum of the City of New York; and the Philadelphia program reproduced in Fig. 38. On Janauschek's rapid mastery of English, see "Fanny Janauschek," *New York Herald*, October 7, 1870; "Janauschek in English Drama," *New York Times*, October 11, 1870; "Theatrical and Musical," *Spirit of the Times*, October 15, 1870; "The Janauschek," *Daily Evening Bulletin* (San Francisco), October 20, 1870; and "Janauschek as Deborah at the Academy," *Israelite*, November 11, 1870.

73. Jerry Vincent Cortez, "Fanny Janauschek: America's Last Queen of Tragedy" (Ph.D. diss., University of Illinois at Urbana-Champaign, 1973).

74. "Deborah," *Salt Lake Daily Herald*, August 2, 1883.

75. See, e.g., *Die Presse* (Brünn/Brno), May 26, 1850; and *Die Wiener Zeitung*, April 20, 1850, or May 1, 1850.

76. J. W., "Deborah," *Didaskalia*, October 10, 1849.

77. See, e.g., *Deutsches Theater-Album* (Munich), April 1, 1860; November 11, 1860.

78. *Deutsches Theater-Album*, May 5, 1861.

79. "Theaterschau: Theater an der Wien," *Blätter für Musik, Theater und Kunst* (Vienna), April 17, 1863.

80. See, e.g., ad, *Sun* (Baltimore), December 13, 1867; "Md'lle Janauschek," *Daily Ohio Statesman* (Columbus), January 3, 1868; ad, *Israelite*, January 17, 1868; ad, *Daily Courier* (Louisville, KY), January 24, 1868; ad, *Milwaukee Daily Sentinel*, February 26, 1868; and ad, *Boston Daily Advertiser*, April 6, 1868.

81. "Janauschek: The Representation of 'Deborah,'" *Chicago Tribune*, February 22, 1868.

82. "Academy of Music—German Drama," *New York Times*, April 28, 1868; and "Janauschek in English Drama," *New York Times*, October 11, 1870.

83. *Deutsches Theater-Album* (Munich), May 5, 1861.

84. "Academy of Music—Fanny Janauschek," *New York Herald*, October 18, 1867.

85. "The German Drama," *Daily Courier* (Louisville, KY), February 2, 1868.

86. "Amusements," *Cleveland Morning Herald*, January 24, 1871.

87. "Janauschek—Her Debut in English Tragedy," *New York Herald*, October 11, 1870.

88. "New-Yorker Bühnenschau," *Belletristisches Journal* (New York), October 18, 1867.

89. "Theatrical Gossip," *Daily Evening Bulletin* (San Francisco), November 11, 1867.

90. "Academy of Music—German Drama—Janauschek in 'Deborah,'" *New York Herald*, October 11, 1868.

91. See, e.g., "Mdll. Fanny Janauschek," *Daily Ohio Statesman* (Columbus), January 11, 1868; "Opera House," *Courier Journal* (Louisville, KY), December 24, 1870; "Amusements: The New National Theatre," *National Republican* (Washington, DC), October 9, 1874; and *Memphis Public Ledger*, January 26, 1875.

92. "Fanny Janauschek as Deborah," *Milwaukee Daily Sentinel*, March 7, 1868.

93. "Theatrical and Musical," *Spirit of the Times* (New York), October 15, 1870.

94. "Janauschek," *Cleveland Morning Herald*, November 25, 1871.

95. "Amusements: Academy of Music," *Inter Ocean* (Chicago), February 17, 1875.

96. See Heather M. McMahon, "Profit, Purity, and Perversity: Nineteenth-Century Child Prodigies Kate and Ellen Bateman" (Ph.D. diss., Indiana University, 2003); John Hanners, *"It Was Play or Starve": Acting in the Nineteenth-Century American Popular Theatre* (Bowling Green, OH: Bowling Green State University Popular Press, 1993), 57–69; Robert Samuel Badal, "Kate and Ellen Bateman: A Study in Precocity" (Ph.D. diss., Northwestern University, 1971); and [Daly,] "A Memoir of Miss Bateman." *The Young Couple* was J. T. Ennis's adaption of Eugène Scribe's *Le marriage enfantin*.

97. Badal, "Kate and Ellen Bateman," 41.

98. [Daly,] "A Memoir of Miss Bateman," 9.

99. For background, see "The Bateman-Daly Controversy: H. L. Bateman, Letter 'To the Editors of the N. Y. Express,'" *New York Saturday Press*, April 28, 1866. On the friendship between the Methuas and Daly, see J. Guido Methua, February 3, 1863, letter to Augustin Daly, Folger Shakespeare Library, Y.c. 4547 (1–12), #1; and letter from Kate Bateman to Augustin Daly, Paris, August 8, 1863, Folger Shakespeare Library, Y.c. 2673 (1–3).

100. See, e.g., "New Yorker Revue," *New-Yorker Criminal-Zeitung und Belletristisches Journal*, May 1, 1863; "Theater und Kunst," *Fremden-Blatt* (Vienna), October 24, 1863; and "Music and the Drama Elsewhere," *Wilkes' Spirit of the Times*, January 23, 1864.

101. "National Theatre: Miss Bateman," *The National Republican* (Washington, DC), January 10, 1870; "National Theater," *National Republican*, January 11, 1870; and "Miss Bateman," *Evening Star* (Washington, DC), January 11, 1870.

102. "Miss Bateman," *New Orleans Times*, February 9, 1870.

103. "Miss Bateman's Leah," *New Orleans Times*, February 13, 1870.

104. "Miss Bateman," *Sphinx* 2, no. 37 (April 24, 1869); and "Miss Bateman; Opinions Differ," *Albion*, March 4, 1865.

105. For positive reviews of Bateman's statuary acting, see "Theater and Things Theatrical: By 'Bayard,'" *Wilkes' Spirit of the Times*, February 14, 1863; "Amusements," *Philadelphia Inquirer*, *Daly Theatre Scrapbooks*, vol. 1 [dated by hand, May 2, 1863, but likely published at least one week earlier]; *Times* (London), October 2, 1863, in *Daly Theatre Scrapbooks*, vol. 1; *Morning Post* (London), October 6, in *Daly Theatre Scrapbooks*, vol. 1; "'Leah' at the Boston Theatre," *Boston Daily Advertiser*, March 9, 1866; and "Miss Bateman in Dublin," *Musical World* (London), November 9, 1867. For critical approaches to the same phenomenon, see "'Leah' at Niblo's," *New York Daily Tribune*, January 17, 1866; "Drama," *Albion*, January 20, 1866; "Theatrical," *Chicago Tribune*, March 15, 1866; "Some of Our Actors," *Galaxy: A Magazine of Entertaining Reading* 5, no. 2 (February 1868): 165; and "Miss Bateman," *Sphinx*, April 24, 1869.

106. The examples here are too numerous to list. See, e.g., "Theatrical," *New York Herald*, January 26, 1863; "The Forsaken One," unnamed New York newspaper, February 7, 1863, Daly, *Correspondence and Documents*, vol. 1; and "Miss Bateman's Last Appearance," unnamed New York newspaper, likely February 22 or 23, 1863, Daly, *Correspondence and Documents*, vol. 1.

107. "The Theatres," *Saturday Review* (London), October 10, 1863. See also "The Drama," *Spectator* (London), October 10, 1863; "Leah," *London Review*, October 24, 1863; "Miss Bateman the Great Attraction in London: From the London Times, Oct. 22," *New York Herald*, November 5, 1863; "Liverpool," *Orchestra* (London), October 8, 1864; and "A Night at the Adelphi and Haymarket Theatres," *S. G. Sharpe's London Magazine of Entertainment and Instruction for General Reading* (February 1865): 99–104.

108. "Drama," *Albion*, January 20, 1866; "'Leah' at the Boston Theatre," *Boston Daily Advertiser*, March 9, 1866; and "Miss Bateman in 'Leah': From an Occasional Correspondent [in New York]," *Boston Daily Advertiser*, March 24, 1866.

109. Mosenthal, "Aus den 'Memoiren' der Deborah."

110. "Kate Josefine Bateman und die 'Leah' auf der englischen Bühne," *Recensionen und Mittheilungen über Theater und Musik* (Vienna), July 29, 1865.

111. Unlike Janauschek or Western, Bateman was never rumored to be Jewish. The fact that she was a committed Episcopalian was mentioned at times in the press. See, e.g., "Miss Bateman," *London Journal, and Weekly Record of Literature, Science, and Art*, March 27, 1869.

112. See *George Henry Lewes's Journal*, London, February 8, 1864, repr. in Gordon S. Haight, ed., *The George Eliot Letters* (New Haven, CT: Yale University Press, 1954–78), 4:132.

113. For Michael Ragussis, Lewes and Eliot's viewing of *Leah* occupies an important place in the development of Eliot as a novelist, as much of the material in *Leah*—the portrayal of antisemitism, the figure of the heroic Jewish maiden, the theme of romance across religious and ethnic boundaries, and the figure of the cowardly crypto-Jew—makes its way into Eliot's *The Spanish Gypsy* (1868) and *Daniel Deronda* (1876). See Michael Ragussis, *Theatrical Nation: Jews and Other Outlandish Englishmen in Georgian Britain* (Philadelphia: University of Pennsylvania Press, 2010), 203–204.

114. See, e.g., the positive comments in "Amusements," *Nashville Daily Union*, February 5, 1864; "The Drama—Avonia Jones—Comments, Not Criticism," *Nashville Daily Union*, March 3, 1864; and "New Theatre," *Nashville Daily Union*, May 17, 1865. See criticism in "Theatrical Matters," *Daily National Intelligencer* (Washington, DC), January 4, 1865; and "Theatres," *Orchestra* (London), May 5, 1866.

115. Clara Morris, *Life on the Stage: My Personal Experiences and Recollections* (New York: McClure, Phillips, 1901), 127; and "National Theatre," *Daily National Intelligencer* (Washington, DC), October 28, 1867.

116. See Bateman's critique of Ristori's *Deborah* in her letter to Augustin Daly, Paris, August 8, 1863, Folger Shakespeare Library, Y.c. 2673 (1–3).

117. "Ristori," *Harper's New Monthly Magazine* 34 (May 1867): 746.

118. "Feuilleton," *Deutsche Allgemeine Zeitung* (Leipzig), February 23, 1858.

119. "Dramatic, Musical, & c," *North American and United States Gazette* (Philadelphia), December 18, 1866; see also "Ristori in Deborah," *New York Herald*, December 29, 1866.

120. [Harry Moss,] "A Vicksburg Editor on Ristori," *Columbus Daily Enquirer* (GA), March 24, 1867. This same article also ran in the *Macon Weekly Telegraph*, March 29, 1867, and in the *Louisville Daily Journal*, April 15, 1867.

121. This occurred on both sides of the Atlantic. See "In General," *Boston Daily Advertiser*, January 12, 1865; *Oswego Daily Palladium*, January 13, 1865; *Milwaukee Daily Sentinel*, January 17, 1865; and *Nashville Daily Union*, March 7, 1866.

122. "Theater," *Daily Arkansas Gazette* (Little Rock), May 19, 1874.

123. "Susan Denin," *Chicago Daily Tribune*, December 5, 1875; *Macon Weekly Telegraph*, December 14, 1875; *Daily American* (Nashville), December 7, 1875; and "Sue Denin's Daughter: Indianapolis Gives a Benefit to the Only Child of the Dead Actress," *Milwaukee Daily Sentinel*, February 18, 1876.

124. Harley Erdman grants special attention to the way Bernhardt's highly sexualized Leah revolutionized the figure of the *belle juive* by bringing together the connections between the actress, the figure, and Jewishness in an unprecedented manner; see Erdman, *Staging the Jew: The Performance of an American Ethnicity, 1860–1920* (New Brunswick, NJ: Rutgers University Press, 1997), 50. The literature on Bernhardt specifically related to star culture is immense. See, e.g., Carol Ockman and Kenneth E. Silver, eds., *Sarah Bernhardt: The Art of High Drama* (New Haven, CT: Yale University Press, 2005); and Rebecca Grotjahn, Dörte Schmidt, and Thomas Seedorf, *Diva: Die Inszenierung der übermenschlichen Frau. Interdisziplinäre Untersuchungen zu einem kulturellen Phänomen des 19. und 20. Jahrhunderts* (Schliengen: Argus, 2011). As I note here, however, Leah was not one of Bernhardt's major roles, and, as a result, few of her biographers tend to pay much attention to this aspect of her career. A major exception here is Janis Bergman-Carton, "Negotiating the Categories: Sarah Bernhardt and the Possibilities of Jewishness," *Art Journal* 55, no. 2 (1996): 55–64.

125. Quoted according to Mary Louise Roberts, *Disruptive Acts: The New Woman in Fin-de-Siècle France* (Chicago: University of Chicago Press, 2002), 210. On Bernhardt as Joan of Arc, see Roberts, *Disruptive Acts*; Arthur Gold and Robert Fizdale, *The Divine Sarah: A Life of Sarah Bernhardt* (New York: Knopf, 1991), 243–245; and, esp., Venita Datta, *Heroes and Legends of Fin-de-Siècle France: Gender, Politics, and National Identity* (Cambridge: Cambridge University Press, 2011), 142–178. Bergman-Carton notes that Bernhardt also was taken to task for playing Mary Magdalene during the same period, "Negotiating the Categories," 64n31. For further background, see Carol Ockman, "When Is a Jewish Star Just a Star? Interpreting Images of Sarah Bernhardt," in Linda Nochlin and Tamar Garb, eds., *The Jew in the Text: Modernity and the Construction of Identity* (London: Thames & Hudson, 1996).

126. Charles E. L. Wingate, "Boston Letter," *Critic*, January 16, 1892.

127. See, e.g., Charles E. L. Wingate, "Bernhardt: Her Reappearance of Leah, the Forsaken," and "Music and Drama: Sarah Bernhardt," 1892, Harvard Theatre Collection, Clippings 13, Folder: Leah, the Forsaken (performances by Sarah Bernhardt), Houghton Library, Harvard University; and "Music and Drama: Sarah Bernhardt in 'Leah,'" *Jewish Messenger*, April 22, 1892.

128. Blakely Hall, "Bernhardt Did Well," *Chicago Daily Tribune*, April 24, 1892; and "Nym Crinkle's Letter: New York's Spring Mélange of Tragedy, Comedy and Music. Sarah Bernhardt in 'Leah,'" *North American* (Philadelphia), April 29, 1892.

129. "The Theatres Last Night," *Philadelphia Inquirer*, April 5, 1892.

130. "Record of Amusements. Dramatic and Musical. Mme. Bernhardt as Leah," *New York Times*, April 21, 1892. On the use of *Deborah* and the curse scene in particularly in acting schools, see "Theater und Kunst," *Berliner Tageblatt*, January 6, 1886; "Kleine Theaterchronik," *Berliner Tageblatt*, February 6, 1890; "Kleine Theaterchronik," *Berliner Tageblatt*, November 30, 1890; ad, *Berliner Tageblatt*, April 25, 1895; and *Der Humorist* (Vienna), July 1, 1918. In the United States, as noted in the Introduction, the curse scene was frequently included in anthologies designed for aspiring actors as well.

131. "Music and Drama," *Chicago Daily Tribune*, March 1, 1892. See also "Amusements: Albaugh's Opera House," *Evening Star* (Washington, DC), January 14, 1892; "Tribute to Bernhardt: Cheer After Cheer Greets Her Impersonation of 'Leah,'" *Washington Post*, January 14, 1892; "Music and Drama," *Chicago Daily Tribune*, March 1, 1892; and Charles E. L. Wingate, "A Notable Night."

132. On Rachel's performance of *Esther*, see the exemplary analysis by Samuels, "France's Jewish Star."

133. See the extensive bilingual, French-English summary of Bernhardt's *Leah* published in conjunction with her 1892 American tour: *Argument of the Play of Leah (Leah, the Forsaken): A Drama in Five Acts by Mosenthal, Adapted from the German by Monsieur A. Albert Darmont. As Presented by Madame Sarah Bernhardt and Her Powerful Company*, trans. Fred[eric] Lyster (New York: Theatre Ticket Office, 1892).

134. Mather seems to have started doing so only in the 1890s, not when she first started performing the play in the early 1880s. See ad for Lee Ave. Academy of Music, New York, November 21, 1890, production of Leah the Forsaken, New York Public Library for the Performing Arts, Billy Rose Theatre Collection, 8-MWEZ 19608, no. 56; ad, April 11–16, 1892, Leah, the Forsaken, at Col. Sinn's New Park Theatre, Brooklyn, New York Public Library for the Performing Arts, Billy Rose Theatre Collection MWEZ n. c. 74, 36; and "Amusements," *Daily American* (Nashville), January 17, 1892.

135. Darmont, *Leah*, 33.

136. Darmont, *Leah*, 35.

137. Darmont, *Leah*, 13. This vision of America, it will be recalled from Chapter 1, is present in Mosenthal's original text as well. But placing a group of emigrants on stage in the final scene makes emigration much more present than in Mosenthal's original, where Deborah leaves the stage simply to set off with her people. In joining a Jewish collective on stage, Bernhardt did have a precursor that she could not have been aware of: R. Moore's *Ruth, the Jewess*, discussed in Chapter 2.

138. See, on this point, Bergman-Carton, "Negotiating the Categories," 60. Bergman-Carton focuses on two of the most widely circulated images of Bernhardt as Leah, the image in front of the cross and the highly sexualized image of her upper body that ran on the June 1906 cover of *Theater Magazine*. She does not discuss Sarony's highly publicized shot of her barefoot in the role of Leah. See, e.g., "Women and the Camera: Sarony's Reminiscences of Brilliant Sitters," *Philadelphia Inquirer*, November 26, 1893; also in *Los Angeles Times*, November 26, 1893. See also Leon Mead, "Sarah Bernhardt's Feet," *St. Louis Republic Sunday Magazine*, December 24, 1905.

139. "Mme. Bernhardt in 'Leah.' The Great French Actress Wins a Triumph. A Large Audience Wildly Enthusiastic over the Artiste's Impersonation of the Jewess—a Fine Version of a Strong Play Beautifully Staged and Well Acted," *Boston Herald*, January 9, 1892.

140. Darmont, *Leah*, 9. The information that this scene was repeated three times in the drama comes from "Nym Crinkle's Letter."

141. "Mme. Bernhardt in 'Leah.'"

142. See, e.g., "Music and Drama," *Chicago Daily Tribune*, March 1, 1892; and "Nym Crinkle's Letter."

143. "Nym Crinkle's Letter" calls this pose "an unworthy piece of sensationalism."

144. A critic in Washington, DC, for instance, celebrated Bernhardt's *Leah* as "spectacular" because it brought "tears to the eyes of all . . . while the curtain rose and fell repeatedly, and roar after

roar of applause rang through the house that broke into a cheer after cheer as the audience, men and women alike, tried to convey to her their thanks for such a display of consummate art, and at the same time relieve their own feelings of the excitement wrought by the events that led up to the noble climax [of the curse scene]." "Tribute to Bernhardt," *Washington Post*, January 14, 1892.

145. "Productions of the Week," clipping from an unnamed New York City newspaper, Harvard Theatre Collection, Clippings 13, Folder: Leah, the Forsaken (performances by Sarah Bernhardt), Houghton Library, Harvard University.

146. "Music and Drama: Sarah Bernhardt in 'Leah,'" *Jewish Messenger*, April 22, 1892.

147. See, e.g., "Leah, the Forsaken," clipping from an unnamed English newspaper, July 22, 1899, Harvard Theatre Collection, Clippings 14, Folder: Leah, the Forsaken (performances by Nance O'Neil), Houghton Library, Harvard University; "Nance O'Neil Proves Powerful but Uneven in 'The Jewess,'" *San Francisco Call*, December 30, 1902; and N. V. R., "'The Jewess' at the Metropolitan," *Minneapolis Times*, May 25, 1903.

148. "At the Theaters," *Los Angeles Times*, January 15, 1899; and "At the Theaters," *Los Angeles Times*, January 22, 1899.

149. See, e.g., "At the Theaters," *Los Angeles Times*, October 23, 1898; and "Music and the Drama," *Los Angeles Herald*, February 2, 1906. For references to the vaudeville version, which O'Neil seems to have performed only in 1907, see "Plays & Players," *Chicago Daily Tribune*, October 20, 1907; and ad, *Los Angeles Herald*, December 9, 1907.

150. For context, see "The Director, the Spectator and the Eiffel Tower," in Kennedy, *The Spectator and the Spectacle*, 26–48.

151. W—f, "Theater, Kunst, Wissenschaft," *Berliner Tageblatt*, May 28, 1889.

152. The connection to the Polish refugees was widely made in the press. See "Theater- und Kunstnachrichten," *Neue Freie Presse*, November 9, 1914; and "Theater, Kunst und Literatur," *Deutsches Volksblatt* (Vienna), November 10, 1914.

153. See, e.g., H. Schl., "Kunst und Leben," *Die Zeit* (Vienna), May 9, 1896; F. E., "Feuilleton," *Berliner Tageblatt*, April 5, 1900; R. S., "Thalia-Theater: Gastspiel der k.k. Hofburgschauspielerin Frl. Adele Sandrock, 'Deborah,'" *Neue Hamburger Zeitung*, May 7, 1900; "Lokales und Chronik," *Der Burggraefler* (Merano), February 17, 1904; and M—z, "Theater, Kunst und Wissenschaft," *Maiser Wochenblatt*, February 20, 1904.

154. See, e.g., Jacob Adler, *A Life on the Stage: A Memoir*, trans. Lulla Rosenfeld (New York: Applause, 2001), 308–309; and Brigitte Dalinger, *Trauerspiel mit Gesang und Tanz: Zur Ästhetik und Dramaturgie jüdischer Theatertexte* (Vienna: Böhlau, 2010), 175. In 1911, Dina Feinman, who played Deborah in Yiddish in both London and the U.S., could still pack the house and send hundreds of fans home disappointed because they were unable to purchase tickets; see "Plays and Players," *Jewish Exponent*, January 20, 1911. An obituary for Liptsin notes that she opened with this role in New York in 1887, rather than 1884. See "Madame Kenny Lipzin Dean," *American Jewish Chronicle*, October 4, 1918.

155. "Theater, Kunst, Wissenschaft," *Berliner Tageblatt*, February 21, 1893.

156. "Künstlerausbeutung in Amerika: Von unserem Korrespondenten," *Berliner Tageblatt*, April 12, 1905.

157. A fragment of the 1908 film is in the collections of the Library of Congress, Vitagraph paper print fragments, No. 7, LC 2002641200. The incomplete copy of the 1912 film in the British Film Institute is a nitrate film not available for viewing, and there are no surviving copies of the 1914 *Deborah*. For a discussion of the films, see "Leah, the Forsaken," *Moving Picture World* 3, no. 15 (October 10, 1908): 288–289; Louis Reeves Harrison, "Leah the Forsaken," *Moving Picture World* 13, no. 13 (September 28, 1912): 1264–1265; and "Deborah, the Jewish Maiden, *Moving Picture World* 21, no. 1 (July 18, 1914): 434, 478. Relying on the discussions in *Moving Picture World*, Patricia Erens offers a brief discussion of these films and sets them in context in her chapter on the "primitive years" in *The Jew in American Cinema* (Bloomington: Indiana University Press, 1984), 29–74, esp. 63–64.

158. "Deborah, the Jewish Maiden," *Moving Picture World*, 434.

159. See, e.g., "Marburger Bioskop," *Marburger Zeitung*, October 19, 1915; and "King's Theatre: West's Pictures," *New Zealand Truth*, March 22, 1913.

160. "Melodramas Set Tonight," *Deseret News* (Salt Lake City), July 29, 1966.

161. See http://www.thop.uni-goettingen.de/sommer2004/200409_deborah.php; and http://www.thop.uni-goettingen.de/sommer2004/200409_deborah_fotos.php.

162. See Ken Jaworowski, "'Leah, the Forsaken' Is an 1862 Drama with Modern Resonance," *New York Times*, February 21, 2017.

163. Victor Gluck, "Leah, the Forsaken," *TheaterScene.Net*, February 26, 2017.

Chapter 4

1. "The Bateman-Daly Case: Theatrical Monopolists and Bohemian Critics," *New York Herald*, April 26, 1866. This article, which alleged to reproduce, in full, Hall's closing statement, ran in several other papers as well, including the *Daily Evening Telegraph* (Philadelphia), April 25, 1866, and the *New York Clipper*, May 5, 1866.

There are no surviving court records for the Marine Court, where this and the other cases discussed here were tried. My reconstruction of the Bateman-Daly case derives from the extensive coverage of these trials in New York and elsewhere in the United States: "The Author of 'Leah, the Forsaken,' and Miss Bateman in Court. Marine Court—Chambers. Before Judge Alker. Augustin Daly vs. Kate Josephine Bateman," *New York Times*, February 8, 1866; "In General," *Boston Daily Advertiser*, February 10, 1866; "'Leah' in Court," *Round Table*, February 17, 1866; "In General," *Boston Daily Advertiser*, February 27, 1866; *New York Herald*, April 20, 1866; "The Memoir of Miss Bateman—Influence of the Press on Theatricals. Marine Court—Trial Term—April 19. Before Judge Gross and a Jury. Augustine Daly vs. Hezekiah L. Bateman," *New York Times*, April 20, 1866; "The Daly-Bateman Case: Liability of a Father as Agent for His Infant Daughter—the Oyster House Critics and Leah," *New York Herald*, April 21, 1866; "The Batemans and the Bohemians in Court," *New York Herald*, April 21, 1866; "The Bateman-Daly Case—Bohemian Criticism and Machinery," *New York Herald*, April 26, 1866; *New York Herald*, April 27, 1866; *New Orleans Times*, April 27, 1866; "Dramatic Feuilleton by Figaro [Henry Clapp, Jr.]," *New York Saturday Press*, April 28, 1866; H. L. Bateman, letter "To the Editors of the N.Y. Express," *New York Saturday Press*, April 28, 1866; *New York Clipper*, April 28, 1866; "Things Theatrical," *Public Ledger* (Memphis), May 8, 1866; *Galaxy: A Magazine of Entertaining Reading*, vol. 1, no. 2 (May 15, 1866): 176–177; "'Leah' Turns Up Again," *New York Herald*, August 18, 1866; "The Authorship of 'Leah, the Forsaken': A Writ of Prohibition to the Marine Court Quashed, Supreme Court, Before Justice Barnard," *New York Times*, August 18, 1866; "'Leah, the Forsaken' Not Forsaken—Two Claimants for Her," *Philadelphia Inquirer*, August 20, 1866; *New York Herald*, November 20, 1866; "The Play of 'Leah' Again in Court—How It Was Translated and What It Cost. Emile Benville [sic] vs. Augustine [sic] J. Daly," *New York Herald*, November 20, 1866; "Marine Court—Nov. 19—Before Judge Alker. LEAH AGAIN IN COURT. Emile Bienville [sic] Against Augustus Daly," *New York Tribune*, November 20, 1866; "'Deborah' and 'Leah the Forsaken' Again in Court. Marine Court—Trial Term—November 20. Before Judge Alker and a Jury," *New York Times*, November 21, 1866; "Marine Court: The Play of Leah—Rights of Translators. Before Judge Alker and a Jury," *New York Herald*, November 21, 1866; "'Leah' Again in Court: Curious Lawsuit Between Playwrights—Another Controversy About the Play of 'Leah'—the Translator Sues the Adapter for a Share of the Profits, &c., &c., &c.," *World* (New York), November 30, 1866; "'Leah' Again in Court," *Daily Evening Bulletin* (San Francisco), December 13, 1866; "Law Reports: Court Calendars," *New York Times*, March 28, 1867; "Marine Court—General Term: Miss Bateman ('Leah, the Forsaken') Again in Court—the Litigation About This Play Not Yet Ended," *New York Herald*, April 26, 1867; *New York Herald*, April 26, 1867; "Leah the Forsaken" and Daly-Bateman Controversy Again—a New Trial Ordered," *New York Times*, September 21, 1867; and "'Leah, the Forsaken,' Again in Court—a New Trial to Be Had. Marine Court—Before Judge Gross," *Milwaukee Daily Sentinel*, September 26, 1867.

2. H. L. Bateman, "To the Editors of the N.Y. Express," *New York Saturday Press*, April 28, 1866.

3. This language was used in numerous ads in the *New York Times* from January 8 on, as well as in the *New York Daily Tribune*. A surviving program from the second week similarly announced Bateman's appearance in her "celebrated role of Leah; A Jewish Maiden," in "Mosenthal's Beautiful Tragedy of that name." See *Stage* 2, no. 20 (January 23, 1866), Theatre Collection, Museum of the City of New York.

4. "Leah, Oxenford and Daly," source not given, *Daly's Theatre Scrapbooks*, New York Public Library for the Performing Arts, 8-MWED+, vol. 1; "Drama: 'Leah' at Niblo's Garden," *Round Table*, January 27, 1866; and "'Leah' in Court," *Round Table*, February 17, 1866.

5. "The Batemans and the Bohemians in Court," *New York Herald*, April 21, 1866.

6. On *Beneville v. Daly*, see the sources listed in n. 1 above.

7. "The Bateman-Daly Case: Theatrical Monopolists and Bohemian Critics," *New York Herald*, April 26, 1866.

8. "Miss Bateman as Leah," *Philadelphia Press*, April 14, 1863, in *Daly's Theatre Scrapbooks*, vol. 1. This piece was attacked and exposed as puffery days after being published. See "Drama," *Albion*, April 18, 1863. The critic in *Albion* notes ironically that it is "gratifying to know that some atonement exists in modern times for 'the prejudiced genius of Shakespeare.'"

9. "The Bateman-Daly Case: Theatrical Monopolists and Bohemian Critics," *New York Herald*, April 26, 1866. The Batemans were from Baltimore, hence Daly branding H. L. Bateman a "Southern Yankee."

10. April 24, 1866, letter of Abraham Oakey Hall to Augustin Daly, Folger Shakespeare Library, Y.c. 4288 (1–7), #1.

11. On December 10, 1875, the case was apparently heard before Judge Davis, who denied the injunction. Daly withdrew the play, however, after Clara Morris earned devastating reviews. See "Miss Bateman's Suit Against Mr. Daly: To the Editor of *The Tribune*," *New-York Tribune*, December 1, 1875; and "Adaptations and Stage Rights: The Suit of Miss Bateman Against Augustin Daly—Judge Davis Denies an Injunction," *New-York Tribune*, December 11, 1875. For evidence of good relations between Daly and the Batemans in the following years, see 1867 [1870] letter from Sidney Frances Crowell Bateman to Augustin Daly, Folger Shakespeare Library, Y.c. 2674 (1–7), #4; and the set of letters from Kate Bateman to Daly in 1894–1895, Folger Shakespeare Library, Y.c. 2948 (1–6)

12. "Miss Bateman," *New Orleans Times*, February 9, 1870.

13. J. W., "Deborah: Volks-Schauspiel in 4 Abth. von S. Mosenthal," *Didaskalia*, October 10, 1849.

14. See, e.g., ads in *Die Wiener Zeitung*, April 20, 1850; and *Die Presse* (Brünn/Brno), May 26, 1850.

15. [Julian Schmidt,] "Deborah von Mosenthal," *Die Grenzboten: Zeitschrift für Politik und Literatur* 8, no. 4 (1849): 139–143.

16. See Andrew G. Bonnell, *Shylock in Germany: Antisemitism and the German Theatre from the Enlightenment to the Nazis* (London: Tauris, 2008).

17. See Judith W. Page, "'Hath Not a Jew Eyes?' Edmund Kean and the Sympathetic Shylock," *Wordsworth Circle* 34, no. 2 (2013): 116–119.

18. See Joel Berkowitz, *Shakespeare on the American Yiddish Stage* (Iowa City: University of Iowa Press, 2010), 172–205.

19. See Bonnell, *Shylock in Germany*; and Peter Kollek, *Bogumil Dawison: Porträt und Deutung eines genialen Schauspielers* (Kastellaun: Henn, 1978).

20. See Hayley Erdman, *Staging the Jew: The Performance of an American Ethnicity, 1860–1920* (New Brunswick, NJ: Rutgers University Press, 1997), 43. On the decision to change the name of Mosenthal's play, see my comments in Chapter 2.

21. On Bandmann's career in the New York German theater scene, see Fritz A. H. Leuchs, *The Early German Theatre in New York, 1840–1872* (New York: Columbia University Press, 1928). For biographical background on Bandmann's early years, see "Daniel E. Bandmann, Tragedian," *Frank Leslie's Illustrated Newspaper*, October 10, 1863, 39; and *New-Yorker Criminal-Zeitung und Belletristisches Journal*, January 23, 1863. Bandmann also spent time performing in Europe, in

German, between his original debut on the New York German-language stage and his appearance in 1863 in English. On Bandmann's performance in *Deborah* at the New Yorker Stadt Theater, see George C. D. Odell, *Annals of the New York Stage* (New York: Columbia University Press, 1827–1949), 7:75.

22. Solomon Bandmann is listed as a "liquor dealer" (and as the father of Daniel's brother Julius, a student admitted to the introductory class) in the *Ninth Annual Report on the Operations and Condition of the Free Academy by the Board of Education of the City of New York* (New York, July 1857), 69.

23. "Music and the Drama," *Spirit of the Times*, January 24, 1863.

24. "Leah, the Forsaken," *Jewish Messenger*, February 6, 1863.

25. Leuchs, *The Early German Theatre in New York*, 207.

26. See "New Yorker Revue," *New-Yorker Belletristisches Journal*, September 25, 1863.

27. See, on this episode, Marilyn Reizbaum, *James Joyce's Judaic Other* (Stanford, CA: Stanford University Press, 1999), 29–31.

28. See Nicole Anae, "'The Majestic Hebrew Ideal': Herr Daniel E. Bandmann's Shylock on the Australian Stage, 1880–1883," *Shakespeare Jahrbuch* 150 (2014): 128–145. See also, for context, Daniel E. Bandmann, *An Actor's Tour: Seventy Thousand Miles with Shakespeare*, 3rd ed. (New York: Brentano Brothers, 1886).

29. "Miss Bateman," unnamed newspaper, undated article, quoted according to *Correspondence of Augustin Daly and Joseph F. Daly and Documents Serving for Memoirs, 1858–1899*, 9 vols., New York Public Library for the Performing Arts, T-Mss 2011-251, vol. 1.

30. Ad for *Leah*, *Jewish Messenger*, January 23, 1863, January 30, 1863, and February 6, 1863.

31. "Leah, the Forsaken," *Jewish Messenger*, February 6, 1863; and ads for *Leah*, *Jewish Messenger*, February 13, 1863.

32. "Musical and Dramatic," *Jewish Messenger*, January 23, 1863.

33. "Leah, the Forsaken," *Jewish Messenger*, February 6, 1863.

34. [Augustin Daly,] "A Memoir of Miss Bateman" (New York: Wynkoop, Hallenbeck & Thomas, 1863), 14.

35. "Dramatic, Musical, & c." *North American and United States Gazette* (Philadelphia), April 20, 1863.

36. Eduard Kulke, "S. H. Mosenthal, eine Studie," *Illustrierte Monatshefte für die gesammten Interessen des Judentums* 2 (1865/1866): 29.

37. Kulke, "S. H. Mosenthal," 30.

38. *Rock Island Daily Argus*, February 26, March 3, March 4, and March 5, 1891.

39. See, e.g., *Philadelphia Inquirer*, April 14, 1863; "Provincial," *Orchestra* (London), July 2, 1864; or "National Theatre—Leah," *National Republican* (Washington, DC), October 28, 1867.

40. London *Punch*, November 21, 1863, repr. in *Spirit of the Times*, December 19, 1863.

41. L. Sp. [Ludwig Speidel], "Feuilleton. Burgtheater. 'Deborah.' Volksschauspiel von Mosenthal," *Neue Freie Presse*, September 13, 1864. The exact date of this theater program is unclear from the article in the *Neue Freie Presse*.

42. *Frankfurter Conversations-Blatt*, September 7, 1852. The article ran in several other newspapers, including *Der österreichische Zuschauer*, September 15, 1852; *Erheiterungen* (Aschaffenburg), September 15, 1852; and *Augsburger Tagblatt*, September 11, 1852.

43. Speidel, "Feuilleton. Burgtheater. 'Deborah.'"

44. *Ben-Chananja: Wochenblatt für jüdische Theologie*, September 21, 1864.

45. See Ludwig Hevesi, *Zerline Gabillon: Ein Künstlerleben* (Stuttgart: Adolf Bonz, 1894), 3–4, 8–12.

46. See "Feuilleton," *Deutsche Allgemeine Zeitung* (Leipzig), April 28, 1853; "Tagesneuigkeiten," *Die Presse* (Vienna), March 18, 1854; "Zur Tagesgeschichte," *Wiener Zeitung*, April 23, 1854; "Baden," *Der Humorist* (Vienna), August 18, 1854; and Hevesi, *Zerline Gabillon*, 28.

47. "Theater, Kunst und Literatur," *Neues Fremden-Blatt* (Vienna), August 25, 1867; "Katharina Frank," *Der Humorist* (Vienna), October 12, 1884; and "Theaterschau," *Blätter für Musik, Theater und Kunst* (Vienna), August 27, 1867. The standard biographical accounts of Frank (see below) typically fail to make note of the fact that Frank made her debut as an adult playing Deborah.

48. On Frank's biography, see Felix Czeike, *Historisches Lexikon Wien in 6 Bänden* (Vienna: Kremayr & Scheriau, 2004), 2:356; and *Über Land und Meer* 59, no. 15 (October 1887): 332. On Frank's performance in *Deborah* at age seven, see, esp., "Aus der Theaterwelt," *Fremden-Blatt* (Vienna), January 6, 1918; and "Wie Kathi Frank zur Bühne kam," *Prager Tagblatt, Abend-Ausgabe*, October 14, 1917. This story was often mentioned in obituaries for Frank as well. See, e.g., "Kathi Frank," *Berliner Tageblatt*, January 2, 1918.

49. Mosenthal, "Aus den 'Memoiren' der Deborah," *Die Gegenwart* 6, no. 46 (November 14, 1874): 312.

50. See Annemarie Stauss, *Schauspiel und Nationale Frage: Kostümstil und Aufführungspraxis im Burgtheater der Schreyvogel- und Laubezeit* (Tübingen: Narr, 2011), 267–269.

51. Mosenthal, "Aus den 'Memoiren' der Deborah, " 311–312.

52. See the review of the Prague premiere in *Bohemia*, June 2, 1849, and June 5, 1849; "Tauwitz," *Jewish Encyclopedia* (New York, 1906), 12:68; and *Hebrew Union College Annual* (1895): 395.

53. An ad for Bateman's appearance in *Leah* at the Brooklyn Academy of Music on February 19, 1866, for instance, lists a certain "Mon. Weingarten" as conductor of the orchestra. See Kate Bateman Portfolio, Billy Rose Theatre Collection, New York Public Library for the Performing Arts, MWEZ+n.c. 13, 071.

54. See ad, *Sun* (Baltimore), March 14, 1864. For background on Rosewald, see obituaries for him, *San Francisco Call*, October 26, 1895; *Sunday Herald* (Baltimore), October 27, 1895. See also Judith S. Pinnolis, "'Cantor Soprano' Julie Rosewald: The Musical Career of a Jewish American 'New Woman,'" *American Jewish Archives Journal* 62, no. 2 (2010): 1–53.

55. Portions of the Stoepel score are pasted in a privately printed copy of *Leah, the Forsaken* in the New York Public Library; see *Leah, the Forsaken: A Play in Five Acts by Augustin Daly. Arranged from the "Deborah" of Mosenthal Expressly for Miss Bateman*, Billy Rose Theatre Collection 9-NCOF+p.v.498, New York Public Library for the Performing Arts. A "rural march" and the organ accompaniment for Deborah's monologues that Josef Töpler composed for a performance of *Deborah* in the German city of Coburg on December 13, 1849, have survived in manuscript form. See Töpler, "Theatermusik zu *Deborah*," Landesbibliothek Coburg, TB Einl 364, bound together with "Theatermusik zur Braut von Messina," http://gateway-bayern.de/BV016476247. Michael V. Pisani notes in *Music for the Melodramatic Theatre in Nineteenth-Century London and New York* (Iowa City: University of Iowa Press, 2014), 117, that Lawrence Barrett was using an uncredited version of Stoepel's score for performances of *Leah* on tour as late as 1881. The score for *Leah, the Jewess* that exists in manuscript at the Harvard Theatre Collection that is attributed to Barrett, however, indicates that Barrett at some point composed original music. See Lawrence Barrett, *Music for* Leah, the Jewess, in *Collection of Musical Scores, ca. 1875–1891*, B MS Thr 649, Box 1, Houghton Library, Harvard University.

56. See, on this issue, Heinrich Laube, "Das Burgtheater von 1848 bis 1867," *Neue Freie Presse*, March 29, 1868; idem, *Das Burgtheater, ein Beitrag zur deutschen Theater-Geschichte* (Leipzig, 1891), 344; and Rudolph Lothar, *Das Wiener Burgtheater* (Leipzig, 1891), 100–102.

57. *Morgenblatt der Bayerischen Zeitung*, September 24, 1864; and Robert von Hornstein, "Memoiren," *Süddeutsche Monatshefte* 4, no. 2 (1907): 30–60, 145–169, 289–316, 453–482, 551–577, here 473.

58. See, e.g., ad, *Wiener Zeitung*, September 11, 1864.

59. Despite my best efforts to locate it, the von Hornstein score appears to be lost. Neither the Burgtheater's archives, nor the music collection of the Austrian National Library, nor the music collection of the Wiener Stadt- und Landesbibliothek has a copy. Special thanks are due here to Rita Czapka in the Burgtheater-Archiv and Thomas Aigner in the Wienbibliothek im Rathaus for their assistance.

60. Em. K. [Emil Kuh], "Feuilleton. Burgtheater," *Die Presse* (Vienna), September 13, 1864.

61. Speidel, "Feuilleton. Burgtheater. 'Deborah.'"

62. "Amusements," *Louisville Daily Courier*, November 27, 1867. This article renders Bien's name incorrectly, as Behna. See also "History of Leah, the Forsaken: A Pathetic Summary," *Louisville Daily Courier*, November 27, 1867.

63. On Bien, see the death notice in the *Publications of the American Jewish Historical Society* 5 (1897): 207–209; and Fred Rosenbaum, *Cosmopolitans: A Social and Cultural History of Jews of the San Francisco Bay Area* (Berkeley: University of California Press, 2011), 23–24. See also, esp., John P. Marschall, "Rabbi on the Comstock: The Irrepressible Herman Bien, 1864–65," *Nevada Historical Society Quarterly* 47, no. 3 (2004): 167–192; and idem, *Jews in Nevada: A History* (Reno: University of Nevada Press, 2008), 28–37. See also Louis Harap, *The Image of the Jew in American Literature: From Early Republic to Mass Immigration* (Philadelphia: Jewish Publication Society of America, 1974), 27, 251–252, 27.

64. My reconstruction of Bien's version of *Leah* takes its cues from "Amusements," *Daily Evening Bulletin* (San Francisco), March 2, 1864; "Amusements," *Daily Evening Bulletin*, March 3, 1864; ad, *Daily Evening Bulletin*, March 16, 1863; ad, *Daily Alta California*, March 16, 1876; "Amusements," *Daily Evening Bulletin*, March 19, 1864; and "Amusements," *Daily Evening Bulletin*, July 22, 1864.

65. The performance of *Leah* on March 19, 1864, was presented as an "author's night and complimentary benefit of Dr. H. M. Bien, author of the English version of Leah." See "Amusements," *Daily Evening Bulletin* (San Francisco), March 19, 1864; and ads in the *Daily Evening Bulletin*, March 16, 17, 18, and 19, 1864. It stands to reason that Bien was in attendance. By April 1864, however, he had already arranged for his play to be performed in Virginia City, Nevada.

66. See Marschall, "Rabbi on the Comstock"; and Margaret G. Watson, *Silver Theatre: Amusements of the Mining Frontier in Early Nevada, 1850 to 1864* (Glendale, CA: Arthur H. Clark, 1964), 328–329.

67. See "Dr. H. M. Bien's Suicide," *San Francisco Call*, April 24, 1895. The reference to Bien as "Rabbi-Poet" is in *In and About Vicksburg: An Illustrated Guide Book to the City of Vicksburg, Mississippi* (Vicksburg, MS: Gibraltar, 1890), 153.

68. Playbill, *Leah, the Outcast*, September 5, 1867, Whitman's Continental Theatre Boston, Harvard Theatre Collection, THE GEN TCS 66, playbills and programs, Boston theatres, ca. 1800–1930, Folder: Continental Theatre, Houghton Library, Harvard University.

69. "Theatrical," *Salt Lake Daily Telegraph*, March 2, 1866. See "Affairs in Salt Lake City," *New York Times*, September 18, 1865; "Theatricals Among the Mormons," *Macon Daily Telegraph*, September 27, 1865, repr. from *Daily Union Vidette* (Salt Lake City), August 21; and ads, *Salt Lake Daily Telegraph*, March 1, March 2, and March 3, 1866. For context, see Horace G. Whitney, *The Drama in Utah: The Story of the Salt Lake Theatre* (Deseret, UT, 1913), 16–20.

70. See "Letter from Tycoon, Idaho City, September 4, 1864," *Idaho Tri-Weekly Statesman* (Boise City), September 6, 1864; and "Theatrical Correspondence," *Idaho Tri-Weekly Statesman*, September 6, 1864.

71. See Jacob Rader Marcus, *United States Jewry, 1776–1985* (Detroit: Wayne State University Press, 1989), 2:159. Wayne C. Sparling reports that a fire in 1865 destroyed 80 percent of the town, "including the newly completed Forrest Theatre"; see Sparling, *Southern Idaho Ghost Towns* (Caldwell, ID: Caxton, 1974), 40.

72. See *The Petroleum Centre Daily Record*, January 31, 1870, and February 1, 1870. S. Sobel owned both "Sobel's Opera House" and the dry-goods store next door in this town, which was rapidly developed in the 1860s but had become a ghost town by 1873.

73. See, e.g., *Examiner* (London), April 2, 1864; *New Orleans Times*, December 2, 1866; *Salt Lake Daily Telegraph*, February 21, 1868; *Memphis Daily Appeal*, March 12, 1869; *Public Ledger* (Memphis), January 26, 1875; *Daily Central City Register*, November 22, 1870; and *Anaconda Standard* (MT), April 7, 1899.

74. Karl Emil Franzos, "Mein Erstlingswerk: 'Die Juden von Barnouw,'" in idem, ed., *Die Geschichte des Erstlingswerks: Selbstbiographische Aufsätze* (Berlin: Concordia Deutsche Verlags-Anstalt, 1894), 227–228.

75. Karl Emil Franzos, *Der Pojaz: Eine Geschichte aus dem Osten* (Stuttgart: J. G. Cotta, 1905), 391–392. See, on this episode, Jeffrey L. Sammons, "Sender Glatteis Reads Lessing and Comes to a Sad End: Some Thoughts on Karl Emil Franzos's *Der Pojaz* and the Problem of Jewish Reading," in

Richard V. Benson, Eric Downing, and Jonathan M. Hess, eds., *Literary Studies and the Pursuits of Reading* (Rochester, NY: Camden House, 2012), 168–186.

76. Franzos, *Der Pojaz*, 418–419.

77. Franzos, *Der Pojaz*, 421.

78. See Jonathan M. Hess, *Middlebrow Literature and the Making of German-Jewish Identity* (Stanford, CA: Stanford University Press, 2010), 72–110; and idem, "Leopold Kompert and the Work of Nostalgia: The Cultural Capital of German Jewish Ghetto Fiction," *Jewish Quarterly Review* 97, no. 4 (2007): 576–615.

79. See Klaus Hödl, "Das 'Jüdische' in der allgemeinen Populärkultur," in idem, *Nicht nur Bildung, nicht nur Bürger*, 7–20.

80. "Kreuz- und Querzüge: Von der Saale, 26. Dezember," *Allgemeine Zeitung des Judenthums*, January 1, 1850.

81. See Hess, *Middlebrow Literature*, 101–102.

82. See, e.g., "Literarischer Wochenbericht," *Allgemeine Zeitung des Judenthums*, May 17, 1864; and "Neuere Dramen mit jüdischen Stoffen," *Allgemeine Zeitung des Judenthums*, February 1, 1876.

83. Wilhelm Goldbaum, *Literarische Physiognomien* (Vienna: Karl Proschaska, 1884), 163–216, esp. 185–195, here 194.

84. Isaak Hirsch, "Der Jude in der Literatur," *Jeschurun* 5, no. 4 (January 1859): 203–207. For context, see Hess, *Middlebrow Literature*, 169–174.

85. [Marcus Lehmann,] "Die moderne jüdische Tendenzpoesie," *Der Israelit*, October 7, 1863.

86. Mosenthal, "Aus dem 'Memoiren' der Deborah," 312.

87. See Salomon Ludwig Steinheim, *Moses Mardochai Büdinger: Lebensbeschreibung eines israelitischen Schulmannes* (Altona, 1844).

88. See, e.g., death notice for Karl Ritter von Weil in *Allgemeine Zeitung des Judenthums*, January 22, 1878.

89. See Josef Weilen, "S. H. Mosenthal: Ein Lebensbild," originally published in the *Wiener Abendpost* and subsequently repr. in *S. H. Mosenthal's gesammelte Werke* (Stuttgart: Eduard Hallberger, 1878), 6:26–27; and Rainer Liedtke, *N. M. Rothschild & Sons: Kommunikationswege im europäischen Bankenwesen im 19. Jahrhundert* (Cologne: Böhlau, 2006), 109.

90. "Leichenbegräbniss Mosenthal's," *Neue Freie Presse*, February 20, 1877.

91. "Leichenbegräbniss Mosenthal's," *Neue Freie Presse*, February 20, 1877.

92. The photographs of Mosenthal with his medals were often singled out for ridicule in the press. See, e.g., Franz Dingelstedt, "Mosenthal, ein Stammbuchblatt," *Die Gegenwart*, April 14, 1877, repr. in Dingelstedt, *Literarisches Bilderbuch* (Berlin: A. Hofmann, 1879), 165–186; and Daniel Spitzer's 1876 essay "Der Vesuv, Mosenthal, Weilen und sonstige Ursachen der Langeweile" and his 1878 essay "Rückblick auf das Jahr 1877," both repr. in Spitzer, *Wiener Spaziergänge* (Leipzig: Julius Klinkhardt, 1879).

93. Mosenthal's request in his will was first mentioned immediately after his death in the obituary "S. H. Mosenthal," *Neue Freie Presse*, February 18, 1877. For Jewish responses, see *Allgemeine Zeitung des Judenthums*, March 6, 1877; "Die Orden Mosenthal's," *Der Israelit*, August 22, 1877; *Israelitische Wochen-Schrift für die religiösen und socialen Interessen des Judenthums*, September 12, 1877; and Adolf Kohut, "Salomon Hermann Mosenthal," in *Berühmte israelitische Männer und Frauen in der Kulturgeschichte der Menschheit. Lebens- und Charakterbilder aus Vergangenheit und Gegenwart: Ein Handbuch für Haus und Familie* (Leipzig: A. H. Payne, 1901), 2:53–56.

94. "S. H. Mosenthal," *Neue Freie Presse*, February 18, 1877. The Lina-Mosenthal-Stiftung was, in fact, first created after Lina Mosenthal's death in 1862 and was administered by the Jewish community as late as 1895. See Carl Ferdinand Mautner Ritter von Markhof, *Die Wiener Stiftungen: Ein Handbuch* (Vienna, 1892), 791; and "Israel: Communal-Schematismus," *Wiener Jahrbuch für Israeliten* 2 (5628/1867–1868). The provision in Mosenthal's will to ensure the continuation of this program in perpetuity was also noted on the other side of the Atlantic. See *Israelite*, June 26, 1877.

95. Mosenthal, "Aus den 'Memoiren' der Deborah," 312. For context on the history of Jews in Graz, see Gerald Lamprecht, *Fremd in der eigenen Stadt: Die moderne jüdische Gemeinde von Graz vor dem Ersten Weltkrieg* (Innsbruck: Studien, 2007).

96. As noted in previous chapters, David Radner's Hebrew translation was first published in 1880, and *Deborah* was performed widely in Yiddish, beginning in 1884.

97. See, e.g., M. Kayserling, *Gedenkblätter: Hervorragende jüdische Persönlichkeiten des neunzehnten Jahrhunderts* (Leipzig, 1892), 58; Kohut, "Salomon Hermann Mosenthal"; and Felix Theilhaber, "Salomon Hermann Mosenthal," *Hamburgisches Israelitisches Familienblatt*, January 13, 1921.

98. Henry Samuel Morais, *Eminent Israelites of the Nineteenth Century* (Philadelphia: Edward Stern, 1880), 245–247.

99. "Ausländische Bühnen," *Blätter für Musik, Theater und Kunst* (Vienna) October 29, 1867; and "New-Yorker Bühnenschau," *Belletristisches Journal*, October 18, 1867.

100. "Amusements: Theatrical," *New York Times*, April 19, 1869; "Theater," *New-Yorker Belletristisches Journal*, April 23, 1869; *Israelite*, April 23, 1869; and "Fanny Janauschek," *New-Yorker Belletristisches Journal*, April 30, 1869.

101. "Local Items," *Jewish Messenger*, April 30, 1869.

102. Program, Viola Wilson Stock Co., Monticello, NY, Billy Rose Theatre Collection, Leah! or, the Jewish Maiden's Wrong (Chas. Smith Cheltingham [sic]), Programme folder, New York Public Library for the Performing Arts. The program lists the performance as taking place on August 4, without naming a year, but references to telephones and motion pictures indicate a date in the late 1920s or early 1930s.

103. "Zion Council to Give Noted Play: 'Leah, the Forsaken' Will Have Vivid Portrayal by Local Thespians," *Pittsburg Press*, November 3, 1910; "Leah the Forsaken in Stock," *Pittsburgh Gazette Times*, March 24, 1911: "Leah, the Forsaken Will Show Special Talent in Dramatic Club," *Pittsburg Press*, May 21, 1911; and "Zionist Dramatic Club in 'Leah, the Forsaken,'" *Pittsburgh Gazette Times*, May 21, 1911.

104. "Leah, the Forsaken Will Show Special Talent in Dramatic Club"; and "Zion Council to Give Noted Play."

105. "Local Items," *Jewish Messenger*, November 23, 1877.

106. "Local Items," *Jewish Messenger*, February 7, 1879.

107. "Testimonial to Mr. Herman Solomon," *Jewish Exponent*, July 26, 1891; and "Music and Reading," *North American* (Philadelphia), June 19, 1891.

108. "A Fashionable Gathering: The First Promenade of the New Hebrew Circle in Allegheny," *Pittsburg Dispatch*, February 21, 1890.

109. The program for this event is reproduced in Eleanor F. Horvitz, "Old Bottles, Rags, Junk!" *Rhode Island Jewish Historical Notes* 7, no. 2 (November 1976): 214–215.

110. "Young Maccabees Awarded First Prize," *Jewish Advocate*, June 28, 1932.

Concluding Remarks

1. Richard Wagner, "Das Judenthum in der Musik" (Leipzig: J. J. Weber, 1869), 9–10. I am using my own translation here, which differs somewhat from Wagner, "Judaism in Music," in *Judaism in Music and Other Essays*, trans. William Ashton Ellis (Lincoln: University of Nebraska Press, 1995), 80–81. Given that the German *Judentum* can refer to Judaism, the Jewish people, and Jewishness, and given Wagner's lack of interest in Judaism as a religion in this essay, "Jewishness in Music" might be a better translation than the standard "Judaism in Music."

2. See, e.g., David Brodbeck, *Defining Deutschtum: Political Ideology, German Identity, and Music-Critical Discourse in Liberal Vienna* (Oxford: Oxford University Press, 2014); and Michael Haas, *Forbidden Music: The Jewish Composers Banned by the Nazis* (New Haven, CT: Yale University Press, 2013).

3. See my comments on this issue in Chapter 1, n. 79.

4. Wagner, "Das Judenthum in der Musik," 13. In the 1869 version of the text, Wagner adds here, in a footnote, some additional disparaging comments about more recent Jewish actors.

5. Friedrich Nietzsche, *The Gay Science*, trans. Walter Kaufmann (New York: Vintage, 1974), 317.

6. Zygmunt Bauman, "Allosemitism: Premodern, Modern, Postmodern," in Bryan Cheyette and Laura Marcus, eds., *Modernity, Culture and 'the Jew'* (Stanford, CA: Stanford University Press, 1998), 144, 146, 148. Bauman here builds on his previous work, including *Modernity and Ambivalence* (Ithaca, NY: Cornell University Press, 1991) and *Modernity and the Holocaust*, 2nd ed. (Ithaca, NY: Cornell University Press, 2000).

7. "Music and Drama: Sarah Bernhardt in 'Leah,'" *Jewish Messenger*, April 22, 1892.

8. Ruth Wisse, *The Modern Jewish Canon: A Journey Through Language and Culture* (Chicago: University of Chicago Press, 2000), 4, 10.

9. See Jonathan Freedman, *Klezmer America: Jewishness, Ethnicity, Modernity* (New York: Columbia University Press, 2008); Lisa Silverman, *Becoming Austrians: Jews and Culture Between the World Wars* (Oxford: Oxford University Press, 2012); and Benjamin Schreier, *The Impossible Jew: Identity and the Reconstruction of Jewish American Literary History* (New York: New York University Press, 2015).

10. Jo-Jacqueline Eckhardt, *Lessing's* Nathan the Wise *and the Critics: 1779–1991* (Columbia, SC: Camden House, 1993), 63–65.

11. *The Governess*, directed by Sandra Goldbacher (Sony Pictures Classics, 1998). My discussion of *The Governess* is limited here to an exploration of the ways it can be read as strategically rewriting Mosenthal's material. A small body of excellent literature on *The Governess* discusses the film in broader terms. See, e.g., Judith Lewin, "Semen, Semolina and Salt Water: The Erotic Jewess in Sandra Goldbacher's *The Governess*," in Nathan Abrams, ed., *Jews and Sex* (Nottingham: Five Leaves, 2008), 88–100; Helene Meyers, "Educating for a Jewish Gaze: The Close Doubling of Antisemitism and Philosemitism in Sandra Goldbacher's *The Governess*," in *Antisemitism and Philosemitism in the Twentieth and Twenty-First Centuries* (Newark: University of Delaware Press, 2008), 103–118; Belén Vidal, "Playing in a Minor Key: The Literary Past Through the Feminist Imagination," in Mireia Aragay, ed., *Books in Motion: Adaptation, Intertextuality, Authorship* (Amsterdam: Rodopi, 2005), 263–286; Nathan Abrams, *The New Jew in Film: Exploring Jewishness and Judaism in Contemporary Cinema* (New Brunswick, NJ: Rutgers University Press, 2012), esp. 59–62, 76–77; Antje Anscheid, "Safe Rebellions: Romantic Emancipation in the 'Women's Heritage Film,'" *Scope* 4 (2006); and Lynette Felber, "Capturing the Shadow of Ghosts: Mixed Media and the Female Gaze in *The Women on the Roof* and *The Governess*," *Film Quarterly* 54 (2001): 27–37.

12. In its exact chronology, Goldbacher's film takes considerable liberties. Rachel did not visit London until 1841; Daguerre had already begun to make his results public in 1838. When Rosina returns to London before the film's final sequence, she encounters a community desiccated in part by a cholera outbreak, which would seem to situate the film in 1832–1833, at a time when Rachel had yet to make her debut in France.

13. Felber aptly describes this pose as a "reclining male 'centerfold,'" "Capturing the Shadow of Ghosts," 32.

14. Salo Baron, "Ghetto and Emancipation: Shall We Revise the Traditional View?," *Menorah Journal* 14 (1928): 515–526.

Index

Page numbers in italics indicate illustrations.

absorption, in theatrical illusion, 32, 111–16, 124, 137–38, 143, 162
acting styles, 24, 110–16, 160–61
actresses, 110–63; criticisms of, 141, 144–45, 147, 157; *Deborah* as a star vehicle for, 125–33, 160; emotions displayed by, 110–16, 125–28, 144–45, 157; identification of, with their roles, 110–12, 116, 118–20, 124, 126, 129, 137; Jewishness of, 118–20, 122, 146–49, 154, 156–57, 178–80; prostitutes linked to, in popular imagination, 1, 203; theatrical range of, 32–33
Adelphi Theatre. *See* Royal Adelphi Theatre, London
Adler, Jacob, *Shylock*, 8, 170
African Americans, 106
Allgemeine Zeitung des Judenthums (newspaper), 187–88, 190
allosemitism, 198–99
ambivalence: of beautiful Jewess figure, 14; about Jews, 10–11, 85–86, 92, 198–200; toward *Leah*'s conclusion, 87; in parodies, 105–8
American Israelite (newspaper), 106, 122
Anczyc, Siegmund, 223n30
anti-Jewish sentiment: in *Deborah*, 43, 49, 82; in *Leah*, 81; *Leah* as antidote to, 227n83; in parodies, 105–8
antisemitism: and ambivalence about Jews, 198–99; Bernhardt's *Leah* and, 156–57; in cultural criticism, 61–62; *Deborah* as threat to, 11–12; philosemitism in relation to, 197–99; portrayals of Shylock in relation to, 170; rationale for, 196; as social context for performances, 7, 148, 162, 168–69; in United States, 81; Wagner's, 61–63, 196–99
Archer, William, *Masks or Faces?* 112

Aristotle, 36
Aschheim, Steven, 20
audience: attendance figures, 212n44; Bernhardt's *Leah* and, 155–56; Cheltnam's *Deborah* and, 97; curtain calls by, 114, 125, 126, 132, 155, 191; identification of, with dramatic characters, 36, 38, 111–12, 115–16; Jewish composition of, 122; melodrama's effect on, 35, 46, 50, 53; nineteenth-century, 114; powerlessness experienced by, 35, 46, 49, 50; relations of Jews and non-Jews in, 19, 87, 163, 174–86, 195; response of, to actresses' virtuosity, 33; response of, to emotional acting style, 112–16; self-awareness of, 109, 112, 114–17, 162; shared experience of, 29; as target of *Deborah*'s script, 42–50, 53, 59–60, 86; tearful response of, to *Deborah/Leah*, 7, 8, 11, 16, 26–29, 31–35, 38, 42, 59–61, 117
authenticity: in acting, 6, 123; of *Deborah*, 6, 10–11, 21, 25, 117, 188, 189; theatricality in relation to, 25, 117–18, 120, 128–29, 137–38, 143, 144, 162

Baison, Maurice, 126
Bandmann, Daniel E., 7–8, 8, 172–74, *172*
Barbier, Jules, *Joan of Arc*, 146
Baron, Salo, 206
Barrett, Lawrence, 181, 244n55
Bârsescu, Agathe, 159–60
Bartels, Adolf, 12, 62
Bateman, Ellen, 139, *139*
Bateman, H. L., 88, 119, 138–40, 164–67, 195, 226n69
Bateman, Kate, 76, 138–44; on acting, 110; as "American Rachel," 119, 143–44; as child actress, 138–39, *139*; criticisms of, 141; Episcopalianism of, 237n111; impact of

Bateman, Kate (continued)
  performances by, 140–44; influence of, 144; international popularity of, 141; lawsuit involving, 164–67; as Leah, 2, 3, 5, 7, 30, 31, 40, *40*, 43, 52, *59*, 65, 67, *68*, 69, *70*, *73*, 87, 91, 92, 95, 100, *101*, 104, 106, 114, 115, 122, 138–44, *142*, 157, 159, 220n2; "memoir" written by Daly for, 81, 119, 164, 174; Mosenthal's personal dealings with, 74, 141–42, 222n23; and Mosenthal's *Pietra*, 89; other roles of, 139–40; parodies of, 100, 104, 106; promotion of, 32, 119; version of *Leah* performed by, 1, 23, 31, 33, 34, *50*, 69, 74, 79, 88–93, 140–44, 149, 165, 174, 222n24, 226n69, 228n97
Bateman, Sidney Frances, 138–39
Bauman, Zygmunt, 198–99
beautiful Jewess (*belle juive*), 13–16, 36, 40, 43, 154, 169, 201, 202–6, 238n124
Beneville, Emile, 76–77, 103, 165, 223n35
Bergman-Carton, Janis, 149
Bernhardt, Sarah: criticisms of, 147; impact of performances by, 113, 122; international celebrity of, 7, 115, 119, 146, 149; and Jewishness, 118, 122, 146–49, 154, 156–57; as Joan of Arc, 146, *147*; as Leah, 146–49, *150–52*, 153–56, *155*, *156*, 238n124; name of, 203; version of *Leah* performed by, 19, 69, 78, 118, 148–49, 151, 153–57, 229n115
Bial, Henry, *Acting Jewish*, 21
Bien, Herman Milton, 77, 182–83
Birch-Pfeiffer, Charlotte, 37
B'nai Brith, 192
Bock, Jerry, 17, 181
Booth, John Wilkes, 140
Booth, Oliver J., 78
Booth's Theatre, New York, 21, *23*, 31, 32
Boucicault, Dion: *After Dark*, 86; *The Colleen Bawn*, 86, 117
Bowers, Elizabeth Crocker (Mrs. D. P.), 144, 180
Brachvogel, Albert Emil, *Narziß* (Narcisse), 26
Brecht, Bertolt, 61, 111–12, 114–16, 162
Britannia Theatre, London, 108
Brooks, Peter, *The Melodramatic Imagination*, 35
Brüll, Ignaz, *Das goldene Kreuz* (The Golden Cross), 197
Buckstone, John Baldwin, 89
Büdiger, Moses, 189
Burbank, Alfred Post, 103, 214n1
Burgtheater, Vienna, 21, 34, 123, *124*, 159, 177, 178, 181

Burkhardt, Lillian, 194
burlesques. *See* parodies of *Deborah/Leah*
Burr McIntosh-Monthly, 149, *151*
Byron, H. J., 231n136

carte-de-visite photographs, *2*, *5*, *30*, *59*, *67*, *68*, 95, 100, *101*, *102*, *113*, *119*, *121*, *145*, *172*, *177*
Cerri, Gaetano, 74, 100, 230n129
Cervantes, Miguel de, *La gitanilla*, 218n55
Cheltnam, Charles Smith, *Deborah; or, the Jewish Maiden's Wrong!* 77–79, 94–98, 148, 160, 226n62
Chicago Tribune (newspaper), 120
Christianity: and beautiful Jewess figure, 14–15; compassion of, 38, 41, 43–46, 90–93; cross as symbol of, 44–46, *45*, 91, 105, 149, 151, *152*, 153–55, *153*, *155*, *156*, 203; in *Leah*, 67, 81–87; in Oxenford's *Leah*, 90–93; persecution of Jews by, 43–44, 53, 58, 65, 151, 156; reconciliation of Jews with, 7, 28, 48, 54–56, 59–60, 79–80, 85, 93, 97; redemption as theme of, 67, 90–91, 98
class, 34, 164
classical drama, 29, 36, 37
Clysbia (play), 77
Coleridge, Samuel Taylor, 116
Collin, James Edgell, *Leah*, *142*
compassion and sympathy: actresses' elicitation of, 117, 122, 127–28, 138, 143; Bernhardt's *Leah* and, 155–56; Christian, 38, 41, 43–46, 90–93; criticisms of, 37; *Deborah/Leah* and, 36–38, 42–50, 63, 86, 90–91, 93, 98; education of theater audience in, 29, 31; for Jewish suffering, 7, 11–12, 60–63, 79, 80, 86, 93, 99, 105, 117, 128, 133, 143, 175–76, 185, 195, 198, 200, 206–7; Lessing's theory of, 29, 31, 36–37; parodies of, 99, 105–8; secular/liberal, 38, 45. *See also* Jews and Jewishness, identification with; liberal feeling, toward Jews
Confederacy, 65–66
Connolly, Charles M. *See* Uncle Schneider
Conquest, George August, *Deborah; or, the Jewish Outcast*, 76, 77, 93, 223n34, 229n117, 229n118
Conway, Sara, 144
copyright, 6, 69, 74, 222n21, 222n24
cross, 44–46, *45*, 91, 105, 149, 151, *152*, 153–55, *153*, *155*, *156*, 203
Crowe, Sidney, 139
Cumberland, Richard, *The Jew*, 13, 42, 133, 169, 170

curse scene: in acting school curricula, 148, 160, 192–93; Bernhardt's performance of, 147–48, 155; in Cheltnam's *Deborah*, 97; in *Deborah*, 10, 33, 34, 37, 51–53, *52*; impact of, 3, 10, 34, 53, 200, 202; parody of, 105; performances of, 33, 69, *73*, 114, 130–31; in popular culture, 1, 3, 185, 193, 194
curtain calls, 114, 125, 126, 132, 155, 191

Daguerre, Louis, 203, 248n12
Daily National Republican (newspaper), 120
Daly, Augustin: early playwriting efforts of, 87–88; and Janauschek, 133; *Judith*, 20; lawsuits involving, 164–67, 195; "memoir" of Bateman written by, 81, 119, 164, 174; *The New Leah*, 167; photograph of, *166*; *Taming a Butterfly*, 103–4; *Under the Gaslight*, 86, 117, 133. See also *Leah, the Forsaken* (Daly)
Daly, Joseph, 77, 223n35
Dambӧck, Marie, 130–32, *130*
Dargon, Augusta, 120, 144
Darmont, Albert, *Leah*, 148–49
Davenport, Fanny, 144
Dawison, Bogumil, 7, 170, *171*, 172, 184, 185
Dean, Julia. *See* Hayne, Julia Dean
Debo-Leah (burlesque), 108, 232n164
Deborah (Mosenthal), 1–12; adaptations and spin-offs of, 6–7, 67–79, 91–94; antisemitic criticisms aimed at, 62, 196–97; audience-oriented nature of, 42–50, 53, 59–60, 86; audience response to, 52, 63, 116–17 (*see also* tears, as response to *Deborah*); authenticity of, 6, 10–11, 21, 25, 117, 188, 189; criticisms of, 6, 21–22, 25, 34, 35, 37–38, 41, 50–51, 53, 61–63, 125, 169–70, 187–89, 196–97, 201; decline in performances of (from late nineteenth century), 159–62, 201; emotional range of, 32–33; ending of, 53–61, 83–85; genesis of, 38–42, 120, 168–69; international popularity of, 65–109; Jewish reception of, 7, 53, 87, 122–23, 168, 186–94; moral and political effects of, 11–12, 19, 38, 63–64, 195, 200, 206; music composed for, 180–81, 244n55; opening of, 43–48; parodies of, 98–109, 184–86, 231n136; reception of, 7–8, 21–22, 34, 60–61, 217n34 (*see also* criticisms of); as a star vehicle, 125–33, 160; study of, 9–10, 22, 187; translations of, 6, 67, 74, 75, 77. See also *Leah, the Forsaken* (Daly)
Deborah, die Jüdin (Deborah, the Jewess) (play), 125

Deborah, oder: die Auswanderung der Juden (Deborah, or: the Emigration of the Jews) (play), 93
Deborah, the Deserted Jewess (play), 77
Deborah, the Jewess (play), 77
Deborah, the Jewish Maiden (silent film), 78, 160
Deborah craze, 11, 12, 16, 21, 22, 24, 25, 69, 74, 75, 79, 98–99, 168, 187, 195, 198–99, 201, 205, 206. See also *Leah* craze
Deborah/Leah (character): actresses' renditions of, 57, 110–63; parodies of, 98–109; portrayals of, *2*, *5*, *30*, *40*, *59*, *68*, *70*, *95*, *101*, *121*, *124*, *132*, *142*, 150–55, *158*, 193
Deborah of Steinmark: or, Curse and Blessing (play), 77
Denin, Susan, 144, 146
D'Este, Helen, 226n62
Devrient, Emil, 129
Devrient, Ludwig, 7, 170
Dexter, E., engraving of Dan Setchell, *102*
Dickens, Charles, *Oliver Twist*, 12, 42
Diderot, Denis, *Paradoxe sur le comédien* (*The Paradox of Acting*), 112
Dingelstedt, Franz, 62
Dresden Court Theatre, 133
Dreyfus affair, 157
Driver, Minnie, 202
Drummond, W., sketch of Rebecca in Scott's *Ivanhoe*, *14*
Dutch dialect, 7, 26

Easter, 90–91, 98
Edict of Tolerance, 54, 60, 80
Eliot, George, 144, 237n113; *Daniel Deronda*, 144
E. Moses & Sons, 107
emotions, theatrical role of, 110–16, 125–28, 144–45, 157, 159
epic theater, 111–12, 116
Erdman, Harley, 238n124
eroticism, of Jewish women, 13–14, 16, 40, 42, 69
Esther, the Jewish Maiden (play), 77
exoticism, Jewish, 3, 4, 6, 7, 11, 13, 36, 40, 43, 48, 69, 120, 126, 129, 131, 181–82, 199, 202, 227n69

Fagin (character), 12, 42
Faucit, Helen, 144
Fealy, Maud, 160
Feinman, Dina, 240n154

Felheim, Marvin, 223n35
Félix, Elisabeth-Rachel, 3, 16, 119, *119*, 125, 148, 157, 178, 197, 202, 248n12
Ferris, Marian, 230n119
Fiddler on the Roof (musical and film), 17, 181
Fleming, Paul, 36
Foerster, Josef Bohuslav, *Debora*, 67
Fontane, Theodor, 21, 126, 235n53
Ford's Holiday Street Theatre, Baltimore, 180
Forrest Theatre, Idaho City, 183
Frank, Kathi, 5-6, 10, 24, 178-80, *179*
Frankfurter Stadttheater, 133
Franz Joseph I, 21, 38
Franzos, Karl Emil, 122-23, 183-84; *Der Pojaz* (The Clown), 184-86
Freedman, Jonathan, 201
Freemont Theatre, Boston, 159
French's Standard Drama, 76, 93
Frey, Marie, 52
Freytag, Gustav, *Soll und Haben* (Debit and Credit), 12, 62-63
Fuller, Mary, 160

Gabillon, Ludwig, 178
Gabillon, Zerline (née Würzburg), *177*, 178
Gamea (play), 19, 20
Die Gartenlaube (magazine), 17, 18, 186
Garthwaite, Fanny, *Rebecca, the Jewish Wanderer*, 223n34
ghetto literature, 17-19, 186, 188
Gilbert, William, *Margaret Meadows*, 140
Gladstane, Mary, 77, 144, 224n41, 226n63
Gledhill, Christine, 35
Goethe, Johann Wolfgang von, 29, 37, 129; *Wilhelm Meisters Lehrjahre* (Wilhelm Meister's Apprenticeship), 184
Goldbacher, Sandra, *The Governess*, 202-6, 248n12
Goldbaum, Wilhelm, 189
Goldberg, Laura, 194
Goldhagen, Daniel, 9
Goldmark, Karl, *Die Königin von Saba* (The Queen of Sheba), 17, 32, 197, 219n79
Goldschmidt, Moritz, 189
Good Friday, 43, 53, 90
Gotzmann, Andreas, 18
The Governess (film), 248n12
Grand Opera House, San Francisco, 159
Grant, Ulysses S., 65, 81, 103, 140, 220n2, 227n75
Grecian Theatre, London, 93

Greville, Augustus, 67, 69; "It Is the Hour: Leah's Song," *72*, 91, 229n106
Grillparzer, Franz, 41; *Medea*, 122, 191
Grover's Theatre, Washington, DC, 113-14
Gutzkow, Karl, *Uriel Acosta*, 19-20
gypsies, 40, 218n55

Hagar, the Outcast Jewess (play), 77
Halévy, Fromental, *La Juive* (The Jewess), 15, 36, 125, 157, 169, 211n34
Halévy, Léon, 74
Hall, A. Oakey, 164-67
Harnick, Sheldon, 17
Harper's Theatre, Rock Island, Illinois, 175
Harper's Weekly (magazine), 65-66, 106
Haskalah (Jewish Enlightenment), 25
Hauff, Wilhelm, "Das kalte Herz" (The Stone Heart), 39
Hawarden, Clementina, *Photographic Study*, 3-4, *4*, 24, 204
Hawthorne, Nathaniel, *The Scarlet Letter*, 81, 174
Hayne, Julia Dean, 78, 144, 182-83
Haza, Ofra, 202
Hazlewood, Colin Henry, 232n164
Hazlitt, William, 117
Hebbel, Friedrich, *Judith*, 20
Hebrew dramas. *See* Jewish plays
Hebrew Free School Association, 191
Heckenast, Gustav, 41-42, 133, 169
Heine, Heinrich, 181
Heraud, Edith, 77
Her Majesty's Theatre, London, 21, 32, 93
Heron, Matilda, 19, 104
Herring, Fanny, 144
Hettner, Hermann, 49-50
Hirsch, Isaak, 189
Hirsch, Samson Raphael, 189
Hödl, Klaus, 20, 187
Holocaust, 9, 10, 162, 207
Hornstein, Robert von, 181
Howard, Rollin, 103, 230n135

Ibsen, Henrik, 61
Iffland, August Wilhelm, 37, 170
impersonation, 118, 122, 124
infant phenomenon, 139
Irving, Henry, 113, 140
Isaacs, M. S., 191
Der Israelit (newspaper), 189, 190
Itzig, Veitel (character), 12

Janauschek, Fanny, 132–38; as Deborah, 78, 118, 122, 132–33, *132*, 135, 141; English-language performances by, 133; as "German Rachel," 119, 132, 135, *136*; impact of performances by, 34, 113, 114, 117, 135, 137–38, 191; international popularity of, 7, 32, 191; Jewish community and, 191–92; Jewishness falsely ascribed to, 118; other roles of, 133; version of *Deborah* performed by, *134*, 222n27

Janin, Jules, 81

Jellinek, Adolf, 190

Jesus, 90–91

The Jewess (play), 31, 78, 157, 159, 160, 161

Jewish literature, 201. *See also* ghetto literature

The Jewish Maiden's Wrong (silent film), 78

Jewish Messenger (newspaper), 156, 173–74

Jewish newspapers, 187, 190

Jewish plays, 19–20, 62, 175, 177, 186

Jewish Record (newspaper), 122

The Jewish Wanderer (play), 77

Jews and Jewishness: acting (role-playing) abilities of, 3, 118–19, 197–98, 209n5; ambivalence about, 10–11, 85–86, 92, 198–200; anti-theatrical sentiments of, 25; ascription of, to non-Jewish actresses, 118–20; as audience members, 122; Christian persecution of, 43–44, 53, 58, 65, 151, 156; collaborations of non-Jews with, 10, 20–21, 24, 168, 174–83, 198–99, 201; compassion/sympathy for suffering of, 7, 11–12, 60–63, 79, 80, 86, 93, 99, 105, 117, 128, 133, 143, 175–76, 185, 195, 198, 200, 206–7 (*see also* identification with); cultural representations of, 12–21; in *Deborah*'s conclusion, 54–61; exoticism of, 3, 4, 6, 7, 11, 13, 36, 40, 43, 48, 69, 120, 126, 129, 131, 181–82, 199, 202, 227n69; identification with, 7, 11, 16–17, 36, 41, 60, 62–63, 107–8, 117, 206–7 (*see also* compassion/sympathy for suffering of); in Lessing's dramas, 36, 41–42; noble Jew figure, 41–42; performance/production of, 10–11, 20–21, 24, 118, 120, 124, 162, 168, 174–83, 194, 197–200; in popular culture, 186–94; reconciliation of Christians with, 7, 28, 48, 54–56, 59–60, 79–80, 85, 93, 97; shared social experiences of non-Jews with, 10, 19, 20, 63–64, 87, 163, 168, 174–86, 190, 195, 207; study of, 200–201, 206; theater's role for, 168; theatricality in relation to, 3, 197–98, 205. *See also* beautiful Jewess

Jones, Avonia, 19, 20, 110, 113–14, *113*, 144, 146, 220n2, 227n75

Jordan, Emily, 144, 182

Joseph II, 54, 60, 80

Joyce, James, *Ulysses*, 173

Junker, Hermann, 18

Kalich, Bertha, 192

Karp, Jonathan, 9

Kean, Edmund, 7, 113, 148, 170

Keller, Gottfried, 61–62

Kenney, Charles Lamb, 32, 34, 76, 88, 91, 93

Knowles, Sheridan, *The Hunchback*, 139–40

Koch, Josephine, 193

Kolár, Jiří, 67

Kompert, Leopold, 17, 188

König, Herbert, *Bogumil Dawison in vershiedenen Rollen* (Bogumil Dawison in various roles), *171*

Königliches Schauspielhaus, Berlin, 160

Körner, Theodor, *Toni*, 39

Kotzebue, August von, 37

Kuh, Emil, 181

Kuhn, Francis X., 162

Kulke, Eduard, 175

Kürnberger, Ferdinand, 62

Kushner, Tony, *Lincoln*, 65, 220n2

Küster, Karl Theodor von, 126, 129

Lacy's Acting Editions, 76

Lawrence, Ada, 78

Lawson, F. W., sketch of Kate Bateman as Leah, 2

Leah, the Forsaken (Bien), 77, 182–83

Leah, the Forsaken (Daly): alterations of *Deborah* made for, 80–87; audience involvement in, 83; authorship of, 87–88; Bateman's version of, 1, *23*, 31, 33, 34, *50*, 69, 74, 79, 88–93, 140–44, 149, 165, 174, 222n24, 226n69, 228n97; Bernhardt's version of, 19, 69, 78, 118, 148–49, 151, 153–57; Bien's adaptation of, 182–83; Cheltnam's *Deborah* in relation to, 94–97; Christian themes in, 67, 81–87; copyright of, 222n24; costume monologue version of, *193*; criticisms of, 88; Darmont's borrowing from, 148; decline in performances of (from late nineteenth century), 159–62; dress rehearsal for, *47*; ending of, 27–28, *27*, 76, 82–87, 89–91, 141–42; genesis of, 76; Jewish reception of, 87, 122–23; lawsuits involving, 164–67; liberal feeling resulting from, 65–66; *The*

Leah, the Forsaken (Daly) (continued)
Merchant of Venice in relation to, 171–74; music composed for, 67, 69, 76, 180–81; opening of, 44, *45*, 46–49; Oxenford's rewriting of, 88–90, 228n97; parodies of, 100–109, 205, 231n136; performances of, 3–4, 19, 20, *52*, 113, 161, 224n36; reception of, 26–29, 31, 34, 87; scholarship on, 22; setting of, 80–81; success of, 74; title of, 226n69; in United States, 65–66, 171–72

Leah, the Forsaken (silent film, 1908), 78, 160–61

Leah, the Forsaken (silent film, 1912), 78, 160

Leah, the Jewish Maiden (anonymous British novel), 69, *73*, 76, 92

Leah, the Outcast (play), 77, 182

Leah craze, 69, 103. See also Deborah craze

Leah the Forsook (burlesque), *102*, 103–8, 231n144

"Leah the Shook, or Was She Forsook" (burlesque), 103

Lehmann, Marcus, 189

Lessing, Gotthold Ephraim: compassion's role in dramatic theory of, 29, 31, 36, 53; domestic dramas of, 32; idealization of Jews by, 36, 41–42; *Die Juden* (The Jews), 41–42; *Miss Sara Sampson*, 32; *Nathan der Weise* (Nathan the Wise), 12–13, 15, 41–42, 133, 169–70, 201–2

Lewes, George Henry, 117, 144

Lewis, Annie, 1, 3, 24, 203

liberal feeling, toward Jews, 7, 36, 56, 59–63, 65–66, 163, 195, 200, 201, 206–7. *See also* compassion and sympathy

liberalism: ambivalence of, toward Jews, 14; compassion stemming from, 38; philosemitic, 163, 168; universalist character of, 11–12

Lincoln, Abraham, 20, 65, 113, 140, 220n2

Lincoln, Mary Todd, 20, 113, 173

Liptsin, Keni, 159

London, Bateman's *Leah* in, 87–93

Longfellow, Henry Wadsworth, 139

Löw, Leopold, 123

Ludovici, Louis, 78

Lustspieltheater, Vienna, 159

Lutzberger, Jakob, 26

Lysiah, the Abandoned (play), 77

Macfarren, George Alexander, *Helvellyn*, 89

Magnet, Cella, 194

The Maiden's Curse (play), 77

Maimonides Library Association, 193

Majestic Theatre, Boston, 159

Malkin, Jeanette R., 20

Manette Club, 194

Maretzek, Max, 135

Marlowe, George, 224n41

Marr, Wilhelm, 12; *Der Sieg des Judenthums über das Germanenthum* (The Victory of Judaism over Germandom), 62

Marra, Kim, 120

Marylebone Theatre, London, 94

Mason Opera House, Los Angeles, 159

Mather, Margaret, 123, 144, 148, *154*, 155

Mayhew, Horace and Augustus, 34

McConachie, Bruce, 116

melodrama: in Anglo-American versions of *Deborah*, 79; Cheltnam's *Deborah* and, 94; *Deborah* as, 16, 21–22, 35, 45, 161; *Leah* as, 86; popularity of, 34; powerlessness of spectator as feature of, 35, 46, 49, 50; scholarship on, 35; in silent films, 160–61; spectator-position for, 46, 50, 53; stereotypes as element of, 10

Mendelssohn, Moses, 36

Mendelssohn-Bartholdy, Felix, 61

Mérimée, Prosper, *Carmen*, 39

Methua, J. Guido, 140; *Narziß* (Narcisse), 26

Methua-Scheller, Marie, 140, 223n35

Metropolitan Playhouse, New York, 162

Meyer, Rahel, 16

Meyerbeer, Giacomo, 61

Meyers, Jonathan Rhys, 202

Michaelson, Hermann, 74, 222n21

Miles, Sophia, 230n119

Miriam, the Deserted (play), 77, 224n41, 226n63

modernist theater, 111–12, 114, 116, 159

Moore, R., *Ruth, the Jewess*, 223n34

Morais, Henry Samuel, 191

Moretti, Franco, 33

Morris, Clara, 167

Mortara, Edgardo, 19

Mosenthal, Lina, 189, 190

Mosenthal, Salomon Hermann: "Aus den 'Memoiren' der Deborah," 222n23, 222n26; awards and honors received by, 21, 190; Bateman's personal dealings with, 74, 141–42, 222n23; career of, 39; death of, 17, 21, 39, 62, 190; *Ein deutsches Dichterleben* (A German Poet's Life), 100; *Erzählungen aus dem jüdischen Familienleben* (Tales of Jewish Family Life), 17, 186, 189; ghetto literature by, 17; *Der Holländer Michel* (Michel, the

Dutchman), 39; Jewishness of, 176, 189–90, 201; Jewish reactions to, 189–91; as "Jewish Schiller," 175–77, 185; libretti by, 17, 32, 39, 197; in Ministry of Education, 38–39; Nazis' banning of works by, 201; on performances of *Deborah*, 10; photographs of, *15*, *176*; *Pietra*, 89, 140; and politics, 39; royalties received by, 74; *Die Sklavin* (The Slave Girl), 39; *Der Sonnwendhof* (Sunny Vale Farm), 89; special effects in dramas of, 45; on Thomas's acting, 126–27. See also *Deborah* (Mosenthal)
Most, Andrea, *Theatrical Liberalism*, 21
Mozart Hall, Cincinnati, 122
music, 67, 69, 76, 180–81, 244n55
Musical World (journal), 91
"Mutter Deborah" (*Figaro*), 99–100, *99*

Naomi (play), 78, 225n46
Naomi, the Deserted (play), 77
Naomi, the Jewish Maiden (play), 77, 226n63
Nast, Thomas, *Leah, the Forsook*, 100, *101*, 103
natural acting, 112, 116, 117, 131–32, 135, 138, 140–41, 144–45, 160
Nazis, 201
Neale, Steve, 35, 46
Nero (dog), 146
Neue Freie Presse (newspaper), 177
The New Leah (play; Brooklyn, 1867), 77
The New Leah (play; New York, 1875), 77
newspapers, Jewish, 187
New York Academy of Music, 133, 191
New York City draft riots, 106
New York Clipper (newspaper), 26, 167
New York Herald (newspaper), 104, 137, 167, 226n69
New York Times (newspaper), 135
Niblo's Garden, New York, 8, 76, 81, 114, 122, 160, 164–65, 171–73, 176
Nicolai, Otto, *Die lustigen Weiber von Windsor* (The Merry Wives of Windsor), 17, 32, 197
Nietzsche, Friedrich, 3, 197–98, 209n5
noble Jew, 41
non-Jews: and beautiful Jewess figure, 14, 16; collaborations of Jews with, 10, 20–21, 24, 168, 174–83, 198–99, 201; ghetto literature read by, 16–17, 186; idealizations of Jews among, 9, 168; involvement of, in *Deborah/Leah*, 4, 7, 11, 20–21, 24; shared social experiences of Jews with, 10, 19, 20, 63–64, 87, 163, 168, 174–86, 190, 195, 207. See also anti-Jewish sentiment; antisemitism; philosemitism

Oettinger, Abraham, 191
O'Neil, Nance, 31, 78, 114–15, 157, *158*, 159, 160, 161
Opera House, Wheeling, West Virginia, *47*
Oppenheim, Moritz Daniel, 17–18, 186, 204; *Bilder aus dem altjüdischen Familienleben* (Scenes of Traditional Jewish Family Life), 17–18; *Der Oster-Abend*, *18*, 204
Otte, Marline, 20
Oxenford, John, 76, 88–90, 140, 228n97

Palmer-Bandmann, Millicent, 173
parodies of *Deborah/Leah*, 98–109, 184–86, 205
Parsloe, Charles T., Jr., 105
Philadelphia Daily Evening Telegraph (newspaper), 167
Philadelphia Press (newspaper), 165
Philippson, Ludwig, 187–88, 192, 201; *Jakob Tirado*, 16
philosemitism: antisemitism in relation to, 197–99; attitudes toward, 9–10, 167, 199; Jews and non-Jews collaborating to produce, 168, 174–83; liberalism and, 163, 168; in marketing and presentation of *Deborah/Leah*, 178; Mosenthal's *Deborah* and, 79, 180, 183, 197, 198
Pike, Samuel Naphtali, 106, 232n153
Pike's Opera House, Cincinnati, 106
pogroms, Russian, 157
popular culture: curse scene in, 1, 3, 185; Jews and Jewishness in, 186–94
Pray, Isaac C., 77
prayer shawls, 6, 10, 179–80, 203
Prechtler, Otto, *Mara*, 39–41, 218n53
Prescott, Vivian, 160
Price, Edward W., *Leah: A Poem in Six Cantos*, 69, 76, 92
Price, Fanny B., 78, 144, 225n46, 226n63
Princess Theatre, London, 94
prostitutes, 1, 203

Rachel. *See* Félix, Elisabeth-Rachel
racism, 65–66, 106
Radner, David, 75
Ragussis, Michael, 144, 237n113
Rankin, McKee, 78
reading fever, 37
Rebecca, the Jewish Wanderer (play), 76, 77, 94, 230n119. *See also* Garthwaite, Fanny, *Rebecca, the Jewish Wanderer*
Richards, Brinley, 67, 69; "Leah's Song," *71*, 91–92

Righton, Edward, 231n136
Ristori, Adelaide: criticisms of, 145; as Deborah, 7, 32, 99–100, 145; fame of, 119; photograph of, *145*; version of *Deborah* performed by, 32, 74–77, 88, 93–94, 98, 108, 223n27, 223n34, 224n41, 229n115, 229n117, 229n118
Roberts, Mary Louise, 146
Rogers, Katherine, 226n62
Rokem, Freddie, 20
Rosewald, Jacob H., 180
Rötscher, Heinrich Theodor, 37
Roumania Opera House, New York, 159
Routledge, William, *Leah, a Hearty Joke in a Cab Age*, 103, 107–8
Royal Adelphi Theatre, London, 2, 31, 34, *40*, 93
Rush, Cecile, 144
Ruth, the Jewess (play), 76, 77, 94, 229n115. See also Moore, R., *Ruth, the Jewess*

Sacher-Masoch, Leopold, 17, 66, 217n34
Sala, George Augustus, 34
"Sally Come Up" (song), 104
Sandauer, Artur, 198
Sandröck, Adele, 159
Sardou, Victorien, *La Papillonne*, 103
Sarony, Napoleon, 115, 149, 193
Sarony, Otto, 193
Sauter, Willmar, 115
Schiller, Friedrich, 29, 31, 37, 175–77, 185; *Die Braut von Messina* (The Bride of Messina), 191; *Maria Stuart*, 116, 126, 131, 133
Schira, Francesco, *Lia*, 67, 76
Schmidt, Julian, 35–36, 37, 169–70
"Schneider Sees Leah" (Uncle Schneider, pseudonym of Charles M. Connolly), 26, 28–29, 31, 103, 214n1
Schönbach, Anton, 217n34
schoolmaster: in Cheltnam's *Deborah*, 95–96; in *Deborah*, 37, 43, 49, 56; in *Leah*, 25, 27, 46–47, *47*, 82–83
Schorsch, Ismar, 17
Schreier, Benjamin, 201
Scott, Walter, *Ivanhoe*, 3, 14, *14*, 36, 169, 209n8
Scribe, Eugène, 15
secularism: Jews accommodated by, 38–39, 42; melodrama grounded in, 35; in outcome of *Deborah*, 38–39, 42, 46, 47–48, 54–56, 59; in outcome of *Leah*, 80, 82
Séjour, Victor, *La Tireuse de cartes* (The Fortune-Teller), 19–20
Selden, Catherine, 77

sensation dramas, 86, 117
Setchell, Dan, *102*, 103, 104, 106, 232n156
Shaftesbury Theatre, London, 159
Shakespeare, William, 1, 165; *The Merchant of Venice*, 7–8, 13, 15, 42, 133, 165–75
Sheva (character), 42, 170
Shylock (character), 7–8, *8*, 12, 42, 166, 169–74, *172*, 184, 185
Silberman, Emma M., 193
silent films, 78, 160–61, 201
Silverman, Lisa, 201
Silverman Brothers Mutual Relief Association, 194
Sklar, Ida, 194
Solomon, Herman, 193
Sonnenthal, Adolf von, 123, *124*, 178
special effects, 45, 117
Speidel, Ludwig, 181
Stanislavski, Constantin, 112
Stein, Joseph, 17
stereotypes, 10–11, 100, 105–8, 117, 200
Stifter, Adalbert, *Abdias*, 54, 219n76
Stoepel, Robert, *Reminiscences of Leah*, 67, 70, 76, 180–81
Stowe, Harriet Beecher, *Uncle Tom's Cabin*, 66
Straßmann-Damböck, Marie. See Damböck, Marie
Strindberg, August, 61
suffering. See compassion and sympathy: for Jewish suffering
Sulzer, Salomon, 190
Sutcliffe, Adam, 9
sympathy. See compassion and sympathy

Tauwitz, Eduard, 180–81
Taylor, Tom, *Mary Warner*, 140
T. B. Peterson & Brothers, 69
tears: Bateman's Leah and, 141–44; collective experience of, 29; critical responses to, 33–34; and Jewish history, 206; melodrama's elicitation of, 35; parodies of elicitation of, 105; as response to *Deborah*, 7, 8, 11, 16, 26–29, 31–35, 38, 42, 59–61, 117
Thaler, Karl von, 21
Theater an der Wien, Vienna, 26
Theatre Magazine, 149
theatricality: authenticity in relation to, 25, 32, 115–18, 120, 128–29, 137–38, 143, 144, 162; Jewishness in relation to, 3, 197–98, 205; Jewish opposition to, 25
Thomas, Bertha, 126–29, *127*
Thompson, Charlotte, 77, 123, 144

Töpler, Josef, 244n55
Twain, Mark, 104

Über Land und Meer (magazine), 17, 18, 186
Uncle Schneider (pseudonym of Charles M. Connolly), 26, 28–29, 31–32, 34, 103, 214n1
Unger, Jozef, 75
United States: antisemitism in, 81; as destination in *Deborah/Leah*, 46, 54–57, 59, 80, 89, 93, 94, 149, 156; *Leah* in, 65–66, 171–72
utopian desires, 36, 47, 59–60

Valman, Nadia, 14
vampirism, 48
vengeance, 50–53, 55–58
Vestvali, Felicia, 19
Viola Wilson Stock Company, 192
Voskuil, Lynn M., 117
Vossiche Zeitung (newspaper), 128

Wagner, Cosima, 219n79
Wagner, Richard, 219n79; "Das Judenthum in der Musik" (Judaism in Music), 61–63, 196–99
Waller, Emma, 144, 225n46
Ward and Lock, 19

Watt, Stephen, 48
Weil, Karl, 189
Weil, Max, 194
Weill, Alexandre, 17
Western, Lucille, 68, 120, *121*, 144, 157
Wheatley, William, 173
"When the Cruel War Is Over" (song), 104
Wilhelmi, Antonie, 120, 125–26
Wilkes' Spirit of the Times (newspaper), 103
Wilkinson, Tom, 202
Williams, Linda, 35, 53
Willis, W. G., *Medea*, 140
Wingate, Charles, 19, 116
Winter Garden Theatre, New York, 100, 106
Wisse, Ruth, 201
Wolff, Pius Alexander, *Preciosa*, 218n55
Wolter, Charlotte, 123, *124*, 129, *153*, 178
Wood, Frank, *Leah the Forsook*, 103–8, 231n144

Yiddish Theater, New York, 159
Young, Brigham, 182
Young Israel All Star Dramatic Night, Roxbury, Massachusetts, 194

Zionist Council of Pittsburgh, 192

Acknowledgments

Deborah and Her Sisters was not a book I intended to write. In the summer of 2011, when putting together a new graduate seminar on sensibility and popular culture, I decided on a whim to place S. H. Mosenthal's *Deborah* on the syllabus. At the time, I knew *Deborah* primarily from the vitriol it provoked in the German Jewish press, the hilarious performance of the drama that featured in Karl Emil Franzos's novel *Der Pojaz* (The Clown), and the brilliant discussion of British adaptations of Mosenthal's material in Nadia Valman's book *The Jewess in Nineteenth-Century British Literary Culture*. As a professor of German and Jewish literature and culture who was originally trained in comparative literature, I was puzzled that this drama that my colleagues and I knew next to nothing about had come to enjoy such popularity abroad. Perhaps, I thought, this might be something to figure out while discussing *Deborah* in the seminar. In my previous monograph, *Middlebrow Literature and the Making of German-Jewish Identity*, I had erroneously referred to *Deborah* in passing as a biblical drama—a sign of my own negligence, to be sure, but also a sign of how little those in my profession have felt obligated to take this work seriously.

Preparing *Deborah* for the final session of the seminar, I developed a fascination with this blockbuster of the nineteenth-century stage that I was reading for the first time. I was amazed by the enormity of the cultural sensation it unleashed, and I was both intrigued and overwhelmed by the extraordinary paper trail that performances of the drama and its various offshoots had left behind on both sides of the Atlantic. I sensed that there was a book to be written, one that would give me the opportunity to tackle the sorts of broad questions about popular culture and liberal attitudes toward Jews that I was grappling with in my research.

I need to begin my acknowledgments, accordingly, by expressing the tremendous debt I owe my students. Both in the 2011 graduate seminar and in a subsequent seminar, "Theatre, Culture, and Commerce," I was privileged to work with an engaged group of students who never shied away from asking difficult questions. I am grateful to be part of such a vibrant graduate program. It is fitting that this project had its first test-drive, as it were, in a fall 2012 works-in-progress presentation for the Carolina-Duke Graduate Program in German Studies. The comments, criticisms, and enthusiasm from my colleagues and our students that evening gave me ample fodder for thought for the next several years (as did some of the initial expressions of skepticism that the project provoked). Ruth von Bernuth, Bill Donahue, Eric Downing, Clayton Koelb, Jakob Norberg, Thomas Pfau, Ann Marie Rasmussen, and Gabe Trop all deserve special thanks here.

I owe the University of North Carolina tremendous gratitude for the generous leave time that enabled me to move forward with my research. Thanks to an R. J. Reynolds Industries Competitive Senior Faculty Leave from the UNC Office of the Provost, a semester-long fellowship at the UNC Institute for the Arts and Humanities, and a research and study assignment from the UNC College of Arts and Sciences, I was able to dedicate three consecutive semesters to my work on this book. As I was struggling to figure out what *Deborah and Her Sisters* was really about in spring 2014, I benefited from being a part of an inspiring cohort of UNC colleagues at the Institute for the Arts and Humanities. My fellow IAH fellows Emily Burrill, Carl Ernst, Sherryl Kleinman, Christopher Nelson, Tommy Otten, Kumi Silva, Benjamin Waterhouse, Brett Whalen, and Rachel Willis all contributed to this project through their questions and comments. Michele Berger, associate director of the IAH, should be singled out for the extraordinary way she led our faculty fellowship seminar.

Robert Dalton of the UNC Libraries gave generously of his time in helping me figure out how to use the digital databases that I ended up spending more time with than I could ever have imagined decades ago. I also need to express my gratitude to the patient and resourceful archivists who assisted me in my research away from Chapel Hill, whether in the Manuscript Collection at the British Library, the Harvard Theatre Collection, the Billy Rose Theatre Collection at the New York Public Library for the Performing Arts, the New York Public Library, the Theatre Collection of the Museum of the City of New York, the Library of Congress, the Folger Shakespeare Library, the Robert E. and Jean R. Mahn Center for Archives and Special Collections at Ohio University, or the St. Louis Public Library. I also owe a special debt to the archivists at the Austrian National Library, the Viennese Burgtheater-Archiv, the Wienbibliothek im Rathaus, the F. N. Manskopf collection at the Universitäts-Bibliothek Johann Christian Senckenberg in Frankfurt am Main, the Bibliothèque nationale de France, the Ohio County Public Library Archives in Wheeling, West Virginia, the Victoria and Albert Museum, the National Portrait Gallery (London), the Bodleian Library at Oxford University, and the State Library of Victoria, Australia, for their help fielding queries and locating materials and images. Without the support of the Moses M. and Hannah L. Malkin Distinguished Professorship in Jewish History and Culture, the frequent research trips to archives in the United States and abroad that this project required would never have been possible. *Deborah and Her Sisters* would also have had many fewer images without the generous support of the Malkin professorship. Brady Lambert at Southeastern Camera in Carrboro did an expert job of preparing high resolution scans of the images in my personal collection. Pam Tharp deserves to be thanked for processing what must have seemed like an endless stream of receipts for reimbursement for research travel and research materials.

While working on this book, I was fortunate to have the opportunity to present my work at the Duke German and Jewish Studies Workshop, the College of William and Mary, Vassar College, Karl-Franzens-Universität Graz, Washington University in St. Louis, the University of Chicago, Sewanee University of the South, Michigan State University, Yale University, Cornell University, the University of Arizona, and the University of California at Davis, as well as at UNC. I thus need to thank Bill Donahue and Martha Helfer at the Duke Workshop, Rob Leventhal and Marc Lee Raphael at William and Mary, Joshua Schreier and Elliott Schreiber at Vassar, Klaus Hödl in Graz, Matt Erlin and Lynne Tatlock at Washington University, Alexandra Zirkle at Chicago, Rick Apgar at Sewanee, Matt Handelman at Michigan State, Eli Stern and Hannan Hever at Yale, Paul Fleming and Jonathan Boyarin at Cornell, Karen Seat at the University of Arizona, and Sven-Erik Rose and Chunjie Zhang at Davis. Those who invited me to speak did not just show me amazing hospitality; they brought together audiences that posed probing and sometimes difficult questions that helped shape the book in significant ways.

Of course, I owe much to my colleagues here in North Carolina who helped the project along in various ways. Along with those mentioned above, Yaakov Ariel, Karen Auerbach, Flora Cassen, and Dick Langston afforded me the opportunity to talk about my project when it was still developing, inevitably providing helpful feedback. Evyatar Marienberg helped me gain a deeper understanding of some of the idiosyncratic ways in which Mosenthal adapted Hebrew liturgical language. Tim Carter provided much needed assistance in analyzing the music that the *Deborah* craze spawned. Cary Levine helped steer me in the right direction in my discussions of much of the visual material in this book. I would have been at a loss analyzing the 1858 Polish translation of *Deborah* I bought from a used bookseller without Ewa Wampuszyc's assistance. Stanislav Shvabrin assisted me with some Russian material, and Lea Greenberg deserves thanks for helping me with the Slovenian translation I got my hands on. Sam Kessler's assistance analyzing the Hebrew version of *Deborah* was invaluable, as was the research support that my former graduate student Erik Grell provided, doing some key initial searches in American newspaper databases.

While working on this book, I have been involved in an informal working group on Jews and popular culture. It is with great pleasure that I express my gratitude to Sharon Gillerman, Klaus Hödl, Paul Lerner, Jonathan Skolnik, Lisa Silverman, and Kerry Wallach for long and fruitful discussions and their reactions to my work. It is difficult to name all the colleagues at other institutions whose comments, criticisms, and conversations have left their mark on this book. Jeff Grossman, Alan Levenson, Maury Samuels, and Nadia Valman all deserved to be singled out here, however.

At the University of Pennsylvania Press, I have had an exemplary editor in Jerome Singerman, who expressed enthusiasm for the project from the moment I first contacted him. I am grateful to Jerry and the editors of the Jewish Culture and Contexts series, David Ruderman and Steven Weitzman, for their initial comments on the project when it was in its final stages. The anonymous readers' reports for the press offered an exceptional level of rigorous engagement with my project. Months later, I discovered that Martha Helfer had authored one of the reviews. I owe Martha tremendous gratitude not just for her enthusiasm for the project but for her trenchant and constructive criticisms, all of which proved enormously helpful in preparing the final version of the manuscript. Janice Meyerson deserves to be singled out for her expert copyediting, and Erica Ginsburg, Managing Editor at Penn Press, was particularly helpful in guiding the manuscript through production. David Luljak deserves thanks for preparing the index.

My family has lived with my own enthusiasm for this project for the last five years, often poking fun at my elation over winning yet another eBay auction for yet another nineteenth-century photograph of Kate Bateman or Sarah Bernhardt posing as Leah. But this book would never have been able to be written without the love of my wife, Beth, and of our three daughters, Rebecca, Lily, and Amelia. To be sure, no one ever agreed to dress up as Deborah or Leah on Halloween or to reenact the Clementina Hawarden photographic study I discuss in the Introduction. Still, Lily and Amelia helped me work through some of the *Leah* vocal selections I discovered at the Harvard Theatre Collection, and Amelia deserves credit for charging me a reasonable rate for helping me inventory the numerous boxes of archival material I collected while doing the research for the book. Our resident basset hounds Tank and Gideon also deserve a special treat for the companionship they offered while napping in comfort as I worked at my computer at home. Without the love, support, and sustenance of my family, writing this book would not just not have been possible; it would not have been worth the effort.

I dedicate this book to the memory of my mother, Frances Aaron Hess, who passed away after a battle with cancer in May 2015, when I was still in the middle of writing. In 2013, I spent a week with my mother in New York while conducting archival research, and she took great interest in my project. This had to do in part with her own love of going to the theater, and even more so with her family connection to the material. After all, Mosenthal, the author of *Deborah*, also wrote the libretto for Karl Goldmark's 1875 popular grand opera *Die Königin von Saba* (The Queen of Sheba). My mother was the great-granddaughter of Karl Goldmark's younger brother Leo, a cantor in the Austro-Hungarian Empire who became an attorney and music impresario in New York. I grew up in an unusual American family where the Viennese composer was both a household name and a revered figure. In my living room as a child, Karl Goldmark's photograph hung on the wall next to my parents' piano and next to the picture of his nephew and my mother's great-uncle, the American composer Rubin Goldmark. To this day, the processional at weddings on my mother's side of the family still consists of selections from the first movement of Karl Goldmark's *Ländliche Hochzeit* (Rustic Wedding Symphony). I am not sure my mother would have deemed the performances of Old Testament vengeance in the celebrated curse scene of Mosenthal's *Deborah* a good way for Jews to put their best foot forward. Nevertheless, she always took enormous pride in the accomplishments of her children and grandchildren. I know that this book would have given her great pleasure and earned a prominent place on the marble coffee table in her New York City apartment.

* * *

Some of the material in *Deborah and Her Sisters* appeared earlier, in "Shylock's Daughters: Philosemitism, Popular Culture, and the Liberal Imagination," *Transversal: Journal for Jewish Studies* 13, no.1 (March 2015): 28–43. I thank De Gruyter and the editors of *Transversal* for permission to use this material here.

Norfolk Public Library

NO LONGER THE PROPERTY
BROAD CREEK BRANCH
OF
Norfolk Public Library
NORFOLK PUBLIC LIBRARY